The Management of Wicked Problems in Health and Social Care

At a time of growing pressure on health and social care services, this book draws together contributions which highlight contemporary challenges for their management. Providing a range of contributions that draw on a Critical Management Studies perspective, the book raises macro-level concerns with theory, demographics and economics on the one hand, as well as micro-level challenges of leadership, voice and engagement on the other. Rather than being an attempt to define the 'wickedness' of problems in this field, this book provides new insights designed to be of interest and value to researchers, students and managers.

Contributions from international researchers explore four main topics:

- identifying contemporary challenges in health and social care;
- managing, leading and following;
- listening to silent voices in delivering change; and
- new methodologies for understanding care challenges.

The concerns discussed in this volume are 'wicked' in so far as they are persistent, pernicious and beyond the curative abilities of any single organization or profession. Such problems require collaboration but also new approaches to listening to those who experience their effects. This book demonstrates such listening through its engagement with policymakers, leaders, followers, professions, patients, forgotten groups and silenced voices. Moreover, it considers how future research might be transformed so as to shine a more inclusive light on 'wicked' problems and their amelioration. This is a timely and engaging book that challenges you—the reader—to think again about how we should look at, engage with and support all those involved in health and social care.

Will Thomas is Associate Professor in the University of Suffolk Business School, UK.

Anneli Hujala is Senior Reseacher in the Department of Health and Social Management at the University of Eastern Finland.

Sanna Laulainen is Senior Lecturer in the Department of Health and Social Management at the University of Eastern Finland.

Robert McMurray is Professor of Work and Organisation at the York Management School, UK.

Routledge Studies in Health Management
Edited by Ewan Ferlie

The health care sector is now of major significance, economically, scientifically and societally. In many countries, health care organizations are experiencing major pressures to change and restructure, while cost containment efforts have been accentuated by global economic crisis. Users are demanding higher service quality, and health care professions are experiencing significant reorganization while operating under increased demands from an aging population.

Critically analytic, politically informed, discursive and theoretically grounded, rather than narrowly technical or positivistic, the series seeks to analyse current health care organizations. Reflecting the intense focus of policy and academic interest, it moves beyond the day-to-day debate to consider the broader implications of international organizational and management research and different theoretical framings.

Managing Modern Healthcare
Knowledge, Networks and Practice
Mike Bresnen, Damian Hodgson, Simon Bailey, Paula Hyde and John Hassard

Challenging Perspectives on Organizational Change in Health Care
Louise Fitzgerald and Aoife McDermott

Healthcare Entrepreneurship
Ralf Wilden, Massimo Garbuio, Federica Angeli, and Daniele Mascia

Medical Professionals
Conflicts and Quandaries in Medical Practice
Edited by Kathleen Montgomery and Wendy Lipworth

The Management of Wicked Problems in Health and Social Care
Edited by Will Thomas, Anneli Hujala, Sanna Laulainen, and Robert McMurray

For a full list of titles in this series, please visit www.routledge.com

The Management of Wicked Problems in Health and Social Care

Edited by Will Thomas, Anneli Hujala, Sanna Laulainen, and Robert McMurray

Routledge
Taylor & Francis Group

NEW YORK AND LONDON

First published 2019
by Routledge
605 Third Avenue, New York, NY 10017

and by Routledge
2 Park Square, Milton Park, Abingdon, Oxon, OX14 4RN

First issued in paperback 2020

Routledge is an imprint of the Taylor & Francis Group, an informa business

© 2019 Taylor & Francis

The right of Will Thomas, Anneli Hujala, Sanna Laulainen, and Robert McMurray to be identified as the authors of the editorial material, and of the authors for their individual chapters, has been asserted in accordance with sections 77 and 78 of the Copyright, Designs and Patents Act 1988.

Library of Congress Cataloging-in-Publication Data
Names: Thomas, Will, 1977– editor. | Hujala, Anneli, editor. |
    Laulainen, Sanna, editor. | McMurray, Robert, 1972– editor.
Title: The management of wicked problems in health and social
    care / edited by Will Thomas, Anneli Hujala, Sanna Laulainen,
    and Robert McMurray.
Description: New York, NY : Routledge, 2019. | Series: Routledge
    studies in health management | Includes bibliographical references
    and index.
Identifiers: LCCN 2018034646 | ISBN 9781138103627 (hardback) |
    ISBN 9781315102597 (ebook)
Subjects: LCSH: Health services administration. | Social work
    administration. | Critical theory.
Classification: LCC RA971 .M3455 2019 | DDC 362.1068—dc23
LC record available at https://lccn.loc.gov/2018034646

ISBN 13: 978-0-367-73318-6 (pbk)
ISBN 13: 978-1-138-10362-7 (hbk)

Typeset in Sabon
by Apex CoVantage, LLC

Contents

List of Contributors   viii
Acknowledgments   xv
Editors' Introduction   xvi

SECTION 1
Contemporary Wicked Challenges to Health and Social Care   1

1   The Concept of Wicked Problems: Improving the
    Understanding of Managing Problem Wickedness in
    Health and Social Care   3
    HARRI RAISIO, ALISA PUUSTINEN AND PIRKKO VARTIAINEN

2   The Politics of Care: Wicked Concerns
    Constituent in Care Reforms   21
    WILL THOMAS AND SUSAN HOLLINRAKE

3   Personalization of Care: A Wicked Problem or a
    Wicked Solution?   34
    JANET CARTER ANAND, GAVIN DAVIDSON, BERNI KELLY AND
    GERALDINE MACDONALD

SECTION 2
Managing, Leading and Following   49

4   The Wicked Problem of Leadership in the NHS   51
    GAURISH CHAWLA AND MARK LEARMONTH

5   Lofty Ideals and Lowly Troubles among Nursing Home Managers   62
    MONICA ANDERSSON BÄCK AND CHARLOTTA LEVAY

6   The Unnoticed Role of Employees in Ethical Leadership   75
    MERJA SINKKONEN AND SANNA LAULAINEN

7   Destructive Leadership as a Wicked Problem in Health Care:
    Can We Blame the Leader Only?   91
    MINNA HOFFRÉN AND SANNA LAULAINEN

8   Health Care Communication Technology and Its Promise
    of Patient Empowerment: Unpacking Patient Empowerment
    through Patients' Identity Constructions   103
    LAURA VISSER, INGE BLEIJENBERGH, YVONNE BENSCHOP AND
    ALLARD VAN RIEL

SECTION 3
Silent Voices: Making the Invisible Visible   117

9   Blame Culture in the National Health Service (NHS), UK   119
    RUTH STRUDWICK

10 A Darker Side to Interorganizational Relations   133
    KRISTINA BROWN

11 Deficit Discourses and Aboriginal and Torres
    Strait Islander Disadvantage: A Wicked Problem in Australian
    Indigenous Policy?   148
    ELIZABETH PYLE, DEANNA GRANT-SMITH AND ROBYN MAYES

12 Unpacking Dependency; Managing 'Becoming': Supporting
    the Experiences of Patients Living with Chronic Disease   160
    WILL THOMAS

SECTION 4
Beyond Conventional Methodologies for
Understanding Wicked Challenges   177

13 Improving Young People's Mental Health? Understanding
    Ambivalence to Seeking Support among Young Adults
    with Asperger Syndrome   179
    EDMUND COLEMAN-FOUNTAIN AND BRYONY BERESFORD

14 Action Research in the Health and Social Care Settings:
    A Tool for Solving Wicked Problems?   194
    MARTA STRUMIŃSKA-KUTRA

15 Four Different Ways to View Wicked Problems   211
    ANNELI HUJALA, SANNA LAULAINEN, ANDY BROOKES, MAARIT
    LAMMASSAARI AND TAMARA MULHERIN

16 The Promise of Visual Approaches in Organizational and
    Management Research   235
    JARI MARTIKAINEN

    Index   250

Contributors

Janet Carter Anand is Professor of International Social Work, University of Eastern Finland. Janet has worked as an academic in Australia, the Republic of Ireland and the United Kingdom. Her key topics of research include global mindedness and international social work practice, refugee quality of life and social integration, abuse of older people and the application of personalization and coproduction in social care. Janet is currently principle investigator for PROMEQ New Start Finland! and director of the UEF summer school, International Migration Studies and Youth, Child and Family Welfare.

Monica Andersson Bäck, PhD, is currently a lecturer in Work Science (previously lecturer in Social Work) at the Department of Sociology and Work Science, University of Gothenburg. Her research centers on the complexity of working life, organization and management of human service organizations, especially in primary, elderly and psychiatric care. Andersson Bäck's and Levay's contribution for this anthology is based on a research project on "Improvement work and leadership within elder care" funded by Vårdalinstitutet. In other current research projects, she has considered financial incentives and professional motivation as well as conditions for management in Swedish psychiatry.

Yvonne Benschop is Professor of Organizational Behavior at the Department of Business Administration of the Radboud University in Nijmegen, the Netherlands. Her research focuses on the functioning of gender and diversity in organizations, specifically on informal organization processes that play a crucial role in the success or failure of gender and diversity management.

Bryony Beresford is a social scientist who has over 25 years' experience of conducting applied policy and practice research concerned with health and social care issues across the life-course. She is a professor based in the Social Policy Research Unit at the University of York, which has an international reputation for the quality and impact of its research in these areas. A mixed-methods researcher, her work includes policy evaluation,

evaluation of alternative models of service delivery and specific interventions, and the lived experience. Her topic areas include: preventive and self-management interventions in social care and mental health and the integration of health and social care, with respect to autism, chronic and life-limiting conditions, disability and aging.

Inge Bleijenbergh is Associate Professor in the Department of Business Administration of the Radboud University in Nijmegen, the Netherlands. She is an expert in participatory research, facilitated modeling, gender and decision-making and social policies, focusing specifically on modeling social policy and diversity to involve decision-makers in analyzing and addressing complex problems.

Andy Brookes (PhD) has more than 30 years' experience as a manager in a number of organizations across the public and private sector. He teaches across a range of subjects in the field of business and management at undergraduate and postgraduate level, as well as providing continuing professional development in corporate programs. He is the Programme Leader for the part-time MBA and has adopted a Critical Management Education approach to develop reflective and independent thinkers. His research area is interorganizational collaboration, particularly in the domain of social problems.

Kristina Brown is currently a final-year PhD student at Durham University, UK, researching the leadership of health and social collaborations in the UK that are mandated as a result of government policy. She also works as a lecturer in leadership and management studies at the University of Northumbria, teaching public sector management and research methods. Her main research areas are critical and emancipatory approaches to leadership and management. Her research focuses on the basic social processes that underpin mandated collaborative processes within a health and social care context. Her current research projects are connected to the integration of UK health and social care services.

Gaurish Chawla (MBBS—Kurukshetra University, India; MSc—University of Manchester, UK) works as Teaching Fellow in the Department of Medical Education at Brighton and Sussex Medical School and is writing up his PhD in Management (University of Durham, UK). A doctor turned academic, his work is situated in what can be described as Critical Management Studies.

Edmund Coleman-Fountain (PhD in Sociology) is Lecturer in Sociology at Northumbria University in Newcastle, UK. His research involves working with disabled and autistic young people, including on applied issues related to mental health and well-being. He was previously a research fellow at the Social Policy Research Unit at the University of York.

Gavin Davidson is Professor of Social Care in the School of Social Sciences, Education and Social Work at Queen's University Belfast in Northern Ireland. His main research interests are in the area of mental health, specifically: the effectiveness of mental health services; the social determinants of mental health; human rights and mental health/mental capacity legislation; and the associations between adverse childhood experiences and mental health.

Deanna Grant-Smith (PhD) is Senior Lecturer in the QUT Business School, Queensland University of Technology, Australia. To explain high levels of regulatory resistance to marine pollution prevention policy concerning the discharge of sewage from recreational vessels, she theorized a new form of wicked policy problem—unspeakable policy problems—characterized by a high degree of psychosocial sensitivity and verbal proscription. As the successful management of these has potentially significant sustainability, social justice and economic impacts, her current research is applying the construct to a range of wicked problems, including death-scapes and innovation in death-related industries, sanitation reform and public acceptance of recycled water, and unpaid internships.

Minna Hoffrén is a PhD candidate in the Department of Health and Social Management at the University of Eastern Finland in Kuopio, Finland. Her research explores destructive leadership, and her research interests are critical and discursive approaches to management in the context of health and social care. Before starting an academic researcher, Minna worked over 20 years as a biomedical laboratory scientist in health care.

Susan Hollinrake is Associate Professor and was Programme Lead for Social Work at the University of Suffolk until she (semi) retired in 2017. She had a long career in social work practice as a practitioner and manager before becoming an academic. Her teaching has covered professional social work values and social work with adults, and her research interests have focused on carers, older people and disabled people. Sue continues to publish on these topics.

Anneli Hujala (PhD in Health Management Science) works as Senior Researcher in the Department of Health and Social Management at the University of Eastern Finland in Kuopio, Finland. Her main research areas are critical and discursive approaches to management in the context of health and social care. Her research focuses on interactional dimensions of management. Her current research projects are connected to the integration of health and social care services for people with multiple complex needs.

Berni Kelly (PhD) is Senior Lecturer in Social Work and Co-Director of the Disability Research Network at Queen's University Belfast. Her main research interests are in the area of disability studies, with a focus on disabled children in care, the effectiveness of disability support services, transitions to adult life and co-production.

Sanna Laulainen (PhD in Social Management Science) is a critical scholar working as a senior lecturer in health and social management sciences in the Department of Health and Social Management, University of Eastern Finland. Her research interests include critical management studies, organizational citizenship, identity, agency theories and enthusiasm for qualitative methods. Currently, she is researching future competencies of health and social professionals and managers.

Maarit Lammassaari holds an MSc in Economics and Business Administration. She is a doctoral student at the Business School, University of Eastern Finland, Kuopio, Finland. Her PhD dissertation focuses on top-management sensemaking in the context of private health care service organizations.

Mark Learmonth (PhD in Organization Studies) works at Durham University Business School as a Professor of Organization Studies. He spent the first 17 years of his career in management posts within the British National Health Service. Prior to taking up his post in Durham, he has worked at the universities of Nottingham and York. His research interests include: Management Discourse, Evidence in Management, Methodological Debates and the Personal Consequences of Work.

Charlotta Levay, PhD, is Associate Professor of Business Administration specializing in organization at Lund University School of Economics and Management. Her research centers on professional work and leadership, especially in health care. Levay has been Harkness Fellow at Harvard Medical School and special advisor to the Commission on the Future of Sweden. She is currently involved in a multidisciplinary research program on the Swedish regulatory principle of 'science and proven experience' and in a research project on the management of health care by numbers.

Geraldine Macdonald is Professor of Social Work in the School for Policy Studies at the University of Bristol. She is a longstanding advocate of evidence-based policy and practice, and much of her research has focused on the evaluation of social interventions, including randomized controlled trials and systematic reviews. She is particularly interested in the evaluation and implementation of complex social interventions. Geraldine is Coordinating Editor of the Cochrane *Developmental, Psychosocial and Learning Problems Review Group*.

Jari Martikainen (PhD in Art History) works as a lecturer in Visual Culture Studies at Ingman College of Crafts and Design in Toivala, Finland. At the moment, he is finalizing his doctoral studies in Social Psychology at the University of Eastern Finland in Kuopio, Finland. His main research areas are teaching methods of art history, visual research methods and visual nonverbal behavior. He is interested in interdisciplinary research applying approaches of visual culture studies to research on social and educational sciences.

Robyn Mayes (PhD in Australian and Cultural Studies) is Senior Lecturer in the School of Management at the Queensland University of Technology. Her research examines interrelationships among community, place, gender and labor mobility grounded in extensive work on social, organizational and geo-political dimensions of mining in Australia. Her current research focuses on paid labor and digital platforms.

Robert McMurray (PhD) is Professor of Work and Organisation at the York Management School, UK. His research interests include the organization of health care, professions, emotion labor, dirty work and visual methods. His related books include *The Darkside of Emotional Labour* (with Dr. Jenna Ward) and Routledge Series on *Women Writers in Organization Studies*.

Tamara Mulherin is doing her PhD in Politics and International Relations in the School of Social and Political Science at the University of Edinburgh. Tamara has more than 25 years' experience in planning, delivery, management and evaluation of national, state, local policies and programs in the public and non-government sectors in Australia, the United Kingdom and internationally. Tamara's PhD is an interorganizational, multi-sited ethnographic account of an integrated management 'team' involved in the implementation of the Public Bodies (Joint Working) (Scotland) Act 2014 in 'Kintra,' Scotland. Her primary research interests lie with collaborative practices in the context of New Public Management and New Public Governance approaches to public management/administration, especially in health and social care. She is also interested in organizational ethnography, practice and socio-material theoretical approaches, feminist theorizing of organizations and critical management.

Alisa Puustinen, PhD, is Senior Researcher at the Emergency Services College. Her research has focused on social networks, complexity sciences, public deliberation, military sociology and security studies. She has published in journals such as *Emergence: Complexity and Organisation* and *Complexity, Governance and Networks*.

Elizabeth Pyle has held senior policy and program roles within the not-for-profit and Queensland Government sectors, particularly in the area of Indigenous Australian Affairs. She has also worked extensively with and within Aboriginal and Torres Strait Islander communities. A part-time student at Queensland University of Technology, Elizabeth's current research examines how the dominant deficit discourses in Australian Indigenous Affairs policy and implementation, framed as a wicked problem, reproduces an ongoing narrative of 'Indigenous disadvantage.'

Harri Raisio, PhD, is Senior Researcher in Social and Health Management at the University of Vaasa and Adjunct Professor at the University of Eastern Finland. His research has focused on the topics of wicked problems, complexity sciences and public deliberation. He has published in journals such as *Landscape and Urban Planning*, *Policy Sciences*, *Administration & Society*, *Journal of Health Organization and Management* and *Scandinavian Journal of Public Administration*.

Merja Sinkkonen (PhD Soc.Sc.) works as Principal Lecturer in the School of Health Care and Social Services at Tampere University on Applied Sciences. Her main research interests are leadership in social services, ethical leadership, inclusion and new ways to teach. Her current research projects are connected to the challenges faced by leaders in integration.

Ruth Strudwick (DProf Health Sciences) is Associate Professor and Subject Lead for Radiography and Interprofessional Learning at the University of Suffolk, Ipswich, UK. Her Professional Doctorate thesis was an ethnographic study of the culture of her own profession, diagnostic radiography. Ruth's main research interests are professional culture, practice-based learning, interprofessional learning and values-based practice.

Marta Strumińska-Kutra, PhD, is Associate Professor at VID Specialized University (Oslo, Norway) and Assistant Professor at Kozminski University (Warsaw, Poland). In the years 2014–2016, she was a Visiting and Associate Fellow at the Institute for Science, Innovation and Society, University of Oxford (Oxford, UK). She conducts research on social and sustainable innovation and on institutional change and organizational learning in public administration. Her interest revolves around questions of a public role of academics and more broadly around science-society relationships. Her book, *Democratizing Public Management. Towards Practice-based Theory*, is going to be published by Palgrave Macmillan in summer 2018.

Will Thomas (PhD Philosophy) is Associate Professor in the University of Suffolk Business School. His current research interests focus on the application of the ethics of care to management, both within the field of health and social care and more widely. His particular interest is in the idea of 'dependency' and how this concept can be used to uncover the responsibilities of those in power (managers, policymakers, decision-takers).

Allard van Riel obtained a PhD in Service Innovation Management (2003) from Maastricht University in the Netherlands. In the past he worked at Maastricht University, the University of Liege and Radboud University. Since 2018, he has been a full professor of Service Innovation Management at Hasselt University in Belgium. He teaches service and service research-related courses. His research focus is on how service users experience innovative health care, education, public and commercial services.

In his research, he uses mixed methods to investigate the user experience in technology-mediated service environments and link this experience to service design choices.

Pirkko Vartiainen, PhD, is a Professor of Social and Health Management at the University of Vaasa. She has held several academic leader positions and has acted as a scientific expert in various organizations. She has edited and published in academic journals internationally and in Finland. Her research has focuses on the topics of evaluation, leadership, wicked problems and public participation.

Laura Visser (PhD) is Lecturer at Monash Business School, Monash University in Melbourne, Australia. Her research interests lie broadly with issues of power and inequality in organizations. More specifically, her research projects are or have been related to the health care sector, technology, gender and diversity, and (post) feminism.

Acknowledgments

The editors would like to extend their thanks to the authors who have contributed work to this volume. They would also like to acknowledge and recognize the contributions of people who have participated in research that is reported here and without whom this work would not be possible.

Editors' Introduction

The idea of the 'wicked problem' has been gaining popularity since it was introduced through the work of Rittel and Webber (1973). Its favor has grown across an increasingly broad range of management domains—see, for example, the literature review conducted by Danken, Dribbisch and Lange (2016). This expansion of the concept has been most noticeable in the discussion of environmental issues, security and terrorism and in health and health care (Danken, Dribbisch and Lange 2016, 19). Despite the attention paid to defining and discussing these complex issues within the field of health and social care, less focus has been given to the implications for public organizations and to how this learning might be applied (Head and Alford 2015).

As critically orientated scholars, informed by the multidisciplinary approach of Critical Management Studies, we must be aware of the criticism of the term 'wicked problem,' summarized by Peters (2017, 394) as becoming something of an "academic fad." We recognize that the term's overuse risks diluting its value and taking the discussion away from policymakers, decision-takers and managers and situating it in an academic realm far away from practice. While it may be true that the idea is one that academics have constructed for themselves—and this book is part of that practice—the concept does offer certain advantages. In properly labeling problems as 'wicked' we are able to offer an explanation for failures to offer a "clear solution" (Danken, Dribbisch and Lange 2016, 18) or a "magic bullet" (Peters 2017, 395) to complex problems that policymakers and managers tackle daily.

The purpose of this book is not to offer new or more advanced definitions of wicked problems—instead, our ambition is to offer a range of contributions that serve a heuristic purpose. It is hoped that the chapters included here will offer the reader new insight into the extent and complexities of the challenges faced by those that seek to manage health and social care systems. We offer this in contrast to attempts to 'tame' wicked problems (Roberts 2000) or to the notion that problems with the management of health care are always best answered through the application of evidence (Sharts-Hopko 2013; Newman and Head 2017).

Typically, there is no shortage of information which might inform decision-making—much management practice is concerned with "confronting a more complex mass of information than we are used to dealing with" (Conklin and Weil 1997). The task of the manager is therefore to try to process this mountain of data in order to resolve problems which are, by definition, hard to define and may "not be solvable in any final and definitive manner" (Peters 2017, 386). In this volume we encourage the reader to use the perspectives from our contributing authors to provoke, challenge and stimulate novel approaches. We accept, and indeed endorse, the calls from those that suggest that the best way to manage wicked problems is through the application of creative, integrative and imaginative thinking (Conklin and Weil 1997; Termeer et al. 2015; Dunne and Martin 2006; Brown, Alfred Harris and Russell 2010). In one sense, this book acts as a resource for stimulating creativity in problem resolution.

This collection of writings draws on the work of authors from across Europe and from Australia to record, report and present empirical and theoretical contributions drawing from health and social care management. Many of the challenges described here will be common to health and social care systems from Africa, Asia and the Americas as well as to the European and Australian systems that they are based upon. While many of the writings are firmly situated within a specific system their conclusions and lessons are applicable across domains. It is hoped that readers from academic and practice backgrounds will find content here that will interest them and which they will find provoking.

The book is organized in four sections, but readers will find clear connections between many of the chapters that go above and beyond a broad focus on wicked problems. The first section offers a discussion of some contemporary challenges facing health and social care systems—exploring and critiquing efforts to understand and respond to the problems faced by care systems and the people that use them. In the second section, the notion of leadership is explored in chapters that discuss relationships between leaders and followers and uncover implicit ethical concerns. In the third section, attention is given to giving voice to marginalized groups, or to unheard voices, and the problems that they face within health and social care systems. The final section considers methodological issues with a focus on techniques and approaches which may prove useful in uncovering the nature of wicked problems and suggesting ways in which we might embrace "the logic of what might be" (Dunne and Martin 2006, 513).

As editors, we offer our warmest thanks to the authors that have contributed to this volume and hope that you, as the reader, will find them interesting and thought-provoking. Below are short summaries of the chapters included in this volume:

Section 1—Contemporary Wicked Challenges to Health and Social Care

Harri Raisio, **Alisa Puustinen** and **Pirkko Vartiainen** lay the ground for our shared understanding by defining what wicked problems are, how, why and from where they arise and what their implications are for health and social care management. The definition of the concept 'wicked problem' is scrutinized thoroughly—with reasonable criticism—and complemented by interesting conceptual expansions. The authors suggest that in the context of health and social care, the concepts of the tame game and the wicked game could be insightful. Similarly, so-called super wicked problems and wicked ethics, i.e. ethical problems confronted by care professionals, deserve special attention. The authors deepen the theoretical foundations of wicked problems by intertwining them insightfully with complexity perspective, contrasting wickedness with the paradigm of order. Their 'wickedness cube' illustrates fascinatingly the different dimensions of a wicked problem. Regarding the management of these problems, Raisio, Puustinen and Vartiainen highlight that wicked problems challenge conventional hierarchies, authorities and evidence-based policymaking. They conclude by suggesting that wickedness and complexity in the context of health and social care should be taken more seriously both by leaders, managers and policymakers and, accordingly, be paid more attention in the research of this field.

Will Thomas and **Susan Hollinrake** bring to the fore wicked problems related to the reforms of social care, a concern identified and discussed in many countries. They familiarize us with the main historical milestones of reforming adult social care in England, starting from the era of Margaret Thatcher in 1979 and ending up with the austerity measures introduced following the 2008 financial crisis. Their focus is on impacts of the changes on care provision for older people—especially in the fourth-age or 'the older old'—who have suffered from significant reductions in funding of social care. The authors describe how cost pressures have resulted in risks that the 'real' care needs of the oldest are not being met by the current delivery of social care services. Thomas and Hollinrake call into question whether the marketization of care has not only increased the freedom of choice and thus independence of individuals, but also increased the responsibility and risks they are supposed to carry by themselves. The underlying policy agenda of personalization of care is therefore questioned by the authors. This doubt will interestingly be extended in the following chapter by Janet Carter Anand and her research colleagues. After raising the concerns arising from social care reforms, Thomas and Hollinrake end their chapter with more optimistic views by proposing the ethic of care as a solution for promoting good care. Not everyone needs to be a fully autonomous decision-maker. Instead of independence, interdependence may be one of the values deserving more appreciation in modern, European-style welfare states of the future.

Janet Carter Anand, Gavin Davidson, Berni Kelly and **Geraldine Macdonald** end the first section of the book by addressing a widely debated social policy topic: the personalization of care. While struggling with how to provide equitable but at the same time cost-effective care for marginalized and oppressed people, politicians, care professionals and other decision-makers face a problem which indeed matches with the definition of a wicked problem. By asking whether personalization is a wicked problem or a wicked solution, the authors question whether personalization has only positive implications. The authors introduce personal budgets as an example of personalization of care and draw on international evidence gathered through a literature review in considering the gains and losses of individual funding arrangements. The chapter is insightfully structured through a series of critical questions addressing diverse aspects of individual funding to be questioned. Anand et al. claim that even though 'the money follows the person' principle increases freedom of choice and gives more control over one's own care, it may not be an ideal solution for everyone with disabilities. Alongside individualized modes of care, directly provided state welfare services may be wanted and needed to be maintained as part of social policy targeting toward both effectiveness and equity.

Section 2—Managing, Leading and Following

Gaurish Chawla and **Mark Learmonth** start the second section of the book with a chapter that explores and unpacks the 'leadership discourse' prevalent in the English National Health Service (NHS). They suggest that the increasing frequency with which the term has come to be used has changed the very language of the organization, and with it, the way in which roles are conceptualized. Usefully, they also highlight the methodological problems associated with asking about workers' experiences of leadership without introducing subliminal, unintended, biases. Coming from the emerging field of Critical Leadership Studies, Chawla and Learmonth's work draws on a variety of techniques to facilitate conversations with NHS employees about the idea of 'leadership.' The analysis that they present puts forward three fantasies: about the self, teams and about leadership itself that provide a thought-provoking start to this section on managing, leading and following.

Monica Andersson Bäck and **Charlotta Levay** explore the way in which managers of nursing homes deal with wicked problems in elderly care. Their chapter exposes the gap between managers' high-minded ideals of respectful, individualized care and the struggles that they face in managing scarce resources and employees' discontent with workloads and work schedules. These tensions represent the practical experience of problems that we might theorize as 'wicked.' Their study is based on qualitative research conducted with nursing home managers and employees working in a variety of different contexts in Sweden. This in-depth work allows them to identify ways in which their participants define the idea of 'good care' and the ways in which they define the troubles that they face in delivering this ideal. Their analysis reminds the reader that managers share the same ambitions of residents, their families and the wider community in wanting to deliver the best possible care. Andersson Bäck and Levay conclude that much of the problem is one of resources—a challenge made all the greater by the increasing demand for elderly care faced by Sweden (and many other states).

Merja Sinkkonen and Sanna Laulainen continue our series of chapters looking at managing and leading by considering the role that employees play in ethical leadership. They question the role of employees in enacting ethics and ethical guidelines within social services. Their purpose is to provide a critique of the assumption of leader-centeredness and draw on the notion of organizational citizenship behavior as a way to construct the role played by individuals in co-constructing an ethical organization. The chapter is in two halves: the first is a review of the literature in which Sinkkonen and Laulainen play close attention to the way in which the role of the employee has been portrayed in the ethical leadership literature. The second part of their chapter presents some empirical data from a study of middle managers working in social services in a large Finnish city. While a lot of attention is typically paid to the role of the manager, the authors argue that the role of employees and even clients in helping to work through, discuss and even resolve wicked problems is critical in addressing them in a meaningful way.

Minna Hoffrén and Sanna Laulainen present an interesting chapter which continues an element from the previous chapter as it questions the role of the 'leader' this time, using the concept of destructive leadership. Their argument is that some of negative behaviors of managers in health care not only serve to make good care difficult, but to create wicked problems in their organizations. Their chapter starts with a discussion of a typology of destructive leadership behaviors before they move on to consider empirical findings from a study of employees in health care services in Finland. Hoffrén and Laulainen's focus is on the employees' responses to the destructive leadership situations that they find themselves facing. Their analysis shows two discourses, that of self-interest and that of collective denial. Just as in the previous chapter, the authors make the case for the crucial role to be played by employees in addressing the quality of leadership in an organization—and remind us that in seeking to address the impact of poor leadership, we should look at employees as well as those holding formal positions of power.

Laura Visser, Inge Bleijenbergh, Yvonne Benschop and Allard van Riel present a view of leadership from a different perspective in the final chapter of this section. Their work concerns the promise that health care communication technology makes to empower patients and improve communication with their health care professionals. In the light of claims that technology might help to put patients at the center of care decisions and to address wicked problems of increased demand, reduced resources and concerns about overall care quality, Visser et al. critically analyze these claims based on their own empirical study conducted in the Netherlands. The authors' work centers on the impact of technology on patients' identity constructions and, in particular, the notion that technology can create empowered identity constructions. Their conclusion is that rather than providing a straightforward way in which patients might be empowered and enabled to take a more active role in the management of their condition, the technology that featured in their study blurs identities while at the same time constraining (in the way the technology is set up) the scope of patients to undertake their own identify work. Importantly, the authors remind us of the impact that the way in which the technology is set up, built and used plays an important part in the extent to which patients can be empowered. In drawing this section to an end with a discussion of how patients might be encouraged to take on a more active leadership role, Visser et al. provide a natural segue into the third section which considers hidden voices and discourses in health and social care.

Section 3—Silent Voices: Making the Invisible Visible

Ruth Strudwick makes visible how the culture of blame is constructed and maintained as a wicked problem within the English National Health Service (NHS). She draws on experiences from her ethnographic study conducted among radiographers, in which she scrutinized how radiographers as medical professionals dealt with safety problems at their work. These professionals took personal responsibility for safety problems and felt guilty about errors causing safety risks. According the author, professionals still have a fear and reluctance to report errors because it may damage their own reputation or that of their colleagues and bring down the reputation of their department. The author draws attention to of the behavior of professionals that sustain blame culture and inhibit learning from the errors, incidents and near misses. She highlights that there is an urge to change organizational culture to be more open and transparent to improve safety and quality of services in health care. Altogether, the question of blame culture in health care turned out to be a complicated wicked problem with no simple solution to deal with it.

Kristina Brown's chapter follows nicely from the previous chapter, as it also looks at unspoken or unnoticed dynamics within a health and social care setting. This work seeks to uncover some of the hidden dynamics of interorganizational teams or groups compelled to work together in addressing complex and often wicked problems. In working to expose the 'darker side' of these relations, Brown provides an interesting account of these mandated (enforced) collaborations that draws on a social psychological perspective to offer insight into group membership, social identity theory, cohesion and pluralistic ignorance. In drawing our attention to the dynamics of relations within an interorganizational group, Brown makes a valuable contribution to the theory and offers insights for practice.

Elizabeth Pyle, **Deanna Grant-Smith** and **Robyn Mayes** pay attention to the deficit discourse constituting 'Indigenous disadvantage' and informing Australian Indigenous Affairs policy development and implementation. They illustrate how the deficit discourse and different aspects of the Australian Indigenous Affairs policy can be seen as wicked problems through history and in the present. However, they also question whether it is justified to use the concept of wicked problems in this context. The authors claim that by underlining the wickedness of the situation of these minorities, there is a risk of turning down their voices instead of making the problems related to the position of Aboriginals and Torres Strait Islander peoples visible. The authors raise a critical point, namely how the discourse of wickedness may prevent strength-based and inclusive approaches of involving indigenous people in dialogue and partnership with policymakers.

Will Thomas discusses the complexity of the concept of dependency, especially through the experiences of people living with chronic disease. He critically scrutinizes the dilemma between dependency and independency as a more philosophical question but also as a more concrete question when dealing with patients and negotiating roles, responsibilities and their inherent entitlements. On the basis of his study, which is based on interviews with individuals with a diagnosis of Inflammatory Bowel Disease, the author illustrates the process of 'becoming' a patient and what kind of wicked features it contains. By applying the dependency framework to the empirical data, the author exposes critical points of balancing between necessary and unnecessary derivative dependency.

Section 4—Beyond Conventional Methodologies for Understanding Care

Edmund Coleman-Fountain and **Bryony Beresford** open the section with a chapter that points to the non-linear nature of wicked problems. They do this by considering the challenges faced by young people who have Asperger Syndrome (AS) and the imperative for doing research with those who are considered 'hard to reach' groups. Drawing on a recent study, Coleman-Fountain and Beresford offer insight into how young people with AS face the challenges of mental health. Through the words of young people themselves, we witness accounts of self-reliance, ambivalence, disappointment and health care systems that struggle to cope with intersecting conditions. The wicked problem is not therefore mental health per se, but a personal-professional-organizational struggle to recognize that established health care interventions do not fit 'all' client sub-groups (in this case, mental health services that do not account for the mediating effects of Asperger syndromes). The result is not just a lack of provision but also the very real danger of negating aspects of individual identity. This brings to light the 'invisibility' of certain people and populations. Therein lies the second contribution of the chapter. In sharing the lives of young people with us, Coleman-Fountain and Beresford point out the importance of actively engaging what are perceived to be 'difficult to access groups' in health and social care research. They rightly assert that such engagement "cannot be replaced by 'proxy informants,' nor wider evidence on young people and mental health being applied to this particular population." What is more, they note that it is not enough just to involve those affected by wicked problems as the subjects of research, but that we must strive to include them as advisors in the creation and conduct of said research if we are to address their wicked problems effectively and sensitively.

Marta Strumińska-Kutra takes up the baton of working 'with' those afflicted by wicked issues when she considers the possibilities for research that both constructs and applies knowledge as it goes along. Specifically, the chapter invites us to consider the potential for 'action research' to be applied to wicked problems. The great advantage of action research is that it moves beyond privileging the knowledge of external experts and instead focuses on the co-creation of joint approaches to tackling difficult issues. Moreover, it is concerned with both theory and practice. Strumińska-Kutra is nonetheless at pains to point out that action research is no magic bullet. Tensions are noted in the critical, pragmatist and constructivist roots of the approach, as conflicting concerns with emancipation, the structural determinants of disadvantage and local verses expert power have the tendency to pull action research in different directions. Having outlined the causes and nature of these tensions, Strumińska-Kutra moves to consider how researchers might work with them to produce socially useful research. This, as we shall see, becomes an inherently ethical issue. The result is a chapter that does not resolve the wicked problems that attend action research in health and social care but, rather, provides a basis on which we may better understand those problems and establish our own route.

Anneli Hujala, Sanna Laulainen, Andy Brookes, Maarit Lammassaari and **Tamara Mulherin** take the issues of research tensions and multiple perspectives a step further as they point out the importance of our underlying assumptions about the nature of reality (ontology) and of knowing (epistemology) for researching health and social care. Their chapter invites us to make these assumptions explicit so that audiences might better appreciate the challenges of confronting wicked problems. They explain this process in relation to the challenges of encouraging collaboration in health and social care. We quickly learn that there is no 'one way' of viewing collaboration as a practice, objective, solution or problem. Depending on how we assume the world works, we may see collaboration as an issue of real things and underlying structures, competing discourses, practices or experiences and feelings. Why does this matter? It matters because, as Hujala et al. remind us, each perspective provides a partial and very particular picture of the wicked problem under investigation. Each perspective prioritizes some things and neglects others. One solution is to attempt to conduct multi-paradigm research. More pragmatically, it reminds us that in research and organizing we often see what we look for, and what we look for is informed by how we look. In this sense, even wicked problems are always multifaceted problems.

Jari Martikainen concludes the section by taking up the theme of looking. The chapter considers the power of the visual in the exploration of wicked problems, paying particular attention to the use of participant-created drawings in the exploration of unspoken organizational problems. Locating itself within the visual turn—which has seen textual research methods supplemented by visual approaches to knowledge construction—the chapter draws on work with hospital workers and managers to tackle organizational issues that are hidden and suppressed. Martikainen makes the point that these non-textual methods are valuable because they allow us to approach wicked problems in a different way: a way that is expressive, emotional and open to collaborative consideration of that which is often tacit or difficult to talk about. With very little prompting, drawing techniques are shown to elicit a wide range of darker organizational issues centered on silence, clouded vision, isolation and narcistic leadership: concerns that are usually left unspoken and unacknowledged. This is juxtaposed with hopefully accounts of individual worth, potential to contribute and commitment. Overall, Martikainen offers a technique for revealing the complex and contradictory nature of working in health and social care organizations. It is a technique that sheds light on the darker side of managing and working while also affording voice (and even catharsis) to those who take part.

Will Thomas
Anneli Hujala
Sanna Laulainen
Robert McMurray

References

Brown, Valerie A., John Alfred Harris, and Jacqueline Y. Russell, eds. 2010. *Tackling Wicked Problems Through the Transdisciplinary Imagination*. London, Washington, DC: Earthscan.

Conklin, E. Jeffrey, and William Weil. 1997. "Wicked Problems: Naming the Pain in Organizations." June 5, 2001.

Danken, Thomas, Katrin Dribbisch, and Anne Lange. 2016. "Studying Wicked Problems Forty Years on: Towards a Synthesis of a Fragmented Debate." *der moderne staat—dms: Zeitschrift für Public Policy, Recht und Management* 9 (1): 15–33.

Dunne, David, and Roger Martin. 2006. "Design Thinking and How It Will Change Management Education: An Interview and Discussion." *Academy of Management Learning & Education* 5 (4): 512–523.

Head, Brian W., and John Alford. 2015. "Wicked Problems: Implications for Public Policy and Management." *Administration & Society* 47 (6): 711–739.

Newman, Joshua, and Brian W. Head. 2017. "Wicked Tendencies in Policy Problems: Rethinking the Distinction Between Social and Technical Problems." *Policy and Society* 36 (3): 414–429.

Peters, B. Guy. 2017. "What Is So Wicked About Wicked Problems? A Conceptual Analysis and a Research Program." *Policy and Society* 36 (3): 385–396.

Rittel, Horst W. J., and Melvin M. Webber. 1973. "Dilemmas in a General Theory of Planning." *Policy Sciences* 4 (2): 155–169.

Roberts, Nancy. 2000. "Wicked Problems and Network Approaches to Resolution." *International Public Management Review* 1 (1): 1–19.

Sharts-Hopko, Nancy C. 2013. "Tackling Complex Problems, Building Evidence for Practice, and Educating Doctoral Nursing Students to Manage the Tension." *Nursing Outlook* 61 (2): 102–108.

Termeer, Catrien J. A. M, Art Dewulf, Gerard Breeman, and Sabina J. Stiller. 2015. "Governance Capabilities for Dealing Wisely with Wicked Problems." *Administration & Society* 47 (6): 680–710.

Section 1

Contemporary Wicked Challenges to Health and Social Care

Becoming increasingly popular in both academic and societal discussions, the approach to problematize 'wickedness' serves as a critical and thought-provoking tool to address and rethink current concerns in the management of health and social care. The first section of the book provides background for understanding wicked problems in a broad sense, starting with insightful reflections on the concept itself and continuing by critical contemplation of important policy-level social issues.

Harri Raisio, Alisa Puustinen and Pirkko Vartiainen deepen our knowledge of the concept of wicked problems and offer insights on how to apply this approach to the context of health and social care management. Next, Will Thomas and Susan Hollinrake take a stand on reforms of social care, a concern faced in many countries. Challenges resulting from reforms are considered from the perspective of service users and professionals and mirrored against the ethical aspects. Janet Carter Anand, Gavin Davidson, Berni Kelly and Geraldine Macdonald highlight a topical worldwide social policy issue, the personalization of care, and challenge us to call into question whether it is always the preferred way to meet the individual and diverse needs of people with disabilities. Using personal budgets as an example, the authors of this chapter claim that, regardless of its benefits, personalization may be a contentious and troublesome concept—and a wicked solution to wicked problems.

Contemporary Wicked Challenges to Health and Social Care

1 The Concept of Wicked Problems

Improving the Understanding of Managing Problem Wickedness in Health and Social Care

Harri Raisio, Alisa Puustinen and Pirkko Vartiainen

Editors of three scientific journals point out in their recent joint editorial that "health care leaders at all levels are faced with some of the most complex and challenging problems confronting leaders" (Hutchinson et al. 2015, 3021). More precisely, they write of *wicked problems* and call for moral courage in tackling problem wickedness. As researchers deeply involved with wicked problems, we share this view and strive to further process the significance of wicked problems in managing health and social care. Our aim is to increase the understanding of the sources of problem wickedness and to explore the implications for leaders in health and social care.

This article consists of four main sections. In the first section, we will define the concept of wicked problems in detail. We also consider the conceptual criticism and provide examples of wicked problems found in the health and social care sector. The second section scrutinizes the conceptual expansions of wicked problems, such as the *super wicked problem*, *wicked ethics*, and the *wicked game*, and assesses their relevance from the health and social care perspective. In the third section, we will deepen the theoretical foundations of the concept of wicked problems by affiliating wicked problems to the complexity science framework. As complexity can be a source of problem wickedness (see Zellner and Campbell 2015), this is an essential aspect of the analysis. The fourth section focuses on the leaders' point of view. Hutchinson et al. (2015) point out the challenge of defining leadership "when there are no easy answers." We conclude with a summary of key insights.

Defining a Wicked Problem

The concept of wicked problems[1] already has a 50-year history. In 1967, an esteemed systems scientist, C. West Churchman, hosted a seminar series at the University of California, Berkeley.[2] In his account of what occurred, Skaburskis (2008) reports how German-born faculty member Professor Horst W. J. Rittel made a presentation at one seminar session that included a description of the differences between social and technical problems, using what came to be known as the ten main features of wicked problems.

Churchman himself became interested in the concept and wrote a guest editorial titled *Wicked Problems* for *Management Science* (Churchman 1967).[3] This was the first reference to wicked problems in the academic literature. Rittel took several years to present his arguments in article form, but finally, in 1973, with his colleague Melvin M. Webber, he published the seminal article *Dilemmas in the General Theory of Planning* in *Policy Sciences*.[4] Today (June 7, 2017), Google Scholar records more than 10,000 citations of the article. Although there are major continental differences on the level of awareness about the concept of wicked problems (Xiang 2013), the overall interest in the concept "seems greater than ever"[5] (McCall and Burge 2016, 200; Danken, Dribbisch and Lange 2016). This is understandable, as the problems we face seem to be in increasing numbers wicked by their very nature (Raisio and Lundström 2015). The dilemma, however, is that these problems are often thought to be tamer than they really are, or the problems are understood as wicked, but even then, the chosen approaches are more like approaches required to address so-called *tame problems* (Rittel and Webber 1973; Raisio 2009).

Rittel and Webber noted that "the problems that scientists and engineers have usually focused upon are mostly 'tame' or 'benign' ones" (1973, 160). The concept of tame problems offers a form of counterpart to the concept of wicked problems. Tame problems can be defined thoroughly and permanently. There is little or no ambiguity. It is relatively easy to reach a common understanding of such problems, so conflict situations are rare. In addition, it is obvious when a tame problem has been solved; there is a clear end solution, and its accuracy can be evaluated objectively. Solving a tame problem is in practice a repetition, in the sense that someone with enough expertise and specialization and using proven solution processes could repeatedly solve similar problems (King 1993; Roberts 2000). It is often also the case that one can start solving tame problems from the beginning, without any major impact, as if the process took place in laboratory conditions. Overall, solving a tame problem can be understood as a rather linear process proceeding step-by-step from problem definition, through gathering information and analysis to identifying different solutions, after which the best solution to the problem is identified and then implemented (Conklin 2005). Think, for example, of an experienced mechanic fixing a familiar model of car.

Wicked problems resist such approaches, as is clear from the ten characteristics attributed by Rittel and Webber (1973) to such issues (see Table 1.1). Owing to the explicit overlapping between the different characteristics, several researchers have condensed them further (see e.g., Conklin 2005; Norton 2012; Xiang 2013). However, Danken, Dribbisch and Lange (2016, 16–17) critique the lack of a clear-cut definition for the concept, as well as the fragmented debate on problem wickedness. Their systematic quantitative literature review strives to collate the existing academic literature so that "we as scholars know what we are talking about when we talk about wicked problems" and thus would be "able to enter more purposefully into a discussion on their management." Three dominant and interrelated thematic clusters of wicked problems' core characteristics emerge from the above review: the challenge of problem definition; non-resolvability; and multi-actor environments.

The challenge of problem definition refers to the cognitive uncertainty (van Bueren, Klijn and Koppenjan 2003) and the content complexity (Stoppelenburg and Vermaak 2009) related to problem wickedness. Wicked problems are by nature so multidimensional, interrelated and ambiguous that understanding them is a considerable challenge. The major uncertainty arises from a lack of knowledge or understanding of the problem and also the solutions; the identification of cause-effect relationships is a particularly challenging exercise (McCall and Burge 2016). *Non-resolvability* refers to the chronic nature of wicked problems. As Danken, Dribbisch and Lange (2016, 16–17) write, "scholars hold that any attempt to resolve [wicked

Table 1.1 The Ten Original Characteristics of Wicked Problems (Rittel and Webber 1973)

1. There is no definitive formulation of a wicked problem. Different approaches to the problem see it differently. Different proposed solutions reflect the fact that it is defined differently.

2. There is a 'no stopping rule.' Unlike in an experiment where you can stop natural processes and control variables, you cannot step outside a wicked problem or stop it to contemplate an approach to answering it. Things keep changing as policy-makers are trying to formulate their answers.

3. Solutions are not true or false, rather they are good or bad. There is no right answer, and no one is in the position to say what is a right answer. The many stakeholders focus on whether proposed solutions are ones they like from their point of view.

4. There is no test of whether a solution will work or has worked. After a solution is tried, the complex and unpredictable ramifications of the intervention will change the context in such a way that the problem is now different.

5. Every solution is a 'one-shot operation.' There can be no gradual learning by trial and error, because each intervention changes the problem in an irreversible way.

6. There is no comprehensive list of possible solutions.

7. Each wicked problem is unique, so that it is hard to learn from previous problems because they were different in significant ways.

8. A wicked problem is itself a symptom of other problems. Incremental solutions run the risk of not really addressing the underlying problem.

9. There is a choice about how to see the problem, but how we see the problem determines which type of solution we will try and apply.

10. Wicked societal problems have effects on real people, so one cannot conduct experiments to see what works without having tangible effects on people's lives.

problems] may exacerbate the problem, reveal new aspects of the problem, and/or generate additional, often unanticipated problems." This is to be understood as a problem of demarcation (see Skaburskis 2008). Waves of consequences can be such that the comprehensive evaluation of solutions becomes virtually impossible (McCall and Burge 2016).

Multi-actor environments refer to the social complexity related to problem wickedness (Conklin 2005). When scholars refer to social complexity, they usually speak of the range of people involved and their diversity, which means the actors concerned have a variety of worldviews, political agendas, educational and professional backgrounds, responsibilities and cultural traditions. This diversity makes the extent of social complexity within the wicked problem overwhelming in most cases (Weber and Khademian 2008). These multi-actor environments include strategic and institutional uncertainty (van Bueren, Klijn and Koppenjan 2003). Strategic uncertainty arises from the presence of a multitude of actors, each with their own perceptions of the problem and the solution, creating many different and sometimes conflicting strategies. Institutional uncertainty develops from the existence of many different arenas—from the local to the global—where wicked problems are discussed. Danken, Dribbisch and Lange (2016, 28) use the three thematic clusters to devise the following formulation of the concept of wicked problems: "[wicked problems] are chronic public policy challenges that are value-laden and contested and that defy a full understanding and definition of their nature and implications."

One significant question debated is the issue of degrees of wickedness. For example, Conklin (2005) considers that problems can be wicked even if they do not include all the original ten features. For Southgate, Reynolds and Howley (2013), while some characteristics might not be as clear as others, it is the sum of these individual characteristics that make the problems wicked. Norton (2012, 450) highlights the involvement of conflicting values as the underlying unifying threat of all the characteristics of wicked problems: "while the characteristics [Rittel and Webber] list for wicked problems are quite disparate, the class of wicked problems are all expressions of diverse and conflicting *values and interests*, which cause individuals to view problems very differently" (italics in the original). For Head (2008, 103), this "divergence and fragmentation of viewpoints, values, strategic intentions" alone might not be enough to make a problem wicked, and an additional high level of "complexity of elements, subsystems and interdependencies" and "uncertainty in relation to risks, consequences of action, and changing patterns" is required. These three dimensions of a problem's wickedness are depicted in Figure 1.1 in the form of a Wickedness Cube.[6] The cube works as a simplified illustration, highlighting the ideal models of three different types of problems.[7] The differentiation of problem types is not as clear-cut in reality as it appears in the cube and in the ideal types described. Boundaries of the ideal types most often blur due to situational

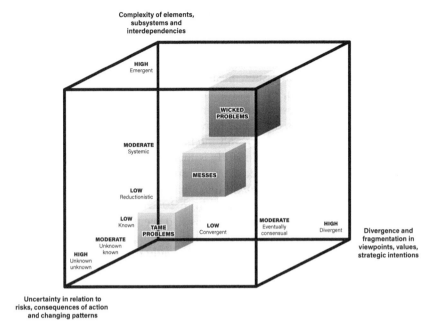

Figure 1.1 A Wickedness Cube

dynamics. Problem types are not static but constantly re-evaluated as part of the dynamic, complex contextual variations.

Tame problems are situated in the bottom left rear corner of the cube. These are issues that can be examined through a reductionist approach. They can be broken into parts and fixed in isolation from other problems. Tame problems are also issues that 'enjoy consensus' (King 1993, 106), in the sense that they are convergent. Additionally, the consequences of solving a tame problem are *known*; for individuals who specialize in solving a particular tame problem, there is no uncertainty around what will happen. In addition, so-called *messes*[8] are added to the cube and situated at the center of the model. Messes can be understood as clusters of problems that cannot be solved in isolation. As King (ibid.) states, "messes demand a commitment to understanding how things going on here-and-now interact with other things going on there-and-later." A systemic approach is needed. This means examining patterns of interaction among the different parts of the problem as well in other, related problems. To illustrate the point, a human mission to Mars is necessarily messier than fixing a car; however, it is still an issue on which consensus could eventually be achieved, at least on some level. After enough time studying the problem, we can, for example, begin to agree on appropriate strategies to go forward. Messes call for interdisciplinarity, which aids not only in formulating solutions, but also in reducing the uncertainty related to the messes. This uncertainty can be depicted as *unknown knows*, meaning that we may not have the knowledge of risks, consequences of actions, or changing patterns, but some other experts might (see Aven 2015).

Wicked problems are situated close to the top right front corner of the cube. These are emergent issues, meaning that even examining patterns of interaction is not enough, as interaction can cause emergent outcomes; the end result is more, or less, than its parts. A holistic approach is needed. Wicked problems are also depicted as divergent issues: "The more it is studied the more people of integrity and intellect inevitably come to different solutions" (King 1993, 112). No study is then sufficient to prompt a broad and sustained consensus. In addition, uncertainty is high, because events that can emerge are *unknown unknowns*, that is, completely unknown, for example, to scientific communities (see Aven 2015).

The very concept of wicked problems has also been criticized: for example, Peters (2017) cautions against conceptual stretching, as it might eventually make the concept of wicked problems analytically meaningless, that is, the analytical capacity of the concept becomes undermined. McCall and Burge (2016, 201) consider that various articles with a critical outlook "portray attempts at hostile takeovers of wicked problems theory by rival theories." An example of such is Coyne's much-cited article (2005), which analyzes the concept from the perspectives of phenomenology and poststructuralism. Based on the analysis, Coyne (2005) considers that almost every problem can be seen to have the character of a wicked problem, making wickedness the norm. McCall and Burge (2016), however, consider these attempts incompatible with the notions of wicked problems. In their own critical outlook, they strive to improve—property by property—the understanding of the strengths and weaknesses of the concept. Among some interesting conclusions, McCall and Burge (2016), for example, redefine the role of trial and error as well the accountability of the individuals trying to tackle wicked problems to move those aspects into a more moderate direction.

Over the last few decades, the concept of wicked problems has been used to describe and explain various societal and organizational issues. Most often these have been issues related to environmental resource management, security and defense, and health and health care. In addition, issues of social care and social policy such as poverty, unemployment and social exclusion are featured in scholarly articles on wicked problems (see Danken, Dribbisch and Lange 2016). To highlight the sector of health and social care, wicked problems have been examined, in relation to the following issues among others: child abuse (Devaney and Spratt 2009), well-being (Bache, Reardon and Anand 2016), reforming health care (Vartiainen 2008; Raisio 2009), mental health policy (Hannigan and Coffey 2011), euthanasia (Raisio and Vartiainen 2015), health promotion (Signal et al. 2013), fragmentation of care (Shaw and Rosen 2013) and institutional abuse (Burns, Hyde and Killett 2013).

Conceptual Expansions

As a fashionable and still timely concept, the notion of wicked problems has inspired various expansions. The best known is that of the *super wicked problem*, coined by Levin et al. (2012, 127–128). To justify the *super* prefix, the authors defined four additional features of wickedness: time is running out; those seeking to end the problem are also causing it; no central authority; and policies discount the future irrationally. The issue of climate change has been identified as a super wicked problem (see Lazarus 2009; Levin et al. 2012). For example, for Pollitt (2016, 78), climate change is the "ultimate wicked issue." Peters (2017) considers the concept of the super wicked problem to be useful, as the four additional features denote a clearly separate category of policy problems. Super wicked problems are then distinguished from different policy issues more easily than traditional wicked problems. Peters (2017, 392) particularly highlights the *time element* as a factor of differentiation.

The concept of the super wicked problem can be particularly useful to describe issues in the context of health and social care. Issues like addressing climate change necessitate multi-sectoral and multilevel governance, in which the "health community has a vital part to play" (Watts et al. 2015, 1862). As Pollitt (2016, 78) states, climate change is a highly interconnected issue that "will directly affect a vast range of government functions, from building regulations to flood defences; from agricultural policy to public health; from border controls to emergency services, and from energy policy through transport policy to the insurance industry and international diplomacy." Climate change will influence health care systems and the health of populations, but the health community can also be part of the solution. The public health perspective on climate change can, for instance, be more tangible than often convoluted environmental concepts and issues. In addition, health professionals already have considerable experience of working on issues such as tobacco usage and HIV/AIDS infection, where they confront what Watts et al. call "powerful entrenched interests" (2015, 1862, 1905). However, despite the super wicked nature of the issue, there is still not enough awareness of climate change as a health issue.

The *wicked game* is one of the recent additions to the conceptual toolbox. The concept has been used in the contexts of urban planning (Lundström et al. 2016) and smart specialization (Lundström and Mäenpää 2017). The wicked game emphasizes the dynamic nature of working with wicked problems. Wicked problems are then not just an abstract issue. As Lundström and Mäenpää (2017, 2) state, "we are all part of the game and can discover some new and interesting ways to understand the wickedness." To concretize the wicked game, Lundström et al. (2016) and Lundström and Mäenpää (2017) use the juxtaposition of a tame game and wicked game, as depicted in Table 1.2.

Table 1.2 Characteristics of a Tame Game and Wicked Game (Lundström et al. 2016; Lundström and Mäenpää 2017).

	Tame game	Wicked game
Rules	Strictly defined set of rules for all situations that can occur. Rules are known by every player. Rules are mechanical.	No coherent set of rules, everybody can play the game by their own rules. Rules are organic.
Players	Limited number of participants recognized by everyone.	Players change all the time. Everyone who is involved in the game is a potential player.
Playing field	Can be defined precisely.	Networked and complex, the spatial scale is relative and can vary.
Practice	Repetition can help one to develop skills. The more you play, the better you get. There is often the possibility of a return tie.	No one can master a wicked game because the game, the rules, and the players change constantly. There is no possibility of a return tie.
Ending point	The game has a clear end point. Answers are right or wrong.	The game does not end. Answers are better, worse, satisfying or good enough.

In the context of health and social care, the concepts of the tame and the wicked game could have value when planning and implementing various reforms. Often, these reform processes resemble more tame games than wicked ones; their distinct features include linear progression, authoritative strategies and the quick identification of problems (see Vartiainen 2005; Raisio 2009). For example, the number of the participants in a planning process is often limited. In Finland, reform processes are mainly controlled by a select few MPs and ministry officials. Not only municipalities and the organizations that provide services, but also the citizens who should be at the center of any process reforming services for their benefit are excluded from the planning processes. Residents, municipal decision-makers and representatives of many organizations are then mere pawns that the state's long arm moves according to its current agenda and political interest.

Wicked ethics appears to be the most relevant conceptual addition in relation to health and social care. Heimer (2013) raises the issue of wicked ethics to illustrate the dilemmas in relation to macro-level official ethics and micro-level ethics on the ground, in the context of the practice of ethics in HIV research. Official ethics are then ethics inherent in the likes of official regulations, policies and operating procedures. Regulators attempt to produce universal solutions and to ensure uniformity across different settings. The idea of ethics on the ground relates more to ethics in action, that is, the ethical problems faced by individual professionals. These are less routinized, more local and beyond the purview of the administration. According to Heimer (2013, 377), "official ethics puts blinders on our eyes." Official ethics can abstract out the wickedness, raising the need for ethics on the ground, that is, for sensitivity and adaption to local conditions. This can become more problematic when the issue at hand includes dimensions that "exhibit high degrees of psychosocial sensitivity." In these situations, problems may not only become wicked, but also *unspeakable* (Grant-Smith and Osborne 2016, 46). If a problem becomes unspeakable, some aspects of that problem can become inaccessible, making it even more wicked.

Integration of Wicked Problems and Complexity

Wicked problems and complexity are intertwined. In recent articles, wicked problems have been combined with a *complex systems* or *complex adaptive systems* (CAS)[9] perspective to offer insight into the nature of such wicked problems (Waddock et al. 2015; Zellner and Campbell 2015). Complex systems and wicked problems seem to have many similar characteristics or properties: defining the problem or its boundaries is difficult; both require a holistic approach; both are characterized by non-linear dynamics; there are no definitive resolutions or outcomes; they seem to follow some kind of pattern, yet remain unpredictable; they are very sensitive to initial conditions and path dependence (see e.g. Cilliers 1998; Rittel and Webber 1973; Waddock et al. 2015; Zellner and Campbell 2015).

Conceptually both wicked problems and complexity stem from a similar world view, the *paradigm of conscious complexity* (see Table 1.3). Whereas wicked problems are most often contrasted with tame ones, conscious complexity is contrasted with the *paradigm of order* (Geyer and Rihani 2010). This notion is also in line with the recent conceptualization of tame games and wicked games (Lundström et al. 2016; Lundström and Mäenpää 2017). In an orderly world, where given causes lead to known effects at all times and in all places, processes flow along predetermined orderly paths and the future can be predicted, we play tame games. In the orderly world, players are limited and known, rules are certain and the playing field is constant and definable. In a world defined by conscious complexity, wicked games become the reality. Games are at the same time orderly and chaotic. The playing field, the space of possibilities, can be partially modeled, but actual outcomes are always uncertain (Puustinen and Lehtimäki 2016). In a complex world, filled with wicked problems and games, the players try to interpret, to make sense of, their surroundings to achieve a collective and common understanding of the situations they face at any given time (see e.g. Hanén 2017; Puustinen 2017). And it is actually the interpretation itself that makes the situation even more complex, as is exemplified by the defining features of wicked problems (see Table 1.1).

In their typology of problems in health and social care settings, Glouberman and Zimmerman (2002) differentiate between simple, complicated and complex problems.[10] The term *complex problem* is used as a synonym for wicked problem. A *simple problem* equates to what we previously called a

Table 1.3 From Order to Conscious Complexity (Original Table by Puustinen and Lehtimäki 2016)

ORDERLY WORLD (Adapted from Geyer and Rihani 2010, 13)	CONSCIOUS COMPLEXITY (Adapted from Geyer and Rihani 2010, 29)
Order: given causes lead to known effects at all times and in all places	**Partial order:** systems exhibit both orderly and chaotic behaviors
Reductionism: the whole is the sum of its parts, no more and no less (the system is reducible to its parts)	**Reductionism and holism:** some phenomena are reducible, others are not (always more or less than the sum of its parts)
Predictability: once global behavior is defined, the future can be predicted by applying the appropriate inputs to the model	**Predictability and uncertainty:** can be partially modeled, predicted and controlled
Determinism: processes flow along orderly paths that have clear beginnings and rational ends	**Probabilistic:** general boundaries, but within these boundaries precise outcomes are always uncertain
	Emergence: systems exhibit elements of co-evolution, adaption and emergence
	Interpretation: actors are aware of themselves, the system and their history and strive to interpret and direct the system

tame problem. A *complicated problem* is somewhere in between, akin to the messes described above. In a health care setting, complicated heart surgery may be an example of a complicated but not a complex problem. According to Glouberman and Zimmerman (2002), we often make the mistake of confusing these different kinds of problems, and hence apply the wrong solutions. Simple or tame problems are easy to detect and also to handle. But differentiating between a complicated and a complex problem can be more difficult. The sophistication of the models and theories suitable to address complicated problems, such as heart surgery, will often fail if we try to apply them to complex or wicked problems (ibid.). Wiping out measles globally or implementing nationwide health care reform are good examples of wicked problems.

Wicked problems also pose knowledge challenges because they are unstructured, in that their causes and effects are extremely difficult to identify and model. The wicked problem space comprises multiple, overlapping and interconnected, embedded subsets of problems and, finally, they are relentless (Weber and Khademian 2008). An incorrect definition or diagnosis of a problem often leads to, and is characterized by, ignorance of some essential features of the case at hand. This in turn may lead to ignorance of complexity, because we prefer to simplify the world and particularly the problems around us to make it easier to cope with the complexity we face (see also Waddock et al. 2015). Complexity thinking or sciences offer assistance in defining problem wickedness, for example by using the concept of *fundamental complexity* as outlined by Cramer (1979, 138), "A system is fundamentally complex if, by a multiplicity of structures or through unfolding of new structures, the number of the parameters to be determined becomes larger than the possibility of measuring or coordinating these parameters." The characterization of wicked problems suggests they are often fundamentally complex, since the number of parameters to be measured in order to understand the problem in its entirety becomes larger than the chance of measuring those particular problem characteristics.

It is quite clear from the complexity perspective that we cannot measure everything. Our understanding and knowledge are always limited (Cilliers 2005), but understanding the fundamentals of complexity and applying "the art of reasoning with complexity" (Zellner and Campbell 2015) would reduce the danger of misdiagnosing a problem and using the incorrect tools. In institutional settings, such as health and social care, the art of reasoning with complexity requires actors make sense of the situation. Sense-making in organizations is fundamentally a social and systemic process that takes place via communication and interaction, and it is always ambiguous (Weick 2015; Weick, Sutcliffe and Obstfeld 2005). It is also always about action, about making sense of what is going on and what should be done next (Weick, Sutcliffe and Obstfeld 2005). Sense-making resonates well with the art of reasoning with complexity, in that it is about finding out what kind of a problem we face, and what might be done next, without ignoring the complexity of problem wickedness. When dealing with wicked problems, ambiguity is permanent, but interpretations of the wickedness are impermanent (see e.g. Weick 2015). Hence, dealing with complex, wicked problems is about the practice of understanding and managing ambiguity.

Implications for Management and Leadership

The question of how to manage wicked problems and complexity in public organizations has been analyzed in numerous publications. Danken, Dribbisch and Lange (2016) summarize the proposed approaches in their literature review. Two extensive intertwined thematic clusters shine through. The first is *cross-boundary collaboration*, which includes such approaches as involving multiple stakeholders, promoting dialogue and deliberation and applying modes of network governance. A second thematic cluster highlights *the role of leadership and management*. Leaders and managers should be able differentiate between different types of problems. They should also understand that tackling wicked problems necessitates the involvement of various stakeholders. Additionally, they should acquire new skills, especially those associated with collaborative governance.

However, Termeer et al. (2015) note that the literature on wicked problems emphasizes *how-to-do* action strategies. In addition, observing and enabling are also necessary. The notion of *observing* in this case refers to the ambiguous nature of wicked problems and the many alternative ways of perceiving problem wickedness. *Enabling* refers to the governance system as a whole and in its capacity to create conditions for both observing and action. For Termeer et al. (2015, 682, 684–686), "to deal wisely with wicked problems" requires these three dimensions to be part of four different governance capabilities, which are *reflexivity* ("to deal with the variety of possible perspectives on wicked problems and to prevent tunnel vision"), *resilience* ("to adapt to a constantly changing flow of problem definitions, solutions, and context conditions,") *responsiveness* ("to react to changing demands while striking a balance between different public values") and *revitalization* ("to unblock unproductive patterns in the governance process").

When managing problem wickedness in health and social care, the focus should be on networks and collaborative governance rather than on hierarchies and authoritarian leadership. For example, Ferlie et al. (2010) conclude that the existence of wicked problems supports the wisdom of constructing networks. Roberts (2000) makes a similar kind of an argument by asking why we always need to realize the prospects of networks and collaboration by first failing in other strategies, that is, in authoritarian or competitive ones. Newman and Head (2017, 423) write about shortcomings in information-based strategies, emphasizing that collecting extensive data does not help decision-makers reduce complex societal problems to "tame, technical puzzles." For example, evidence-based policymaking would then always lag behind in the attempt to address wicked problems.

Nevertheless, Daviter (2017, 584) asks an important question: "If wicked problems cannot be solved [see Table 1.1], what should the governance of wicked problems aim to accomplish?" Emphasizing that there must be a better understanding of the alternatives, Daviter identifies *three different strategies of problem governance*: problem-solving, coping and taming with the aims of resolving, reflecting and reducing, respectively. The three strategies have contrasting intellectual premises and practical implications and, according to Daviter (ibid.), in essence, no strategy is better than any other. Instead of one correct strategy, the question is then more about the trade-offs between the different strategies, and if the different kinds of wicked problems require different kinds of responses.

Problem-solving strategies include (often overly optimistic) holistic approaches such as whole-of-government and collaborative or network governance. According to Daviter (2017, 578), these strategies "aim to resolve wicked problems as comprehensively as possible." However, the literature rarely explicitly defines the stopping rule, that is, what would be a sufficient level of goal attainment. In addition, these holistic strategies include major challenges for resolving wicked problems, such as collective action problems and gridlocks. As for coping strategies, these "aim to reflect the fragmented, uncertain, and ambiguous nature of wicked problems by relying on a more disjointed and tentative process of formulating policy responses" (ibid.). Such incremental and less coherent approaches are then not seen negatively, but as a natural approach that views wicked problems as essentially a never-ending process. In taming strategies, the aim is "to reduce wicked problems to make them more controllable and manageable" (ibid.). Such strategies often unnecessarily reduce the complexity of the situation, hence ignoring some essential features of the complex whole. However, they do facilitate quick and efficient decision-making, but with the risk of volatile results, as interdependencies are neglected and the problem of reflectivity decreased (see e.g. Hanén 2017; Puustinen 2017). For example, Conklin (2005) highlights various taming strategies, such as freezing the problem definition prematurely or assuming that the problem is the same kind as was faced before.

All the aforementioned strategies of taming, coping and problem-solving were also presented in Raisio (2009), where the planning of the Finnish national health service reform was analyzed from the perspective of problem wickedness. The study highlighted that the wickedness was in the most part noted, but it was not taken as seriously as it should have been. A taming strategy was clearly present, in that the problems were defined by a few people, who then attempted to implement a linear solution. In addition, the conflict between the coping and problem-solving strategies emerged from interviewees' statements that no one could have taken everything into consideration and others to the effect that if the approach had been truly holistic, perhaps nothing would have happened. The situation poses a dilemma over which approach is preferable: a swift taming approach with possible volatile results, an incremental approach with only small incremental changes or a holistic problem-solving approach targeting fundamental change but which may never happen. Daviter (2017) notes how these alternative strategies and related trade-offs need to be better understood.

Conclusion

The significance and use of the concept of the wicked problem seem to grow year by year. As a concept it has not, however, become static, but has both been challenged and developed. The concept of wicked problems does not exist in isolation, but is a part of similar frameworks, such as that of complexity sciences. As the world becomes more networked and as the quantity of information as well as the speed of its transfer grows, the complexity and wickedness gain strength (see Say and Pronk 2012). Increased connectivity means small, local-level triggers can have powerful unintended and unforeseeable wave-like consequences throughout the system. The quantity of information and the speed of data flows, in turn, bring significant challenges to our ability as humans to address the complexity of the operating environment.

The increase in wickedness and complexity should be acknowledged more than it is currently in management theory and practice. There should, for example, be more empirical research on managing problem wickedness in the context of social and health care. In addition, the connections between the theoretical framework and the existing management culture need to be strengthened. As pointed out in Raisio and Lundström (2015, 4), "through theory-practice dialogue . . . a more in-depth understanding of complexity, chaos, and wickedness could be obtained." However, in the worst case, these concepts are used only as window-dressing; nothing really changes.

Notes

1. Some academics also refer to a *theory of wicked problems* (e.g., McCall and Burge 2016).
2. The seminar series was a part of Churchman's research project, funded by NASA, which explored how the technology from the US space program could be transferred to the context of urban problems (Skaburskis 2008).
3. Skaburskis (2008, 277) points out that it might have actually been Churchman who gave wicked problems their striking name: "At the end of Rittel's presentation, West Churchman responded with that pensive but expressive movement of voice that some may well remember, 'Hmm, those sound like wicked problems.'"
4. Note, Rittel had also published an article in the Norwegian journal *Bedriftsøkonomen* in 1972, which received considerably less attention (see Rittel 1972).
5. It is important to note that regardless of the attention the concept of wicked problems has received since its first publication, it was not the sole factor in the paradigm shift of that time; consider, for example, Herbert Simon with his suggestion of "bounded rationality" and Charles E. Lindblom with his approach of "muddling through." Scholars have considered just what influenced the popularity of the wicked problem concept: for Zellner and Campbell (2015, 488), "one source of the article's power is its unequivocal writing and explicit argument: that we have tried to confront (urban) social problems with the wrong tools because we have misunderstood the very nature of the problems." Skaburskis (2008, 279) sees the contribution in "the clarity, directness and timing of [Rittel's] message."
6. Inspired by Fung's Democracy Cube (Fung 2006).
7. In the Wickedness Cube, only tame problems, messes and wicked problems are illustrated. They are depicted as ideal types. For example, Alford and Head (2017) present a two-dimensional matrix encompassing nine different problem types.
8. Originally coined by Ackoff (1974).
9. The study of complex adaptive systems has been popular since the establishment of the renowned Santa Fe institute. However, complexity thinking has existed far longer. For instance, well-known examples of complexity thinkers include Mary Parker Follett (see Mendenhall, Macomber and Cutright 2000) and Carl von Clausewitz (see Hanén 2017).
10. See also Snowden and Boone (2007), whose *Cynefin* framework differentiates between simple, complicated, complex and chaotic domains.

References

Ackoff, Russell L. 1974. *Redesigning the Future*. New York: John Wiley & Sons.
Alford, John, and Brian W. Head. 2017. "Wicked and Less Wicked Problems: A Typology and a Contingency Framework." *Policy and Society* 36 (3): 397–413.
Aven, Terje. 2015. "Implications of Black Swans to the Foundations and Practice of Risk Assessment and Management." *Reliability Engineering and System Safety* 134: 83–91.
Bache, Ian, Louise Reardon, and Paul Anand. 2016. "Wellbeing as a Wicked Problem: Navigating the Arguments for the Role of Government." *Journal of Happiness Studies* 17 (3): 893–912.
Burns, Diane, Paula Hyde, and Anne Killett. 2013. "Wicked Problems or Wicked People? Reconceptualising Institutional Abuse." *Sociology of Health and Illness: A Journal of Medical Sociology* 35 (4): 514–528.
Churchman, C. West. 1967. "Wicked Problems." *Management Science* 14 (4): 141–142.
Cilliers, Paul. 1998. *Complexity and Post-Modernism: Understanding Complex Systems*. London: Routledge.
Cilliers, Paul. 2005. "Knowledge, Limits and Boundaries." *Futures* 37 (7): 605–613.
Conklin, Jeff. 2005. *Dialogue Mapping: Building Shared Understanding of Wicked Problems*. New York: Wiley-Blackwell.
Coyne, Richard. 2005. "Wicked Problems Revisited." *Design Studies* 26 (1): 5–17.
Cramer, Friedrich. 1979. "Fundamental Complexity. A Concept in Biological Sciences and Beyond." *Interdisciplinary Science Reviews* 4 (2): 132–139.
Danken, Thomas, Katrin Dribbisch, and Anne Lange. 2016. "Studying Wicked Problems Forty Years on: Towards a Synthesis of a Fragmented Debate." *der moderne staat—Zeitschrift für Public Policy, Recht und Management* 9 (1): 15–33.
Daviter, Falk. 2017. "Coping, Taming or Solving: Alternative Approaches to the Governance of Wicked Problems." *Policy Studies* 38 (6): 571–588.
Devaney, John, and Trevor Spratt. 2009. "Child Abuse as a Complex and Wicked Problem: Reflecting on Policy Developments in the United Kingdom in Working with Children and Families with Multiple Problems." *Children and Youth Services Review* 31 (6): 635–641.
Ferlie, Ewan, Louise Fitzgerald, Gerry McGivern, Sue Dopson, and Chris Bennett. 2010. "Public Policy Networks and 'Wicked Problems': A Nascent Solution?" *Public Administration* 89 (2): 307–324.
Fung, Archon. 2006. "Varieties of Participation in Complex Governance." *Public Administration Review* 66 (s1): 66–75.
Geyer, Robert, and Samir Rihani. 2010. *Complexity and Public Policy: A New Approach to 21st Century Politics, Policy and Society*. New York: Routledge.
Glouberman, Sholom, and Brenda Zimmerman. 2002. "Complicated and Complex Systems: What Would Successful Reform of Medicare Look Like?" Discussion Paper no. 8. Commission on the Future of Health Care in Canada.
Grant-Smith, Deanna, and Natalia Osborne. 2016. "Dealing with Discomfort: How the Unspeakable Confounds Wicked Planning Problems." *Australian Planner* 53 (1): 46–53.
Hanén, Tom. 2017. *Yllätysten edessä: kompleksisuusteoreettinen tulkinta yllättävien ja dynaamisten tilanteiden johtamisesta* [Faced with the Unexpected—Leadership

in Unexpected and Dynamic Situations: An Interpretation Based on Complexity Theory]. Helsinki: The National Defence University.

Hannigan, Ben, and Michael Coffey. 2011. "Where the Wicked Problems Are: The Case of Mental Health." *Health Policy* 101 (3): 220–227.

Head, Brian. 2008. "Wicked Problems in Public Policy." *Public Policy* 3 (2): 101–118.

Heimer, Carol Anne. 2013. " 'Wicked' Ethics: Compliance Work and the Practice of Ethics in HIV Research." *Social Science & Medicine* 98: 371–378.

Hutchinson, Marie, John Daly, Kim Usher, and Debra Jackson. 2015. "Leadership When There Are No Easy Answers: Applying Leader Moral Courage to Wicked Problems." *Journal of Clinical Nursing* 24 (21–22): 3021–3023.

King, Jonathan B. 1993. "Learning to Solve the Right Problems: The Case of Nuclear Power in America." *Journal of Business Ethics* 12 (2): 105–116.

Lazarus, Richard J. 2009. "Super Wicked Problems and Climate Change: Restraining the Present to Liberate the Future." *Cornell Law Review* 94 (5): 1153–1233.

Levin, Kelly, Benjamin Cashore, Steven Bernstein, and Graeme Auld. 2012. "Overcoming the Tragedy of Super Wicked Problems: Constraining Our Future Selves to Ameliorate Global Climate Change." *Policy Sciences* 45 (2): 123–152.

Lundström, Niklas, and Antti Mäenpää. 2017. "Wicked Game of Smart Specialization: A Player's Handbook." *European Planning Studies* 25 (8): 1357–1374.

Lundström, Niklas, Harri Raisio, Pirkko Vartiainen, and Juha Lindell. 2016. "Wicked Games Changing the Storyline of Urban Planning." *Landscape and Urban Planning* 154: 20–28.

McCall Raymond, and Janet Burge. 2016. "Untangling Wicked Problems." *Artificial Intelligence for Engineering Design, Analysis and Manufacturing* 30 (2): 200–210.

Mendenhall, Mark E., James H. Macomber, and Mark Cutright. 2000. "Mary Parker Follett: Prophet of Chaos and Complexity." *Journal of Management History* 6 (4): 191–204.

Newman, Joshua, and Brian W. Head. 2017. "Wicked Tendencies in Policy Problems: Rethinking the Distinction Between Social and Technical Problems." *Policy and Society* 36 (3): 414–429.

Norton, Bryan G. 2012. "The Ways of Wickedness: Analyzing Messiness with Messy Tools." *Journal of Agricultural and Environmental Ethics* 25 (4): 447–465.

Peters, B. Guy. 2017. "What Is So Wicked About Wicked Problems? A Conceptual Analysis and a Research Program." *Policy and Society* 36 (3): 385–396.

Pollitt, Christopher. 2016. "Debate: Climate change—The Ultimate Wicked Issue." *Public Money & Management* 36 (2): 78–80.

Puustinen, Alisa. 2017. *Voiko verkostoa johtaa? Tapaustutkimus sosiaali—ja terveydenhuollon yhteistoiminta-alueen hallinnan yhteenkietoutuneesta luonteesta* [Can Networks Be Managed? Case Study on the Complexity of Governance in a Cooperation District of Health and Social Care]. Kuopio: University of Eastern Finland.

Puustinen, Alisa, and Hanna Lehtimäki. 2016. "Success and Failure? A Complexity Perspective on an Organizational Innovation Blockage." *Emergence: Complexity and Organization* 18 (3–4): 1–9.

Raisio, Harri. 2009. "Health Care Reform Planners and Wicked Problems: Is the Wickedness of the Problems Taken Seriously or Is It Even Noticed at All?" *Journal of Health Organization and Management* 23 (5): 477–493.

Raisio, Harri, and Niklas Lundström. 2015. "Real Leaders Embracing the Paradigm of Complexity." *Emergence: Complexity & Organization* 17 (3): 1–5.

Raisio, Harri, and Pirkko Vartiainen. 2015. "Accelerating the Publics Learning Curve on Wicked Policy Issues: Results from Deliberative Forums on Euthanasia." *Policy Sciences* 48 (3): 339–361.

Rittel, Horst W. J. 1972. "On the Planning Crisis: Systems Analysis of the 'First and Second Generations'." *Bedriftsokonomen* 8: 390–396.

Rittel, Horst W. J., and Melvin Webber. 1973. "Dilemmas in a General Theory of Planning." *Policy Sciences* 4 (2): 155–169.

Roberts, Nancy. 2000. "Wicked Problems and Network Approaches to Resolution." *International Public Management Review* 1 (1): 1–19.

Say, Mick, and Ben Pronk. 2012. "Individual Decision-Making in Complex Environments." *Australian Army Journal* 9 (3): 119–140.

Shaw, Sara E., and Rebecca Rosen. 2013. "Fragmentation: A Wicked Problem with an Integrated Solution?" *Journal of Health Services Research & Policy* 18 (1): 61–64.

Signal, Louise N., Mat D. Walton, Cliona Ni Mhurchu, Ralph Maddison, Sharron G. Bowers, Kristie N. Carter, Delvina Gorton, Craig Heta, Tolotea S. Lanumata, Christina W. McKerchar, Des O'Dea, and Jamie Pearce. 2013. "Tackling 'wicked' Health Promotion Problems: A New Zealand Case Study." *Health Promotion International* 28 (1): 84–94.

Skaburskis, Andrejs. 2008. "The Origin of 'Wicked Problems'." *Planning Theory & Practice* 9 (2): 277–280.

Snowden, David J., and Mary E. Boone. 2007. "A Leader's Framework for Decision Making." *Harvard Business Review* 85 (11): 69–76.

Southgate, Erica, Ruth Reynolds, and Peter Howley. 2013. "Professional Experience as a Wicked Problem in Initial Teacher Education." *Teaching and Teacher Education* 31 (1): 13–22.

Stoppelenburg, Annemieke, and Hans Vermaak. 2009. "Defixation as an Intervention Perspective: Understanding Wicked Problems at the Dutch Ministry of Foreign Affairs." *Journal of Management Inquiry* 18 (1): 40–54.

Termeer, Catrien J. A. M., Art Dewulf, Gerard Breeman, and Sabina J. Stiller. 2015. "Governance Capabilities for Dealing Wisely with Wicked Problems." *Administration & Society* 47 (6): 680–710.

van Bueren, Ellen M., Erik-Hans Klijn, and Joop F. M. Koppenjan. 2003. "Dealing with Wicked Problems in Networks: Analyzing an Environmental Debate from a Network Perspective." *Journal of Public Administration Research and Theory* 13 (2): 193–212.

Vartiainen, Pirkko. 2005. "Wicked Health Care Issues: An Analysis of Finnish and Swedish Health Care Reforms." *Advances in Health Care Management: International Health Care Management* 5: 163–186.

Vartiainen, Pirkko. 2008. "Health Care Management in Finland: An Analysis of the Wickedness of Selected Reforms." *Review of Business* 28 (2): 41–55.

Waddock, Sandra, Greta M. Meszoely, Steve Waddel, and Domenico Dentoni. 2015. "The Complexity of Wicked Problems in Large Scale Change." *Journal of Organizational Change Management* 28 (6): 993–1012.

Watts, Nick, W. Neil Adger, Paolo Agnolucci, Jason Blackstock, Peter Byass, Wenjia Cai, Sarah Chaytor, et al. 2015. "Health and Climate Change: Policy Responses to Protect Public Health." *The Lancet* 386 (10006): 1861–1914.

Weber, Edward P., and Anne M. Khademian. 2008. "Wicked Problems, Knowledge Challenges and Collaborative Capacity Builders in Network Settings." *Public Administration Review* 68 (2): 334–349.

Weick, Karl E. 2015. "Ambiguity as Grasp: The Reworking of Sense." *Journal of Contingencies and Crisis Management* 23 (2): 117–123.

Weick, Karl E., Kathleen M. Sutcliffe, and David Obstfeld. 2005. "Organizing and the Process of Sensemaking." *Organization Science* 16 (4): 409–421.

Xiang, Wei-Ning. 2013. "Working with Wicked Problems in Socio-Ecological Systems: Awareness, Acceptance, and Adaptation." *Landscape and Urban Planning* 110 (1): 1–4.

Zellner, Moira, and Scott D. Campbell. 2015. "Planning for Deep-Rooted Problems: What We Can Learn from Aligning Complex Systems and Wicked Problems?" *Planning Theory & Practice* 16 (4): 457–478.

2   The Politics of Care

Wicked Concerns Constituent in Care Reforms

Will Thomas and Susan Hollinrake

The purpose of this chapter is to provide a summary and critical commentary of reforms to the system of adult social care in England. The drivers of reforms, economic and demographic pressures, are classically 'wicked' (Rittel and Webber 1973) in the way that they interface, are non-linear and overlap. Even defining the nature of the problem is difficult, particularly if we seek to identify the root causes of the challenges that we now face. This is not unique to the English situation, of course: the same problems are faced in many jurisdictions. As a result, concerns often overlap and compete; we see people living longer with multiple or complex health conditions which increases pressure on social care systems as they seek to provide support to people who 10, 20 or 30 years ago may not have survived for nearly as long. We cannot, and indeed should not, roll back the clock—but in seeking to improve the quality of care that is provided should recognize the complexity, indeed the wickedness, of the problem we face. The result is that a neat, linear solution may not exist, and we might instead focus on ways in which we can manage our way *through* some of this complexity.

The main focus will be on the period since 2010, which saw a Labour government replaced by a Conservative-Liberal Democrat coalition and later replaced by a Conservative government in 2015. However, reference will also be made to longer-term reforms and changes, particularly where they reflect ambitions that cross party-political lines. We consider concerns or challenges that result from these reforms from the points of view of both users of care services and professionals (largely social workers) involved in their delivery. The final section of the chapter will discuss the suitability of the ethic of care as a response to the challenges raised, paying close attention to the quality and effectiveness of caring relationships. This analysis will help to codify the nature of the issues raised by the reforms and will help move from a specific, English, context toward conclusions which are more generally applicable to other settings.

Reform in England

The reform of social care in England has been influenced by two long-term trends—firstly the neo-liberal project, introduced by the government of

Margaret Thatcher in 1979, to achieve a small state with a residual rather than a universal approach to welfare provision and social care and with an anti-collectivist agenda (George and Wilding 1994). Secondly, there has been a series of responses to economic crises since the 1970s, where the social care needs of the population have not been prioritized for financial support and have in fact been used as a means of saving money and cutting costs to the state (e.g. after the oil crisis in the early 1970s, the recessions of the early 1980s and 1990s as well as the austerity measures introduced in 2011) and transferring more of the responsibility for addressing social needs on to the individual and their networks.

The dynamics of servicing and caring within the private sphere of family life have, for centuries, delivered a gendered expectation for women's role as carer and have been highlighted by feminist writers as socially constructed as a normal and natural activity for women, unpaid and undervalued, performed by women in support of the male breadwinner as an essential but unrewarded component within the organization of capitalism (e.g. see Fraser 2013, 213). This was extended to expectations within community care policy development in the 1980s, with family or informal carers as a major stakeholder in 'care in the community' (Finch and Groves 1980; Dalley 1996). Additionally, paid care work, as 'body work,' is seen as 'dirty work' culturally (Fine 2007) and part of women's work (essentialists see caring in all its forms as deriving from women's natural abilities with the mother-child relationship as the blue-print for caring relationships) and as such tends to be poorly paid and unrecognized for the skills involved, based on a cultural value of 'a labour of love' (Hollinrake 2013, 184–185).

The next section of the discussion will explore the impact of these two trends on social care provision for older people (particularly those in the fourth-age or the 'older old' i.e. frail and dependent with more complex needs who have to rely on the discretion and benevolence of others to care for them (Gilleard and Higgs 2000)).

Increased Pressure on Budgets

The number of people aged 65 and over in the UK is projected to rise by over 40% in the next 17 years, so that by 2040, nearly one in four people in the UK will be aged 65 or over (AgeUK 2018). The Office for National Statistics (Office for National Statistics 2017) predicts a 36% growth in people aged 85 and over between 2015 and 2025, from 1.5 million to two million. While being 'old' is not in itself problematic, it brings with it an increased likelihood of health problems and frailty with older people increasingly living with multiple co-morbidities (Care Quality Commission 2016, 13). These demographic changes are expected to lead to a substantial increase in demand for care home services between 2015 and 2025 of between 14% and 34% (Competition and Markets Authority 2017), and demand for non-residential social care services is expected to show similar increases in the same period.

Despite these figures, there have been significant reductions in funding for social care for older people as they become more dependent on others for their care. In response to the global economic crisis in 2008, the Conservative-Liberal Democrat coalition government (2010–2015) introduced a policy of austerity with a view to reduce the nation's debts and to 'balance the books,' and, in 2011, local government's budget was reduced by 27%. According to Bassel and Emeijulu (2018), this resulted in annual expenditure on social welfare being cut by £18 billion. Demand continues to outstrip resources. In considering the future resilience of adult social care, the UK's social care regulator, the Care Quality Commission (CQC), commented in 2016 that:

> In adult social care, an ovespend was reported by councils of £168 million (out of a budget of £13.65 billion). It has been calculated that public funding for adult social care will rise by an average of 0.6% per year in real terms from 2015/16 to 2019/20—a welcome increase, but lower than the projected increase in demand pressures of 4% per year.
>
> (CQC 2016, 41)

Age UK reported in 2015 that disability-free life expectancy is rising more slowly than life expectancy meaning that people are living for more years with disabilities (Mortimer and Green 2015, 4), thereby likely to require more funding for support to manage these needs. Despite this, there has been a fear in successive governments of the electoral consequences of facing up to the costs of an increasingly aging population for some decades now. There have been longstanding debates, especially in terms of how much should people pay toward their own care (Royal Commission 1999; Wanless et al. 2006; Dilnot 2011), but no clear policy on the matter has emerged, though a Green Paper (for consultation) has been promised from the current Government in the summer of 2018.

The Impact of Funding Pressures

Funding issues within the English Social Care sector are a result of demographic pressures and ideologically driven ambitions to reduce the extent of the state's involvement in care service delivery. The Audit Commission Report of 1986 noted the heavy dependence on institutionalized care (in hospitals or small residential homes funded by Supplementary Benefit Payments (central government funded income support)) for those older people unable to live independently in their own homes (Audit Commission 1986, 2). Social security spending on residential care increased from £10m in 1974 to £1bn by 1989 (Evandrou, Jane and Glennerster 1991). This indicated a perverse incentive for those caring for older people to encourage them to move into residential care where all their needs would be met, and thereby move the costs away from the Local Authority to the Department of Social Security, rather than rely on informal care and some local authority care in the community (already under some financial strain during this period). The Conservative Government in 1990 closed this 'gap' in spending control through the NHS and Community Care Act 1990, which sought to make residential care a last resort and emphasized care within the community. This saw the introduction of care management and the marketization of care, which was facilitated through the creation of quasi-markets (as a result of the Act, 85% of financing for community care had to be spent in the independent sector), introducing competition between providers of services to drive down costs. This change represented a consistency in the philosophy underpinning social care that has been maintained, across party lines, over decades, with a move away from large-scale residential settings (a residue of the 19th century) to smaller residential homes and home care. Care within the community is supplemented by specialist residential or nursing home care only for those for whom living in their own homes can no longer provide sufficient care and protection (Jones 2007). However, by 2006, the Kings Fund (Wanless et al. 2006, 54) reported an increase in the level of need of people in receipt of social care services, a fall in the number of care home placements and an increase in home care for more dependent older people.

The introduction of national eligibility criteria within the Care Act 2014 represented an attempt to move away from local inconsistencies in funding decisions across England but has nonetheless resulted in a policy framework which continues to promote 'less eligibility.' It sees bureaucratic processes that seek to minimize the number of people who qualify for assistance rather than seeking to ensure that all those who need help receive it.

The reduction in the number of older people in care homes (and nursing homes) has continued. In 2015, Age UK reported that the numbers of older people with public support in nursing homes had slightly fallen between 2012 and 2015, alongside a more significant fall in the total numbers of older people in care homes. The CQC Report for 2015–2016 confirms this trend (CQC 2016, 45). Worryingly, there had been a much higher reduction in community and home care services and recipients. It was also reported that unmet need has risen since 2010, with more than a million older people in England having at least one unmet need for social care which meant they receive no help from their local authority or from family, neighbors or friends. The risk of having an unmet care need was greatest for the oldest and those who live alone (Mortimer and Green 2015, 5).

Marketization of Care

Social care in the UK is paid for through a combination of individual and government payments. The majority of services are now provided by private sector agencies, either via contract with local authorities or directly with individuals through a mix of public and private funding (Johns 2011). Of course, some older people can afford to pay for their own home or residential care, but for those dependent on some state support, social care has become harder to obtain and choice has been eroded (Rogowski 2010), with government spending on home care for older people reduced by a fifth between 2010/11 and 2013/14.

These cuts reflect a political philosophy that underpinned the actions of governments from both sides of the political spectrum. From the 1990s onwards, there was a consistent policy of developing and supporting markets in social care through neo-liberal policies, first introduced by the Conservative Government, under Prime Minister Margaret Thatcher, from 1979. These prioritized a small state, increasing privatization of public services and the rebranding of users of services as 'consumers.' Social work has had to embrace these changes as policy has driven the personalization of services (SCIE 2011; Lymbery 2012). Consumer choice, assumed to promote quality saw care needs 'managed' by social workers who assessed needs and referred service users to social care services largely outsourced from the local authority as part of a more active social care market. As Houston aptly states:

> through the medium of personalization, service users take more responsibility for their problems, implement their own solutions and manage the accruing risk. Social workers, in this modernised form of 'active welfare' are individualised quasi-marketers whose role is to broker and advocate.
>
> (2010, 842)

A recent report shows that more than 90% of support is now provided by a diverse range of more than 19,000 independent organizations, ranging from big corporate chains to small, family run businesses, charities and social enterprises (Skills for Care 2016).

The risks borne by the individual older service user were tragically demonstrated through the collapse of Southern Cross in 2011, as one example of the disastrous effects of a major private care provider failing within a complex and volatile world of private equity finance, against the ramifications of the global financial crisis of 2008 and the local authorities driving down fees as described above (for details, see Wearden 2011). Since then, the *Guardian* has continued to report on the continuing risk of care home closures (for example, Ruddick 2017). The closure of residential care homes causes significant stress and risk to the well-being of vulnerable residents, who face major upheaval when they may not have the resilience to cope with the consequences.

In a continuation of attempts to reduce costs and improve efficiency, the management of social care has been increasingly informed by models emphasizing personal choice and control through personalization (Lead-beater, Bartlett and Gallagher 2008). Organizations have also been put under pressure to manage expectations in a 'smarter' way through the adoption of managerial principles taken 'from industry'. Introduced as a result of the Labour government's (1997–2010—so-called 'New Labour') preoccupation with improving quality within public services, the NHS and Local Authorities have grappled with a performance-based and 'target-driven' culture to increase the quality of service for service users and carers. These policies have promoted managerialism, (ever tightening) eligibility criteria and funding inequalities across different local authorities (post code lotteries), alongside the continuing expectation of the integration of health and social care. These changes of increased competition, preoccupation with quality of services and promotion of support to maintain independence in the community have all been in response to a perceived need to contain and reduce costs in health and social care due to demographic pressures.

The independence of the individual 'consumer' of social care is a narrative that has run alongside the marketization of the system. Neo-liberal ideology emphasizes the ability of the individual to pursue their own self-interest independent of state intervention—based on the liberal values of liberty and autonomy (Rogowski 2010, 29). This has been translated into the social care system through the policy of personalization (Leadbeater, Bartlett and Gallagher 2008) emerging from the New Labour think-tank 'Demos' and representing New Labour's adherence to the market economy in continuation with the reforms carried out by previous Conservative administrations (Rogowski 2010, 104). As Rogowski comments:

> Although personalisation may be sold on the basis that it improves 'choice' and 'independence,' the underlying policy agenda is more about reducing expenditure and maximising the care provided by family, friends and neighbours and thereby minimising the need for state-funded support.
>
> (Rogowski 2010, 105)

For those older people who are able to remain active and independent the ambitions of personalization are indeed positive. They are able to engage with the agenda of individual responsibility and self-care with minimal need for formal support to maintain their health, well-being and an active lifestyle.

This active and independent group, the third-age, is not only able to manage any care needs in a fairly independent manner, but they are able to be part of the self-supporting communities expected by these policies. For more frail older people, those in the fourth-age, when dependency on others becomes more the norm, then this emphasis on independence has little meaning and 'inter-dependence' (also see Thomas 2018, this volume) is a more accurate description of daily needs. For many of these people, relatives, friends and neighbors become the first port of call as providers of support. The CQC report concerns about the increased reliance on unpaid care and levels of unmet needs (CQC 2016, 45).

In cases where dependency on state funding becomes necessary for the individual, dependency on the market to provide a solution, given the pressure that is placed on their budgets, becomes a precarious situation to be in. Again, the CQC (2016, 45) comments:

> The number of contracts that providers are terminating early is concerning as this gives an indication of the fragility of the social care sector. Providers tell us that increasingly they are making the decision to hand back contracts where they feel they cannot meet the fundamental standards of care while maintaining profitability.

Threats such as care home closures, standardized thresholds and assessments of eligibility for the individual to gain access to support serve to undermine an holistic approach to that individual's uniqueness and well-being. This system is one that is unable to deliver true personalization to those who can effectively self-manage or who have the financial and social resources to supplement funded social care services. As Beresford and Slasberg comment:

> [the Secretary of State] says he wants a system that addresses the 'whole person' and gives them control. Neither can happen under a system where 'need' is standardized and rooted in personal deficits. It can only occur if the lived experience of need becomes the foundation of all that happens.
>
> (Beresford and Slasberg 2018)

This quote is particularly interesting in the way that it seems to indicate a change of approach away from standardized care that is provided on the basis of eligibility toward personalized approaches that are based on need. The use of the concept of 'lived experience of need' recalls the importance of the way in which the social care system is experienced by those that encounter it, whether as service users (or those that are 'cared-for') or by those providing care as a professional or in an informal manner. These are elements that will be explored from a more theoretical perspective in the following section, which will use the 'ethic of care' as an analytical device to draw conclusions that will apply beyond the English context.

The Ethic of Care

The 'ethic of care' is best thought of as a family of ethical frameworks, which share core ontological assumptions and make similar normative claims about how best to promote 'good care.' It is a teleological approach: actions are 'good' in so far as they promote good outcomes rather than because they conform to rules of conduct. Key authors, including Joan Tronto (1993), Nel Noddings (2002), Virginia Held (2006), Eva Feder Kittay (1999) and Fiona Robinson (2011), largely agree on important aspects, particularly on the focus on the relational nature of ontology, the importance of caring relationships and on the value of particularity in decision-making and care planning. Below, we consider whether reforms informed by this ethical perspective might address some of the concerns raised in previous sections.

The starting point for discussions situated within the ethic of care is an ontological position which recognizes the naturalness and importance of interdependence. From this standpoint the continued promotion of independence might be problematized as well as applauded. The position of theorists working in this tradition emphasizes the importance of listening to the needs and preferences of those that are in receipt of care; what Tronto calls "attentiveness" (1993, 127–131). At the same time, we acknowledge the multiple ways in which we can be dependent on one another, not just in periods of illness or through frailty or disability, but perhaps due to power relations, time, access to information or other causes. This position emphasizes the complexity of questions of dependence and autonomy, reminding us of the danger of expressing choices and decisions in binary terms.

The notion of service users (or indeed anyone else) as fully autonomous decision-makers is therefore rejected. Autonomy is acknowledged as an important element within the ethic of care, but it is understood in terms of having an input into decision-making processes rather than in having sole responsibility (see Tronto 1993, 162–164 for a discussion about the relationship between dependence and autonomy through interdependence). Individuals have a right to be involved, but the neo-liberal ideal of the autonomous decision-maker fails to give full account of the ways in which the input of professionals, family and friends *adds value to* the choices made by individuals.

Within the ethic of care, emphasis is placed on the value of caring relationships whether they exist between a service user and a professional, between family members or otherwise. When they work most effectively, these relationships ensure and promote a responsiveness and a quality of care that cannot consistently be achieved when there is no pre-existing relationship in the care setting. Such relationships are frequently complicated, particularly in family settings, when individuals may act as a caregiver and as a recipient of care at the same time. Such complexity is not easily captured or recognized within a system which understands relationships in purely economic or market-based terms and so placing economic value on these shifting and complex roles is also problematic.

These ideas challenge the current understanding of the service user as commissioner, client or employer—someone who is expected to take on responsibility for organizing their own care. In a shifting network of relationships, it is not possible to define roles in such a clear and static manner, particularly when individuals may not self-define as 'carers' despite regularly performing care tasks. Indeed, such attempts also fail because they imply a simple, mono-directional relationship. The reality, at least outside formal settings, is that relationships are more complex and more dynamic than terminology implies.

Straightforwardly, the emphasis on the quality of caring relationships implies a need for adequate time to develop and build confidence and understanding between those providing care and those in receipt of services. This cannot happen in very short (15-minute) appointments, especially if there is no consistency in terms of who provides the care. Less obviously the same thought-process also emphasizes the highly skilled nature of providing care—balancing attentiveness to the needs and desires of individuals with a need to exercise professional judgment and experience and attention to budgetary and other concerns. Care provision is not simply a matter of the adequate application of skills and knowledge; it is *emotional labor* (Hochschild 2003) which makes demands on the empathetic and interpersonal skills of caregivers. The organizations that employ caregivers must pay attention to the needs of those that they employ and recognize that a type of caring relationship should also exist at the heart of the employer-employee relationship. Failure to do so, as noted by Kittay (1999), will result in burnout, illness, staff turnover and threats to the quality of care provision—many of the same challenges that face the care system in England (and in many other settings) currently (Slawson 2017).

A third central feature of the ethic of care is particularity to the needs of the individual. Much importance is placed on listening to and engaging with the needs and desires of the person that is to receive care. One result of this is to reject the use of standardized packages of care which seek to provide *equal* care to each person who meets a threshold test. This conflation of fairness or justice with equality highlights a weakness in the current system and provides an opportunity to make improvements to the system, informed by this ethical position, without necessarily increasing the overall costs of care.

A focus on providing equal care is problematic in two ways. Firstly, it fails to recognize that, even amongst those who have moderate or serious care needs, different people will have different priorities and preferences for the support that they receive. For example, in the period after discharge from hospital, some people will need daily care for a short period (available and funded by the National Health Service), while others will need a different pattern of care or care only with certain tasks (harder to secure). Unless the available care packages are able to respond to these needs, they will fail to meet the care needs of those they seek to support.

Secondly, in treating everyone equally, injustices and inequalities are reinforced not addressed: those that are better off financially and socially will do better than those who are not. Those who are totally reliant on the care that they receive will do worse than those whose formal care is supplemented by family, friends and self-funded additional support. This is not just an argument in favor of means-testing access to care but rather to say that if someone meets the threshold for access to care, the package of support must meet and respond to their needs rather than relying on this care being supplemented through some other means. The system, then, should seek to be 'fair' not in its provision of equal or standardized care packages but through responsiveness to the needs of individuals.

The ethic of care provides a way of looking at the concerns of those in receipt of care and of those who provide care services in both formal and informal settings. It advocates a focus on caring relationships rooted in mutual interdependence which seek to respond to the needs of individuals. In doing so, it promotes care at a personal level through principles which can be applied at an organizational or system level. It also addresses some of the theoretical concerns which were raised above particularly in response to the problematic nature of the relationship between service users and professionals. Here, it is argued, there is value in both the skills and knowledge of the professional and in listening to the needs and desires of individuals—but this value is best realized through a system of co-production rather than one of economic transaction.

Conclusion

This chapter addresses a classic 'wicked' problem—that of resourcing social care provision within a modern, European-style, welfare state. We have discussed the case of social care in England, but have done so not simply because it provides an interesting case, but because an understanding of the concerns in *this* system helps expose the challenges faced in *many other* systems. In demonstrating how economic and demographic concerns relate to one another we have seen that trying to meet obligations to support an increasing number of older people with care needs while trying to cut the overall (absolute) cost of social care creates a number of problems. While the fact that the system is facing problems in terms of quality and sustainability is not a new or particularly insightful conclusion, the use of the ethic of care to help understand specific concerns provides a way to move from the consideration of a single case to draw more general conclusions.

In starting from an ontological position which understands humans as relational beings, we must recognize that the value of these relations holds a particularly significant value and creates a normative imperative. Promoting the quality of these relationships, whether they are based in a professional context or are the result of family, friends or neighbors being supportive is central to ensuring high-quality care for all. Principles such as autonomy can only be protected from within a supportive environment in which caring relationships are established and nurtured so that they provide the opportunity for everyone to make choices about the care that they need. This creates a space in which the needs of individuals can be recognized and, while they cannot always be acted upon, used to create a care plan which is truly personalized.

Finally, the analysis provided here suggests that an obsession with defining fairness through recourse to the notion of equality is fallacious on two counts: different people with different problems, circumstances and preferences will need different types of care; and that provision of equal care serves to deepen social inequalities rather than reduce them. It is, of course, paramount that care services should be provided in a fair manner. However, fairness should be considered in terms of equity—that is, whether people's needs are given appropriate and equal consideration—rather than in terms of equality.

In the case of reforms to the English system, our central criticism is that they have served to reduce the scope for professionals to establish strong caring relationships; that they emphasize independence (when interdependence is a more helpful concept); and that those people with strong personal networks of support can do well, while those that are entirely reliant on state support are likely to do much worse. An appreciation and sensitivity to the issues raised in our analysis will, we believe, start to reverse the damage caused by at least four decades of reforms.

References

Age UK. 2018. "Later Life in the United Kingdom Factsheet April 2018." Accessed May 27, 2018. www.ageuk.org.uk/globalassets/age-uk/documents/reports-and-publications/later_life_uk_factsheet.pdf.

Audit Commission. 1986. *Making a Reality of Community Care.* London: Audit Commission for Local Authorities in England and Wales.

Bassel, Leah, and Emeijulu Akwugo. 2018. "Caring Subjects: Migrant Women and the Third Sector in England and Scotland." *Ethnic and Racial Studies* 41 (1): 36–54.

Beresford, Peter, and Colin Slasberg. 2018. "Are Social Care Services Improving People's Wellbeing?" *The Guardian*, April 23, 2018. Accessed May 28, 2018. https://www.theguardian.com/social-care-network/2018/apr/23/are-social-care-services-improving-peoples-wellbeing

Care Quality Commission. 2016. "The State of Health Care and Adult Social Care in England 2015/16." Accessed May 29, 2018. www.cqc.org.uk/sites/default/files/20161013b_stateofcare1516_web.pdf.

Competition and Markets Authority. 2017. "Care Homes Market Study: Summary of Final Report." Accessed May 28, 2018. www.gov.uk/government/publications/care-homes-market-study-summary-of-final-report/care-homes-market-study-summary-of-final-report.

Dalley, Gillian. 1996. *Ideologies of Caring: Rethinking Community and Collectivism.* London: Palgrave Macmillan.

Dilnot, Andrew. 2011. "Fairer Care Funding Report: The Report of the Commission on Funding of Care and Support (Dilnot Report)." Accessed May 29, 2018. http://webarchive.nationalarchives.gov.uk/20130221121529/www.wp.dh.gov.uk/carecommission/files/2011/07/Fairer-Care-Funding-Report.pdf.

Evandrou, Maria, Jane Falkingham, and Howard Glennerster. 1991. "The Personal Social Services: Everyone's Poor Relation but Nobody's Baby." In *The State of Welfare*, edited by John Hills. Oxford: Clarendon Press.

Finch, Janet, and Dulcie Groves. 1980. "Community Care and the Family: A Case for Equal Opportunities." *Journal of Social Policy* 9 (4): 487–514.

Fine, Michael. 2007. *A Caring Society? Care and the Dilemmas of Human Service in the 21st Century*. Basingstoke: Palgrave Macmillan.

Fraser, Nancy. 2013. *Fortunes of Feminism: From State-Managed Capitalism to Neoliberal Crisis*. London: Verso.

George, Victor, and Paul Wilding. 1994. *Welfare and Ideology*. Hemel Hempstead: Harvester Wheatsheaf.

Gilleard, Chris, and Paul Higgs. 2000. *Cultures of Ageing: Self, Citizen and the Body*. Harlow: Pearson Education.

Held, Virginia. 2006. *The Ethics of Care: Personal, Political and Global*. Oxford: Oxford University Press.

Hochschild, Arlie. 2003. *The Managed Heart: Commercialization of Human Feeling*. Berkeley, CA: University of California Press.

Hollinrake, Sue. 2013. "Informal Care." In *Key Concepts in Medical Sociology*, edited by J. Gabe and L. F. Monaghan, 2nd ed. 183–188. London: Sage Publications.

Houston, Stan. 2010. "Beyond Homo Èconomicus: Recognition, Self-Realization and Social Work." *British Journal of Social Work* 40 (3): 841–857.

Johns, Robert. 2011. *Social Work, Social Policy and Older People*. Exeter: Learning Matters.

Jones, Ray. 2007. "A Journey Through the Years: Ageing and Social Care." *Ageing Horizons* 6: 42–51. Accessed March 27, 2018. www.ageing.ox.ac.uk/files/Ageing%20Horizons%206%20%20Jones.pdf.

Kittay, Eva Feder. 1999. *Love's Labor: Essays on Women, Equality and Dependency*. London: Routledge.

Leadbeater, Charles, Jamie Bartlett, and Niamh Gallagher. 2008. *Making It Personal*. London: Demos.

Lymbery, Mark. 2012. "Social Work and Personalisation." *British Journal of Social Work* 42 (4): 783–792.

Mortimer, Jill, and Marcus Green. 2015. *Briefing: The Health and Care of Older People in England 2015*. London: Age UK.

Noddings, Nel. 2002. *Starting at Home: Care as the Basis for Social Policy*. Berkeley, CA: University of California Press.

The Office of National Statistics. 2017. "Overview of the UK Population." www.ons.gov.uk/peoplepopulationandcommunity/populationandmigration/populationestimates/articles/overviewoftheukpopulation/july2017.

Rittel, Horst W. J., and Melvin Webber. 1973. "Dilemmas in a General Theory of Planning." *Policy Sciences* 4 (2): 155–169.

Robinson, Fiona. 2011. *The Ethics of Care: A Feminist Approach to Human Security*. Philadelphia: Temple University Press.

Rogowski, Steve. 2010. *Social Work: The Rise and Fall of a Profession?* Bristol: Policy Press.

Royal Commission on Long Term Care for the Elderly. 1999. *With Respect to Old Age: Long Term Care—Rights and Responsibilities*. London: The Stationary Office.

Ruddick, Graham. 2017. "Care Home Closures set to Rise as Funding Crisis Bites." *The Guardian*, January 11, 2017.

Skills for Care. 2016. "The Size and Structure of the Adult Social Care Sector and Workforce in England, 2016." www.skillsforcare.org.uk/NMDS-SC-intelligence/NMDS-SC/Workforce-data-and-publications/Size-and-structure-of-the-adult-social-care-sector.aspx.

Slawson, Nicola. 2017. "UK Social Care Sector in Crisis Due to Staff Shortages." *The Guardian*, March 8, 2017.

Social Care Institute for Excellence (SCIE). 2011. *Personalisation Briefing: Personalisation, Productivity and Efficiency*. London: Social Care Institute for Excellence.

Tronto, Joan. 1993. *Moral Boundaries: A Political Argument for an Ethic of Care*. Oxford: Routledge.

Wanless, Derek, Julien Forder, Jose-Luis Fernandez, Teresa Poole, Lucinda Beesley, Melanie Henwood, and Francesco Moscone. 2006. *Securing Good Care for Older People: Taking a Long Term View*. London: King's Fund.

Wearden, Graeme. 2011. "The Rise and Fall of Southern Cross." *The Guardian*, June 1, 2011.

3   Personalization of Care

A Wicked Problem or a Wicked Solution?

Janet Carter Anand, Gavin Davidson,
Berni Kelly and Geraldine Macdonald

The personalized provision of equitable and effective social care to the marginalized and oppressed represents both a wicked problem (Churchman 1967) and a wicked solution. Western policymakers, economists and social care professionals struggle to address the costs and resources associated with the provision of quality social care. Limited outcomes of social services in addressing the changing and complex needs of the most excluded groups of people in countries of the global north is of ongoing concern to politicians, policymakers and professionals. On the other hand, countries of the global south, such as Indian and China, are only just coming to terms with the question of universal social care service provision on a scale not previously negotiated, and the concept of personalization at this stage may appear as a distant pipe dream.

Equitable and effective social care remains an intractable problem. Personalization of service delivery appears as both a vision and strategy in response to the issues involved. People with disabilities indeed have individualized and diverse needs. Some (Rittel and Webber 1973) would have us believe that personalization is the preferred solution to the inadequacies traditional models of welfare delivery. International evidence does suggest that personalization may well contribute to a radical transformation of social care however, the costs and complexities of implementing products such a personal budgets alongside traditional resource allocation systems, service provision and culture presents major challenges. Personalization is potentially a wicked solution giving power and control back to the recipients of social care. Yet, the initial enthusiasm for radical social care reform has somewhat waned in light of the complex reality. Issues around the provision of personal payments continue to generate considerable debate and discussion amongst the multiple stakeholders including people with disabilities, professionals, politicians, policymakers and academics (Scourfield 2005). A critique of personalization and its inadequacies to address the ineffectiveness and inequity of traditional welfare delivery modes is therefore warranted, and, in the process, an understanding as to why personalization has not reached its potential may be provided.

The concept of 'personalisation' first emerged in the early 1990s, initially for people with learning disabilities as a means of achieving increased levels of choice and control in tailoring solutions to individual need through direct management of the care budget. Its subsequent introduction across social policy for adults also came with the anticipation that it would deliver much hoped for, but far less prominently advertised, cash savings in the welfare bill of adult social care support. However, the term personalization is in a contentious and troublesome term. Divergent policy trajectories of personalization across the UK, Europe and internationally has resulted in it being implemented and perceived in a variety of ways. It has become associated with a range of products: for example, direct payments; personal budgets; individual budgets; and self-directed support. Personalization appears to reflect the provision of welfare services from a ground-up approach, but exactly who sets the agenda and models of care provision represents a very much top-down approach dictated by economists and policy-makers (Anand et al. 2012).

In order to examine the impact or lack of impact of personalization, a rapid systematic literature review of the experiences and outcomes of personalization for people with disabilities occurring across different jurisdictions, namely the UK, ROI, Netherlands, the USA and Australia. The international evidence is summarized and critiqued in response to a series of wicked questions relating to the promotion of social equity and human rights in relation to personalization.

What Are Personal Budgets?

Personal budgets involve an individualized system of funding, based on assessments of need of individuals, and of their changing needs over time (Anand et al. 2012). A personal budget is an amount of funding allocated to a service user to enable them to determine which services they wish to purchase to meet their expressed needs. The money provided should follow the needs of service users. There are a range of different models, but usually needs are assessed by health and social care professionals, in partnership with the service user. This assessment provides the basis for the personal budget. The idea is that the individual then has some flexibility to meet the needs for which the budget is granted in ways which they choose, giving them greater control over their own social care provision.

A personal budget may be paid directly to a service user in the form of a direct payment, or paid indirectly, through another person, broker or agency or a combination of both. Personal budget schemes vary considerably but often share common characteristics. Internationally, there is a variety of funding models for the provision of personal budgets, such as 'direct payments' in the United Kingdom (Rabiee, Moran and Glendinning 2009; Spandler and Vick 2006), 'consumer directed care' or 'self-directed care' in states of Australia (Fisher et al. 2010) and 'cash and counselling schemes' in the USA (Dale and Brown 2006). A range of models has been generated, including, at the one end if a continuum, large-scale national programs, such as the Netherlands model, with its links to the national insurance system, and, at other end, regional or small-scale community based programs, such as those being developed in states and provinces of Australia and Canada.

In principle, personal budgets may be used irrespective of the person's age (e.g. older adults, working aged adults, young adults or children) or disability, i.e. illness, chronic health conditions, intellectual disability, mental health conditions, sensory impairment, and physical disability, but in reality, their availability is limited to certain age groups, disabilities or geographical areas, i.e. urban rather than rural areas. The implementation of personal budgets aims to promote personal responsibility, independence, capability and resilience through the delivery of cost-effective and innovative services chosen by the service user.

Personal Budgets and Human Rights

The principle of self-determination for all people is enshrined in the Universal Declaration of Human Rights. The International Convention on the Rights of Persons with Disabilities, adopted by the United Nations General Assembly (2006), included the general principle, "Respect for inherent dignity, individual autonomy including the freedom to make one's own choices and independences of persons" (Article 3). One of the claims made is that personal budgets facilitate opportunities for personal development and greater independence for people with disabilities through increased responsibility, flexibility and choice (Egan 2008). However, there are concerns that complicated personal budget schemes can reduce control and oversight for some service user groups (Ungerson 2004).

Some UK user groups have criticized government plans to introduce personal budgets into health care as being too restrictive and bureaucratic in administration. Galpin and Bates (2009) point out that there are "winners and losers" in every model of social care provision, with service users who lack the essential attributes and support to make rational and strategic choices, being less able to benefit from personal budgets compared to other groups. Those without the ability or capacity to manage personal budgets may be excluded from access to this type of funding, unless support (such as advocacy, financial assistance and protective policy/legislation) is in place to facilitate their participation. Personal budgets provide opportunities to enable people with significant cognitive disabilities to exercise their preferences, but they may also present unique challenges for supporting and communicating decision-making.

The successful introduction of personal budgets depends on the positive response of existing disability services to adopt new care philosophies. This requires not only moving from professionally driven (case management) to person-centered (service user directed) models of provision, but also the emergence of new types of services and categories of service providers that can respond to the demands of service users. In order to take control of budgets, service users may require a range of advocacy, brokerage, planning, administrative and independent living support services, depending on their individual needs.

The introduction of personal budgets can have the effect of helping to create new services and means of support, effectively breaking down the near monopoly of existing home care organizations (Timonen, Convery and Cahill 2006). The introduction of personal budgets can increase the demand for personal assistants (Spandler 2004), a human resource which may or may not exist in local communities. In some cases, personal assistants may be drawn from informal support networks, such as family members and significant others, but the use of paid, informal personal carers has implications for the standard of care provided and raises issues of regulation and accountability.

Existing service providers may find the introduction of new market models and the prospect of having to 'sell' their care services somewhat challenging. For example, service providers in Australia have criticized their Government for wanting control of agencies, but distancing themselves from the risks and responsibilities of care provision (Aged and Community Services 2008). Promoting the 'growth' of new support services and a flexible care workforce involves developing a culture of collaboration between government and service providers.

Public bodies are obliged to ensure that public funds are fully accounted for, and used by people with disabilities and organizations for the purposes intended (Egan 2008). Personal budgets are thought, by some, to have the potential to increase opportunities for the misuse of funding or budget allocation difficulties. However, it also has the potential for cost saving and greater flexibility to respond to the needs of people with disabilities and to prevent inappropriate institutionalization and hospital admission.

Methodology

A critique of personal budgets was undertaken using the following methods (Anand et al. 2012). Key jurisdictions were selected to illustrate and compare a range of models of personal budget frameworks. The United Kingdom (including England and Wales, Scotland, Northern Ireland), the United States of America (Washington, Arkansas), Canada (Ontario) and the Netherlands were included because they have personal budget programs in place. For this review, a Rapid Evidence Assessment (REA) was undertaken. REAs provide more thorough syntheses than narrative reviews and are valuable where a robust mix of evidence is required but the time or resources for a full systematic review are not available. The reviewers develop and then specify search strategies and each study is quality assessed using standardized instruments. Only studies that provided directly relevant data were included. The majority of studies include small sample sizes which may limit the generalizability to the population of people with disabilities. Reliable evidence on long-term social care costs and implication was at the time not available. The result of the review are outlines in response to critical questions as to the effectiveness of personalization to deliver rights and equity.

What Are the Outcomes for Service Users and Carers?

Service users' responses to the introduction of personal budgets vary according to scheme and service user group. Overall, the evidence suggests that personal budgets outperform traditional services in meeting service users' needs, given the right kind and level of information and support.

The UK National Personal Budget Survey (Hatton and Waters 2011) found that service users reported more positive outcomes if they were themselves managing their personal budget, although there have been exceptions regarding older people (Poll and Duffy 2006). Sikma and Young (2003) US study reported high levels of satisfaction with personalized budgets, emphasizing freedom and the opportunity to take control of important aspects of life and daily care. Glendinning et al. (2008)'s evaluation of the Individual Budgets pilot in England reported that generally service users reported improvements in quality of life, care and control although there were differences between groups as will be further discussed below. Likewise, Laragy and Ottmann's (2011) small-scale Australian study reported that the self-esteem of the five participant families was enhanced because they were no longer reliant on a case manager. However, the families in this study also reported a need for more information and support than was available. Ensuring service users are well informed of their financial allocations and providing them with adequate support to implement care plans and services were identified as critical factors in this study. A large survey of over 1,700 people in the USA found that the ability to employ paid personal assistants was highly valued by service users (Foster et al. 2003). In Australian study, different forms of employment options are available to service users included hiring through a company, association or cooperative, or directly. Different employment models suit individuals at different points in time. Services users require knowledge and information to support informed decisions as to what model suits them at a particular time and to support the transition between arrangements as required or desired.

A Scottish study on dementia patients involving local authorities (Innes, Kelly and Dincarslan 2011) found that payments were used for personal care, social/recreational activities, domestic tasks and respite. In this study, personal budget recipients used their payments more often to employ personal assistants than to purchase services. It also indicated perceived benefits to be tailored outcomes; improved value for money; improved quality of care; and improved health outcomes. Considerable work has also been done by In Control (Hatton and Waters 2011) on the impact of personal budgets for carers. Most carers reported a positive impact of the personal budgets on their quality of life and physical and mental health. Carers reported that the receipt of personal budgets by the person they cared for had no impact on their own capacity to get and keep a paid job. However, they did express concerns about other aspects of the personal budget process—particularly the stress and worry associated with personal budgets. For the family carers of older service users, the impact of personal budgets was less positive. The impact on carers appears to be linked to factors such as whether the carer is living in the same house as the service user, and how much care and support the carer is providing. The critical factor for in achieving positive outcomes for service users managing their own personal budgets appears to be the availability of adequate information and support. Of course these findings raise further questions as to what is meant by adequate support for whom and by whom?

Are Issues of Equity and Diversity Addressed?

There has been an assumption that personal budgets will improve choice and control for all people with disabilities. However, recent UK research has failed to yield significant findings on the implications of individual budget schemes for members of minority groups (SCIE 2011). In fact, there is a suggestion that the introduction of personal budgets may result in further inequalities, such as a two-tiered system of service provision, in which some (the majority community) are able to avail of personal budgets; and others (minority groups) are not (Galpin and Bates 2009; Bloche 2000). Not only do different service user groups report different levels of outcomes, but there appears to be significant variations in access to personalization. Groups that face inequity of access to personalization include older people and people with a mental health diagnosis.

Glendinning et al. (2008, 2) reported that

> mental health service users reported a significantly higher quality of life; adults with physical disabilities reported receiving higher-quality care; people with learning disabilities were more likely to feel they had con-trol over their daily lives; and older people reported lower psychological well-being, possibly because they felt that the processes of planning and managing their own support were burdens.

The evidence suggests that uptake of personal budgets in the UK remains highly variable between countries, across local authorities within coun-tries, and between different groups of social care service users. For exam-ple, rates of uptake are highest in England and lowest in Northern Ireland, and the uptake of direct payments by people with physical and intellectual disabilities is highest in areas with lower population density (Fernandez et al. 2007). People with physical and sensory impairments have had consistently higher rates of uptake, while older people, people with intellectual disabilities and people with mental health problems have had much lower average take-up rates (Riddell et al. 2006; Priestley et al. 2006; Davey et al. 2007). In a national Australian study (Fisher et al. 2010), it was found that individual funding is more likely to be used by people of working age with low support needs, by male and non-Indigenous service users, by people with a single impairment and by people across all disabilities without informal care networks.

Older people and people with complex needs require greater time and support to help them get the most from personal budget schemes. Alzheimer Scotland (2011) identified that the main barriers to take up of personal budgets for older people included the need for an appropriate person to manage the direct payment as the illness (dementia) progressed. Many of those interviewed acknowledged the issue of not being able to get a direct payment unless the person with dementia had the capacity to consent or the family carer had appropriate legal powers in place.

People with mental health problems also face considerable inequities as to access. Not all Local Authorities extend personal budget schemes to all health services. UK research suggests that some practitioners may perceive some groups as 'risky,' particularly people with mental health problems, and limit their access to personal budgets (Taylor 2008). One study found that people with mental health problems were more likely to receive a personal budget if they had family or a 'significant other' to help manage it (Spandler and Vick 2006).

One of the challenges to the implementation of personal budgets is that some models appear to work well for some categories of service users and not for others. It is therefore important to attempt to address these different needs, while preventing the fragmentation of service provision. Service providers need support to negotiate personal budgets because of possible barriers including complexity of needs, geographic distance, racial and ethnic bias, cultural barriers, mental capacity issues and discriminatory attitudes. Information and support, clear policy guidance, legislation and advice on decision-making capacity are all key issues for the equitable provision of personal budgets.

Will Personal Budgets Improve Health Outcomes?

Evidence as to personalization resulting in improved health outcomes is again tenuous. Findings from the evaluation of Cash and Counselling schemes in the USA suggest that people in receipt of a personal budget may be more likely to use health services (Robert Johnson Wood Foundation 2007). This could be due to the improved identification of health needs arising from the assessment process and the greater availability of funding which, in the context of the USA, may address some of the financial barriers to accessing health care. In the same study, recipients employing their own personal assistants were more likely to experience positive health outcomes, such as a reduction in falls and bedsores due to personal care provided. Alakeson (2008), in a discussion of the USA and UK systems, compared self-directed care with the traditional system and found that people using the former make greater use of routine services, and that there is a shift toward prevention and early intervention. This can lead to efficiency gains by avoiding costly acute interventions. The Australian Government's (Fisher et al. 2010) evaluation found that most service users using individual funding experienced personal well-being and physical and mental health at levels similar to the Australian general population norm, and participants attributed these positive results to their increased control over the organization of their disability support.

Are Personal Budgets Cost-Effective?

The introduction of personal budgets is based on the assumption that they should be at least cost neutral. However, the variation in models and service users makes it difficult almost impossible to compare costs. Small-scale studies in the UK by Jones et al. (2011) and Stainton, Boyce and Phillips (2009) indicate that personal budget schemes were cheaper than services delivered by the local authority, and relatively cost neutral when compared with independent sector provision. However, both research teams warn of the need to adequately budget for start-up costs.

Potential cost savings have been suggested through the stimulation of business processes such managing access to services, auditing and IT systems, together with reduction in waste, overhead cost reduction and greater value for money (SCIE 2011). Stainton, Boyce and Phillips (2009) conclude that there is some evidence to suggest that direct payments are cheaper than traditional in-house service provision and relatively cost neutral when compared with independent sector provision. After performing the Individual Budgets Evaluation Network (IBSEN) evaluation of the individual budget pilots in 13 Local Authorities, Glendinning et al. (2008) reported that there appears to be a small cost-effectiveness advantage over standard support arrangements for younger people with a physical disability and people with mental health problems. However, there is virtually no reliable evidence on the long-term social care costs and outcomes of personal budgets in England (SCIE 2011). In the Australian context, individual funding has not resulted in an increase in the total specialist disability support cost to government (Fisher et al. 2010). In their US study, Dale and Brown (2006) report that the additional costs involved in the provision of personal budgets could be offset by the associated prevention of the need for some nursing home places. Based on a scan of the relevant research, the Health Foundation concluded that "[t]here is limited information about value for money, largely because there are few rigorous effectiveness studies and the costs of traditional care and personal budgets tend to be underestimated" (2010, 3).

In the Netherlands, the estimated state expenditure on personal budgets in 2007 was considerably less than the budgets for nursing homes or residential care services and equivalent to home care services (Kremer 2006). However, van Ginneken et al. (2012) cite the Dutch Ministry of Health, reporting that personal budgets had become unsustainable. "Between 2002 and 2010 the number of personal budget holders increased 10-fold, and spending increased on average by 23% a year, a rate that was much faster than for those without budgets."

What Are the Perceptions of Frontline Staff?

The attitudes of professional service providers who gate keep access to personal budgets was highlighted in many of the reports reviewed. Spandler and Vick (2006) discovered early in their pilot research that, in order for it to be successful, Local Authority senior managers, practitioners and care co-coordinators had themselves to be willing and able proactively to support direct payment implementation. The reluctance of frontline staff to offer direct payments is evident in several research studies. As early as 2006, Kremer highlighted that training for frontline staff and first-line managers is pivotal to the successful implementation of personal budget schemes. Training is needed to manage change, improve knowledge and assessment practice and promote equality and diversity awareness (Glendinning et al. 2008). It is also needed in order to challenge erroneous perceptions about risk for certain groups (particularly older people, people with mental health problems and/or severe intellectual disabilities) whom professionals might assume are not able to benefit from a personal budget. Tyson (2009), in a study of the introduction of personal budgets in Hartlepool between 2006 and 2009, reported that "there are four areas which must be addressed in the early days: leadership; legitimacy (shared understanding and ownership); a system for resource allocation; and a system for support planning and brokerage" (p. 4).

Evidence suggests that the adoption of the philosophy of personalization and person-centered approaches is critical for the implementation of personal budgets.

What Are the Implications for the Availability and Quality of Support Infrastructure?

The availability of qualified support workers for disability support and of new types of support services is fundamental for implementing of personal budgets (Timonen, Convery and Cahill 2006). The experience in the Netherlands was that the growth of the care market has been slower than originally anticipated (Kremer 2006). In the Australian context, particular supply issues for personal budget users living in rural areas have been a challenge (Laragy and Ottmann 2011).

As for the nature and quality of care, evidence suggests that personal assistants employed by budget holders regard themselves able to provide a better care than is possible when employed by a care organization, and service users are more satisfied with their support than with traditional personal assistance programs (Kremer 2006; Hatton and Waters 2011). Personal assistants tend to be either known to the service user though family or social networks. Kremer observes that personal assistants "employed via direct payments sometimes feel obliged, like unpaid family carers, to undertake certain tasks or duties which may be beyond their skills or which may go against their professional standards," because "clients did not always understand their role as employers" (Kremer 2006, 394).

Concerns that personal budgets may undermine the professionalism of care are valid. For example the lack of opportunities for professional development for personal assistants, who cannot consult other professionals or train and educate themselves, and the lack of control over "development of professional knowledge" (Kremer 2006, 395). One potential problem that may arise from informal care giving is that caregivers may feel reluctant to exercise their social rights such as taking the annual leave to which they are entitled. The emergence of an unregulated market of personal assistants may present concerns about not only the quality assurance or care, but also the employment conditions, training and low wages of care providers. Kremer (2006) reported that, in the Netherlands, the state no longer regulates domiciliary care, with half of the caregivers in this study saying they were overburdened because of living in the same house with the care receiver.

The Dutch government is increasingly wary of the 'monetarization' of informal care, because, in some cases, people are being paid in circumstances where they would provide care without payment. The debate around payment for previously unpaid, informal carers is complex and involves ethical, budgetary and social rights issues. The availability of sufficient high-quality, trained and skilled personal assistants who are able to offer the type of choice required by personal budget employers presented challenges in most of the programs reviewed.

Personalization as a Wicked Solution to Welfare Rights and Equity

In conclusion, any opportunities that promote the equity and rights of people requiring support and care must be considered in light of the complexity of welfare provision and the multiple interests involved. Good intentions and ideas should always be subject to critique, especially at the interface where technical solutions to welfare provision intersect with professional norms, service providers' cultures and service users' responses (Head and Alford 2015). Contrary to policy claims, the evidence base for personalization, identified in this paper, is limited, and so it is difficult to draw strong conclusions about the implementation, management and impact of personal budgets. However, it can be said that qualitative findings from service users tend to be positive. The introduction of personal budgets provides an opportunity to promote a greater level of choice and control services and facilitate people's inclusion in society. Personalization should be prefaced with an acknowledgment that people with disabilities have individualized and diverse needs and that the age old tenet that a 'one model fits all' approach is unlikely to be adequate to address complex social welfare problems. Evidence suggests that personal budgets are not appropriate for everyone with disabilities and there is a need for a range of service delivery options responsive to the needs of people with physical, sensory, mental health and/or intellectual disabilities (Anand et al. 2012). The unbridled acceptance of personalization as the solution to welfare ills may unintentionally reproduce the deficiencies of past welfare delivery. Just who gains or who loses in the personalization stakes of social care is still a matter of considerable debate. Developing individually tailored and accessible support arrangements should not detract from necessary investment in improving directly provided state welfare services for those who still want and/or need them.

The authors wish to acknowledge to contributions of Victoria Clift-Matthews, Alison Martin and Maria Rizzo of Matrix Evidence, London, UK.

References

Aged and Community Services. 2008. "Consumer Directed Care in Community Care." Discussing Paper for ACSA Policy Development. Canberra, Australia.

Alakeson, Vidhya. 2008. "Self-Directed Care for Adults with Serious Mental Illness: The Barriers to Progress." *Psychiatric Services* 59 (7): 792–794.

Anand, Janet, Gavin Davidson, Geraldine Macdonald, and Berni Kelly. 2012. "The Transition to Personal Budgets for People with Disabilities: A Review of Practice in Specified Jurisdictions." National Disability Authority, Working Paper, Dublin, Ireland.

Audit Commission. 2006. *Choosing Well: Analysing the Costs and Benefits of Choice in Local Public Services.* London: Audit Commission for Local Authorities and the National Health Service in England and Wales.

Bloche, Gregg M. 2000. "Consumer-Directed Health Care and the Disadvantaged." *Health Affairs* 26 (5): 1315–1327.

Burrow, Elizabeth. 2009. "Direct Payments an Older People: Developing a Framework for Practice." In *Social Work Practice with Adults*, edited by D. Galpin and N. Bates. Exeter: Learning Matters.

Churchman, Charles West. 1967. "Free for All." *Management Science* 14 (4): 141–146.

Dale, Stacy B., and Randall Brown. 2006. "Reducing Nursing Home Use Through Consumer-Directed Personal Care Services." *Medical Care* 44 (8): 760–767.

Davey, Vanessa, Tom Snell, José-Luis Fernández, Martin R. J. Knapp, Roseanne Tobin, Debbie Jolly, Margaret Perkins, Jeremy Kendall, Charlotte Pearson, and Nicola Vick. 2007. *Schemes Providing Support to People Using Direct Payments:*

A UK Survey. London School of Economics and Personal Social Science Research Unit.

Department of Health (England). 2006. *Guide to Action: Direct Payments for People with Mental Health Problems*. London: CSIP and Department of Health. www.socialinclusion.org.uk/publications/Direct_Payments_web.pdf.

Duffy, Simon. 2005. "Individual Budgets: Transforming the Allocation of Resources for Care." *Journal of Integrated Care* 13 (1): 8–16.

Egan, D. 2008. "Issues Concerning Direct Payments in the Republic of Ireland." A Report for The Person Centre. www.dublincil.org/Documents/DP%20Report.pdf.

Fernández, José-Luis, Jeremy Kendall, Vanessa Davey, and Martin Knapp. 2007. "Direct Payments in England: Factors Linked to Variations in Local Provision." *Journal of Social Policy* 36 (1): 97–121.

Fisher, Karen R., Robyn Edwards, Ryan Gleeson, Christiane Purcal, Tomasz Sitek, Brooke Dinning, Carmel Laragy, Lel D'Aegher, and Denise Thompson. 2010. *Effectiveness of Individual Funding Approaches of Disability Support*. Canberra, Australia: Department of Families and Housing Community Services and Indigenous Affairs.

Foster, Leslie, Randall Brown, Barbara Phillips, Jennifer Schore, and Barbara Lepidus Carlson. 2003. "Improving the Quality of Medicaid Personal Assistance Through Consumer Direction." *Health Affairs*. http://content.healthaffairs.org/content/early/2003/03/26/hlthaff.w3.162.citation.

Galpin, Di, and Natalie Bates. 2009. *Social Work Practice with Adults*. Exeter: Learning Matters.

Glasby, Jon, Julian Le Grand, and Simon Duffy. 2009. "A Healthy Choice? Direct Payments and Health care in the English NHS." *Policy & Politics* 37 (4): 481–497.

Glendinning, Caroline, David Challis, J. Fernandez, Sally Jacobs, Karen Jones, Martin Knapp, Jill Manthorpe et al. 2008. *Evaluation of the Individual Budgets Pilot Programme: Final Report*. Individual Budgets Support Networks Evaluation (IBSEN). York: Social Policy Research Unit and University of York.

Hatton, Chris, and John Waters. 2011. *The National Personal Budget Survey*. Lancaster: Lancaster University.

Head, Brian W., and John Alford. 2015. "Wicked Problems: Implications for Public Policy and Management." *Administration & Society* 47 (6): 711–739.

Health Foundation. 2010. *Personal Budgets: Research Scan*. London: Health Foundation.

Health Service Executive. 2009. "National Review of Health Services Executive Funded Adult Day Services, Republic of Ireland." www.hse.ie/eng/services/list/4/disability/day-service-review/.

Innes, Anthea, Fiona Kelly, and Ozlem Dincarslan. 2011. "Care Home Design for People with Dementia: What Do People with Dementia and Their Family Carers Value?" *Aging & Mental Health* 15 (5): 548–556.

"International Convention of the Rights of Persons with Disabilities and Its Optional Protocol." U.N. GAOR, 61st Sess., Item 67(b), U.N. Doc. A/61/611, December 6, 2006.

Jones, Karen, Julien Forder, James Caiels, Elizabeth Welch, Karen Windle, Jacqueline Davidson, Paul Dolan, Caroline Glendinning, Annie Irvine, and Dominic King. 2011. *The Cost of Implementing Personal Health Budgets*. Canterbury: Personal Social Services Research Unit, University of Kent.

Joseph Rowntree Foundation. 1995. *Increasing User Control in Social Services: The Value of the Service Brokerage Model—Findings.* York: Joseph Rowntree Foundation.

Kodner, Dennis L. 2003. "Consumer-Directed Services: Lessons and Implications for Integrated Systems of Care." *International Journal of Integrated Care* 3 (2): 3–12.

Kremer, Monique. 2006. "Consumers in Charge of Care: The Dutch Personal Budget and Its Impact on the Market, Professionals and the Family." *European Societies* 8 (3): 385–401.

Laragy, Carmel, and Goetz Ottmann. 2011. "Towards a Framework for Implementing Individual Funding Based on an Australian Case Study." *Journal of Policy and Practice in Intellectual Disabilities* 8 (1): 18–27.

National Disability Authority. 2010. *Advice Paper to the Value for Money and Policy Review of Disability Services Programme: A Contemporary Developments in Disability Services Paper.* Dublin: NDA.

National Economic and Social Council. 2005. *The Developmental Welfare State.* Dublin: The Stationary Office.

Parker, Sarah, and Karen Fisher. 2010. "Facilitators and Barriers in Australian Disability Housing Support Policies: Using a Human Rights Framework." *Disability Studies Quarterly* 30 (3/4).

Poll, Carl, Simon Duffy C. Hatton, H. Sanderson, and M. Routledge. 2006. *A Report on in Control's First Phase, 2003–2005.* London: In Control Publications.

Priestley, Mark, Debbie Jolly, Charlotte Pearson, Sheila Ridell, Colin Barnes, and Geof Mercer. 2006. "Direct Payments and Disabled People in the UK: Supply, Demand and Devolution." *British Journal of Social Work* 37 (7): 1189–1204.

Rabiee, Parvaneh, Nicola Moran, and Caroline Glendinning. 2009. "Individual Budgets: Lessons from Early Users' Experiences." *British Journal of Social Work* 39 (5): 918–935.

Riddell, Sheila, Mark Priestley, Charlotte Pearson, Geof Mercer, Colin Barnes, Debbie Jolly, and Victoria Williams. 2006. *Disabled People and Direct Payments: A UK Comparative Study.* ESRC Award RES-000-23 263. https://www.researchgate.net/publication/255612758

Ridley, Julie, and Lyn Jones. 2010. "Direct What? The Untapped Potential of Direct Payments to Mental Health Service Users." *Disability & Society* 18 (5): 643–658.

Rittel, Horst W. J., and Melvin M. Webber. 1973. "Dilemmas in a General Theory of Planning." *Policy Sciences* 4 (2): 155–169.

Robert Johnson Wood Foundation. 2007. *Choosing Independence: A Summary of the Cash & Counseling Model of Self-Directed Personal Assistance Services.* Princeton: Robert Johnson Wood Foundation.

Scottish Government. 2008. *Personalisation: A Shared Understanding.* Edinburgh: Scottish Government.

Scourfield, Peter. 2005. "Implementing the Community Care (Direct Payments) Act: Will the Supply of Personal Assistants Meet the Demand and at What Price?" *Journal of Social Policy* 34: 469–488.

Sikma, Suzanne K., and Heather M. Young. 2003. "Nurse Delegation in Washington State: A Case Study of Concurrent Policy Implementation and Evaluation." *Policy, Politics, & Nursing Practice* 4 (1): 53–61.

Social Care Institute of Excellence. 2009. *SCIE Research Briefing 20: The Implementation of Individual Budget Schemes in Adult Social Care.* London: SCIE.

Social Care Institute of Excellence. 2011. *Personalisation, Productivity and Efficiency*. London: SCIE.

Spalding, Karen Lynn, Alan Paul Williams, and Jillian R. Watkins. 2006. *Self Managed Care Programs in Canada: A Report to Health Canada*. Ottawa: Health Care Policy Directorate and Health Canada.

Spandler, Helen, and Nicola Vick. 2005. "Enabling Access to Direct Payments: An Exploration of Care Co-Ordinators Decision-Making Practices." *Journal of Mental Health* 14 (2): 145–155.

Spandler, Helen, and Nicola Vick. 2006. "Opportunities for Independent Living Using Direct Payments in Mental Health." *Health & Social Care in the Community* 14 (2): 107–115.

Stainton, Tim, S. Boyce, and C. J. Phillips. 2009. "Independence Pays: A Cost and Resource Analysis of Direct Payments in Two Local Authorities." *Disability & Society* 24 (2): 161–172.

Taylor, Nicholas D. 2008. "Obstacles and Dilemmas in the Delivery of Direct Payments to Service Users with Poor Mental Health." *Practice* 20 (1): 43–55.

Timonen, Virpi, Janet Convery, and Suzanne Cahill. 2006. "Care Revolutions in the Making? A Comparison of Cash-for-Care Programmes in Four European Countries." *Ageing and Society* 26 (3): 455–474.

Tyson, Andrew. 2009. *Self-Directed Support in Hartlepool 2006–2009*. In Control and Hartlepool Borough Council.

Ungerson, Clare. 2004. "Whose Empowerment and Independence? A Cross-National Perspective on Cash for Care Schemes." *Ageing and Society* 24 (2): 189–212.

Ungerson, Clare, and Susan Yeandle. eds. 2007. *Cash for Care in Developed Welfare States*. Basingstoke: Palgrave Macmillan.

van Ginneken, Ewout, Peter P. Groenewegen, and Martin McKee. 2012. "Personal Health care Budgets: What Can England Lfrom the Netherlands?" *BMJ: British Medical Journal (Online)* 344: e1383.

Section 2

Managing, Leading and Following

The chapters in this second section share an attention to the roles played by those who manage, lead and follow in response to a variety of wicked problems in the field of health and social care. These discussions prompt us to think about who can, or should, take responsibility for formulating approaches to their resolution. We start by problematizing the overuse of the idea of leadership within the English NHS. Gaurish Chawla and Mark Learmonth consider the impact of this fascination on the experiences of employees. In the second chapter, we continue looking at the role of the leader as Monica Andersson Bäck and Charlotta Levay weigh up the aspirations of managers to provide high-quality care with their day-to-day concerns.

The next chapter, from Merja Sinkkonen and Sanna Laulainen, questions the extent to which leaders should be expected to deliver ethically attuned organizations. Their conclusion is that employees have a critical role to play in delivering ethical leadership. We see this theme continue and develop in the fourth chapter, authored by Minna Hoffrén and Sanna Laulainen, in which the destructive capacity of poor leadership is explored and considered from the viewpoint of the employee. In paying attention to the way that destructive leadership affects the actions and behaviors of employees they remind us of the important role that both groups play in addressing the complex problems of managing in this sector. The final chapter of this section provides a thought-provoking link to the question of leadership and to chapters that follow and consider those voices that are often unheard. Laura Visser, Inge Bleijenbergh, Yvonne Benschop and Allard van Riel consider the scope of technology to empower patients and to give them the chance to manage and lead their own treatment. As they consider the results of an empirical study they are able to explore the potential of new technology as well as to highlight some of its risks.

4 The Wicked Problem of Leadership in the NHS

Gaurish Chawla and Mark Learmonth

For many throughout health care systems across the world, 'leadership' has become what Ford, Harding and Learmonth call 'a way of being' (2008, 4) rather than merely a job. In the last few years, rather than managerialism being the dominant way people with power think about their influence, what O'Reilly and Reed (2010, 962) call 'leaderism' has taken its place. As they argue: "whereas management necessarily involves the conundrum of aligning principal and agent, the change in discourse to leadership resolves this conundrum through re-definition by making the issue the establishment of a passion for a common goal between leaders and led" (2010, 962). Indeed, the word leadership is now used for pretty much any kind of activity that is thought of by officials as 'positive' such that leadership is becoming an almost meaningless term (Learmonth and Morrell 2017). Indeed, the rhetoric is so widespread that as Morrell and Hewison (2013, 70) show, "it becomes impossible to see an alternative to 'leadership' . . . leadership is, seemingly, anything and everything."

Indeed, Gemmill and Oakley (1992) question the very existence of leaders—why are they necessary? They problematize the need of a leader in an organization: "*exactly what underlying existential needs or problems the concept of a leader is meant to address has not been clearly articulated*" (p114), calling leadership a product of reification. The purpose of the myth of leadership, they suggest, is to act as a social defense mechanism against social anxieties caused by uncomfortable emotions that, they argue, arise when people work together (building upon Gemmill 1986 and Jacques 1955). Therefore, leadership is a sign of "social pathology," an "iatrogenic social myth that induces massive learned helplessness among members of a social system" (Gemmill and Oakley 1992, 115).

Nevertheless, it is good to be able to think of oneself as a radical and empowering leader—not as (merely) administering something like paper-work. Furthermore, and relatedly, being known as a leader is more likely to construct the sort of public image that others may see as legitimate—and to which they will therefore acquiesce (Harding and Learmonth 2000). As Clarke and Newman have pointed out, the "discourse of managerialism . . . is part of the process through which 'administrators,' 'public servants' and 'practitioners' come to see themselves as 'business managers' . . . 'strategists,' 'leaders' and so on" (1997, 92). All this is important because it may well not be in the interests of health care professionals to define themselves as leaders or to use the language of leadership—as attractive as it may be on certain levels so to do (Learmonth 2004, 2005). After all, identifying as a leader involves conformity to the wider logics of leadership: an acceptance of the legitimacy of the top leader's (the chief executive's) right to lead, as well as an acquiescence to the elites who get to define 'what the NHS requires.'

This chapter is dedicated to exploring the *"wicked problem"* (Grint 2005) of understanding Leadership discourse in the English National Health Service (NHS). "Leadership Development" has been the focus of the NHS for a while: but the extent to which this Leadership Development addresses the above concerns of Gemmill and Oakley is debatable. Martin and Learmonth (2012), for example, present a criticism of Leadership in the NHS and how the term has come to be over-used (perhaps due to its powerful cultural connotations) and is increasingly being used to describe various frontline professionals, managers and executives in the NHS: similar to how 'management' replaced 'administration' (Learmonth 2005). In the contemporary NHS, everyone can be, and is, a Leader. For the worker, the received language of Leadership is becoming the language of the organization.

To a student of organizational lives, this poses another wicked problem: how does one study worker experience (part of which would be their experience of *Leadership*) without talking about *Leadership*? For example, Gordon et al. (2015) asked 65 medical trainees in the UK about "their experiences of leadership and followership." It can be argued that by asking them about their experience of leadership and followership, the interviewers may have subliminally encouraged the participants to make sense of their experience using the language of leadership and followership, which, if asked independently, the participants may or may not have chosen. Indeed, on page 1, Gordon et al. acknowledge this limitation. Following on from Parker (1997), it can be deduced that the respondents have been provided with the discourse by the interviewer within which to construct their answers, hence influencing the results. Therefore, we decided that we need to step away from the traditional qualitative interview, and use a method that could help us bring out worker stories, but with minimal questioning from the researcher.

In so doing we are working in the tradition of what has come to be known as Critical Leadership Studies (CLS). CLS has recently emerged from the more established tradition of Critical Management Studies (CMS). Briefly, CMS is a diverse set of ideas which, rather than being concerned primarily with increasing organizational efficiency, seeks to reveal, challenge and overturn the power relations within organizational life by which individuals and collectives are often constrained and dominated (King and Learmonth 2015). CLS, as Collinson (2011, 182) argues, broadly shares CMS's political aims and intellectual traditions, but it attempts to broaden CMS's range, in that it:

[E]xplicitly recognizes that, for good and/or ill, leaders and leadership dynamics (defined . . . as the shifting, asymmetrical interrelations between leaders, followers and contexts) also exercise significant power and influence over contemporary organizational and societal processes. . . [whereas] many CMS writers ignore the study of leadership, focusing more narrowly on management and organization.

Free Association Interviews: Wicked Solution to a Wicked Problem?

In the introduction of their book *doing qualitative research differently* (lowercase in original), Hollway and Jefferson (2000) ask provocatively about using interviews as research methods:

> Will you believe everything you are told? If not, how will you distinguish between truth and untruth? Even if you believe everything you are told, will you be satisfied that you have been told everything that is relevant? . . . What do you assume about the effect of people's motivations and memory on what they tell you? What will you assume about your effect as an interviewer on the answers given?

This demonstrates the limitation of a standard qualitative interview: it can potentially influence individual's opinion and choice of discourse. Arguably, this limitation can be minimized by using the Free Association Narrative Interview. In the following paragraphs, we discuss Free Association Interview based on Hollway and Jefferson's (2000) work and present some evidence which makes a case for its suitability compared to other kinds of qualitative interviews.

Free association, Storey et al. write ((2012, 231), borrowing from Malan (1979)) "refers to whatever comes to mind when a person is asked to think and talk about a particular issue: analysis focused on why certain aspects came to the forefront rather than others."

The use of free association as a way to access the thought processes before their conscious manipulation goes back to Freud, who used free association as a method of choice to understand his clients' 'subconscious' thought patterns and circumvent 'conscious' sense-making, which may make the individual defensive and/or make them feel like they have to offer a 'coherent and sensible' narrative, and inadvertently altering the discourse. Campbell (2007, 58) sums it up:

> When we ask clients to free associate, we are really asking them to access unconscious affective memory with all the images and fantasies it entails

By asking the respondent to speak what comes to their mind in which-ever order it appears, the idea is to reduce the 'conscious control' over responses. This can have significant advantages over the traditional inter-view. For example, Hollway and Jefferson (2000) had mixed success with standard interviews, before having to resort to Free Association Interviews. They write (Hollway and Jefferson 2000, 300) that although their semi-structured questionnaire was directed at eliciting the same anxieties and fan-tasies (in their case fear of crime) as the (later conducted) Free Association Narrative Interviews, asking "What's the crime you most fear" straightaway puts the research subject into a position of conscious alert and defense, as the topic is "Introduced abruptly, devoid of context, and prior to the build-up of any rapport." They theorize that such an abstract and abrupt ques-tioning is likely to be met with an 'uncertain,' disengaged answer.

In contrast (they continue on p. 309), using an approach similar to Freud (who allowed his patients to start the therapy session with whatever was presenting to the patient's subconscious at that moment) helped them gain access to participants fears and concerns much more effectively. They (Hol-lway and Jefferson 2000, 310) conclude that a semi-structured interview primes the interviewee to offer a coherent narrative which forces them to indulge in critical conscious faculties instead of letting the researcher hear their free flowing thoughts. Free association, however, aims to minimize such requirement of coherence and welcomes incoherent, intra-contradictory stories as they indeed add richness to the account which is being sought.

Similarly, Menzies Lyth (1988, 117) argues that adding 'structure' to interviews, by means of specifying questions, or preceding them with ques-tionnaires or surveys, can be suggestive to the individual and can influence their choice of the discourse that they might use for their narrative. This is likely to engage the conscious thinking of the individual and they are more likely to use the vocabulary and the kind of sentences that they might think are relevant for the kind of discussion that they perceive is about to happen.

To avoid these pitfalls, the interviews were based on Free Association, attempting to follow the interviewee's lead and only asking exploratory questions to help them develop their narrative. To begin the interview, instead of simply enquiring about the interviewee's experience of work in their organization, the method involved asking them to think about their experience of working in the NHS and pick one (or many) photo (photos) (from a set of photos preselected by the researcher) that represents their experience and talk about it/them.

Photo Elicitation

Visual methods of eliciting subconscious thoughts have found their use in various psychotherapeutic and organizational research contexts (see Bell and Davison 2013 for a review). Photo elicitation has also been used in combination with other qualitative research methods to enrich the data and access deeper, subconscious thoughts (Harper 2002, 23–24). Davison, McLean and Warren (2012, 3–5) review the literature using visual research methods to explain the advantages of using such methods. They give the example of Slutskaya et al.'s exploration of "dirty work" among butchers in the UK (Vol. 7, 16–33), which exemplifies how use of photographs helped elicit emotions and thoughts that may have been otherwise difficult to comprehend. Another example is provided by Warren (2012): Armstrong's (2007) study of the 'organisational mind.'

Inspired by these studies, photos were used as a conversation starter for a free association interview. Seven anonymous interviews were conducted by Gaurish (any mentions of 'I' below are his reflections) and the interviewees were employees of the NHS from across England. Participants reserved the right to withdraw a month after the interview was conducted. The interviewees were shown 50 random photos (selected from public domain using google image search with keywords 'random images') and asked to select one/many that remind them of their organizational lives and talk about them. In addition to audio, a video was also recorded of the interviewees' hands interacting with the photos.

In interacting with the interviewees, I didn't ask questions about 'leadership' or 'management' or even 'teams.' After they started talking about a photo, I mostly made remarks that were aimed at clarifying their stories (such as "Tell me more about that?"). If the interviewee finished their statement, I allowed for the silence to precipitate. Mostly, the interviewees would break the silence themselves, often by asking for further guidance; but they would tend to do it in a suggestive manner. For example, commonly, the interviewees will themselves ask something to the effect of "Shall I pick more photos now?" (As opposed to 'what should I do next?') In that case, I would interpret this as a subconscious suggestion that they would like to pick more photos, I would duly oblige by giving them the permission that they seem to seek.

I paid a close attention to how the interviewee would seem to be interacting with the photos. If they seemed to be mulling over a few, I would ask them to talk me through what they were thinking. If I saw them 'narrow down' their choices to a few and then prioritize the order to talk in, I would ask them to clarify their decision-making process. In conversation, I would then follow the individuals' narrative and encourage them to follow the train of their thought freely. At times, individuals would seek permission to do so (e.g. "Is this the sort of thing you are looking for?," "Shall I keep going?" etc.) which I would happily grant.

At the end of the interview, I would also ask the individuals about their thoughts on participating in the process ("How was this interview process for you?"), and I have had some useful feedback about the method itself. For instance, I received comments like *"the photos help me remember things I wouldn't have thought about," "The questions are more open than open,"* etc. which encouraged me about the usefulness of the method.

The interviews were approached with psychodynamic theory which has been described as one of the "hermeneutics of suspicion."

> Psychoanalysis can be seen as belonging to the hermeneutics of suspicion which, apart from Freud, is also represented by Marx and Nietzsche. All three have probed behind what they conceived as an illusionary self-consciousness to a deeper lying, more unpleasant or shameful one. In Freud, the latter appears as libido, in Marx the economic interest, and in Nietzsche the will to power.

Use of psychodynamics to study organizations is not new (for some classic studies, see Menzies Lyth 1960; Carr 1998; Diamond 1993; Gabriel 1999; Kets de Vries 1988). Menzies Lyth (1988, 10) writes in justification of use of psychodynamics for organizational studies:

> It may be too hard for workers to focus on the basic problem, and they pick the ambience of the job as a means of expressing something of their discontents

Arnaud (2012, 1122) reviews plenty of examples and concludes that

> [Psychodynamic theory can help] . . . researchers to develop a richer comprehension of organizational functioning and managerial issues by taking the effects of the unconscious into account. Second, psycho-analysis can guide them on different 'terrains' of intervention, by trans-posing aspects of the analytical treatment, integrating transference, and so on. Third, it allows them to re-question organizational issues and managerial ends from a slightly skewed point of view attributable to psychoanalytic ethics and the recognition of the subject.
>
> (Arnaud 2012, 1129–1130)

Examining interview transcripts was a lengthy, messy process of reading, rereading, making notes, reflecting over the interview transcripts and deducing (or indeed assigning) meaning (in shape of fantasies, myths and defense mechanisms) to the transcripts in light of the psychodynamic theory. Below, I present some of the results: fantasies noted in people's narratives about themselves and the people they work with as well as of leadership.

Self-Fantasies

Immediately apparent were fantasies about the self. Almost everyone I spoke to represented themselves as a, dare I say, 'good,' 'well-intentioned' worker who 'goes the extra mile' and 'does what's required to the best of their abilities.' The self was almost always kindly portrayed. Frequently, people tended to cast themselves as the 'underdog' in their fantasies about the self.

For instance, on one occasion, the language of playground was used where the boss was framed as the bully and the self as the helpless schoolboy. On another occasion, the self was the helpless prisoner whereas the boss was the distant prison officer, the work environment being described as 'suffocating,' 'dull' and 'like prison cells.'

The self was portrayed as a survivor of institutional hardships. The meanings attached to things done by 'those above' were more reminiscent of the 'powerful owner making us do things we don't like,' as opposed to 'my democratic/servant leader trying to distribute his power/ leadership etc.' For instance, in one example, the manager bought certain food items for their subordinate workers for Christmas—and that was an act viewed with suspicion ('What did they want in exchange?') by the worker.

It is, at this point, important to note several things. Firstly, I am not trying to make value judgments about either my interviewees or their bosses, or the NHS in general. Thinking about my own experience of working in multiple sectors and in two different countries, I can't say I can't relate to any of these fantasies myself. Anecdotal conversations with colleagues and friends have been affirmative—so I am sure the reader, if they manage to set aside their initial anxieties, would be able to recall several such narratives from either their own life, and/ or from the lives of others. Our narratives about ourselves often involve portraying ourselves as well-meaning, righteous beings.

Secondly, this is not a 'call for self-improvement' or a 'warning to managers that workers need to be improved,' or an admission that my experience/ experience of NHS workers are 'negative.' What I am trying to describe here is that most of us frame our narratives of ourselves in similar manner, and it is not something 'wrong' that 'needs to be improved' by ways of 'staff engagement initiatives' or 'team working days.' This is the way our narrative selves maintain our self-esteem or, as Freud would say, our ego tries to justify why we are not at our ego-ideal stage yet to our super ego. Since ego ideals are almost always mythical and therefore almost always non-attainable (no matter how much a person achieves, in their own subconscious, they are almost always yearning for another target (that life is a journey with destinations to be 'reached' is another fantasy on its own) or justifying why they can't reach it any more).

So, what are the implications? The first is to take a critical look at attempts to 'improve' organizational participation of workers, or 'followership' or 'team engagement' based on 'satisfaction.' If we are to believe that most interventions that are initiated by the 'managers' or 'people at the top' are perceived as a 'threat' by the workers, the more one tries to improve the organization by such means, the more threatened the worker is likely to feel. Indeed, whether explicit or implicit, the aim of most of such initiatives is to 'improve' organizational performance, which, could easily be perceived as just another way to coerce more work out of the workers. Is there a way to make the workers change their opinions about such interventions? One can surround the workers with narratives of 'leadership,' 'teamwork' and 'followership' and so on and take words such as 'exploitation' out of the language. However, taking the language of contestation away doesn't take away the discontents of the organization: it just seeps out through alternative channels.

Similarly, several interviewees described themselves as an individual who was comfortable with organizational changes (while other employees weren't, and were more like 'dinosaurs,' like one interviewee said), individuals who 'take initiatives' (or couldn't because of some limiting factors) and 'try to do my best with members of my team.' This is similar to what Sveningsson and Larsson (2006) discuss: how the organizational worker can construct a fantasy of leadership and of themselves as a leader. They present how such fantasy can serve the purpose of creation of an identity that serves the subconscious drives of the individual and therefore (in psychodynamic terms) brings them closer to their ego-ideal, hence contributing toward raising their self-esteem.

Team Fantasies

Another notion to strike me within the narratives was how people portrayed their experience of working within their immediate groups ('teams,' as many prefer to call it: henceforth we shall refer to them as 'teams' too, although we remain skeptical as to what each individual meant when they said 'team.' Also worth noting is that in each of the interviews, the word 'team' was brought up by the interviewee themselves (and not suggested by the interviewer) while talking about the people who they work with). It is perhaps not surprising to note that different people had different fantasies of their teams depending upon a whole lot of different factors: for instance, where they've worked before they worked for the health service, where they worked after they worked for the health service, their position, number of people they work with and their jobs, the day-to-day stress being faced by these teams etc.

For instance, one professional working in a 'multi-disciplinary' team dealing with mental health crisis situations as their primary role, was very appreciative of their team and how 'lucky' it was that their team members rarely had 'differences of opinions.' The person described themselves as "extremely lucky" to have been working with people who were so congruent and that this team was "absolutely great."

This was, however, quite different from the narrative about 'teams in general' and their 'past teams' that this individual had worked in. While talking about these, the interviewee held the opinion that 'all teams can be improved upon' and then went on to describe what these things might have been, in those teams. Looking at these notions psychodynamically—there are two fantasies here—first being that 'my team is great, everyone gets along so well and we don't have disagreements,' and the second, that all teams can be 'improved.'

It is perhaps easy to see the romanticization of the current team and group of people. I would describe it as a defense against the needs of the 'front-line firefighting' role that they find themselves in: the demand of this role meant that the individuals have to subconsciously create this comfortable safe space offered by the fantasy of 'we are all a family' to cope with the emotional labor they carry out on a day-to-day basis.

Fantasies about Leadership

Although not directly questioned about their experience with 'Leaders,' most interviewees talked to varying degrees about their experience of work-ing with colleagues. In quite a few of these stories, people talked about interpersonal interactions where power was being exercised—which could be taken to mean as examples of Leadership.

For example, rarely anyone spoke of themselves as a 'Leader' (or equiva-lent). Stories of what might be called Leadership were often about how power was being exercised upon the people rather than how they were exer-cising power themselves. This apparent denial was quite interesting because to an external observer, a lot of these workers would appear to have roles that involved exercising some sort of 'Leadership.' 'Leaders' were almost always 'they' or 'them' who were doing things 'to us.'

Whenever it came up, the way people perceived the idea of 'Leadership' was also fascinating. For example, when asked about their experiences of working in their organization, 'Alex' (pseudonym) asked me to clarify: *"You want me to talk about my experience through 'lens of leadership?'"*

I had asked Alex to tell me his story of working in his organization. It was quite interesting how they presented their understanding of Leadership with the metaphor of a 'Lens.' The metaphor of lens suggests that their fantasy of Leadership is perhaps not that of actions to be enacted, but that of a newer way to perceive organizations. They are beginning to reframe their organi-zational knowledge through this 'lens of leadership': they are revising their language about organizational working from something else to that of being a 'newly developed leader.' Perhaps a shift to the language of 'leadership' is happening—similar to the shift from the language of 'administration' to that of 'management,' as Learmonth (2005) describes.

Conclusion

Knowledge produced within alternative epistemologies are indeed crucial in order to critique prevalent hegemonies. This chapter describes one such attempt and as such hopes to contribute to Critical Management/Lead-ership Studies. We find ourselves agreeing with Gabriel and Carr (2002, 348), who write that psychodynamics offers original insights and expla-nations and helps us move away from the organizational theory that is "centred on rationality, hierarchy and authority" and helps us understand the "symbolic, irrational, emotional and discursive dimensions of organisational life."

References

Armstrong, David. 2005. *Organization in the Mind: Psychoanalysis, Group Relations and Organizational Consultancy*. London: Karnac.

Arnaud, Gilles. 2012. "The Contribution of Psychoanalysis to Organization Studies and Management: An Overview." *Organization Studies* 33 (9): 1121–1135.

Bell, Emma, and Jane Davison. 2013. "Visual Management Studies: Empirical and Theoretical Approaches." *International Journal of Management Reviews* 15: 167–184. doi: 10.1111/j.1468-2370.2012.00342

Campbell, Jan. 2007. *Psychoanalysis and the Time of Life: Durations of the Unconscious Self*. London: Routledge.

Carr, Adrian. 1998. "Identity, Compliance and Dissent in Organizations: A Psychoanalytic Perspective." *Organization* 5 (1): 81–99.

Clarke, John, and Janet Newman. 1997. *The Managerial State: Power, Politics and Ideology in the Remaking of Social Welfare*. London: Sage Publications.

Collinson, David. 2011. "Critical Leadership Studies." In *The Sage Handbook of Leadership*, edited by Alan Bryman, David Collinson, Keith Grint, Brad Jackson and Mary Uhl-Bien. 181–194. London: Sage Publications.

Davison, Jane, Christine McLean, and Samantha Warren. 2012. "Exploring the Visual in Organizations and Management." *Qualitative Research in Organisations & Management* 7: 5–15. doi: 10.1108/17465641211223528

Diamond, Michael A. 1993. *The Unconscious Life of Organizations: Interpreting Organizational Identity*. London: Quorum Books.

Ford, Jackie; Nancy Harding, and Mark. Learmonth. 2008. *Leadership as Identity: Constructions and Deconstructions*. Houndmills: Palgrave Macmillan.

Gabriel, Yiannis. 1999. *Organizations in Depth: The Psychoanalysis of Organizations*. London: Sage Publications.

Gabriel, Yiannis and Adrian Carr. 2002. "Organizations, Management and Psychoanalysis: An Overview." *Journal of Managerial Psychology* 17 (5): 348–365.

Gemmill, Gary. 1986. "The Mythology of the Leader Role in Small Groups." *Small Group Behavior* 17 (1): 41–50.

Gemmill, Gary, and Judith Oakley. 1992. "Leadership: An Alienating Social Myth?" *Human Relations* 45: 113–129. doi: 10.1177/001872679204500201.

Gordon, Lisi J., Charlotte E. Rees, Jean. S. Ker, and Jennifer Cleland. 2015. "Leadership and Followership in the Health care Workplace: Exploring Medical Trainees' Experiences Through Narrative Inquiry." *British Medical Journal Open* 5 (12): e008898.

Grint, Keith. 2005. "Problems, Problems, Problems: The Social Construction of 'leadership'." *Human Relations* 58 (11): 1467–1494.

Harding, Nancy, and Mark Learmonth. 2000. "Thinking Critically: The Case of Health Policy Research." *Technology Analysis & Strategic Management* 12 (3): 335–341.

Harper, Douglas. 2002. "Talking About Pictures: A Case for Photo Elicitation." *Visual Studies* 17: 13–26. doi: 10.1080/14725860220137345.

Hollway, Wendy and Tony Jefferson. 2000. *Doing Qualitative Research Differently: Free Association, Narrative and the Interview Method*. London: Sage Publications.

Jacques, Elliott. 1955. "Social Systems as a Defence Against Persecutory and Depressive Anxiety." In *New Directions in Psychoanalysis*, edited by M. Klein, P. Heimann, and R. E. Money-Kyrle. London: Tavistock.

Kets deVries, Manfred F.R., 1988. "Prisoners of Lleadership." *Human Relations* 41 (3): 261–280.

King, Daniel, and Mark Learmonth. 2015. "Can Critical Management Studies Ever Be 'practical'? A Case Study in Engaged Scholarship." *Human Relations* 68: 353–375.

Learmonth, Mark. 2004. "The Violence in Trusting Trust Chief Executives: Glimpsing Trust in the UK National Health Service." *Qualitative Inquiry* 10 (4): 581–600.

Learmonth, Mark. 2005. "Doing Things with Words: The Case of 'management' and 'administration'." *Public Administration* 83 (3): 617–637.

Learmonth, Mark, and Kevin Morrell. 2017. "Is Critical Leadership Studies 'critical'?" *Leadership* 13 (3): 257–271.

Malan, David. H. 1979. *Individual Psychotherapy and the Science of Psychodynamics*. London: Butterworths.

Martin, Graham P. and Mark. Learmonth. 2012. "A Critical Account of the Rise and Spread of 'leadership': The Case of UK Health Care." *Social Science & Medicine* 74 (3): 281–288.

Menzies Lyth, Isabel. 1960. "A Case Study in Fuctioning of Social Systems as a Defense Against Anxiety." *Human Relations* 13: 95–121.

Menzies Lyth, Isabel. 1988. *Containing Anxiety in Institutions: Selected Essays*. London: Free Association Books.

Morrell, Kevin, and Alistair Hewison. 2013. "Rhetoric in Policy Texts: The Role of Enthymeme in Darzi's Review of the NHS." *Policy and Politics* 41: 59–79.

O'Reilly, Dermot, and Mike Reed. 2010. "'Leaderism': An Evolution of Managerialism in UK Public Service Reform." *Public Administration* 88: 960–978.

Parker, Ian 1997. "Discourse Analysis and Psycho-Analysis." *British Journal of Social Psychology* 36: 479–495.

Roper, Michael. 1996. "'Seduction and Succession': Circuits of Homosocial Desire in Management." In *Men as Managers, Managers as Men: Critical Perspectives on Men, Masculinities and Managements*, edited by David. L. Collinson and Geoff. Hearn, 210–226. London: Sage Publications.

Slutskaya, Natasha., Alexander. Simpson, and Jason Hughes. 2012. "Butchers, Quakers and Bankrupts: Lessons from Photo-Elicitation." *Qualitative Research in Organizations and Management* 7 (1): 16–33.

Storey, Judith, Mary-Ann Collis, and Jennifer Clegg. 2012. "A Psychodynamic Interpretation of Staff Accounts of Working with People Who Have Learning Disabilities and Complex Needs." *British Journal of Learning Disabilities* 40: 229–235. doi: 10.1111/j.1468-3156.2011.00697.x.

Sveningsson, Stefan, and Magnus Larsson. 2006. "Fantasies of Leadership: Identity Work." *Leadership* 2 (2): 203–224. doi: 10.1177/1742715006062935.

Warren, Samantha. 2012. "Psychoanalysis, Collective Viewing and the 'Social Photo Matrix' in Organizational Research." *Qualitative Research in Organizations and Management* 7 (1): 86–104.

Wozniak, Anna. 2010. "The Dream That Caused Reality: The Place of the Lacanian Subject of Science in the Field of Organization Theory." *Organization* 17: 395–411.

5 Lofty Ideals and Lowly Troubles among Nursing Home Managers

Monica Andersson Bäck and
Charlotta Levay

Introduction

Elderly care is riddled with wicked problems. Most industrialized countries face a demographic challenge with a rapidly growing share of elderly in the population and no obvious sources of increased funding. In the UK, Ferlie et al. (2013) noted that prolonged difficulties in tackling inter-sectorial complexities mark the care of older people as an intractable 'wicked issue.' In Sweden, which is discussed in this chapter, local authorities responsible for elderly care provision have tried to manage rising costs by directing funds from elderly care homes to less expensive home-based services. Care at nursing homes is kept to a minimum and mainly provided to elderly with high care needs, such as older people with dementia. This strategy does not solve the problem for society as a whole, however. As is typical for wicked problems, lower costs for local authorities are balanced out by higher costs for hospital care and informal care provided by relatives, who thereby work less and pay less taxes (Swedish Agency for Health and Care Services Analysis 2015). At the same time, just as in the UK (Ferlie et al. 2013), there are serious quality concerns and comprehensive national efforts to enhance quality of care. In the nursing homes, wicked problems take the form of constant pressures to keep costs down and at the same time improve care for increasingly vulnerable residents.

In this chapter, we explore how nursing home managers grapple with local manifestations of the wricked problems that plague elderly care. Drawing on a qualitative case study of six nursing homes, we show the tension between managers' lofty ideals of high-quality, individualized care and their continuous struggle to handle very basic troubles that ultimately appear to be grounded in a lack of resources, such as high personnel turnover and staff complaints about inconvenient work times. We explain and illustrate the gap between lofty ideals and lowly troubles among managers which we found at most investigated nursing homes but which was more or less absent from one of them, a private non-profit home with relatively ample resources and a strong focus on concrete quality work. We claim that the contrast between managers' ideals and everyday reality reflects the underlying conflict between mounting demands and limited resources in elderly care as a whole.

Wicked Problems from the National to the Local Level

In Swedish elderly care, the squeeze between increasing numbers of elderly, limited resources and pressing needs to improve quality of care qualifies the problems of elderly care as 'wicked' (cf. Rittel and Webber 1973). The situation is complex. While Swedish health and social care has a deserved reputation of being among the best in the world, the funding dilemma is more serious than in most other OECD countries; with one of the world's highest life expectancy, about 83 years for women and 79 for men, the share of elderly is higher than almost everywhere else (OECD 2013). By 2020, the proportion of Swedes aged 65 or older will approach 25%, and from 2015 to 2060 the number of over 75-year-olds is expected to more than double (Statistics Sweden 2012). The expectation for the future is that this country, with one of the highest spending on elder care as share of GDP (3.6%) and the highest number of care workers per capita, will face a shortage of manpower and escalating financial pressure. Yet, neither national nor local authorities, managers nor experts have the knowledge or experience to resolve such thorny problems (cf. Swedish Agency for Health and Care Services Analysis 2015).

Swedish elderly care of today is also discussed in terms of insufficient quality because of scarce availability, limited patient involvement in decision-making and deficient coordination between different organizations of health and social care (Commonwealth Fund 2017). Scandalous media reports of elderly suffering from maltreatment or left in inhuman conditions have caused public outrage and demands for robust systems enabling transparency and control, prompting governmental action and national quality programs (Lloyd et al. 2014; Winblad, Mankell and Olsson 2015; Jönson 2016).

In the nursing homes focused on in this chapter, wicked problems take the form of constant pressures to keep costs down and at the same time aim at high quality of care for increasingly vulnerable residents. Despite the heavy burden of care to be provided, nursing homes generally confront austere budget constraints. In addition, they need to answer to a range of national initiatives to raise quality of care. There are comprehensive nationwide programs for enhancing the professional competence of caregivers, stimulating the use of quality registers and quality indicators and promoting core values to ensure the dignity of the elderly (Swedish Ministry of Health and Social Affairs 2010; Fejes 2012). Apparently, national governance aims high in seeking to set forth ideals and aspirations representing the very best of what managers and employees can offer. As a consequence, nursing home managers need to balance financial targets with quality indicators, more task-oriented procedures for staff and growing standardization and monitoring systems to document and measure performance (Hvid and Kamp 2012).

A Study of Local Managers Confronting
Wicked Problems

With the aim of exploring how wicked problems are dealt with at the local level of elderly care, this chapter takes the perspective of those working close to elderly residents, the ambitions they express, and the challenges they experience in everyday settings. We draw on a qualitative study of managers at nursing homes in Sweden. The homes and interviewees have been de-identified and provided with pseudonyms. Our study comprises six nursing homes with 30–100 residents living in their own studio apartments. Two were public homes operated by local authorities (Oakshott and Seashott); two were private for-profits owned by a large corporation (Hillside and Bernside), and two were private non-profits run by charitable trusts (Danora and Sanora). In line with the Swedish system for health and social care, all services were publicly funded and universally offered to inhabitants considered to qualify for institutional care after a formal assessment, which meant that they were either physically fragile with multi-morbidities and bad physical condition or mentally instable because of dementia, or both. The study did not handle any personal data on residents or staff counted as sensitive in the Swedish Personal Data Act, and so it was not considered as needing ethical approval.

In the study, 12 mangers and 20 employees were interviewed. All managers and most of the employees were women. Managers' positions ranged from general managers responsible for a home to unit managers responsible for one or several wards and group managers working in daily care with added responsibility for personnel. Most of the employees were nursing assistants, but some were nurses, physiotherapists or occupational therapists. We also conducted observations during meetings and coffee breaks and studied documents such as quality protocols and policy papers. The interviews were semi-structured, inviting respondents to talk about their work conditions, ambitions and practices, with a focus on management and quality improvement. Managers were also asked about their role and experiences as managers, and employees were asked about their expectations on managers. Each interview was opened up with a question and follow-up queries about what good elderly care means, which yielded rather lengthy descriptions of interviewees' ideals and their efforts to achieve them. Quotes from the interviews have been lightly edited for readability.

Based on the case study, we have problematized the ideals, values and everyday challenges expressed by elderly care managers and staff involved in services for older people. The contrast between managers' engaged explanations of their guiding ideals and the many signs of very concrete, often mundane problems confronting them struck us early on in the analysis. With that in mind, we sifted the material and extracted relevant passages. When reflecting on the excerpts, we found that the emergent issues could be roughly subsumed under three themes related to ideals and three related to everyday problems. Our analysis is mainly focused on similarities between cases, but we also note that one of the homes showed a different pattern and discuss what that implies.

In the next section, we present descriptions and quotes showing managers' high ideals and ambitions along the three themes identified: 1) abstract descriptions of the meaning of good elderly care, 2) a belief in systematic tools, methods and procedures to ensure high-quality care and 3) concrete examples of good elderly care on an interpersonal level. We then present the much more down-to earth problems that seemed to plague managers' everyday reality, again along the three main themes identified in the analysis: 1) staff not following routines or doing as agreed, 2) predicaments of working together and 3) complaints and controversies regarding high workloads, temporary staff and contested schedules. In the concluding discussion, we trace the contradictions between high ideals and everyday challenges to the wicked problems of elderly care.

Lofty Ideals . . .

Caring Ideals in the Abstract

First, all interviewed managers reflected on good elderly care on a quite abstract level related to the dignity of elderly nursing home residents. They spoke of the rights of older people to receive care that respects their autonomy and contributes to their well-being and meaningful existence. Managers emphasized that good care means that individual needs and wishes are considered. In order to guarantee the best possible quality of life, the goals of elderly care should be expressed "through person-centred work, according to their needs and aspects that make them feel good" (unit manager, Sanora).

The critical change that moving into a nursing home represents in a person's life was a repeated theme in the interviews. Some managers voiced high ambitions that the elderly should be able to continue their lives as before as much as possible. It could be about small habits, perhaps hobbies and interests from more active phases of life, but also about maintaining one's personal identity. Self-determination was seen as important, in the sense of deciding for oneself and finding life manageable and within one's own control. As one manager expressed it:

> For my part, the starting point is always, always, always the individual, to consider the individual's wishes, the individual's special needs, in order to make a care action plan that enables us to work according to the individual's needs and providing a sense of coherence. How to make my daily life meaningful to me after moving into a nursing home? How does it become manageable and understandable? Because it's very tough to move for an older person at the end of life, when you're over

90 maybe, and to acclimatize to this new context. The care action plan should help providing good care to this person.

(unit manager, Oakshott)

Managers' views on the essence of good care reflected precepts laid out in national and organization-specific policy documents. Several brought up the importance of 'the good encounter' between caregiver and care recipient and connected it to well-being, satisfaction and dignity of life. Their reasoning also appeared anchored in theory from the field of caring. For example, the ideas expressed by the manager in the previous and next quotes can be traced to a classic medical-sociological theory on 'salutogenesis' which expounds positive factors that help people cope with difficult situations and maintain good health.

Instruments of Caring

Second, managers discussed how good elderly care could be provided in terms of tools, methods, means and procedures. Most managers had completed a national, mandatory training related to dignity and respect for elderly care-takers that was meant to secure that such core values were addressed in all nursing homes. In order to achieve that, the staff's education and training were regarded as essential.

> It's also a question of having well-educated staff, who know what it is to work in a salutogenic way, starting from the needs of the individual. That staff know how to do that, that you talk about what will be best for this person, in consultation with the person him- or herself.

(unit manager, Oakshott)

The systematic side of elderly care work was consistently brought up as the preferred way to fulfill the ideals of good care. The private for-profit homes in particular had developed plenty of routines, systems and detailed instructions. Their systems were materialized in written text classified in binders to guide all staff in their daily duties. One manager emphasized that it was important to "express the care in text by a care action plan, to follow-up on agreements, to measure quality by surveys and deviation reports in order to guarantee that things function as expected by all actors at all levels" (unit manager, Hillside). Another manager saw systematic work with quality and processes as central to her role.

> If you don't do systematic work you can't see any effects—has there been an improvement or has there been a deterioration, or how are we doing? It's a way to take the temperature on our operations. [—] It's incredibly important with deviation reports, for example. If they

don't write deviation reports, it's very difficult to do any change work.

(general manager, Bernside)

The systematic quality work was also described in detail at one of the private non-profit nursing homes, Danora. The general manager underlined that it took systematic work to put the definitions of good care according to the Social Care Act and the National Board of Health and Welfare into practice.

> If we put it like this, what is self-determination? Then we need to have some form of goal for it, how to evaluate it and follow it up. It's followed up by questionnaires, so I can say that we are measuring and setting goals a lot. Then we use different types of materials for staff development at internal workplace meetings and planning days to discuss these various areas. We follow up through surveys such as focus groups, interviews, complaints and deviations reports.

(general manager, Danora)

Caring Eye-to-Eye

Third, managers set high ambitions for hands-on activities in everyday care to make life better for the elderly. They encouraged staff to make small gestures and actions to help residents continue their daily life. A favorable, concrete activity might be getting a suitable seat pad to release pressure and reduce the risk for ulcers. It might also be finding fun things to do and motivation for activities that make the elderly feel inspired and move a bit more, or perform alternative movements, sometime as little as changing regularly between staying in bed, getting up and sitting down.

> Good care is that I can go home and feel I've made a difference, that I've done my utmost for the customers I'm with during the day, that I've been able to make a difference to their day. [. . .] It doesn't have to be something big, but if you go in to someone, maybe she's just happy to get an extra hug, or you sit down for five minutes and talk about something. [. . .] Just to be seen sometime during the day. You're seen all the time of course, but maybe you're not being confirmed.

(group manager, Bernside)

The needs are often caused by residents being hindered by fragility and disability that come with age, and caregivers can provide help to carry out basic everyday doings or find out new ones. Interviewed employees generally shared managers' attention to the everyday helpful practices that make up good care.

> Perhaps this elderly man can't walk so well and needs physiotherapy or rehab, just so he can walk from the bed to the toilet or from the toilet to the living room, and he needs to practice on that. Or maybe he can't hold the fork, then you need to assist in some way. [. . .] So that's what good care does, it creates a feeling of security and makes the person feel safe.
>
> (nursing assistant, Bernside)

. . . And Everyday Vexations

Staff Not Following Routines or Set Responsibilities

Notwithstanding managers' high ideals, it is clear from interviews and observations that they and their staff were struggling to handle everyday work reality. To start with, managers often found it difficult to make employees accept and carry out certain required tasks such as deviation reporting, risk assessment and documentation in general. This occurred among nursing assistants as well as nurses critical of a certain system and 'a bit older nurses' who felt uncomfortable using the computer. When confronted about missing routines and forgotten activities, staff reportedly referred to lack of time but also to finding the tasks unnecessary or to feelings of discomfort. From time to time, they admitted that they tried to avoid documentation and took shortcuts. One manager mentioned that it is not so fun for staff to sit by the computer. Some people do not automatically see the computer as a tool, she said, although they have been given the prerequisites for using it at work. "It goes without saying that we expect staff to take responsibility for maintaining their skills," she asserted. The different reasons for avoiding to conduct documentation are difficult to disentangle and were probably interrelated. In any case, managers seemed to invest a lot of time and energy in convincing staff of the whys and hows of routines and procedures they believed were essential.

> It depends very much on the person how much you take responsibility for making it a routine. Unfortunately, I have to say. We have some stars who are really engaged and take responsibility, but some sort of try not to want to attend to it. And then it's my role as manager to press on.
>
> (unit manager, Oakshott)

The managers talked of various ways to address the challenges by trying to identify, address, and kindly remind those who slink off or forget what the manager believed they had all agreed upon. Some managers had also approved documentation on paper copies when staff found it difficult to start documenting electronically, even if they would have preferred that notes were made directly on the computer.

At one of the nursing homes, however, the private non-profit Danora, staff shared managers' fervor for structured quality work and procedures. They found formal instructions useful and talked enthusiastically about adherence to routines and participation in collaborative quality improvement projects.

> I haven't worked here for long, but I was fascinated, you know, there are routines for everything! If you're wondering about something, you know you can just go to the quality handbook and check it out. Everything is already regulated, you can't get lost. You know that there's someone who's already thought of it.
>
> (nursing assistant, Danora)

Predicaments of Working Together

Managers also struggled to make collaboration and coordination in day-to-day work function as it should. Team meetings, for instance, were considered important to deal with risks and collaborative preventive work, and they were an integral part of governmental programs for quality enhancement. From our interviews and observations, however, it was clear that such meetings were actually quite rare. The reasons appeared mundane. Differing work schedules, high personnel turnover and many temporary staff made it difficult to regularly convene all those involved in the care of the residents meant to be discussed at each team meeting. When asked about the introduction of a new quality assurance program that included team meetings, one manager explained:

> We've had a bit of a rough start, we've had problems with recruitment and such things. You need to have a fairly continuous group to work with this, you can't have too many temporary staff who aren't informed, because then too much is put on the ordinary personnel.
>
> (unit manager, Oakshott)

One manager talked of continuous nagging between the night and day shifts and said that she often heard "the night hasn't done this, the day hasn't done that. If they didn't do it then I'm not doing it either" (group manager, Bernside). Discussions of a fair workload got in the way of service improvements, she thought. For example, when she had suggested that the day shift cook breakfast so that each resident could get the food they liked, the day shift objected and asked what the night shift would do instead. The general manager at the nursing home meant that there was a tradition among employees to work as they wished rather than as they were told, with a focus on practical chores rather than documentation or interacting with the elderly. She put it down to problematic group processes and an unwillingness to change.

> There has been a culture of not writing deviation reports because you don't want to get reprisals from colleagues. [—] You don't change that overnight. If you've worked for ten or twelve years and don't want to get into a clinch with each other, then of course it takes time to understand why to do it.
>
> (general manager, Bernside)

Again, the nursing home Danora was something of an exception. In our interview with a group of employees, they talked appreciatively about the collaborative climate and even connected it to the existence of sensible routines. The nursing assistant quoted in the previous section thus continued her praise of formal routines:

> You know that there's someone who's already thought of it. Someone with goals, a plan, someone who's written it down, and that's how it should be. It's great, it's really important. Everyone's following the same goal, it feels like we're all a team, we know where we're going.
>
> (nursing assistant, Danora)

High Workloads, Temporary Staff and Contested Schedules

Managers set high goals for individualized care and quality development, but they also needed to keep strict budgets. In most of the homes, the consequences of limited resources were felt by employees in terms of staff shortage, high personnel turnover, temporary employees and demanding work schedules, which made it difficult for them to live up to expectations. The extra attention to residents' everyday wishes for a stroll or a shower every day was hard to provide given the workload of ordinary, necessary task.

> If we're fully booked, we are two working with nine residents. Maybe an older man wants to get out every day, but you need more resources to get out every day. We cannot get out every day because there are nine. So maybe we're going out today but not more than that.
>
> (nursing assistant, Bernside)

At the public nursing homes in particular, staff witnessed of a tough work situation because of too many temporary staff. When a large part of the work was carried out sporadically by new people or temporary staff who required a lot of instructions and practical knowledge in order to carry out their work, the ordinary staff became exhausted, missed important activities and felt that they did twice the work. At one for-profit nursing home, there was an open disagreement between management and the staff about working times. The employees insisted that more staff and better schedules were necessary to realize the general manager's declared goal of making the home into the best workplace:

> We have many long work shifts, from eight to eight or half past six to nine, and if you work for twelve, thirteen hours in a dementia ward, I don't think anyone can do a good job. [—] OK, I'm here, I can change diapers, give medicine, give food, but what I would give from my heart, it's not possible. We're humans too, we work with humans. Sometimes it's not so calm, sometimes it's really anxious here, you just can't do it.
>
> (nursing assistant, Bernside)

Once more, non-profit Danora stood out in a positive sense. As a long-standing, well-known institution, Danora had a steady flow of incoming residents and apparently relatively ample resources. In our interview with a group of staff, they voiced complaints about low salaries and the low status of working in elderly care, but they thought that conditions at Danora were unusually good, both for residents and themselves. They talked of sufficient staffing and a good work climate, with close collaboration in teams and open communication with managers at all levels. One nursing assistant mentioned the beautiful environment and that the elderly really appreciated it, even those who suffered from dementia. A nurse declared:

> I've worked in many places, but here there's plenty of resources, they don't economize but even add money to operations. Those who come here, the residents, they drew the winning ticket, absolutely.
>
> (nurse, Danora)

Discussion and Conclusion

The nursing home managers in this study had high hopes to secure the well-being, autonomy and meaningful daily life of their elderly residents through engaged, high-quality care adapted to individual needs and wishes. They were echoing the importance attached by Swedish policymakers to ensuring the dignity, integrity and security of older persons. Managers aspired to good practice based on evidence and professional training, and they had much faith in the kind of structured, systematic quality work that is promoted by current national programs. To an outside observer, their goals and preferred methods seem sensible and no doubt worthy to pursue. However, in contrast with the everyday, concrete problems they faced, their ideals appear strangely detached from reality.

In contrast with their high-minded ideals, managers experienced considerable difficulties in actually offering good care. The problems they struggled with were remarkably down to earth—getting staff to follow routines, making collaboration work and managing employees who felt overburdened with high workloads. While several managers tended to highlight social and psychological aspects such as entrenched work cultures hindering staff from carrying out their work as needed, employees themselves had more concrete complaints, centered on issues such as staff shortage, temporary staff and over-demanding schedules. These issues are well-known from Swedish elderly care in general (e.g. Elwér, Aléx and Hammarström 2010). Ultimately, they are all related to restricted resources.

The contrast between managers' lofty ideals and lowly troubles can be seen as a consequence of more fundamental and wicked problems in elderly care. The national gridlock caused by the need to provide more and better care without expending more resources were transposed to the local level, where it had to be dealt with one way or another. The wicked problems that still remain to be resolved nationally were thus landed on managers' lap. When confronted with the next-to-impossible challenge of improving care of increasingly demanding elderly without raising costs, managers in this study apparently took an optimistic outlook that seems decoupled from the serious and concrete difficulties they obviously struggled with.

The connection between managers' contradictions and the underlying, inextricable problems of elderly care is strengthened if we consider the one home in our study where managerial ideals were not that far from everyday realities—Danora, the private non-profit institution which enjoyed sufficient resources and successful quality work. In this nursing home, there was less of a struggle to balance the budget with ambitions for high-quality care. The surroundings were pleasant and the home's reputation brought status, pride and financial security. It was an attractive employer that could keep qualified staff satisfied and give them adequate conditions for offering professional care. We have no grounds to conclude that this nursing home was in any way flawless, but compared to the other homes, managers had much less difficulties to secure collaboration among staff. In this setting, the wicked problems of elderly care were relatively subdued. With sufficient resources, a good work climate and well-established routines to ensure quality, managers' opportunities to realize their aims were quite favorable, and daily care practices actually appeared to approach their ideals.

In their seminal article, Rittel and Webber (1973, 165) underline that every wicked problem can be considered to be a symptom of another, more general problem, which in its turn has a range of potential causes. While there is nothing like a natural level of wicked problems, they recommend that one should try to settle the problem on as high a level as possible. Our study illustrates how fundamental societal problems that are left unresolved on the higher level make themselves felt locally, in the bodies and minds of less powerful actors who cannot escape them. The study further shows how local actors, in this case nursing home managers, can respond to thorny issues they are hardly equipped to deal with by maintaining lofty ideals that seem disconnected from their everyday reality—incorporating, as it were, the wicked problems into their own managerial personas.

References

Commonwealth Fund. 2017. *International Health Policy Survey of Older Adults in 11 Countries*. New York: The Commonwealth Fund.

Elwér, Sofia, Lena Aléx, and Anne Hammarström. 2010. "Health Against the Odds: Experiences of Employees in Elder Care from a Gender Perspective." *Qualitative Health Research* 20 (9): 1202–1212.

Fejes, Andreas. 2012. "Knowledge at Play: Positioning Care Workers as Professionals Through Scientific Rationality and Caring Dispositions." In *Elderly Care in Transition: Management, Meaning and Identity at Work: A Scandinavian Perspective*, edited by Helge Hvid and Annette Kamp, 83–105. Frederiksberg: Copenhagen Business School Press.

Ferlie, Ewan, Louise Fitzgerald, Gerry McGivern, Sue Dopson, and Chris Bennett. 2013. "Networks for Older People's Care: A Really Wicked Problem." In *Making Wicked Problems Governable? The Case of Managed Networks in Health Care*, edited by Ewan Ferlie, Louise Fitzgerald, Gerry McGivern, Sue Dopson, and Chis Bennett, 119–143. Oxford: Oxford University Press.

Hvid, Helge, and Annette Kamp, eds. 2012. *Elderly Care in Transition: Management, Meaning and Identity at Work: A Scandinavian Perspective*. Frederiksberg: Copenhagen Business School Press.

Jönson, Håkan. 2016. "Framing Scandalous Nursing Home Care: What Is the Problem?" *Ageing & Society* 36 (2): 400–419.

Lloyd, Liz, Albert Banerjee, Charlene Harrington, Frode Jacobsen, and Marta Szebehely. 2014. "It Is a Scandal! Comparing the Causes and Consequences of Nursing Home Media Scandals in Five Countries." *International Journal of Sociology and Social Policy* 34 (1/2): 2–18.

OECD (Organisation for Economic Co-Operation and Development). 2013. *OECD Reviews of Health Care Quality: Sweden 2013: Raising Standards*. Paris: OECD Publishing. Accessed January 11, 2018. http://dx.doi.org/10.1787/9789264204799-en.

Rittel, Horst W., and Melvin M. Webber. 1973. "Dilemmas in a General Theory of Planning." *Policy Sciences* 4 (2): 155–169.

Statistics Sweden. 2012. *Sveriges framtida befolkning 2012–2060* [Sweden's Future Population 2012–2060]. Demografiska rapporter 2012: 2. Stockholm: Statistics Sweden.

Swedish Agency for Health and Care Services Analysis. 2015. *Hemtjänst, vård—och omsorgsboende eller mitt emellan? Ett kunskapsunderlag för planeringen av morgondagens äldreomsorg* [Home Services, Residential Care or in Between? A White Paper for Planning Tomorrow's Elderly Care]. Report 2015: 8. Stockholm: Swedish Agency for Health and Care Services Analysis.

Swedish Ministry of Health and Social Affairs. 2010. *Värdigt liv i äldreomsorgen: Regeringens Proposition 2009/2010:116* [Dignified Life in Elderly Care: Government Bill 2009/2010: 116]. Stockholm: Riksdagens tryckeriexpedition.

Winblad, Ulrika, Anna Mankell, and Fredrik Olsson. 2015. "Privatisering av välfärdstjänster: Hur garanteras kvalitet i vård och omsorg?" [Privatization of Welfare Services: How Is Quality in Health and Social Care Guaranteed?] *Statsvetenskaplig tidskrift* 117 (4): 531–554.

6 The Unnoticed Role of Employees in Ethical Leadership

Merja Sinkkonen and Sanna Laulainen

Introduction

The prerequisites for working as a professional and as a leader in social services are constantly changing and under negotiation. For example, Finland is currently preparing for a major and unprecedented nationwide reform integrating health and social services and partly also public and private services; discussions are ongoing concerning, e.g. the division of labor and service production, organizing integration more intensively and also between the public and private sectors, de-centralization of services and incentives or barriers to strengthening interorganizational collaboration. These discussions linked to fundamental changes and reforms highlight a requirement for new competencies to respond to the complex needs of clients, to demands for productivity and effectiveness and to endeavors to strengthen multi-actor-based processes. This may necessitate revising management structures and practices and investigating what factors are critical to the successful implementation of changes and reforms and solving ethical problems emerging in the process.

Working in the social services entails ethical challenges, underlining the importance of shared codes of ethics (Alahmad 2010; Beeri et al. 2013) as a basis for professional work and management. We argue that adherence to the codes of ethics and ethical guidelines is generally taken for granted among public servants and professionals, e.g. in the field of health and social services. However, we, too, like Ireni-Saban and Berdugo (2017), question if it is realistic to assume that following the ethical codes is an unproblematic task given the complexity of the field of social services. Hence the line between ethical and unethical decisions both at the grassroots level and for management purposes may be blurred and fluctuating. We argue that these ethical dilemmas can be called wicked problems with no certain, guaranteed and sustainable solutions to them (see Chapter 1 in this book; however, it is noticeable that the traditional view on wicked problems contains no moral emphases, see, e.g. Rittel and Webber 1973). Based on this argument, we ask what this means for ethical leadership.

When we consider the complexity and wicked nature of working in social services, it is reasonable to ask how this affects ethical leadership and the roles of leaders and employees. Are there particular expectations regarding the change from the traditional leader-centric view to a more collective and reciprocal perspective on leadership? How does ethical leadership as one example of virtue-based behavior emphasize different roles and the role of employees in particular?

The purpose of this chapter is to deconstruct how the role of employees is portrayed in the ethical leadership literature, which is traditionally focused on leaders' virtuous behavior. To take a closer look at that particular and less noticed perspective, we reviewed articles encompassing ethical leadership and employees' views. For the latter we deploy the concept of organizational citizenship behavior (OCB) as a construction of the virtuous behavior of a worker as a good and useful member of a work organization (Organ 1988; cf. Vigoda-Gadot and Beeri 2012). We interpret it here as a kind of counterpart to ethical leadership from the perspective of employees even though we are aware of differences between the premises of these two theoretical concepts.

In addition to reviewing the literature on ethical leadership, we utilize empirical material gathered by one of the authors from middle managers in social services to enrich our examination. Inspired by critical management studies (Prasad et al. 2016), we question the basic assumption of leader-centeredness as a premise of ethical leadership and pay special attention to the less prominent role of employees in constructing this phenomenon. It has recently become more common to scrutinize the role of employees when studying and discussing leadership (e.g. Uhl-Bien 2006). However, the tradition of acknowledging the reciprocal nature of the leader-employee relationship is much more widespread, for example, in the work of Follett (1919; see also Hujala 2008).

Ethical Leadership in Social Services

The role of ethics has always been important in social services. Leaders of social services are regularly faced with a variety of ethical questions. While the law stipulates the limits of operations, resources and ethical guidelines determine the more precise content of actions and decisions. Ethical situations can be divided into three groups (Banks 2006, 12–13). The first of these consists of ethical subject fields in which the worker implements the actions prescribed by law or according to the ethical conceptions prevailing in society or takes decisions without conflict. The second group consists of ethical problems in which the conflict emerges between the worker's own ethical views and the generally accepted instructions for action. The worker cannot as an individual act as s/he thinks fit. The third group consists of ethical dilemmas, problem situations in which both solution options entail some transgression against the ethical principles. Frequently the interests of the individual and the public interest are juxtaposed. Typical conflict situations in the field of social services give rise to situations in which the interests of the client are at odds with economic resources and situations in which the interests of a client group are in conflict with the organization's modes of operation.

There is a difference in the approaches to ethics among moral philosophers and social workers, yet these two are related. An ethical dilemma entails a difficult choice between two equally unwelcome alternatives and it is not clear which choice will be the right one. Some philosophers argue that there are 'irresolvable' dilemmas. When the decision is taken the moral loss is enormous. Banks and Williams (2005) prefer to characterize this as "resolvable with remainder." They also concede that in these situations social workers reflexively construct their own identities as ethical practitioners. This suggests that 'virtues,' notions of professional roles and emotional responsiveness, are important features of the accounts given by social workers about ethically difficult situations in practice.

Leadership challenges in social services are moreover in many ways ethically loaded. In their work social services leaders come up against not only the ethical views prevailing in society on the bases and objectives of social services, but also against the various ethical guidelines of different professional groups, the ethical dilemmas arising in work with clients and ethical issues pertaining to leadership itself. Ethical leadership in the field of social services has been researched mostly from the perspective of ethical dilemmas (Pawlukewicz and Ondrus 2013), from the perspective of the professional codes of ethics of social work (Gough and Spencer 2014) and from the ethical decision-making perspective (Yeung et al. 2010).

Brown, Treviño and Harrison (2005, 120) define ethical leadership as follows: "The demonstration of normatively appropriate conduct through personal actions and interpersonal relationships, and the promotion of such conduct to followers through two-way communication, reinforcement, and decision-making." They stress that ethical leadership is also closely connected to the workers' ethical decision-making and to their job satisfaction, work motivation, and commitment. They state that of the characteristic features of ethical leadership honesty, incorruptibility and trustworthiness are closely connected to the efficacy of leadership.

It is the task of the manager to identify workers' strengths and to promote their professional development and also to support workers in making morally right choices. The manager should also intervene in time in unethical actions. In addition to the manager's declared objectives and ethical actions and the harmony between these, ethical leadership is influenced by one-off and culture bound factors and the manager's own personality and level of moral development (Yukl 2002, 409–410; on moral development see Kohlberg 1984). On the other hand, Burns (1978) perceives one of the most important tasks of ethical leadership to be to increase awareness in the work organizations and also to provide workers with support in ethical dilemmas.

Ethical leadership traditionally focuses on ethical leaders and their actions and behavior (Brown and Treviño 2006; Gerpott et al. 2017; Ko et al. 2017). We find this to be a fairly leader-centric approach to a phenomenon that also involves employees. Theoretical and empirical studies of ethical leadership underline a normative view of an appropriate leader as a key component in the implementation of ethical principles among subordinates (e.g. Brown, Treviño and Harrison 2005). Recent studies have provided some irrefutable evidence that ethical leaders can reduce deviant employee behaviors and promote organizational citizenship behavior (Mayer et al. 2009; Mayer et al. 2012; Stouten et al. 2013). But this is not the whole truth.

The Role of Employees in Ethical Leadership Studies

The scientific literature on ethical leadership is relatively new and empirical research on ethical leadership has burgeoned since the beginning of the 2000s and the number of publications has increased particularly since 2005. The research has traditionally been normative, focusing on ethical leaders, their actions and behavior and its impact on employees (Brown and Trevino 2006; Stouten et al. 2013).

To deconstruct how the roles of employees are described in the literature on ethical leadership, we analyzed scientific articles containing among their keywords "ethical leadership" and "organizational citizenship behavior/ employee" (or articles with these words mentioned in the abstract) from the years 2010–2017. By focusing on the articles that connect these two concepts, we aimed to find literature discussing both views simultaneously, thereby reiterating our purpose in this chapter.

As stressed by Brown, Treviño and Harrison (2005, 120), ethical leadership is closely connected to the workers' job satisfaction, work motivation and commitment, and many of the articles from the years 2010–2017 deal with ethical leadership and job satisfaction (Ogunfowora 2014) or/ and commitment (Kalshoven, Den Hartog and De Hoogh 2011; Neubert, Wu and Roberts 2013; Philipp and Lopez 2013; Resick et al. 2013). Hartog and Belschak (2012, 35) tested a model suggesting that work engagement acts as a mediator in the relationships between ethical leadership and employee initiative (a form of organizational citizenship behavior, see, e.g. Choi 2007) and found support for this model. In several studies the effects of ethical leadership on employee behavior have been studied through the mediating role of ethical climate (Shin 2012; Dinc and Aydemir 2014; DeConinck 2015; Shin et al. 2015). All these results show that ethical leaders exert a positive influence on employees' job attitudes and behaviors.

The characteristic features of ethical leadership, honesty, incorruptibility and trustworthiness, are also closely connected to the efficacy of leadership (Brown, Treviño and Harrison 2005, 120). Mozumder (2016) developed and tested a multilevel trust-based model of ethical public leadership outcomes. He found a positive relationship between ethical leadership and employees' trust in leaders. Newman et al. (2014) found that ethical leadership leads to higher levels of both affective and cognitive trust. Beeri et al. (2013) found that ethical leadership was positively related to employees' awareness of the code of ethics, increased inclusion of employees in ethical decision-making and was conducive to greater organizational commitment (on increased awareness see Burns 1978).

Ethical leadership is moreover characterized by fairness and setting an example (Brown and Treviño 2006, 596–597; see also Yukl 2002, 404–405; Alahmad 2010). The process through which ethical leaders influence employees is commonly explained with social learning theory (Brown, Treviño and Harrison 2005; Mayer et al. 2009) or social exchange theory (Ruiz-Palomino, Ruiz-Amaya and Knörr 2011; Kacmar et al. 2011; Ahn, Lee and Yun 2018) or both (Mo and Shi 2017).

The concepts of morality and ethics are closely interrelated but the relationship between ethical leadership and moral process/moral personality/moral ideology is extremely complex (Chuang and Chiu 2018; Gerpott et al. 2017). The relationship between ethical leadership and OCB is also much more complex than some studies suggest. Ethical leadership has been documented as a crucial factor influencing employee behavior (Ko et al. 2017) and studies in the 2010s aim to expand on previous research by investigating the effect of ethical leadership on different aspects of OCB (Ko et al. 2017; Steinmann, Nübold and Maier 2016).

A less normative perspective on ethical leadership was presented in a study that dealt with the relationship between supervisor moral disengagement and employee perceptions of ethical leadership (Bonner, Greenbaum and Mayer 2016). According to this study, morally engaged supervisors and employees still recognize the danger of unethical behavior and thus are more likely to exemplify ethical leadership. The study dealing with employees' reactions to supervisors' unfair treatment of peers (Zoghbi-Manrique-de-Lara and Suárez-Acosta 2014) highlights the importance not only of the victim's reactions to injustice, but also of the reactions of third parties. Wang and Sung (2016) examined the relationships of perceived ethical leadership, work jealousy and organizational citizenship behaviors. The study showed that workplace jealousy, a consequence of social comparison, can mediate the effects of ethical leadership on employee organizational citizenship behavior.

Piccolo et al. (2010, 270–271) found support for a model in which the positive effect of ethical leadership on follower effort was mediated by task significance. By giving employees a voice in organizational decisions, using rewards to encourage ethical behavior and injecting ethical values into regular business activity, ethical leaders enhance the autonomy and significance of work.

The most interesting articles from our point of view are those that explore ethical leadership from a critical perspective. Stouten et al. (2013, 691–692) claim that their research is the first to explicitly address the unintended negative effects of ethical leadership. Their results show that highly ethical leaders reduced participants' deviant behavior more than did less ethical leaders. Their study also revealed that ethical leadership showed a curvilinear pattern for people's OCB. Moderately ethical leaders were found to encourage OCB more than less and more ethical leaders. It seems important for ethical leaders not to appear to be passing moral judgment on employees. Instead, leaders may express their recognition of employees' values and respectfully support employees' behavior. This can be done by encouraging employees to voice their opinions on the enactment of ethics in the workplace.

Babalola et al. (2017) also highlight that empirical studies examining ethical leadership and employee OCB have yielded mixed results. They claim that the influence of ethical leadership is more complex than initially assumed. Stouten et al. (2013) found that ethical leaders sometimes communicate such a strong ethical conviction as to undermine employees' own moral values, and Babalola et al. (2017) found that when leaders were perceived to be rigid or strong in their ethical convictions, employees responded to them less positively. Their findings also demonstrate that the interaction between ethical leadership and the leader's perceived ethical conviction relates to feelings of personal control and the opportunity to have a voice, which is one of the characteristics of change-oriented OCB (e.g. Van Dyne and LePine 1998).

Empirical Example of the Role of Employees in Ethical Leadership

To enrich our examination of the role of employees in ethical leadership we re-utilized research material gathered by one of the authors a few years ago, by applying the method of empathy-based stories, also known as non-active role-playing (e.g. Eskola 1988). Through this material, we illustrate how the role of employees is constructed in descriptions of ethical and unethical leadership.

When applying the method of empathy-based stories the idea is to ask informants to write their own short stories inspired by a given orientation text, called a frame story. In the frame story, the idea is to give hints for writing based on the aim of the research and the theoretical understanding of the phenomenon of interest, ethical leadership. There are usually at least two versions of frame stories in which one significant element varies, and the purpose is to study how informants' accounts change according to that variation. In our study we composed the frame stories in such a way that one was constructed according to the idea of ethical leadership and the other according to the opposite, unethical leadership. Each of the informants was randomly given only one of the two frame stories and instructed to empathize with the situation of the given story, and write a short account based on it. Informants were given 20 minutes' time to write their own accounts with traditional paper and pen.

The frame stories were:

A. Story about ethical leadership

Employees are committed to their work community and the job satisfaction is high. They trust their supervisor, and the profitability of the organization is increasing. Empathize with the situation and continue the story in a way you wish. Write a story (1 page) on this paper about what has happened and what has been leader's course of action.

B. Story about unethical leadership

Employees are not committed to their work community and the job satisfaction is low. They do not trust their supervisor and the profitability of the organization is decreasing. Empathize with the situation and continue the story in a way you wish. Write a story (1 page) on this paper about what has happened and what has been leader's course of action.

We composed the frame stories so that they contained hints of the critical factors related to ethical leadership such as commitment (Kalshoven, Den Hartog and De Hoogh 2011; Neubert, Wu and Roberts 2013; Philipp and Lopez 2013), job satisfaction (Resick et al. 2013; Ogunfowora 2014), trust (Brown, Treviño and Harrison 2005, 120; Newman et al. 2014; Mozumder 2016) and employee outcomes (Neubert, Wu and Roberts 2013; Ogunfowora 2014).

The informants worked as middle managers in social services in a big city in the southern part of Finland. We gathered the research material from middle managers by utilizing their regular official meetings in different parts of the organization and with different participants. One of the researchers attended a few of these meetings and gathered the research material. In each meeting, the researcher told all the participants about the purpose of the research and its ethical conduct. She also pointed out that participation was optional and made sure that each of the informants had all the information required to give informed consent.

The amount of research material gathered was 23 written accounts of ethical leadership and 21 accounts of unethical leadership: altogether, 44 accounts from 44 middle managers. The accounts varied in length from 22 words to over 200 words. Even though the written accounts were quite short, the content was informative. Most of the accounts illustrated the situation from the leaders' perspective following the instruction in the orientation to describe how the leader acts in that particular situation. However, inspired by one or the other frame story, the informants illustrated how employees, too, were part of the situation.

We re-analyzed these accounts applying thematic analysis (Braun and Clarke 2006). We focused on how employees were portrayed explicitly e.g. as part of success or failure in implementing ethical leadership or how they constructed the phenomenon more implicitly, e.g. by highlighting the actions of the leader as one-sided. We are aware of restrictions concerning our research material, and the findings and interpretations which it permits. Due to the data gathering method selected we can see the accounts of middle managers in social services as possible descriptions of 'real' life. This therefore prevents us from generalizing the results in a broader context. In addition, we cannot know how these descriptions will stand the test of time even though they appear to propose views which we could deem contemporary.

In keeping with the purpose of the chapter, our aim is to analyze how the role of employees was constructed in the written accounts of ethical or unethical leadership. We need to consider that the context of writing the accounts, the form of the frame stories and the orientation task also provide a frame for analysis. For example, the emphasis on leader-centric descriptions in the written accounts is probably a result of the leader-centric assignment in the frame story. In retrospect, it might have been reasonable to exclude the final hint concerning the leader's action in the situation, thereby giving informants more options to freely illustrate the phenomenon from a perspective of their own choice. However, due to this restriction, it is particularly interesting to see how employees were constructed, explicitly and more implicitly, as part of the phenomenon.

Employees as Followers or Initiators in Ethical Leadership

At first glance, the written accounts underlined the significant role of the leader in constructing both ethical leadership and unethical leadership. The social services leaders stressed that success or failure when implementing ethical leadership was mainly dependent on the actions of the leader him/ herself or of leaders more collectively. The emphasis of the leader-centric approach in the accounts is obvious when we take into consideration our frame stories and the request to write about the leader's perspective. However, it was illuminating to read the research material more closely paying special attention to how middle managers portray employees as a part of ethical or unethical leadership. From a critical stance, we want to question the prevailing assumption of employees as not so significant in constructing leadership. We therefore intend to scrutinize how the role of employees emerges in the accounts illustrating ethical or unethical leadership.

Our analysis enabled us to discern a diversity in the descriptions illustrating the role of employees in constructing the phenomenon with two main categories, followers and initiators. We concede that these categories are simplifications, but as such they highlight significant characteristics of the employees' role in leadership relations. The main difference between these categories is that employees are seen either as objects of leadership practices or as more active agents in constructing and re-constructing these practices.

Employees as Followers

In the written accounts based on both ethical and unethical descriptions, middle managers frequently portrayed employees as mere objects of leadership practices. In that sense, the descriptions reveal employees as followers passively waiting for their leaders' actions, such as instructions, support and feedback to deserve the trust and commitment of employees in return (see extract below).

> Employees do not trust their supervisor if he/she does not 'earn' it. The supervisor did not give any positive feedback, or he/she failed to prioritize and encourage employees.
>
> (Story B24)

Even though we interpreted this as an example of passive followership, we are aware that it may also contain many more active and conscious solutions, even if it seems to underline minimal agency. Waiting for something to occur, as a prerequisite for one's own restricted contribution can be a way to strengthen the sense of control and power. However, the image of non-active agency is quite opposite to the current expectations of active promotive voice behavior (see e.g. Vigoda-Gadot and Beeri 2012). If we had gathered research material from people in employee positions instead of in middle management we might have been able to evince a more many sided interpretation of followership.

One of the middle managers' main justifications of unethical leadership was a leader-centric, and even an authoritarian, approach to employees (see more on the phenomenon in Chapter 7). The employees were enforced followers with no opportunities to display initiative in the strategic and development processes, not even in circumstances that were unfair to the employees themselves or to clients. The extracts below illustrate both an almost total lack of 'space' for active agency on the part of employees and how the 'costs' of non-interference cause passive followership.

> The manager did not involve employees in decision-making and even ended up taking unjust decisions. The strategy process focused on the manager's work without the involvement of employees.
>
> (Story B41)

> The supervisor was informed of the problems of the unit [. . .] the supervisor had no time to intervene sufficiently [. . .] work with clients is suffering [. . .] everyone finds the situation poor. Everyone is helpless.
>
> (Story B25)

Even though a quite large part of the leader-centric examples of middle managers' written accounts embodied a passive view of the role of employees in ethically loaded situations, we noticed that this interpretation was too one-sided. Particularly in the written accounts of ethical leadership there were examples in which the leader was also in focus, but more as a facilitator than as a dictator in enhancing employees' opportunities for involvement and supporting the interests of an organization. This appears in the extract below. In the extract, as in other examples illustrating the same phenomenon, the role of the employees appeared more like that of an active partner waiting for opportunities to occur.

> The supervisor earned the respect and trust of the work community by his/her actions. [. . .] He/she has strength and courage to handle things in a democratic way but at the same time authority enough to outline and conclude in a way that employees commit to. Job satisfaction in the work community is high when everyone has a say and can see their role in the entity and achieving a common goal.
>
> (Story A3)

Employees as Initiators

In the written accounts based on ethical descriptions, there were examples that emphasized employees more as initiators, active subjects and agents. Hints of critical agency actually emerged. In these examples, the role of the leader as an enabler was still emphasized.

> He or she [leader] supports diversity, creativity, and allows employees experiments and mistakes.
>
> (Story A4)

> Enabling the polyphony is important, there is no single truth in achieving a good result.
>
> (Story A19)

However, the role of employees as potential, even critical, active agents was confirmed by permitting them to work in a novel and experimental way.

> Employees were encouraged to express opinions, to take a stand, to question and to make innovative suggestions [. . .] they are encouraged to take risks.
>
> (Story A7)

Risk-taking and a critical innovative approach to work requires support and trust from a leader which means e.g. "*a certain kind of laziness without direct answers and orders*" (Story A9). In an open work community, employees are willing and able to express opinions (to have a voice) and share out-of-the-box thinking and engage in critical change-oriented organizational citizenship behavior (see Vigoda-Gadot and Beeri 2012). However, this 'laziness' does not mean laissez faire leadership, which may cause deviant behavior among employees and include the exercise of informal and unjustified power (see more in Chapter 7).

In some accounts of unethical leadership, the middle managers described showing favor to employees as one form of unethical behavior on the part of leaders in which unpopular employees were obliged to obey and acquiesce to inconsistent decisions, whereas favored employees had exceptional opportunities to manipulate the decisions of the leaders. As a consequence of experiences of injustice among less well-liked employees, lack of motivation and commitment to the organization increased. Even cynicism emerged (see extract below). Indifference to the interests of the organization is presented as an inevitable consequence of unethical leadership.

> The supervisor true to form persisted with his/her favoritism. [. . .] It has nothing to do with how well the work is done. The decision-making of the supervisor was inconsistent and unfair. [. . .] Little by little this led to cynicism and resentment among employees and distrust of the organization. It is inevitable that lack of motivation and authentic interest led to indifference regarding productivity.
>
> (Story B38)

Employees were mostly portrayed as 'victims' of unfair treatment or occasionally as undeserving beneficiaries of favor. Even though the latter represents employees as an active force of leadership in a negative sense, there was another exceptional example of deviant behavior among employees (e.g. Robinson and Bennett 1995). Employees may deliberately obstruct leaders' work. One of the middle managers described the phenomenon as torpedoing. It stresses the employees' role in unethical leadership. In that same account, the middle manager highlighted a problem of "narcissistic employees who are almost impossible to deal with" (Story B36). This example points out one significant but often unnoticed aspect affecting the ethicality of leadership. It can be called the dark and unnoticed side of leadership embodied in leader-employee dynamics (see Clements and Washbush 1999).

The Crucial Role of Employees in Ethical Leadership

The role of ethics will be even more important in the future as complexity and 'wickedness' increase in the context of social services and more generally in working life. Ethical issues are emphasized in a complex environment, and the role of ethical leadership assumes greater importance. Dealing with ethical dilemmas frankly together reduces the employees' stress and improves their well-being. The studies dealing with ethical leadership in the early 2000s are either very normative and leader-centered or they are statistical analyses of how ethical leadership correlates with trust, job satisfaction, commitment and so on. The faith in the positive influence of the leaders' conducting ethical leadership has been self-evident.

However, we found some critical studies from the 2010s showing ethical leadership to have unintended negative effects (Stouten et al. 2013) and studies reporting mixed results for ethical leadership (Babalola et al. 2017). These studies reveal the importance of employees having a say, which is one feature of change-oriented OCB (e.g. Vigoda-Gadot and Beeri 2012), and feelings of personal control.

The purpose of this chapter is to deconstruct how the role of employees appears in the ethical leadership literature and in descriptions of ethical leadership or its opposite in written accounts by middle managers in social services. Our examination highlights the fundamental role of employees in constructing and implementing ethical leadership even though the mainstream of the research of ethical leadership has been based on leader-centeredness. Employees exert influence intentionally and unintentionally, e.g. by assuming active, supportive or passive, following roles in leader-employee relations, in how ethical leadership emerged in practice. Based on this, we conclude that employees have unnoticed and underestimated power in enabling but also of impeding ethical leadership. Thus, employees invariably have opportunities to wield power in a positive or negative way. The latter is illustrated, e.g. in the discussions of deviant or counterproductive work behavior.

The scrutiny of the role of employees in ethical leadership also revealed its paradoxical nature. The new studies in the 2010s show that ethical leadership as a concept is much more multidimensional than was previously thought. We already know that identifying ethical dilemmas, which we called wicked problems, and dealing them collaboratively is extremely important, and this is even more so in the complex field of social services. An ethical leader listens to and supports employees but does not give them too strict instructions or restrict them too much. As pointed out earlier in the chapter, a leader may even act too ethically and so reduce the ethicality of the employees. From an ethical leadership point of view, it is not enough that the leader acts ethically or thinks that s/he is ethical. The question is much more complex.

Especially in social services, if ethical leadership is understood as too narrowly leader-centered, by focusing only on the leader's virtuous actions, it does not help to resolve the ethical dilemmas encountered in social services. We argue that it is extremely important to recognize the critical role of employees and expand the perspective from leader to the organizational level and as a collective shared phenomenon. By involving employees actively in dealing with ethical dilemmas, the tacit knowledge from the grass-roots level is taken into account. Wicked problems in social services, and the associated ethical dilemmas, are often related to clients. This suggest a need to include clients in research on ethical leadership. Both of these can be significant factors in countering the wickedness of the problems and in resolving them.

In the future, ethical leadership should be studied from an organizational perspective including leaders, employees and clients, especially when dealing with the context of social services beset by wicked problems and challenges.

Bibliography

Ahn, Jaehyung, Soojin Lee, and Seokhwa Yun. 2018. "Leaders' Core Self-Evaluation, Ethical Leadership, and Employees' Job Performance: The Moderating Role of Employees' Exchange Ideology." *Journal of Business Ethics* 148 (2): 457–470.

Babalola, Mayowa T., Jeroen Stouten, Jeroen Camps, and Martin Euwema. 2017. "When Do Ethical Leaders Become Less Effective? The Moderating Role of Perceived Leader Ethical Conviction on Employee Discretionary Reactions to Ethical Leadership." *Journal of Business Ethics*, published online: February 22, 2017.

Banks, Sarah. 2006. *Ethics and Value in Social Work*, 3rd ed. Hampshire, New York: Palgrave Macmillan.

Banks, Sarah, and Robin Williams. 2005. "Accounting for Ethical Difficulties in Social Welfare Work: Issues, Problems and Dilemmas." *The British Journal of Social Work* 35 (7): 1005–1022.

Beeri, Itai, Rachel Dayan, Eran Vigoda-Gadot, and Simcha B. Werner. 2013. "Advancing Ethics in Public Organizations: The Impact of an Ethics Program on Employees' Perceptions and Behaviors in a Regional Council." *Journal of Business Ethics* 112 (1): 59–78.

Bonner, Julena M., Rebecca L. Greenbaum, and David M. Mayer. 2016. "My Boss Is Morally Disengaged: The Role of Ethical Leadership in Explaining the Interactive Effect of Supervisor and Employee Moral Disengagement on Employee Behaviors." *Journal of Business Ethics* 137 (4): 731–742.

Braun, Virginia, and Victoria Clarke. 2006. "Using Thematic Analysis in Psychology." *Qualitative Research in Psychology* 3 (2): 77–101.

Brown, Michael E., Linda K. Treviño, and Harrison David. 2005. "Ethical Leadership: A Social Learning Perspective for Construct Development and Testing." *Organizational Behavior and Human Decision Processes* 97 (2): 117–134.

Burns, James M. 1978. *Leadership*. New York: Harper & Row.

Choi, Jin N. 2007. "Change-Oriented Organizational Citizenship Behaviour: Effects of Work Environment Characteristics and Intervening Psychological Processes." *Journal of Organizational Behavior* 28 (4): 467–484.

Chuang, Pei-Ju, and Chiu Su-Fen. 2018. "When Moral Personality and Moral Ideology Meet Ethical Leadership: A Three-Way Interaction Model." *Ethics & Behavior* 28 (1): 45–69.

Clements, Christine, and John B. Washbush. 1999. "The Two Faces of Leadership: Considering the Dark Side of Leader-Follower Dynamics." *Journal of Workplace Learning* 11 (5): 170–175.

DeConinck, James B. 2015. "Outcomes of Ethical Leadership Among Salespeople." *Journal of Business Research* 68 (5): 1086–1093.

Den Hartog, Deanne N., and Frank D. Belschak. 2012. "Work Engagement and Machiavellianism in the Ethical Leadership Process." *Journal of Business Ethics* 107 (1): 35–47.

Dinc, Muhammet S., and Aydemir Muzaffer. 2014. "Ethical Leadership and Employee Behaviours: An Empirical Study of Mediating Factors." *International Journal of Business Governance and Ethics* 9 (3): 293–312.

Eskola, Antti. 1988. "Non-Active Role-Playing: Some experiences." In *Blind Alleys in Social Psychology*, edited by Antti Eskola, Anna Kihlström, David Kivinen, Klaus Weckroth, and Oili-Helena Ylijoki, 239–311. Advances in Psychology 48. Amsterdam: Elsevier Science Publishers B.V.

Follett, Mary P. 1919. "Community Is a Process." *The Philosophical Review* 28 (6): 576–588.

Gerpott, Fabiola H., Niels van Quaquebeke, Sofia Schlamp, and Sven C. Voelpel. 2017. "An Identity Perspective on Ethical Leadership to Explain Organizational Citizenship Behavior: The Interplay of Follower Moral Identity and Leader Group Prototypicality." *Journal of Business Ethics*, published online: July 7, 2017.

Gough, Jim, and Elaine Spencer. 2014. "Ethics in Action: An Exploratory Survey of Social Worker's Ethical Decision Making and Value Conflicts." *Journal of Social Work Values and Ethics* 11 (2): 23–40.

Hujala, Anneli. 2008. *Johtamisen moniäänisyys: Johtaminen vuorovaikutuksena ja puhuntana hoivayrityksissä* (Polyphonic Management. Management as Interaction and Discourse in Care Enterprises). Kuopio University Publications E. Social Sciences 149. Kuopio.

Ireni-Saban, Liza, and Berdugo Galit. 2017. *Ethics Management in the Public Service: A Sensory-Based Strategy*. Routledge Critical Studies in Public Management. New York: Routledge.

Kacmar, K. Michele, Daniel G. Bachrach, Kenneth J. Harris, and Suzanne Zivnuska. 2011. "Fostering Good Citizenship Through Ethical Leadership: Exploring the Moderating Role of Gender and Organizational Politics." *Journal of Applied Psychology* 96 (3): 633–642.

Kalshoven, Karianne, Deanne N. Den Hartog, and Annabel H. B. De Hoogh. 2011. "Ethical Leadership at Work Questionnaire (ELW): Development and Validation of a Multidimensional Measure." *Leadership Quarterly* 22 (1): 51–69.

Ko, Changsuk, Jianhong Ma, Mingu Kang, Alexander S. English, and Mark H. Haney. 2017. "How Ethical Leadership Cultivates Healthy Guanxi to Enhance OCB in China." *Asia Pacific Journal of Human Resources* 55 (4): 408–429.

Kohlberg, Lawrence. 1984. *The Psychology of Moral Development: The Nature and Validity of Moral Stages*. New York: HarperCollins.

Mayer, David M., Maribeth Kuenzi, Rebecca Greenbaum, Mary Bardes, and Rommel (B.) Salvador. 2009. "How Low Does Ethical Leadership Flow? Test of a trickle-Down Model." *Organizational Behavior and Human Decision Processes* 108 (1): 1–13.

Mayer, David M., Karl Aquino, Rebecca L. Greenbaum, and Maribeth Kuenzi. 2012. "Who Displays Ethical Leadership, and Why Does It Matter? An Examination of Antecedents and Consequences of Ethical Leadership." *Academy of Management Journal* 55 (1): 151–171.

Mo, Shenjiang, and Junqi Shi. 2017. "Linking Ethical Leadership to Employees' Organizational Citizenship Behavior: Testing the Multilevel Mediation Role of Organizational Concern." *Journal of Business Ethics* 141 (1): 151–162.

Mozumder, N. A. 2016. "A Multilevel Trust-based Model of Ethical Public Leadership." *Journal of Business Ethics*, published online: October 6, 2016. https://doi. org/10.1007/s10551-016-3341-1

Neubert, Mitchell J., Cindy Wu, and James A. Roberts. 2013. "The Influence of Ethical Leadership and Regulatory Focus on Employee Outcomes." *Business Ethics Quarterly* 23 (2): 269–296.

Newman, Alexander, Kohyar Kiazad, Qing Miao, and Brian Cooper. 2014. "Examining the Cognitive and Affective Trust-Based Mechanisms Underlying the Relationship Between Ethical Leadership and Organisational Citizenship: A Case of the Head Leading the Heart?" *Journal of Business Ethics* 123 (1): 113–123.

Ogunfowora, Babatunde. 2014. "It's All a Matter of Consensus: Leader Role Modeling Strength as a Moderator of the Links Between Ethical Leadership and Employee Outcomes." *Human Relations* 67 (12): 1467–1490.

Organ, Dennis W. 1988. *Organizational Citizenship Behavior: The Good Soldier Syndrome*. Lexington: Lexington Books.

Pawlukewicz, Justine, and Sherri Ondrus. 2013. "Ethical Dilemmas: The Use of Applied Scenarios in the Helping Professions." *Journal of Social Work Values and Ethics* 10 (1): 2–12.

Philipp, Beverly L. U., and Patricia D. J. Lopez. 2013. "The Moderating Role of Ethical Leadership: Investigating Relationships Among Employee Psychological Contracts, Commitment, and Citizenship Behavior." *Journal of Leadership & Organizational Studies* 20 (3): 304–315.

Piccolo, Ronald F., Rebecca Greenbaum, Deanne N. den Hartog, and Robert Folger. 2010. "The Relationship Between Ethical Leadership and Core Job Characteristics." *Journal of Organizational Behavior* 31 (2–3): 259–278.

Prasad, Anshuman, Pushkala Prasad, Albert J. Mills, and Jean H. Mills, eds. 2016. *The Routledge Companion to Critical Management Studies*. New York: Routledge.

Resick, Christian J., Michael B. Hargis, Ping Shao, and Scott B. Dust. 2013. "Ethical Leadership, Moral Equity Judgments, and Discretionary Workplace Behavior." *Human Relations* 66 (7): 951–972.

Rittel, Horst W. J., and Melvin M. Webber. 1973. "Dilemmas in a General Theory of Planning." *Policy Sciences* 4 (2): 155–169.

Robinson, Sandra L., and Rebecca J. Bennett. 1995. "A Typology of Deviant Workplace Behaviors: A Multidimensional Scaling Study." *Academy of Management Journal* 38 (2): 555–572.

Ruiz-Palomino, Pablo, Carmen Ruiz-Amaya, and Helena Knörr. 2011. "Employee Organizational Citizenship Behaviour: The Direct and Indirect Impact of Ethical Leadership." *Canadian Journal of Administrative Sciences* 28 (3): 244–258.

Shin, Yuhyung. 2012. "CEO Ethical Leadership, Ethical Climate, Climate Strength, and Collective Organizational Citizenship Behavior." *Journal of Business Ethics* 108 (3): 299–312.

Shin, Yuhyung, Sun Y. Sung, Jin N. Choi, and Min S. Kim. 2015. "Top Management Ethical Leadership and Firm Performance: Mediating Role of Ethical and Procedural Justice Climate." *Journal of Business Ethics* 129 (1): 43–57.

Steinmann, Barbara, Annika Nübold, and Günter W. Maier. 2016. "Validation of a German Version of the Ethical Leadership at Work Questionnaire by Kalshoven et al. (2011)." *Frontiers in Psychology* 7 (March): art. no. 446.

Stouten, Jeroen, Marius van Dijke, David M. Mayer, David De Cremer, and Martin C. Euwema. 2013. "Can a Leader Be Seen as Too Ethical? The Curvilinear Effects of Ethical Leadership." *The Leadership Quarterly* 24 (5): 680–695.

Uhl-Bien, Mary. 2006. "Relational Leadership Theory: Exploring the Social Processes of Leadership and Organizing." *The Leadership Quarterly* 17 (6): 654–676.

Van Dyne, Linn, and Jeffrey A. LePine. 1998. "Helping and Voice Extra-Role Behaviors: Evidence of Construct and Predictive Validity." *Academy of Management Journal* 41 (1): 108–119.

Vigoda-Gadot, Eran, and Itai Beeri. 2012. "Change-Oriented Organizational Citizenship Behavior in Public Administration: The Power of Leadership and the Cost of Organizational Politics." *Journal of Public Administration Research and Theory* 22 (3): 573–596.

Wang, Yau-De, and Wen-Chuan Sung. 2016. "Predictors of Organizational Citizenship Behavior: Ethical Leadership and Workplace Jealousy." *Journal of Business Ethics* 135 (1): 117–128.

Yeung, Kit Sum Syrine, Amy Po Ying Ho, Man Chun Hui Lo, and Engle Angela Chan. 2010. "Social Work Ethical Decision Making in an Inter-Disciplinary Context." *British Journal of Social Work* 40 (5): 1573–1590.

Zoghbi-Manrique-de-Lara, Pablo, and Miguel A. Suárez-Acosta. 2014. "Employees' Reactions to Peers' Unfair Treatment by Supervisors: The Role of Ethical Leadership." *Journal of Business Ethics* 122 (4): 537–549.

7 Destructive Leadership as a Wicked Problem in Health Care

Can We Blame the Leader Only?

Minna Hoffrén and Sanna Laulainen

Research into leadership studies has presented variable outcomes of destructive leadership (Schyns and Schilling 2013, 148–149; see also Einarsen, Skogstad and Schanke Aasland 2010). These outcomes include negative attitudes of employees toward their job and their organization, which can lead to significant costs for the organization. Moreover, studies have presented organizational outcomes such as increased employee turnover, actual or intended, and decreased employee performance. Absenteeism, tardiness and reduced job input (Einarsen, Skogstad and Schanke Aasland 2010), as well as counterproductive work behavior (CWB; e.g. general misbehavior or unethical behavior), all increase (Schyns and Schilling 2013).

In addition to the negative organizational outcomes, destructive leadership has effects on employees' personal lives. These effects are related to negative affectivity and to the experience of occupational stress. The personal well-being of employees decreases (see also Einarsen, Skogstad and Schanke Aasland 2010), and job satisfaction diminishes (Schyns and Schilling 2013). Low levels of job satisfaction are associated particularly with destructive leadership behavior, such as high levels of tyrannical, derailed and laissez faire leadership (Einarsen, Skogstad and Schanke Aasland 2010, 161–162). Because of destructive leadership, employees cannot use their abilities at work, and misgivings and dissatisfaction increase. Their confidence in their own abilities and trust in themselves also waver. The employees must either adjust to the organization culture, submit to the leader or try to find a new job. (Hoffrén and Laulainen, n.d.) Due to variable outcomes, and limited possibility to respond to these negative leadership situations, destructive leadership can be seen, in a way, as a wicked problem without a single clear or linear solution to manage it. The causes of this problem can be explained in numerous ways (see also Rittel and Webber 1973), and it involves a broad range of various actors (See Danken, Dribbisch and Lange 2016, 20). Therefore, dealing with this wicked problem, also destructive leadership requires collaborative leadership processes, where every member of the work community must participate and share responsibilities (see also Grint 2005, 1478).

Existing research recognizes the crucial role played by the leader, and in research into destructive leadership, this wicked problem is seen mainly as a leader-centric phenomenon (see also Padilla, Hogan and Kaiser 2007). Although some research has been carried out on the critical role played by the organizational context of destructive leadership (e.g. Padilla, Hogan and Kaiser 2007; Mulvey and Padilla 2010), very little attention has been paid to the role of the social context, such as the work community and employees. Hitherto, there has been little discussion about the role of employees as a part of the development of destructive leadership (see also Thoroughgood et al. 2012).

From the lens of critical management studies, we challenge the leader-centric approach, which has generally been taken for granted in the field of destructive leadership. The purpose of this chapter is to deepen the level of research knowledge about destructive leadership, which can represent a dark side of organizational behavior (see Linstead 2014), and to generate understanding about how the role of employees is illustrated in discourses related to destructive leadership. We utilize leadership descriptions from employees of health care services as a research material to illustrate this phenomenon.

The Features of Destructive Leadership

Einarsen, Schanke Aasland and Skogstad (2007, 208) defined destructive leadership (DL) as "systematic and repeated behavior by a leader, supervisor or manager that violates the legitimate interest of the organization by undermining and/or sabotaging the organization's goals, tasks, resources, and effectiveness and/or motivation, well-being or job satisfaction of subordinates." They developed a theoretical model of destructive leadership behavior, presenting four categories of destructive leadership behavior: supportive-disloyal, laissez faire, derailed and tyrannical. Figure 7.1 shows some of the main characteristic features of destructive leadership behavior in this model. In addition, White and Lippitt (1960, 26–27) highlighted some features of laissez faire leadership behavior, which have been attached to Figure 7.1 to broaden the characteristic features of laissez faire leadership.

In this chapter, we consider destructive leadership as a harmful leadership behavior that violates the legitimate interests of the organization, harms the organization and employees or both and is embedded in the process of leading (see also Krasikova, Green and LeBreton 2013, 1310–1311). In addition, we consider destructive leadership as a result of the leadership process, to which the destructive leader, employee(s) and the work environment all contribute (see Padilla, Hogan and Kaiser 2007). Destructive leadership takes advantage of obedience, discipline and guilt; employees may suffer from humiliating, subjugating or underestimating leadership activities, which damage both the organization and the workforce (Padilla, Hogan

Supportive-disloyal leadership	Laissez faire leadership
• reveals itself when a leader motivates, stimulates and supports employees through individualized or inspirational consideration and motivation • a leader grants employees more benefits than appropriate or may courage low work ethics and misconducts	• the leader fails to fulfill expectations embedded in the role of a leader • the leader does not participate in activities or discussion in the work community, and does not provide voluntary feedback (White and Lippitt 1960) • decision-making and distribution of work are absent (White and Lippitt 1960)

Derailed leadership	Tyrannical leadership
• is shown through behaviors such as bullying, humiliating, manipulating, deceiving or committing to fraud • the leader uses his/her charismatic qualities for personal gain and exploits both employees and the employer	• the leader manipulates, humiliates or intimidates employees in order to get a job done • the leader may be a superior strategist or high-performing leader but obtains results at the cost of employees

Figure 7.1 Categories of Destructive Leadership Behaviors
(adapted from Einarsen, Schanke Aasland and Skogstad 2007, 211; Einarsen, Skogstad and Schanke Aasland 2010, 151–155; White and Lippitt 1960, 26–27).

and Kaiser 2007; Krasikova, Green and LeBreton 2013; Schyns and Schilling 2013; Hoffrén 2015). Destructive leadership probably does not concretely destroy organizations or employees (Einarsen, Skogstad and Schanke Aasland 2010, 160–165). However, previous definitions of destructive leadership emphasize the role of the leader as an active agent, and regard employees more as followers and sufferers of consequences.

In our previous research (Hoffrén and Laulainen, n.d.), we have specified the features of destructive leadership. In addition to the characteristic features of the theoretical model of Einarsen, Skogstad and Schanke Aasland (2007, 2010), our research revealed that supportive-disloyal leadership manifests itself in different kinds of inequalities, and strong segmentations into the leader's favorite and non-favorite employees. The favorites receive bonuses and special assignments regardless of their real abilities and know-how. The inner circle attacks the non-favorites by making arrogant comments and calling them names. Laissez faire leadership reveals itself through passive and absent leadership actions. The leader is lazy in human resource management, and ignores or fails to react to problems. The employees quarrel, squabble among themselves, discourage others and are malicious in the work community. In derailed leadership, the leader may, for example, groundlessly take all duties away from an employee and try little by little to get rid of him/her. The leader silences all protest and criticism at the workplace. The other co-workers do not help or support their discriminated colleague, and avoid those who are on the firing line. Tyrannical leadership manifests itself in a strong hierarchical command relationship between the leader and the employees. The leader obtains results by dictating and controlling, and the employees should obey. (Hoffrén and Laulainen, n.d.) In this chapter, we explore destructive leadership, particularly from the point of view of employees' actions.

Empirical Findings

The following is a brief description of the research material through which we illustrate the special role of the employees in destructive leadership. The research material consists of 17 leadership descriptions gathered in 2015 (April to December) from employees of health care services in Finland. These written descriptions were collected by placing research information on a Facebook website "To obey, be silent or resist" (in Finnish: "Totella, vaieta vai vastustaa"). The research information could be distributed by clicking the Facebook actions Like or Share and, in addition, via other methods, such as work-oriented websites and electronic mail. The informants were asked to describe what had happened, who were involved, what kind of consequences the situation had and how this situation had affected the informant, the work community or the leadership. The informants could also reflect on what kind of factors could have an ameliorating effect on the situation at the workplace and on the leadership. A free-form story could be sent via a Webropol-based web platform, by email or by post.

Most of the 17 informants worked in a public hospital or health center in Finland, as employees or managers, and two of them were male. Three stories were written from the perspectives of a local health care elected official, health care student and health care educator. The informants described situations which had occurred between 2004 and 2015, mainly in 2014.

In the analysis, we were interested in a discursively constructed description of work life reality, and emphasized language as a central component of the construction process (see also Alvesson and Deetz 2000, 36; Alvesson and Karreman 2000, 1126). We focused on the role of the employees from the premises of critical discourse analysis (e.g. Fairclough 2003). In the analysis process, we utilized the theoretical model of Einarsen, Schanke Aasland and Skogstad (2007, 2010) to identify destructive leadership. To begin the analysis, we focused on the negative situations or actions embedded in the process of leading and extracted these situations from the data by using Atlas.ti software for the qualitative analysis.

After this, we categorized situations and actions by using the theoretical model of destructive leadership behavior, including categories such as supportive-disloyal, laissez faire, derailed and tyrannical leadership. In the third step, we applied close reading of particularly employees' actions in the face of these destructive leadership situations. The main categories were supportive-disloyal and laissez faire leadership behavior. Finally, we analyzed how the roles of employees were discursively constructed through words (e.g. sucking up, backstabbing, black list), phrases (e.g. crying scene, turning into bosses) and metaphors (e.g. stirring up bad blood, setting the devil free). We then constructed an analytical frame based on these discursive practices. This frame helped us to gather and analyze a specific employee's or work community's actions in destructive leadership situations. As a result, we identified two discourses: the self-interest discourse and collective denial discourse.

Self-Interest

The self-interest discourse highlights a single employee's action, such as sucking up, backstabbing and turning into bosses. A description of opportunism and dominance constructs this discourse. In the descriptions, the informant describes how other employees react to and represent negative leadership actions. These employees participate actively in destructive leadership, and seek personal utility such as areas of responsibility and bonuses. In the excerpt below, this utility seeking is expressed as the habit of sucking up to a superior, so that an employee can gain a number of areas of responsibility with his/her action. This kind of action underlines some of the features of supportive-disloyal leadership.

Excerpt

Pretty soon it became clear that the superior only had certain employees he/she[1] favoured. Not so much workstations. At first, I did not pay much attention to the situation, but ultimately it began to open up, in all its horror, in front of my eyes. At our workplace, areas of responsibility were divided and this, of course, also led to thoughts about the complexity of the work, and *it also affects the personal salary element*. I had become friends with an employee at the unit, and I began to notice that *he/she received a great number of these areas of responsibility*. I also began to wonder out loud about *his/her habit of 'sucking up' to our superior*, and the person said that he/she had wondered him/herself why he/she is suddenly good for anything, when previously he/she had even feared the superior. Now the situation was different, and he/she obviously enjoyed the situation. Our relationship began to go cold, and I eventually realized that *he/she reported all of my thinking and wondering to the superior*.

(S13)

In the descriptions, rhetorical elements also illustrate how the informants alienate themselves from the actions of the other employee (e.g. sucking up). This alienation can be identified in the excerpts above through categorization into others (he/she, they, male-female) and the informant (personal pronoun I). Thus, the discourse generates distance between the informant and the others.

Furthermore, the informant describes sucking up as an action in which another employee reports all his/her thinking and wondering to the superior (excerpt above). This reporting or giving feedback is also highlighted as "back-stabbing stuff" like children of primary school age (excerpt below).

Excerpt

I said that I would never go to a 'boss's office' to give feedback on anyone or send e-mails. I do not take part in *'backstabbing stuff' like children of primary school age.* If I feel something wrong has been done, or if something does not go right, in my opinion, I will talk about the matter right away with the person in question, and we do not discuss it after that. [. . .] they [female nurses][2] garner respect for themselves in our work community with this 'backstabbing technique.' Add to that a *'crying scene,'* and *the culprit* is obvious. This is an accepted practice.

(S16)

The informant refers to the crying scene and the culprit (excerpt above), and constructs a metaphor to the actions of children of primary school age. By using the metaphor, the informant questions the accepted practices at the workplace, and contrasts these actions with grown-up work performance. In the situations, the crying scene and identifying the culprit represent how employees seek to obtain personal advantage in supportive-disloyal leadership situations and act in their own self-interest.

The phrases such as turning into 'bosses' and taking control, but with no responsibility (excerpts below), highlight the self-interest discourse in the descriptions of laissez faire leadership. The informant questions employees' position of dominance and constructs a contrast to the true supervisor by using the word 'bosses' in quotes (the first excerpt below). In addition, the situation at the workplace is defined as an uncontrollable chaos. Thus, in the leadership situations, anything can happen.

Excerpt

[O]n the other hand, working for a boss like this, they ((employees)) can *turn themselves into 'bosses'* whereby uncontrollable chaos prevails in the work community.

(S7)

Excerpt

I was elected as a head nurse. *The devil* broke free. *This one nurse* had decided to *sabotage* all my decisions whatever I did. He/she *slandered* me for the other staff in the ward. I said that he/she was completely narcissistic in his/her character, who knew how to dictate the other staff. He/she *took control, but no responsibility.*

(S8)

In the descriptions of the employee's dominance position, the informant produces a description of this one nurse as the devil, who takes control, sabotages and slanders the head nurse (excerpt above). The description defines the employee as the "boss," and the informant, as a real superior, must succumb to the dominance of an employee. In this excerpt, the self-interest discourse highlights the description of the deposition of the superior; the employee takes real control and power in leadership situations.

Collective Denial

In the collective denial discourse, the work community and its members' actions are positioned as a part of anonymous subjects such as the other employees and they. The discourse emerges from metaphors and verbs that represent actions such as stir "bad blood" or single out (excerpt below). In particular, the metaphor of stirring bad blood refers to denial and especially to anxiety that the informant can cause trouble to the others with his/her actions such as talking about negative things or seeking for support and help. Talking and seeking for help disturb the others and inflict irritation and anger. The metaphor produces a description according to which the other employees actively try to avoid going along with the leadership actions or they do not support others. In addition, talking and seeking for help discommode the whole work community or unbalance the steady state at the workplace. Because of seeking help, the informant is singled out and placed in a jam (excerpt below), or on the superior's blacklist.

Excerpt

I ended up on *the superior's blacklist*, and when I tried to talk about things, one male employee said I was *stirring up 'bad blood.' The other employees* understood this because *they* had seen the same thing happen to many other employees. I was *singled out* and *placed in a jam.*

(S13)

The collective denial discourse is represented through the perspective of a work community. For example, negative leadership situations such as in the case of laissez faire produce a description of different forms of collective cover up and lack of support. In the excerpt below, a collective coverup emerges from the expression in which the employees try to conceal the leader's omissions and mistakes, even though they should seek help.

Excerpt

Those who have it worst with a superior like this are *the employees* who do not realize that *they* should seek help or even *cover up* the closest *superior's omissions and mistakes. The work community* becomes distressed and feels uncertainty about the future, they also have to ascertain all things

(S7)

As discussed above, the descriptions represent that some of the work community members seek support and help. However, rhetorical elements, such as words like no support, refer explicitly to lack of support (excerpt below). The excerpt below presents the role of the employees exceptionally as an active agent and that of the leader as a sufferer of consequences. The employees deny their support to the head nurse. In retrospect, the employees describe their actions in the situation naively (blue-eyed) and unfairly.

Excerpt

I [a head nurse] talked to my director of nursing, who I thought I was getting support [. . .] I would have needed more support in that situation. There was *no support*. [. . .] I think the whole process went so wrong that I did not see any survival opportunities. I resigned myself. Later, when I have met my former employees, they have recognized how *they were blue-eyed* [naïve] and how *they acted unfairly*. I asked them to learn their lesson, and support the next immediate superior.

(S8)

In the situation, the employees comply with the other employee, who takes control and dominance in the work community. The real superior is powerless and remains without support from his/her supervisor or employees. In this excerpt above, the collective denial discourse confirms the previously mentioned description of the deposition of the superior. The employee takes actual control and power in leadership situations, with the support of the other employees. In this wicked situation, the employees are main concern of the problem. The collaborative leadership processes have been degenerated into destructive leadership.

Discussion and Conclusions

In this chapter, we examined how the role of employees was illustrated in the leadership descriptions from the employees of health care services. These descriptions were related to destructive leadership. By applying the theoretical model of destructive leadership behavior (Einarsen, Schanke Aasland and Skogstad 2007, 2010), and by using discursive interpretation, this chapter focused on the role of employees in constructing destructive leadership. As a result, we identified two discourses related to employees' actions: self-interest discourse and collective denial discourse.

The findings suggest that the role of the employees can appear in behavior such as a passive non-intervention and settling for the situations. This role is emphasized in the collective denial discourse, which is based on a prerequisite for employees to "stop rocking the boat." The self-interest discourse constructs an idea of the role of employees that can be embodied as an active and conscious opportunism, at the cost of the other employees, however. Thus, collective or individual responses do not address to destructive leadership or other leadership problems at the work community. Nor these responses do not solve the problems. As Grint (2010, 305) describes, the responses emerge other wicked problems. By following the nature of wicked problems, there is an assumption that wicked problems do not have a well-described set of potential solutions (Rittel and Webber 1973). However, based on the lens of critical management studies (Alvesson 2003), we question that destructive leadership as an example of wicked problem would not be manageable. It requires collaborative leadership approach to solve this problem by involving employees, too (see also Danken, Dribbisch and Lange 2016, 24).

The analysis of the leadership descriptions revealed two dimensions of destructive leadership supportive-disloyal and laissez faire leadership. By contrast, the features of derailed and tyrannical leadership were missing in this particular research material. We recognize the limitations of our research material concerning, e.g. the number of leadership descriptions. Even though we focused especially on the role of the employees, the research material provided an adequate view of destructive leadership situations as a whole. However, based on our methodological premises, we are not able to generalize our results to a broader context, and we cannot argue that the wickedness of destructive leadership concerns only health care organizations.

In a practical context, due to an ongoing reform of Finnish health care and social welfare services, destructive leadership can currently be manifested explicitly in health care and social welfare organizations. The reform concerns the structure of health care and welfare services, and, for example, it brings together all levels of entities. Furthermore, steering and operating models will be reformulated. The aim of the reform is to achieve cost-effective, better coordinated and custom-oriented services. (Ministry of Finance 2018). However, organizational changes such as restructuring and reformulating can easily highlight internal competition with micro-political behavior (e.g. bullying or destructive leadership) that aims to improve the competitive position of certain individuals or to eliminate non-desirable persons from the work community (Salin 2003).

The results support the idea that employees have an essential role in the process of destructive leadership. This role can be a result of intentional and active actions in the destructive leadership situations, even though these actions may appear outsiders to be quite small and minimal (followers' disguised agency, see Collinson 2014, 37). Based on these results we question the traditional view of employees' role as a follower in leader-employee relationships in the context of destructive leadership. Inspired by critical management studies, even though we are aware that the field of CMS is extensive, and that there is a critical debate concerning its shortcomings (e.g. Klikauer 2015; Prasad et al. 2016), we challenge the biased power relations between leaders and employees (see also a discussion concerning Critical Leadership Studies, Collinson 2014). We question the idea of employees as passive followers and managerial objects, which has generally been taking for granted in the field of destructive leadership and in wider leadership studies. The idea of passive followers can be interpreted as an insult in the context of health care crowded with intelligent actors (Learmonth 2003, 112). Thus, we underline the significant role of employees as intentional and active agents in destructive leadership situations and in the associated power relations. Therefore, consideration of the phenomenon of destructive leadership from the perspective of the leader only can restrict both the comprehension of this wicked problem theoretically and tackling it in practice.

Notes

1. The Finnish gender-neutral third-person singular pronoun *hän* (he/she) refers to either a man or a woman, and, therefore, the subject can be either he or she.
2. [Brackets] contain information that clarifies a subject or the context.

References

Alvesson, Mats. 2003. "Critical Organization Theory." In *The Northern Lights—Organization Theory in Scandinavia*, edited by Barbara Czarniawska and Guje Sevón, 151–174. Trelleborg: Copenhagen Business School Press.
Alvesson, Mats, and Stanley Deetz. 2000. *Doing Critical Management Research*. London: Sage Publications.
Alvesson, Mats, and Dan Karreman. 2000. "Varieties of Discourse: On the Study of Organizations Through Discourse Analysis." *Human Relations* 53 (9): 1125–1149. doi: 10.1177/0018726700539002.
Collinson, David. 2014. "Dichotomies, Dialectics and Dilemmas: New Directions for Critical Leadership Studies?" *Leadership* 10 (1): 36–55.
Danken, Thomas, Katrin Dribbisch, and Anne Lange. 2016. "Studying Wicked Problems Forty Years on: Towards a Synthesis of a Fragmented Debate." *Zeitschrift für Public Policy, Recht und Management* 9: 15–33.
Einarsen, Ståle, Merethe Schanke Aasland, and Anders Skogstad. 2007. "Destructive Leadership Behaviour: A Definition and Conceptual Model." *The Leadership Quarterly* 18: 207–216.
Einarsen, Ståle, Anders Skogstad, and Merethe Schanke Aasland. 2010. "The Nature, Prevalence, and Outcomes of Destructive Leadership: A Behavioral and Conglomerate Approach." In *When Leadership Goes Wrong: Destructive*

Leadership, Mistakes, and Ethical Failures, edited by Birgit Schyns and Tiffany Hansbroughn, 145–171. Charlotte, NC: Information Age Publishing.

Fairclough, Norman. 2003. *Analysing Discourse: Textual Analysis for Social Research*. London: Routledge.

Grint, Keith. 2005. "Problems, Problems, Problems: The Social Construction of 'leadership'." *Human Relations* 58 (11): 1467–1494. doi: 10.1177/0018726705061314.

Grint, Keith. 2010. "The Cuckoo Clock Syndrome: Addicted to Command, Allergic to Leadership." *European Management Journal* 28 (4): 306–313. doi: 10.1016/j.emj.2010.05.002.

Hoffrén, Minna. 2015. "Totella, vaieta vai vastustaa? Diskurssianalyysi johtamisen kielteisistä piirteistä hoitotyöntekijöiden haastattelupuheessa (To Obey, to Be Silent or to Resist? Discourse Analysis of the Negative Features of Leadership in the Care Workers Interviewing Speech)." *Työelämän tutkimus* 13 (1): 20–37.

Hoffrén, Minna, and Sanna Laulainen. n.d. *"Role of the Work Community in the Construction of Destructive Leadership."* Unpublished manuscript.

Klikauer, Thomas. 2015. "Critical Management Studies and Critical Theory: A Review." *Capital & Class* 39 (2): 197–220.

Krasikova, Dina V., Stephen G. Green, and James M. LeBreton. 2013. "Destructive Leadership: A Theoretical Review, Integration, and Future Research Agenda." *Journal of Management* 39 (5): 1308–1338.

Learmonth, Mark. 2003. "Making Health Services Management Research Critical: A Review and a Suggestion." *Sociology of Health & Illness* 25 (1): 93–119. doi: 10.1111/1467-9566.00326.

Linstead, Stephen. 2014. "Theorizing and Researching the Dark Side of Organization." *Organization Studies* 35 (2): 165–188.

Ministry of Finance. "About the Reform: Health and Social Services Reform." Accessed March 9, 2018. http://alueuudistus.fi/en/social-welfare-and-health-care-reform/about-the-reform.

Mulvey, Paul W., and Art Padilla. 2010. "The Environment of Destructive Leadership." In *When Leadership Goes Wrong: Destructive Leadership, Mistakes, and Ethical Failures*, edited by Birgit Schyns and Tiffany Hansbroughn, 49–71. Charlotte, NC: Information Age Publishing.

Padilla, Art., Robert Hogan, and Robert B. Kaiser. 2007. "The Toxic Triangle: Destructive Leaders, Susceptible Followers, and Conducive Environments." *The Leadership Quarterly* 18 (3): 176–194.

Prasad, Anshuman, Pushkala Prasad, Albert J. Mills, and Jean Helms Mills. 2016. "Debating Knowledge: Rethinking Critical Management Studies in a Changing World." In *The Routledge Companion to Critical Management Studies*, edited by Anshuman Prasad, Pushkala Prasad, Albert J. Mills, and Jean Helms Mills, 3–41. London, New York: Routledge.

Rittel, Horst, and Melvin Webber. 1973. "Dilemmas in a General Theory of Planning." *Policy Sciences* 4 (2): 155–169.

Salin, Denise. 2003. "Ways of Explaining Workplace Bullying: A Review of Enabling, Motivating and Precipitating Structures and Processes in the Work Environment." *Human Relations* 56 (10): 1213–1232. doi: 10.1177/00187267035610003.

Schyns, Birgit, and Jan Schilling. 2013. "How Bad Are the Effects of Bad Leaders? A Meta-Analysis of Destructive Leadership and Its Outcomes." *The Leadership Quarterly* 24 (1): 138–158.

Thoroughgood, Christian N., Art Padilla, Samuel T. Hunter, and Brian W. Tate. 2012. "The Susceptible Circle: A Taxonomy of Followers Associated with Destructive Leadership." *Leadership Quarterly* 23 (5): 897–917.

White, Ralph K., and Ronald Lippitt. 1960. *Autocracy and Democracy: An Experimental Inquiry*. New York: Harper & Brothers.

8 Health Care Communication Technology and Its Promise of Patient Empowerment

Unpacking Patient Empowerment through Patients' Identity Constructions

Laura Visser, Inge Bleijenbergh, Yvonne Benschop and Allard van Riel

A major development affecting the organization of health care today is the implementation of technologies in daily care provision, especially those that focus on improving communication between patients and health care professionals (Schwamm 2014; Bishop et al. 2013; Krist and Woolf 2011; Dedding et al. 2011). Implementing communication technology is often seen as a promising avenue for dealing with the current wicked challenges faced by health care systems in many countries in the Global North (i.e., combining aging populations, increase of patients with long-term illnesses, cost reductions and increased quality of care). These expectations are based on the assumption that technology can give patients a more central role, by empowering them to become better informed and involved patients, striving for what is often called 'integrated care' (Kodner and Spreeuwenberg 2002). Although there is much speculation about the empowering benefits of technology, we know little of how the technology is actually used and what the implications for patients are (Berwick 2009; Davies 2012). From a Critical Management Studies perspective, however, we know that 'empowerment' is often a more complex issue than generally assumed (Alvesson and Willmott 1996; Hardy and Leiba-O'Sullivan 1998; Henwood et al. 2003), one not easily or necessarily achieved through implementing technology. Therefore, we argue that it is important to critically analyze claims of increased empowerment and see what actually happens when communication technologies are introduced in health care to question if they actually provide a better alternative for long-term illness management. This chapter will provide this critical analysis and ask, based on an empirical study, how patients' role in health care is affected by using health care communication technology.

To understand the use of technology and its effect on roles of patients, we are especially interested in examining how the use of communication technology affects patients' identity constructions. We use patients' identities as a way to unpack the supposed empowering effects of the technology, taking a critical approach to the idea of patient empowerment through technology. As a result, we show the complexity of using communication technology and its effect on health care management. To understand patients' identities, we make a distinction between identity work and regulation (Alvesson and Willmott 2002) as we see patients' identities both in the light of the day-to-day work they do to construct their identity (i.e., identity work) and how these identities are regulated by the larger social and organizational context of the health care technology and health care management in general (i.e., identity regulation). While our empirical question is related to understanding patients' empowerment through technology, the related theoretical question asks how identities are constructed in environments that are explicitly meant to be empowering. In other words, the context of this technology might create a 'wicked' environment in which identity work of patients is messier than the empowered identity constructions assumed by the advocates of health care technology. As we will discuss in the coming sections, our case provides an interesting environment in which to link to a recent debate around the instability and incoherence of identity work (Daskalaki and Simosi 2018; Beech et al. 2016; Brown and Coupland 2015; Carollo and Guerci 2017) and to further question the division between (controlling) regulation and (empowering) identity work.

The communication technology we examine is that of Personal Online Health Communities (POHCs). The online communities allow an individual patient to communicate with her or his own health care professionals in a secured online space. As such, the POHCs are designed to give patients easier access to their health care professionals, no longer bound by restrictions in time and space or by a gatekeeper (e.g. secretary), which existed before.[1] We collected data from a pilot project set up by ParkinsonNet, an organization aiming to improve the lives of patients with Parkinson's disease. We followed 18 patients, who we interviewed and who allowed us to follow the communication on the POHC.

In the next sections, we will discuss our position in the literature, our methods for data collection and analysis and the findings based on that analysis. In the final section of this chapter, we discuss the theoretical and practical relevance of our findings.

Identity Work and Regulation

Critical literature has a long tradition in showing how people's organizational identities are constructed through an interplay between regulatory control and identity work (Alvesson and Willmott 2002). In many studies on organizational identities, Alvesson and Willmott's (2002) model, which relates identity regulation, identity work and self-identity to each other, is drawn upon (e.g. Brown and Coupland 2015; Gotsi et al. 2010; Watson 2008; Essers, Doorewaard and Benschop 2013). In their model, they make a distinction between identity regulation at the organizational (and societal) level and identity work at the individual level (Ybema et al. 2009). Identity regulation is seen as a way through which organizations exert control, as identity regulation sets standards for appropriate behavior (e.g. how to 'professionally' communicate a diagnosis to a patient) that organizational members are influenced by. Importantly, organizational members do not just undergo this regulation, their constructed identities are also an effect of the identity work done in a relational process to identity regulation. Individuals engage in conforming and/or resisting identity work, meaning they comply with the regulation and/or find ways to subvert or circumvent the regulation on their identity construction (Alvesson and Willmott 2002; Zanoni and Janssens 2007). Identity work is defined by the active participation of individuals in "forming, repairing, maintaining, strengthening or revising [identities]" (Alvesson, Lee Ashcraft and Thomas 2008, 626). As such, identity work is a constant activity that individuals engage in to ensure that their constructed identities align with norms. Both the organizational-level identity regulation and the individual-level identity work are, therefore, important for identity construction.

Identity Work in Changing Environments

When we relate this theoretical framework to our empirical case, there is an important difference to note, especially when it comes to the notion of empowerment. In the framework constructed by Alvesson and Willmott (2002), identity regulation through organizational practices are positioned as maintaining the status quo whereas identity work sits on the opposite side as the individual's attempt to disrupt this. Although a potentially useful distinction, it also creates a separation between identity regulation as controlling and identity work as potentially empowering. In our empirical context such a separation seems less useful as we have a case where the POHCs form a regulatory environment that itself is geared to change and the disruption of norms: identities are expected to change through regulation in POHCs. As empowerment is no longer solely up to the individual patient, but part of the organizational agenda (and therefore, identity regulation) as well, we suggest that the concept of empowerment becomes more ambiguous, potentially leading to the exacerbation of conflicts and tensions in individuals' (ambiguous) identity work.

To further understand the ambiguity of this identity work, we link up with and contribute to a recent debate that attempts to complicate the concept of identity work, by challenging the assumed coherence and stability of identity work (Carollo and Guerci 2017; Beech 2011; Beech et al. 2016; Daskalaki and Simosi 2017). As the concept is commonly used, identity work explains ways to repair and adjust one's self-identity in a changing context, aiming to restore a sense of coherence (e.g. when a manager goes through a merger (Beech 2011)). However, recent empirical work challenges this idea that identity work is mostly geared toward constructing a coherent sense of self and instead argues that some might feel comfortable sitting in a space of ambiguity and constant questioning and restructuring of their sense of self (Beech et al. 2016; Clarke, Brown and Hailey 2009; Carollo and Guerci 2017). For example, Beech et al. (2016) show that individuals (in their case, indie musicians) constantly engaged in identity work that was self-criticizing and at times, self-deprecating, and this questioning was part of their self-identity. This literature is useful to help understand patients' identity constructions when using communication technology, because POHCs also present a context of change, where patients' identity work is affected by the environment (but also strongly affects the environment). Moreover, patients with chronic degenerative diseases (such as Parkinson's disease) are constantly changing themselves as their disease progresses, increasing the 'wickedness' of their identity work. As such, it might be more useful to see patients' identity construction on the POHCs as a process of "self-questioning [that is] ongoing and unresolved; it [is] not a means to an end; it [is] an end in itself" (Beech et al. 2016, 519). We will use this lens of ambiguity and tensions to explore the complexity of patients' identity constructions when using the assumed empowering context of POHCs.

Methods

To answer our research question (how the patient's role is affected by using health care communication technology), we draw on data from 18 patients with Parkinson's disease using a POHC. These patients represent a sample from one hundred patients who joined a pilot project on POHCs in the Netherlands from 2011 to 2013. The criterion for selecting patients was the frequency with which they used their community. By focusing on frequent users (which applied to only a third of the participants in the pilot project), we ensured to have enough data to analyze patients' identity construction using communication technology. The data collection consisted of in-depth interviews with patients and long-term observations of their POHCs. The combination of two types of data collection allows us a multisided understanding of patients' use of their communities. The local hospital's medical ethics committee approved the research project before starting.

Parkinson's Disease and the POHC System

The POHCs used by our sample of patients were set up by the ParkinsonNet foundation. ParkinsonNet aims to improve care for patients with Parkinson's disease by finding innovative ways to organize the current complex and multidisciplinary care provision process (ParkinsonNet 2012). The technological system of the communities provides patients and health care professionals with a menu of options (ParkinsonNet 2012).

These options consist of sections called 'files,' 'diary,' 'meeting,' 'apps,' 'problem list' and 'team.' Patients use the diary and meeting sections most frequently. The 'diary' section allows patients to provide updates on their well-being. In the 'meeting' section, patients or health care professionals can start a virtual meeting and invite specific health care professionals to participate.

Collecting the Data

We combined interviews with 18 patients with observations of their POHCs. For the interviews, we used a topic list, which focused on how patients experience the use of their POHC, how they experience their relationship with their health care professionals, and how they experience their role in the care provision process. Since all patients were Dutch native speakers, interviews were performed in Dutch and lasted between 45 and 90 minutes, with an average duration of 60 minutes. After the interview, we asked all interviewees permission to observe their POHC. All interviewees, except for four, gave the interviewer permission to access their POHCs. Some patients stipulated that they would only give access to the POHC for a limited amount of time. These patients stated that they preferred not to be observed constantly, but allowed the interviewer temporary access to save the necessary data. The patients who gave permission for observations only granted access to the first author and added her to their virtual team on the POHC. This allowed her to receive notifications and read new postings. Patients' data were anonymized before the first author shared them with the other authors. The names used in Table 8.1 are aliases to protect the privacy of the interviewees.

Table 8.1 Overview of Characteristics of the Patients

Name	User since	Number of health care professionals	Number of diary entries	Number of virtual meeting entries	Number of documents
Adam	Oct 2011	6	6	12	2
Kristina	Apr 2012	4	22	13	4
Camille	Feb 2013	4	11	1	1
Sarah	Jan 2012	5	108	11	4
Julia	Dec 2011	6	33	8	26[i]
Victor	May 2012	5	4	7	8
Nora	Nov 2011	5	8	26	3

i This patient has posted a large number of documents in her capacity as a patient advocate. These documents are not related to her own health, but are meant for distribution among the patient population.

Analyzing the Data

We analyzed the verbatim transcripts of the interviews and patients' writings on their POHCs using a critical discourse analysis approach. Going beyond the superficial content of quotes, we analyzed how patients phrase their sentences in the interviews and on the POHCs. Critical discourse analysis allows for the examination of power processes embedded in use of language by paying close attention to not only what was said (or not said), but also to how it is said and how it is embedded in a specific place and time (Alvesson 2010). It enables us to reflect on how language constitutes patients' identities and relations with others (Fairclough 1993). Therefore, we treat the text produced by our interviewees not as a reflection of a stable reality, but as language created in that specific context in relation to the interviewer (Alvesson 2010).

When analyzing how patients talked about their use of the online communities three themes emerged, namely reflections on the frequency of their postings, the content of their postings, and intersections of online and offline space. Using these themes as guiding principles, we analyzed how patients displayed hesitations, assertiveness and/or contradictions in discussing those themes. In this chapter, we analyze quotes from seven different patients that best expressed the main findings, but represented patterns in the entire sample. We translated the Dutch quotes to English only in the last stage of writing, trying to preserve the subtle character of the used language (including grammatical errors and punctuation) and to identify (in the analysis) when Dutch expressions have a slightly different meaning than English ones.

Results

As mentioned above, our analysis revealed three themes linked to the patients' identity work. We successively discuss the number of postings, the content of postings and online-offline intersection.

Number of Postings

Patients show variations in the number of postings in the different sections of their POHCs. Some use their diary to present updates multiple times a week; others only use the virtual meeting space to ask questions. To illustrate how the number of postings is a topic that patients explicitly reflect on, we first introduce Adam, who started using his POHC two years ago, and posted 12 times in the virtual meeting. He uses his diary much less often, only having posted six diary entries. When asked about the frequency of his postings, he states:

> To me it's also about not too much . . . Because if you ask too many questions to . . . but then they [health care professionals] will also think 'here's that nuisance again.'
>
> (Adam, interview)

Adam talks about what the result would be if he makes 'too much' use of his POHC: his health care professionals thinking "here's that nuisance again." Even though the POHCs are supposed to allow patients to ask questions when and where they want to ask them, Adam clearly identifies a norm here: there are limits to posting. If we delve into this, we note that patients discuss limits to the number of postings mostly in relation to the activity of asking questions. The POHC system is set up in such a way that when patients ask questions (in the virtual meeting section), their health care professionals receive a notification, setting the expectation for receiving a response. In contrast, when patients write in the diary section, health care professionals do not receive a notification and generally a response to these messages is not required nor provided. Therefore, patients who talk about limiting the number of postings refer to the activity of asking questions in the 'virtual meeting' section. Interestingly, while writing in their diary, patients are regulated by a different norm from what we have seen so far: informing your health care professionals as frequently as possible. We illustrate this with the excerpts below:

It's been a while since I last wrote something in my diary
                                                        Camille, diary

From today on, going back again to writing a short diary entry regularly
Had no energy to write for a couple of days. Wasn't feeling well at all
                                                        Sarah, diary

Already 16 days since I last wrote
                                                        Kristina, diary

Already been a while since I last wrote in my diary, but was in Portugal for 4 weeks, next time I'll write there as well, if there's ever going to be a next time
                                                        Julia, diary

---

In these excerpts, we notice the role of the design of the POHC in shaping norms. The label 'diary,' literally translated from Dutch, actually means 'day journal,' implying one should write in it on a daily basis. Indeed, as we see above, patients start some of their diary entries referring to the regularity with which they write in this section of their POHCs. These postings often contain justifications and apologies. Julia even apologizes for not posting while she was on vacation, promising that next time she will also update her diary from over there. These excerpts expose an interesting development: the meticulous recording of one's symptoms over time is not something that patients usually do or share with their health care professionals. Progression of symptoms are generally discussed in a more limited way, for example, during the biannual consultation with the neurologist. The availability of the diary section in the POHC, and the implicit suggestion that it should be used on a daily basis, seems to impose extra duties on patients.

The patients, therefore, relate to strict norms around the number of postings. Even though the POHCs are meant to facilitate increased frequency of contact and empower patients to choose when and about what to contact their health care professionals, their identity work suggests the coexistence of other regulatory norms, which, in a sense, limits the possibilities offered by the technology.

Content of Postings

Patients do not only carefully reflect on the number of postings, but also on the content of their postings. The design of the POHC does not allow for nonverbal communication, meaning that what patients say cannot be nuanced by other methods of communication. Therefore, patients consciously reflect on how the content of their postings comes across to their health care professionals. What is considered appropriate content is conceived of differently by different patients, as we illustrate below.

One concept that came up frequently during the interviews and the observations of the POHCs, is that of 'complaining.' Victor brings this issue up during an interview. He started using his POHC a year and a half ago, and makes the following statement:

> You are . . . very consciously thinking . . . should I bother him [the neurologist] with this, yes or no? [I: Do you hesitate when posting?] Yes. [silence] Yes . . . I am not someone who complains quickly.
>
> (Victor, interview)

The excerpt shows the conscious thought process going into posting on the POHC. When asked if he ever hesitates, Victor links his hesitation to coming across as a complainer. As such he, and other interviewees, identify a norm of not complaining about issues related to their illness. Even though Parkinson's disease has had an enormous impact on these patients' lives, they suggested on multiple occasions their desire to avoid expressing negative emotions around this impact, for fear of coming across as a complainer.

We compare his identity work with another patient named Nora. She has been using her POHC for over a year. Nora also hesitates about complaining, saying earlier in the interview that she would rather be a bit 'tough' than complain. Below she relates the lack of face-to-face contact to making it more difficult to nuance her postings:

> [In face-to-face interactions] I am there as my whole person interacting with someone and that person will see some sort of . . . I also often use self-mockery. [. . .] And you include that in your story [. . .] and on the

electronic [system], you have to put that into words, if you want to include that aspect. [. . .] With that surgery on my foot, I make a little bit of a dramatic . . . how should I put it . . . story out of it. [laughing:] because it needs to be a taken a bit serious of course. So I use my negative mood to really emphasize my worries, like gosh, I am really worried about that.

(Nora, interview)

Nora states that she finds it easier to avoid coming across as a complainer by interacting face-to-face with her health care professionals. This allows her to display 'self-mockery' and her 'whole person' through which she can both express emotions and nuance them simultaneously. She states that she "should be taken a bit serious of course" while she starts laughing. She frames her storytelling as a way to express fears ("emphasize my worries") and convince her health care professionals of the severity of her symptoms. Such emphasizing ensures that her health care professionals take her seriously. In fact, with her use of the word 'should,' Nora voices an expectation that she has of her health care professionals; they *should* take her seriously.

As such, as patients consciously consider the content of their posts, the idea of complaining frequently comes to the surface. In this online space, patients reflectively navigate the thin line between reaching out to their health care professionals and disturbing them with too much irrelevant or inappropriate information.

Intersection of Online and Offline Spaces

As we have seen in Nora's case, the online space does not exist separately from the offline space where health care provision takes place (i.e., the doctor's office). To understand how the offline and online spaces intersect, we need to provide more background information about the common pattern of interaction between Parkinson patients and their health care professionals. Almost all patients have biannual appointments with their neurologist for which they tend to save up questions. Most patients also see other health care professionals, but the intensity of contact with them varies and fluctuates.

In this section, we move on to Kristina. She has been using the online community for about a year and a half and mainly uses the diary section to keep track of how she is doing. She wrote one of her diary entries in preparation for the first meeting with her new neurologist. The title of this diary entry is "Is everything actually fine?" and in it she writes:

Tomorrow first time to Dr. [name neurologist]. Knowing myself, I will say that everything's going fine. It is going fine, but I haven't been sleeping well lately because the tremor is becoming more apparent.

Kristina, diary excerpt

The excerpt indicates that Kristina is aware that she will probably find it difficult to articulate that she has not been sleeping well lately, during the face-to-face meeting with the neurologist. Although she does not articulate it specifically, her reasoning behind this behavior might be similar to the patients we discussed before: she wants to avoid coming across as a complainer. She recognizes she is inclined not to discuss her well-being openly, and counteracts this tendency by making this comment in her diary. Through this statement, she (deliberately) loses the opportunity to pretend she is fine in the offline consultation room. In a rather complex way, Kristina uses the online space to change her offline behavior. She avoids transgressing the norm of coming across as a complainer, but is still able to transfer that she is not doing 'fine.' During the interview, Kristina shows another example of impacting her activities in the consultation room through using her online community:

> Before I go there, I write down some things [on the POHC], that I want to discuss for a bit. So he has . . . he prints it out and has it there with him. And that's what I also think is very convenient. Because, I think, if I come in myself with a piece of paper, then I always think 'that's so [self-important].' But then he has that piece of paper with him [. . .] and just the other day as well, I had forgotten something and then he said as well 'we haven't talked about that yet.'
>
> (Kristina, interview)

Kristina describes how she uses her POHC to post an overview of issues she would otherwise bring in print. She signals that her questions are not that worthy of attention when she states that she feels "so self-important" when she comes to the consultation and brings out a piece of paper. However, through Kristina's words, it becomes clear that the neurologist *is* deserving of this importance because he can bring a printout of her issues. By appreciating that he uses a printout, she ascribes him the importance necessary to possess such physical evidence of her problems. In these excerpts, we witness Kristina engage in identity work that is specifically geared to impacting her offline identity. The POHCs create a complex environment in which patients' identities are regulated by both online and offline spaces. As a result, patients' identity work now interacts with both worlds at the same time. The POHC disrupts the common, face-to-face communication with the neurologist and offers space to reflect on oneself as a patient, engaging in identity work that downplays certain issues, but also makes sure that some issues are discussed, as we see Kristina doing. Although she partly leaves it to the neurologist to bring up her issues, Kristina navigates the identity regulation embedded in the POHC in a way that is comfortable to her. Where she, in the past, left it completely up to the neurologist to initiate the conversation, she now gives stronger suggestions online for what she wants to discuss offline.

Discussion

Based on the excerpts analyzed above, we can conclude that patients' identity work is based on reflecting on what they post, how frequently and to whom. Their identity work is done in interaction with the identity regulation embedded in the care provision through POHCs. However, we find that the disrupting ways of working introduced by the POHC have blurred the regulation of their identities. Although the POHCs are supposed to lead to empowerment, patients' identity work does not automatically follow this identity regulation. Our analysis shows that the communication technology comes with ambiguous norms dictating that patients should provide more information, without asking more questions. Therefore, the material structure of the POHC also restricts patients' identity work because the website sends email alerts for certain postings (virtual meetings) and not for others (diary entries), patients make decisions about what and when to post based on the level of intrusiveness for health care professionals. Equally ambiguous is the norm that emotional elements (in patients' words 'complaining') should not appear in postings unless one explicitly includes humor into accounts of daily life. Lastly, the offline integration of online communication shows that by posting about certain topics online, patients create space for discussing these topics during the offline consultations. Although the online space seems to take away some barriers to address certain issues, there is a layer of ambiguity as the initiative to discuss those issues still remains with the health care professional.

The POHCs, being the vehicles through which this empowerment is supposed to be organized, present a new regulatory context. Regulation on POHCs is not done by an external actor (such as a secretary), as was the case before, but by the presence and design of the technology. This makes POHCs highly empowering at first sight (individuals are free to act as they wish) but it simultaneously creates a responsibility for the patient to become empowered. Phrased in theoretical terms, although some argue that such 'blurred lines' provide space for actively resisting restricting norms (Fleming 2007), we argue that in empowering contexts—where individuals are encouraged, but left to their own devices to become empowered—the idea of empowerment moves away from a 'right' that individuals possess to a 'duty' that they themselves are made partly responsible for. Therefore, we can theorize that identity regulation through POHCs in combination with patients' identity work produces a complex web where especially the responsibility for this empowerment becomes a site for contestation.

The contestation over responsibility for empowerment becomes clear through examining the increased ambiguity of patients' identity work. When using the POHCs, patients displayed identity work that often showed tensions, further substantiating the idea that identity work is not always aimed at developing a coherent self (Beech et al. 2016). The ambiguity is central to their identity of an 'empowered' patient; while patients work to become

more active, and use some of the options that the POHCs present to contact their health care professionals, patients also remain wary of bothering
their health care professionals 'too much.' As the regulation of what 'good
patients' do and are is disrupted by the introduction of the POHCs, incoherence, ambiguity and self-questioning became an integral part of patients'
identity work. Part of their identity work involved creative ways of embracing this ambiguity, for example by writing on the online communities about
experiences that the neurologist could later bring up for discussion in the
offline consultation room.

We want to emphasize that the introduction of POHCs is not merely
driven by 'humanistic' ideals of liberating patients from organizational
power processes. The other side of introducing the POHCs is one of
increased efficiency and cutting costs. Empowering patients through encouraging them to play an active, self-managing role in their care, is expected
to come with financial benefits. The limited research on empowerment at
the organizational level has argued that organizations saying they promote
'empowerment' need to be examined in light of neoliberalist ideals (Fleming and Sturdy 2009). Empowering discourses may merely mask new forms
of organizational control, ultimately aimed at further tying individuals to
organizations to increase profit (Fleming and Sturdy 2009; Fotaki 2006;
Ezzamel and Willmott 1998). From a neoliberalist standpoint, patients taking on some of the care may save professionals some time (and thus, money)
and may increase the quality of the care itself because it is explicitly adjusted
to the patients' individual needs and desires. Although we were specifically
interested in the micro-level of patients' identity work, this economic discourse, and its ties to neo-liberal celebrations of the individual and the
market (Gleadle, Cornelius and Pezet 2008), could provide an interesting
avenue for future research.

Lastly, we want to reflect on ways on moving forward with technology
in health care, as it seem inevitable that technology such as this will be part
of the future of health care provision, especially for management of chronic
illnesses. Chronic illness, and the frequent doctor and hospital visits that
might accompany it, do lend itself for some kind of technology implementation based on convenience. We noted that patients appreciated being able
to contact their health care professionals from their own space at times that
were convenient to them. This might create a sense of some empowerment
for patients, but we also feel we need to think beyond this 'convenience' to
address the other issues that we have raised in this chapter. We feel that it is
important to bring in the perspective of the health care professionals in as
well, because their practices help to (re)produce patients' roles. Although we
have no simple recipe for patients' empowerment, we recommend that users
of this technology (both health care professionals and patients) engage in an
open dialogue, to voice their expectations and wishes with regard to using
the system. As opposed to setting up user guidelines (which could be seen
as another, but strongly regulatory, alternative) such conversations could

create a space where both parties can express their ideal use of the communication technology. Although we have no illusions that such conversations are devoid of power, they might make each party more aware of the assumptions they hold about the abilities the other parties have in terms of using the technology. This dialogue might create innovative ways of managing care and supporting patients in the navigation of their chronic illness to ultimately have a more meaningful impact on patient empowerment.

Note

1. Previously, a patient would have to go through the process of contacting a secretary, setting up an appointment and ultimately talking to a health care professional over the phone or face-to-face at a time that was convenient for both.

References

Alvesson, Mats. 2010. *Interpreting Interviews*. London: Sage Publications.
Alvesson, Mats, Karen Lee Ashcraft, and Robyn Thomas. 2008. "Identity Matters: Reflections on the Construction of Identity Scholarship in Organization Studies." *Organization* 15 (1): 5–28.
Alvesson, Mats, and Hugh Willmott. 1996. *Making Sense of Management: A Critical Introduction*. London: Sage Publications.
Alvesson, Mats, and Hugh Willmott. 2002. "Identity Regulation as Organizational Control: Producing the Appropriate Individual." *Journal of Management Studies* 39 (5): 619–644.
Beech, Nic. 2011. "Liminality and the Practices of Identity Reconstruction." *Human Relations* 64 (2): 285–302.
Beech, Nic, Charlotte Gilmore, Paul Hibbert, and Sierk Ybema. 2016. "Identity-in-the-Work and Musicians' Struggles: The Production of Self-Questioning Identity Work." *Work, Employment & Society* 30 (3): 506–522.
Berwick, Donald M. 2009. "What 'Patient-Centered' Should Mean: Confessions of an Extremist." *Health Affairs* 28 (4): w555–w565.
Bishop, Tara F., Matthew J. Press, Jayme L. Mendelsohn, and Lawrence P. Casalino. 2013. "Electronic Communication Improves Access, But Barriers to Its Widespread Adoption Remain." *Health Affairs* 32 (8): 1361–1367.
Brown, Andrew D., and Christine Coupland. 2015. "Identity Threats, Identity Work and Elite Professionals." *Organization Studies* 36 (10): 1315–1336.
Carollo, Luca, and Marco Guerci. 2017. " 'Activists in a Suit': Paradoxes and Metaphors in Sustainability Managers' Identity Work." *Journal of Business Ethics* 148 (2):249–268.
Clarke, Caroline A., Andrew D. Brown, and Veronica Hope Hailey. 2009. "Working Identities? Antagonistic Discursive Resources and Managerial Identity." *Human Relations* 62 (3): 323–352.
Daskalaki, Maria, and Maria Simosi. 2018. "Unemployment as a liminoid Phenomenon: Identity Trajectories in Times of Crisis." *Human Relations* 71 (9):1153–1178.
Davies, Peter. 2012. "Should Patients Be Able to Control Their Own Records?" *British Medical Journal* 345: e4905.
Dedding, Christine, Roesja van Doorn, Lex Winkler, and Ria Reis. 2011. "How Will e-Health Affect Patient Participation in the Clinic? A Review of e-Health Studies

and the Current Evidence for Changes in the Relationship Between Medical Professionals and Patients." *Social Science & Medicine* 72 (1): 49–53.

Essers, Caroline, Hans Doorewaard, and Yvonne Benschop. 2013. "Family Ties: Migrant Female Business Owners Doing Identity Work on the Public—Private Divide." *Human Relations* 66 (12): 1645–1665.

Ezzamel, Mahmoud, and Hugh Willmott. 1998. "Accounting for Teamwork: A Critical Study of Group-Based Systems of Organizational Control." *Administrative Science Quarterly* 43 (2): 358–396.

Fairclough, Norman. 1993. "Critical Discourse Analysis and the Marketization of Public Discourse: The Universities." *Discourse & Society* 4 (2): 133–168.

Fleming, Peter. 2007. "Sexuality, Power and Resistance in the Workplace." *Organization Studies* 28 (2): 239–256.

Fleming, Peter, and Andrew Sturdy. 2009. "'Just Be Yourself!': Towards Neo-Normative Control in Organisations?" *Employee Relations* 31 (6): 569–583.

Fotaki, Marianna. 2006. "Choice Is Yours: A Psychodynamic Exploration of Health Policymaking and Its Consequences for the English National Health Service." *Human Relations* 59 (12): 1711–1744.

Gleadle, Pauline, Nelarine Cornelius, and Eric Pezet. 2008. "Enterprising Selves: How Governmentality Meets Agency." *Organization* 15 (3): 307–313.

Gotsi, Manto, Constantine Andriopoulos, Marianne W. Lewis, and Amy E. Ingram. 2010. "Managing Creatives: Paradoxical Approaches to Identity Regulation." *Human Relations* 63 (6): 781–805.

Hardy, Cynthia, and Sharon Leiba-O'Sullivan. 1998. "The Power Behind Empowerment: Implications for Research and Practice." *Human Relations* 51 (4): 451–483.

Henwood, Flis, Sally Wyatt, Angie Hart, and Julie Smith. 2003. "'Ignorance Is Bliss Sometimes': Constraints on the Emergence of the 'informed patient' in the Changing Landscapes of Health Information." *Sociology of Health & Illness* 25 (6): 589–607.

Kodner, Dennis L., and Cor Spreeuwenberg. 2002. "Integrated Care: Meaning, Logic, Applications, and Implications—A Discussion Paper." *International Journal of Integrated Care* 2: e12.

Krist, Alex H., and Steven H. Woolf. 2011. "A Vision for Patient-Centered Health Information Systems." *JAMA* 305 (3): 300–301.

ParkinsonNet. 2012. "MijnP@rkinsonZorg." Accessed December 13, 2012. www. parkinsonnet.nl/video's/parkinsonnet-video's/mijnp@rkinsonzorg.

Schwamm, Lee H. 2014. "Telehealth: Seven Strategies to Successfully Implement Disruptive Technology and Transform Health Care." *Health Affairs* 33 (2): 200–206.

Watson, Tony J. 2008. "Managing Identity: Identity Work, Personal Predicaments and Structural Circumstances." *Organization* 15 (1): 121–143.

Ybema, Sierk, Tom Keenoy, Cliff Oswick, Armin Beverungen, Nick Ellis, and Ida Sabelis. 2009. "Articulating Identities." *Human Relations* 62 (3): 299–322.

Zanoni, Patrizia, and Maddy Janssens. 2007. "Minority Employees Engaging with (Diversity)Management:AnAnalysisofControl,Agency,andMicro-Emancipation." *Journal of Management Studies* 44 (8): 1371–1397.

Section 3

Silent Voices

Making the Invisible Visible

One aim of diverse critical approaches and raising wicked problems for discussion is giving a hearing to silent voices and making visible unnoticed, and
even marginalized, and stigmatized, groups and their experiences. The third
section of the book is devoted to listening to these voices and comprehend-
ing how the approach to wicked problems can support taking these special
groups and particular experiences into account at the political level and in
everyday encounters. It is also questioned here if the approach to wicked
problems is just another way to marginalize.

Ruth Strudwick makes visible one of the marginalized cultures in health
care, the culture of blame among specialist radiographers within the NHS.
She illustrates how the blame culture is constructed and maintained at a
personal and cultural level. The blame culture turns out to be an unnoticed
wicked problem that has an impact on the safety and quality of services.
Kristina Brown's chapter continues the theme of uncovering hidden dynamics in a study of the darker side of interorganizational teams that draws
on social psychology to offer valuable insights into mandated groups. In
the third chapter Elizabeth Pyle, Deanna Grant-Smith and Robyn Mayes
give a voice to indigenous people by portraying the wickedness of the deficit discourse in Australia and Australian Indigenous Affairs policy. They
also raise the critical point of the risk of re-marginalizing when relying on
the discourse of wickedness. Will Thomas makes a stimulating contribution
to the discussion on making the invisible visible by critically exploring the
complexity of dependency, claiming that there is both necessary and unnecessary dependency. Scrutinizing the experiences of individuals with chronic
disease enriches the understanding of wicked problems.

9 Blame Culture in the National Health Service (NHS), UK

Ruth Strudwick

Introduction

The aim of the chapter is to discuss the 'wicked problem' of the culture of blame within the NHS.

This chapter outlines the theory and literature around the subject of blame culture and specifically blame culture in the NHS. The literature included will be papers that were written both before and after the Francis report, Keogh review and Berwick report (Francis 2013; Keogh 2013; Berwick 2013).

The phrase 'blame culture' comes from the author's doctoral thesis which was an ethnographic study of the culture in a diagnostic imaging department, researching the professional culture of diagnostic radiographers. It was evident from observing the behavior of the radiographers that there was an inherent culture around blame for mistakes or errors and the radiographers, along with their colleagues from other health care professions behaved in a specific way when an error or mistake occurred in practice. The behaviors associated with this were labeled as a sub-theme within the data from the thesis. This will be further explained later in the chapter.

A blame culture consists of a set of attitudes in an organization which is characterized by a lack of risk-taking or accepting responsibility for mistakes. This is often due to a fear of criticism and punishment.

This is a wicked problem. It does not appear to be a solvable problem, no matter what is done within the organization to try to change the culture, there is always some resistance. We are dealing with human beings, who by their very nature are fallible and make mistakes. It is also part of human nature to want to find someone to blame or to 'point the finger at.' Since the Francis report, Keogh review and Berwick report (Francis 2013; Keogh 2013; Berwick 2013), there have been attempts to make the culture more open and transparent within the NHS. The duty of candor is an important step toward ensuring the open, honest and transparent culture in the NHS (CQC 2015). However, the question is if this will make a difference long term. Processes and systems can be put in place to reduce errors and mistakes, but such systems cannot prevent errors and mistakes, they can only reduce the risks.

Many have tried to change the culture of a profession or organization, but few have succeeded. To transform the culture of a whole health care system like the UK NHS would be a complex, multilevel and uncertain process, it would take years (Scott et al. 2003). The problem is that the NHS has a recognizable overall identity and certain apparent core values, but within that overall 'NHS culture,' there are a number of distinct subcultures that can be discerned whose relationship to the overall organizational culture is hard to disentangle (Scott et al. 2003). There are multiple cultures within the NHS, there are different professions, different departments, different hospitals and different ways of doing things.

Ideally, there would be a learning culture within the NHS where human nature is acknowledged and mistakes or errors are learned from rather than a culture of blame.

However, due to its wicked nature, it is difficult to solve. By solving one part of the problem, you can end up making another worse. We can end up with litigation, professional rivalries, weakening of relationships between professionals and departments and people becoming scapegoats.

Problem-solving is not encouraged if there are too many systems are in place to follow, this makes the workplace rigid and inflexible, and, there-fore, people do not have the opportunity to think for themselves. Safeguards rely on human beings not messing up.

Within a culture of blame, reporting errors may result in a damaged pro-fessional image and self-confidence for the individual (Waring 2005). The author sees the health service as a competitive environment where error is seen as poor performance. When there is a blame culture and something goes wrong, those involved want to hold someone accountable. People working in such an environment often want to blame others in order to protect themselves. They may also worry about doing something wrong and the implications that this might have for them. There is a fear of being 'struck off'; don't 'mess up,' patients are involved, and there are peoples' lives at stake.

The risk from errors or mistakes is more significant in the NHS, as we are dealing with people whose lives could be at risk; there is risk of harm or even death. Professionals do not want to hurt, injure or kill people. It is more than just 'looking over your shoulder'; health care professionals don't want to mess up, so there is a temptation to cover up anything that shows mistakes have been made. Therefore, nobody learns from this.

Data from the author's doctoral research will be used to provide examples and illustrate blame culture in practice (Strudwick 2011).

The themes from the doctoral study can be seen in Figure 9.1.

There were four overarching themes from the doctoral study of the cul-ture within the diagnostic imaging department. These were: relationships with patients, relationships with colleagues, structure and environment, and characterizing the role of the diagnostic radiographer. Within the

Relationships with patients	Relationships with colleagues

Involvement with patients
Task focussed interactions
Time pressures and waiting times
Avoiding confrontation
Categorizing patients
	Use of dark humor
	Team working and communication
	  between diagnostic radiographers
	Interprofessional relationships
	Diagnostic radiographer—radiologist
	  relationships
	Discussion and storytelling
	Role modeling

Structure and environment	**Characterizing the role of the diagnostic radiographer**

Blame culture
Structure, organization, routine—the
  way things are done
Workflow
Behavior in different areas
	Visible product
	Diagnostic radiographers' views about
	  research, CPD and evidence-based
	  practice
	Extended role and barriers
	Dealing with radiation

Figure 9.1 The Overarching Concepts and Themes

overarching theme 'structure and environment,' 'blame culture' was the primary theme, upon which this chapter is focused. Examples from the thesis will be used to illustrate blame culture.

The issue of blame culture and how errors are managed in the NHS is not a new issue. However, in the past five years, three high-priority government reports have been published (Francis 2013; Keogh 2013; Berwick 2013). This recent catalogue of events, investigations and reports into the NHS has highlighted a lack of transparency and an underlying blame culture.

Whenever we talk about errors we tend to use emotive words or language such as; error, mistake, problem, blame, risk, harm and damage. All of these words have negative connotations and we associate them with something bad. Use of such emotive language has an effect on the way in which errors are understood.

This chapter will focus on one diagnostic imaging department and the culture and behavior amongst the diagnostic radiographers around blame and errors within this department using data from an ethnographic study. These findings can be extrapolated to the NHS as a whole when looking at workplace culture with respect to blame. In order to understand blame culture within a health care environment, we need to consider how safety is perceived.

Safety

The notion of safety is important within all societies and cultures. Safety of others, particularly those entrusted to your care transcends all cultures (Clawson and Vinson 1978; Cieciuch, Schwartz and Vecchione 2013). This is a key consideration in health care where patient safety is the responsibility of the health care professional. Edwards, Davey and Armstrong (2013) suggest that safety is a state in which individuals are protected from the likelihood of harm. The World Health Organisation (WHO 2009) takes the safety concept further when considering safety within health care, suggesting that safety is the prevention of errors and adverse effects to patients. This implies that errors and adverse effects may be prevented and that these errors or adverse effects have outcomes for those involved (Wachter 2012). Safety, it could be argued then becomes a personal, social and also a professional value for health care professionals.

Health care providers have an obligation to ensure that patients are kept safe by managing their environment; this involves carrying out risk assessments, having a reporting system for errors and mistakes and ensuring that their staff are trained and are competent (CQC 2016). Senior management commitment is essential for a positive 'safety culture.' If a positive 'safety culture' is in place then errors are expected, and when an error occurs, there should not be individual blame but instead an investigation into why systems fail. A positive 'safety culture' is the direct opposite of a blame culture.

Information From the Literature

Radiography or, more specifically, radiographic imaging, involves the use of ionizing radiation, in the form of X-rays, which have the potential to cause harm. The biological effects of ionizing radiation are widely known about. There are risks, both deterministic and stochastic associated with the use of ionizing radiation to image patients. Although rare, patients can suffer radiation induced skin injuries (Rehani and Srimahachota 2011). Also, there have been some reported errors in Computed Tomography (CT) which have resulted in patients having skin reddening and hair loss (US Food and Drug Administration 2010).

In recognition of this potential for harm, the International Commission on Radiological Protection (ICRP) requires three principles to underpin radiographic practice: i) justification—there must be a valid reason for the examination which will impact on the patient's treatment or management, ii) optimization and iii) limitation of the radiation dose (ICRP 2007; Boyd 2012). Patients expect the diagnostic radiographer to be knowledgeable about their role, and they should have trust and confidence in the radiographer.

It is in this area of the practice that the diagnostic radiographer works. They are made aware during their training about the risks associated with the use of ionizing radiation, and mistakes are perceived to be dangerous and also poor practice.

There is very little in the way of literature regarding blame culture within the profession of radiography. Mayles (2003) wrote a commentary about the culture in radiotherapy, and points out that radiographers need correct training in the use of X-rays to reduce the potential for harm but he feels that a blame culture still exists within the NHS with regard to radiation incidents. Fitzgerald (2001) concurred with this in his literature review about errors in radiology. He indicates high levels of error within radiology and outlines the overall blame culture within the NHS.

> While the traditional medical culture of personal responsibility and autonomy of action has certain strengths, it has led to a belief that mistakes should not be made, and that they are indicative of personal and professional failure.
>
> (Fitzgerald 2001, 938)

This makes health care professionals anxious about errors and consequently increases their feeling of guilt should they make a mistake. However, Fitzgerald (2001) points out that "errors fall into recurrent patterns" (p 938), and, therefore, error traps need to be uncovered in order to prevent similar mistakes in the future. This can be seen in the way that the media reacts to situations where they see that blame can be attributed. For example, any perceived error or story of a poor service within the NHS receives high profile coverage. It appears that the media just want to blame, and not understand and learn from the situation. This was evident with the Staffordshire Enquiry (Francis 2013).

Rix, Crane and Severs (2003) also comment that there is a lot of repetition of errors in the NHS in their communication about a radiographic incident. They outline two approaches to reviewing an incident: a person-centered or systems approach. The person-centered approach focuses on failings and weaknesses of the individual and fosters a culture of blame. The systems approach accepts that individuals make mistakes and tries to counteract these by systems and procedures. Writing in 2003, they state that there is still a perception amongst NHS staff that a person-centered blame culture is present. They feel that one of the major cultural barriers to the system approach is professional and group allegiances.

Waring (2005) explored the attitudes of medical physicians toward adverse incident reporting in health care and looked at inhibiting factors or barriers to participation in such reporting. He found that there was a reticence among doctors to be open and honest about their errors and believed this was due to them having a 'deep-seated assumption' that they would be 'found out' and would be held personally responsible for any mistake that they had made and be punished.

This assumption may also be true for other professions, and very little has changed since these papers were written in 2003 or 2005. There still appear to be professional allegiances where professionals protect colleagues from their own profession.

A person-centered approach, where the individual involved is blamed rather than focussing on the system or procedure is a pattern of behavior which can be observed and copied by others. This is an example of learned behavior (O'Reilly 2005).

Study Design

It is important to understand the context in which the following data were collected which comes from the methods used in the study. The data discussed comes from an ethnographic study of the culture in a diagnostic imaging department (Strudwick 2011).

The study began with four months of participant observation with the department. The author observed diagnostic radiographers working in practice. The departmental and professional culture was observed and explored. The observations continued until saturation point was reached. After this, semi-structured interviews were carried out with ten key informants.

The observational notes and the interview transcripts were analyzed to elicit themes. The transcripts were scrutinized by the researcher and labeling of text was carried out; these labels were used to form themes from the data.

Results

One of the key themes that arose from the data, under the overarching theme of 'structure and environment,' was that of blame culture. It was felt by the researcher that many of the behaviors in the department were influenced by the overriding blame culture within the NHS. There appeared to be a culture of being worried about making a mistake or doing something that might need to be dealt with by 'management.' Some of the behaviors that were observed lead to this belief by the researcher. Radiographers were concerned on a daily basis about waiting times; they did not like it when patients had to wait for their examination or were late for their appointment time. The radiographers were concerned that there would be 'breaches' to waiting times and this would reflect badly on their department. Radiographers apologized to patients on a regular basis and they tried to avoid any complaints from or confrontations with patients. Complaints from patients and from other staff were frequently discussed, as there was a fear amongst the radiographers about having a complaint made against an individual. Radiographers were worried about this and also about how it might be dealt with by 'management.' There was pressure to 'perform' and not to make any mistakes, but also to do the work as quickly as possible in order to reduce waiting times.

Two incidents were observed in the department where blame for error was discussed.

> A member of staff from the intensive therapy unit (ITU) came to the imaging department to find out who had X-rayed a particular patient. All of the radiographers were immediately defensive in case they had

done something wrong, or that their images weren't optimal. Actually the patient had tuberculosis (TB) and the nurse wanted to arrange for the radiographers he had come into contact with to be screened. After this one radiographer discussed with me the whole 'feeling of guilt' idea further and said that as a profession we can be quite defensive, always worrying about what we have done wrong and worried about the consequences, when we should be happy to admit that we are human and sometimes we make mistakes, but move on from it.

(Observation 13/8/08)

It was interesting that the radiographers reacted in this way initially and were immediately on the defensive; they were worried that there was a complaint coming. It seemed that their reaction was learned behavior from previous incidents. The radiographers appeared to be concerned primarily that other professionals had a problem with their work. This 'feeling of guilt' seemed prevalent amongst the radiographers in this department.

The second incident occurred a week later.

There was a machine fault and the patient was exposed to an unnecessary dose of radiation. The radiographers discussed how they felt about this and how guilty they felt.

(Observation 20/8/08)

Once again there was a defensive reaction from the radiographers involved. Guilt was one of the feelings expressed. Each time it seemed that the radiographers involved were personally taking the blame. The radiographer using the equipment at the time came across as feeling particularly guilty, even though the incident was proven to be due to an equipment fault, and it was not the radiographer's error. This illustrates how the 'finger pointing' culture operates: there needs to be someone responsible, so either you take the blame or someone else is blamed. However, there was also a lack of safety here, and so the researcher feels that this made the situation worse and the radiographers were concerned that they had not afforded the patient the protection that they should have given them from harm. These two observed incidents support the findings in the literature (Mayles 2003; Waring 2005).

The radiographers involved on these two occasions appeared to take the blame for what had happened and continually 'beat themselves up' about it. The second incident, where there was a machine fault, was mentioned several times by staff members during the days that followed, and each time it was discussed, the radiographer involved was mentioned when discussing the incident, as if it was their fault. This follows the person-centered approach where the focus is on the failings of the individual. It seemed that the radiographers felt it necessary to blame someone and to take on the responsibility for what had happened. They needed someone to 'carry the can.'

So why is it that the radiology department and the wider NHS still seem to foster a blame culture and look to blame the individual? It appears that people like to have someone to blame, rather than blaming the system. Bauman (2001), in his book entitled *The Individualised Society*, says that people find it easier to blame one person than society or the system.

This could be due to previous experiences of incidents and the way in which they were dealt with by both colleagues and managers. Hogg, Hogg and Bentley (2007) in their paper about leadership in radiography suggest that this culture is changing and that gradually, a 'no blame culture' is being engendered. However, they also acknowledge that mistakes can still lead to punishment rather than learning, resulting in perpetuation of traditionalism and hierarchy which will hold back progress within the profession of radiography. Socialization is seen to be the cause of blame culture in that individuals become socialized into a pattern of behavior through their experiences (Guimond, Begin and Palmer 1989).

This blame culture was discussed further with the radiographers during a quiet period.

> Blame culture and admitting to mistakes was discussed. One of the radiographers brought up the machine fault from last week as the feeling of guilt remained. The other radiographers reassured this radiographer that it was not their fault, although admitted that if it was them they would still be worried about what had happened. We also discussed the filling in of incident forms. The radiographers seemed to be worried about how an incident form would reflect on their practice and also the consequences for them of filling out the form and how it might be handled by management.
>
> (Observation 29/8/08)

The radiographers appeared to behave in this way regarding the incidents observed because they were worried about how these incidents might reflect badly on them. French (2004) in an article about occupational stress amongst therapy radiographers identifies the 'potential to make errors' as a source of stress for radiographers. She says that this is due to the acute awareness amongst radiographers of the damaging effects of X-rays if an error is made. It seems that this potential to make a mistake coupled with how this might reflect on the staff is a concern amongst diagnostic radiographers and has become a part of the culture, so much so that radiographers are anxious about anything that could be seen as an error in their work. This would explain the reaction of the radiographers to the nurse from ITU where they became very defensive about their work.

It seemed that the culture within this department fostered concern about errors, mistakes, complaints and things going wrong. This resulted in the radiographers becoming worried and anxious. There appeared to be an overall feeling of guilt amongst the radiographers, particularly when it came to keeping patients waiting. One of the radiographers expressed this in their interview.

> I hate it when I'm late and you keep well you just think that if that was you in the waiting room 'cause somehow when you come for an appointment you do kind of get resigned to the fact that you're gonna be kept waiting but when you see other people going in and out you just get really really agitated and what only might be a couple of minutes seems like forever doesn't it? So I do find that pressure quite hard sometimes and I just don't like the thought that if it was me sat there I wouldn't like it. I do usually try and explain especially if you can pick up that someone's getting agitated and I always apologise when they come in because if you don't they're gonna get aggressive.
>
> (Interview with radiographer)

The radiographer said that the pressure of the demands on the service and keeping patients waiting was hard to deal with and felt that apologies to patients were necessary. This was linked to blame in that radiographers did not wish to be reprimanded if a patient made a complaint.

This feeling of personal guilt and the need to apologize was also talked about by another radiographer.

> [T]here is a lot going on it's a very busy department and um and you know we all are under pressure you know to again uphold the service to the patients.
>
> (Interview with radiographer)

This radiographer obviously felt that the service provided by the department was their responsibility as a radiographer and felt under pressure to ensure that the service provided was a good one.

This was also observed in the department.

> Radiographers say that they are fed up with apologising to patients about the long wait this afternoon.
>
> (Observation 11/11/08)

The culture within the department extended to the first author who also experienced personal guilt. On one occasion, this was written in the observational notes.

> There is only one radiographer left in this part of the department, the others are off at tea break or busy. I wish I could help out, I have a feeling of guilt as I am not able to help, and this is not why I am here.
>
> (Observation 17/11/08)

Performance measurement	Patient safety	Public perception
Speed of work and throughput	Radiation dose	Press
Accuracy of work	Patient injury	Reputation
Quality of work		
Management intervention		
Regulator and being 'struck off'		

Figure 9.2 Factors Influencing the Radiographer's Perception of Blame

It seems that this feeling of guilt is part of the culture within the radiography profession and influences behavior.

From the data, it appears that in the NHS at the time this study was undertaken, there was still an underlying culture of blame, and that the staff members conform to expected patterns of behavior. This includes how errors and mistakes are accounted for, and how the staff members feel about a less than perfect service for their patients. The radiographers in this department considered delays and long waiting times to be poor service. So, this culture of blame continues to exist within the organization of the NHS.

This can be defined as a wicked problem due to all of the influencing factors at play; see Figure 9.2.

Discussion

So there is evidence of a blame culture in the data derived from this one center. The literature suggests that this is something that has come from the dominant medical profession (Waring 2005). The radiography profession was and is still to some extent a profession which fits in to the professional hierarchy below medicine. This culture of blame also comes from the responsibility that comes from dealing with radiation on a daily basis; and from the inherent risks, safety considerations and potential for harm that can occur due to errors. Whatever the source, it is clear that a culture of blame still exists within this department and that radiographers appear to seek for an individual to blame or take the blame themselves.

It also may be that the blame culture and attitude toward blame and error comes from the way in which the NHS is viewed by the public via the media. The NHS is constantly being criticized by the media. A lot of this criticism is about failure to meet targets and minimum standards expected by the public. There have also been high profile incidents that included some form of cover up, such as the Bristol Royal Infirmary Inquiry (Kennedy 2001), and when the public reads these cover-up stories in the press, it might well influence them to believe that NHS staff are involved in cover up. This could result in NHS staff being reluctant to report errors for fear of punishment or being personally blamed. Radiography, like all public professions, is tightly regulated, and any poor or malpractice is dealt with by the regulator, the Health and Care Professions Council. Radiographers can be removed or 'struck off' from the professional register for a short period of time or indefinitely if their error is deemed to be serious enough.

The feeling of guilt appears to be linked to this culture in that radiographers seem to take personal responsibility for issues such as waiting times, patient complaints and equipment breakdown. Their way of dealing with these issues was to apologize to the patients in the hope that a complaint would not follow. They seemed to be concerned about their own reputation, the reputation of their profession and the reputation of the department.

A systems approach to errors is needed to shift the balance. A systems approach accepts that people have the potential to make mistakes. Attention focusses to incorporating systems to reduce the potential for error, e.g. in order to ensure that the correct patient is having the correct X-ray examination the radiographer has to check three forms of identity: full name, date of birth and first line of address. This should reduce the chances of the incorrect patient being imaged and is a system to reduce errors. Attention is focused on human behavior in relation to the workplace context (Wachter 2012). The workplace as a whole, the team and the different individuals are all examined to understand where mistakes could occur (Reason 2000; Vincent 2010).

In a systems approach, the focus shifts from individual culpability and blame to exploring what can be done within the system to prevent the errors and also learn for the future. Analysis of incidents in this way has revealed in many settings that a chain of events can be triggered which results in an unintended outcome (Vincent, Taylor-Adams and Stanhope 1998). In this systems investigation of errors, it is anticipated that there would be a more fair and transparent system which supports reporting of incidents and concerns (Dolansky et al. 2013). This can only occur if there is a shift in culture from blaming individuals to supporting openness.

Since the implementation of clinical governance in the late 1990s (DH 1997), a no blame culture should have emerged within the NHS. Clinical governance aimed to improve the quality of NHS services and safeguard high standards (Scally and Donaldson 1998). The series of high profile failures and errors in the NHS reported in the 1990s threatened to undermine public confidence in the NHS. Since the late 1990s the National Institute for Health and Care Excellence (NICE) and the National Service Frameworks (NSFs) have been important in setting quality standards within the NHS. The Commission for Health Improvement (CHI) has also been instrumental in inspecting clinical governance within NHS organizations. Along with the NHS Plan, NICE, CHI and professional regulatory bodies have sought to improve the quality of the service provided to patients by setting performance targets. Then, in 2008, Lord Darzi's report (DH 2008) looked at the quality of the service provided to patients along with maintaining performance targets.

It is in this current climate of bureaucracy, with accountability and targets that the NHS sits. From the results of this study, it seems that professionals still have a fear and a reluctance to report errors that may damage their own reputation or that of their colleagues and bring down the standing of their department.

More recently, there have been three high-profile government reports (Francis 2013; Keogh 2013; Berwick 2013). This recent catalogue of events, investigations and reports into the NHS has highlighted a lack of transparency and an underlying blame culture.

Conclusion

It appears, from the doctoral study carried out in one department, that diagnostic radiographers foster a culture of blame. The radiographers in this department appeared to take the blame for any errors or anything that was not as good as it could be. While it is important to acknowledge that none of us is perfect and that mistakes do happen, we need to be aware that fostering a blame culture does not help us to move forward.

Utilizing a systems approach should result in reduced attribution of blame to individuals and a review of systems, policies and procedures. This review should help to prevent future errors and improve the care patients receive.

A systems approach acknowledges that individuals do make mistakes but policies and procedures need to be robust enough to reduce the impact of these mistakes. Adoption of a systems approach should also reduce the feeling of guilt and personal responsibility which appeared to be evident amongst the radiographers in this study.

Garner (2014) suggests that lessons need to be shared and patterns of events and errors publicized in the wider NHS. The lack of learning from mistakes within diagnostic radiography leads to the blame culture seen within this study. All health care professionals need to be supported to report errors, incidents and near misses without fear of blame or repercussions. In this way trends and common errors can be recorded and then learned from. This will result in greater safety, improvements in practice, better systems, more openness and transparency and a better-quality service.

How can this be done? This is, indeed, a 'wicked problem,' as there are so many contributing and influencing factors. The organizational culture within the NHS is complex. The current state of austerity measures, coupled with the climate of bureaucracy, with accountability and targets in the NHS does not assist in conquering this problem.

References

Bauman, Zygmunt. 2001. *The Individualised Society*. Cambridge: Wiley-Blackwell.
Berwick, Don. 2013. *A Promise to Learn—A Commitment to Act: Improving the Safety of Patients in England*. London: NHS.

Boyd, Mary Ann. 2012. "A Regulatory Perspective on Whether the System of Radiation Protection Is Fit for Purpose." *Annals of the ICRP* 41 (3–4): 57–63.

Cieciuch, Jan, Shalom H. Schwartz, and Michele Vecchione. 2013. "Applying the Refined Values Theory to Past Data: What Can Researchers Gain?" *Journal of Cross-Cultural Psychology* 44 (8): 1215–1234.

Clawson, C. Joseph, and Donald E. Vinson. 1978. "Human Values: A Historical and Interdisciplinary Analysis in Hunt Kent and Abor Ann (eds.)." *NA-Advances in Consumer Research* 5: 396–402.

CQC. 2015. "Regulation 20: Duty of Candour." Accessed May 2018. www.cqc.org.uk/sites/default/files/20150327_duty_of_candour_guidance_final.pdf.

CQC. 2016. "The Fundamental Standards." Accessed May 2017. www.cqc.org.uk/content/fundamental-standards.

DH. 1997. *The New NHS*. London: HMSO.

DH. 2008. *High Quality Care for All*. London: HMSO.

Dolansky, Mary A., Kalina Druschel, Maura Helba, and Kathleen Courtney. 2013. "Nursing Student Medication Errors: A Case Study Using Root Cause Analysis." *Journal of Professional Nursing* 29 (2): 102–108.

Edwards, Jason R. D., Jeremy Davey, and Kerry Armstrong. 2013. "Returning to the Roots of Culture: A Review and Re-Conceptualisation of Safety Culture." *Safety Science* 55: 70–80.

Fitzgerald, Richard. 2001. "Error in Radiology." *Clinical Radiology* 56: 938–946.

Francis, Robert. 2013. *The Report of the Mid Staffordshire NHS Foundation Trust Public Enquiry*. London: The Stationary Office.

French, Helen C. 2004. "Occupational Stresses and Coping Mechanisms of Therapy Radiographers—A Qualitative Approach." *Journal of Radiotherapy in Practice* 4: 13–24.

Garner, Jane. 2014. "Some Thoughts and Responses to the Francis Report." *Psychoanalytic Psychotherapy* 28 (2): 211–219.

Guimond, Serge, Guy Begin, and Douglas L. Palmer. 1989. "Education and Causal Attributions: The Development of 'Person-Blame' and 'System-Blame' Ideology." *Social Psychology Quarterly* 52 (2) (June): 126–140.

Hogg, Peter, Diane Hogg, and Brian Bentley. 2007. "Leadership in the Development of the Radiographic Profession." *Imaging and Oncology*: 54–60.

ICRP. 2007. "The 2007 Recommendations of the International Commission on Radiological Protection: ICRP Publication 103." *Annals of the ICRP* 37: 2–4.

Kennedy, Ian. 2001. *The Report of the Public Inquiry into Children's Heart Surgery at the Bristol Royal Infirmary 1984–1995: Learning from Bristol*. London: HMSO.

Keogh, Bruce. 2013. *Review into the Quality of Care and Treatment Provided by 14 Hospital Trusts in England*. London: NHS.

Mayles, W. P. M. 2003. "Commentary—Changing the Culture in Radiotherapy." *The British Journal of Radiology* 76: 587–589.

O'Reilly, Karen. 2005. *Ethnographic Methods*. London: Routledge.

Reason, James. 2000. "Huma Error: Models and Management." *BMJ* 320: 768–770.

Rehani, Madan M., and Suphot Srimahachota. 2011. "Skin Injuries in Interventional Procedures." *Radiation Protection Dosimetry* 147 (1–2) (September): 8–12.

Rix, Richard, Sue Crane, and Martin Severs. 2003. "A Case of Mistaken Identity." *Radiography* 9: 63–66.

Scally, Gabriel, and Liam J. Donaldson. 1998. "Clinical Governance and the Drive for Quality Improvement in the New NHS in England." *BMJ* 37: 61–65.

Scott, Tim, Russell Mannion, Hugh T. O. Davies, and Martin N. Marshall. 2003. "Implementing Culture Change in Health Care: Theory and Practice." *International Journal for Quality in Health Care* 15 (2) (1 March): 111–118.

Strudwick, Ruth M. 2011. "An Ethnographic Study of the Culture in a Diagnostic Imaging Department (DID)." DProf thesis, unpublished, University of Salford.

US Food and Drug Administration. 2010. "Safety Investigation of CT Brain Perfusion Scans: Update 11/09/2010." Accessed December 2017. http://wayback. archive-it.org/7993/20170111092743/www.fda.gov/MedicalDevices/Safety/ AlertsandNotices/ucm185898.htm.

Vincent, Charles. 2010. *Patient Safety*, 2nd ed. Hoboken: Wiley-Blackwell.

Vincent, Charles, Sally Taylor-Adams, and Nicola Stanhope. 1998. "Framework for Analysing Risk and Safety in Clinical Medicine." *BMJ* 316: 1154.

Wachter, Robert M. 2012. *Understanding Patient Safety*, 2nd ed. New York: McGraw-Hill.

Waring, Justin J. 2005. "Beyond Blame: Cultural Barriers to Medical Incident Reporting." *Social Science and Medicine* 60: 1927–1935.

WHO. 2009. "The Conceptual Framework for the International Classification for Patient Safety." Version 1.1, Technical Annex 2, Glossary of Patient Safety Concepts and References. WHO.

10 A Darker Side to Interorganizational Relations

Kristina Brown

Introduction

This chapter explores the darker side to mandated interorganizational relations, specifically mandated groups, in health and social care integration and the basic social processes that are at play. Provan' (2008) defintion of the darker side being the processes or behaviours which can leave members feeling disempowered and isolated, creating suspicion, conflict and distrust and being pressured into behavior they do not fully support, is used to highlight where instances of this may occur in mandated inter-organizational relations. I use the case study of a Health and Wellbeing Board in the North East of England, UK, as an example of a mandated interorganizational relation, which brings together health and social care system leaders and democratic representatives to influence the integration of health and social care provision. Given that there is little attention placed on the difference between voluntary and mandated forms of interorganizational relations, specifically, how the interactions in mandated interorganizational relations differ from the interactions in voluntary interorganizational relations, this study explored the gap and identified a darker side to the interactions that take place. The findings presented within this chapter are based on 12 months of observations of the North East Health and Wellbeing Board meetings and 25 qualitative interviews with the board members. Taking a social psychological perspective, a small insight is offered which considers the group processes exerted on members to identify with a group they have been mandated to join and become cohesive with. It further argues that mandating individuals to conform to group norms results in a discord with certain group process normally used to explain the workings of groups in interorganizational relations, such as group membership, social identity theory, cohesion and pluralistic ignorance, which results in wicked behavior. These group processes are associated with social psychology and organizational psychology and have explored interorganizational relations, but are yet to explore group processes in mandated interorganizational relations or to explore whether a darker side to these processes might exist. This chapter has the significant potential to contribute to the literature on groups, mandated interorganizational relations and the darker side of interorganizational relations.

Mandated Interorganizational Relations

Despite the considerable attention that has been paid to interorganizational relations in health and social care integration and in particular the analysis of partnership and collaborative working, the exploration of interorganizational relations as a condition of mandate, has received little attention. That is, the extant research literature has largely ignored the prominent role that mandate has in mobilizing interorganizational relations and the implications this has on its processes (Vaughan, 2011; Brummel, Nelson and Jakes, 2012; Guro, Cook and Kirchhoff, 2018). The implications of such a study are important, as they have a direct bearing in explaining the ways in which groups function under these conditions and may advance the discussion on why current arrangements in interorganizational arrangements are ineffective in solving wicked issues in health and social care (Hunter et al. 2011, Cook, Mulherin, and Seditas, 2015).

Mandated forms of interorganizational relations are now a significant policy tactic of most governments, especially in the UK (Ranade and Hudson, 2003; Dickinson and Glasby, 2010; Humphries, 2013). Generally, there is a growing consensus that organizations need to work together to integrate funding and resources for a better health for the population (Clarke and Glendinning, 2002; Glendinning, Dowling, and Powell, 2005; Perkins, Smith, Hunter, Bambra, and Joyce, 2012). Policy mandated interorganizational relations in health and social care are mostly triggered by a constant and growing demand on public finances, more recently with an aging population and poverty rates and wicked issues growing over the last decade (Baggott, 2013; Runer, Salway, Mir, Ellison, Skinner, Carter and Bostan, 2013). There appears to be no contra-argument from any stakeholder regarding the integration of funding and resources that leads to a reduction of health inequalities and a better life chance for all. The concept of integrating the two areas of care has been a popular choice of policy for labor, conservative and coalition governments as well as the organizations and statutory bodies directly involved in the provision and commissioning of care. So why is it, that when the belief in the principle of integration is so strong, that the behavior in mandated interorganizational relations, specifically mandated intergroup membership can act to the contrary, with interorganizational behavior showing a 'dark side' involving conflict and secrecy as opposed to harmony and transparency?

There are many excellent reviews documenting efforts to integrate the provision health and social across sectors, disciplines and professions (Evans, 2004; Peckham, 2007; Smith, Bambra, Joyce, Perkins and Blenkinsopp, 2009; Hunter and Perkins, 2014). While many of these reviews focus on the form or purpose of the interorganizational relation *per se* (i.e. partnership, collaboration, network etc.), with a notable exception in the literature being the impetus for it, such as are the memberships of these interorganizational relations voluntary, with members gravitating to each other as a result of a sense of shared organizational social identity, or are these relations a consequence of 'a mandate,' where members will be expected to act as a group that shares a social identity without necessarily having this conceptual element.

Studies examining where interorganizational relations are mandated traditionally find these types interrelations in areas of social issues, such as health and social care, environments, planning, education etc. In health and social care mandates to interact usually come from a higher authority such as government or a statuary agency which often leaves little room to negotiate guidelines and implementation at the local level (Taylor and Schweitzer 2005; Ivery 2008; Genskow 2009). With this kind of mandated top-down approach, interorganizational members are at risk from disowning policy objectives, unable to take complete ownership of something decided for them which in some studies has shown the effect on outcomes as being poor and short-lived (Gray 1989; Yaffee and Wondolleck 2000; Brummel et al. 2010). Studies examining who is more likely to benefit from mandating interorganizational relations and how have identified mandated networks as enjoying benefits such as the opportunity to raise important issues, the transfer of knowledge and skills to have a more reaching impact on issues at stake and the opportunity to network with members they might never have interacted with (Ivery 2008). Such benefits are indeed noteworthy particularly when the main goals is to improve life chances and outcomes, but even these outcomes can be deterred if governing arrangements are not varied throughout the mandated relations to account for the individual identities and ways of working that members bring to the party (Rodríguez et al. 2007). Such information is useful to inform our understanding of these relations and how they work, as too little attention is placed on the difference between voluntary and mandated interorganizational relations to understand if interactions differ as a direct consequence of this (McNamara 2015). For this reason, exploring the process that can play a key role in mandated interorganizational relations can inform our understanding of why 'mandatedness' might put the interrelation at risk from a darker side of organizational behavior.

Interorganizational Groups

Groups and group working account for the majority of efforts to integrate funding and service provision in health and social care both locally and globally. While individual organizational circumstances and characteristics play an important part, an interorganizational relation is above all, a group phenomenon (Goldman, Giles and Hogg 2014). Because the interaction of individual and group processes is important in understanding all forms of interorganizational groups, exploring these group process can help build an understanding of the behavior in mandated groups and why this is at times observed as having a 'dark side' to group behavior. Part of the reason for a void in our understanding is that there is much less known about the processes that occur within groups when organizations inter-relate with each on a mandated as opposed to voluntary basis. A recent exploration of a mandated interorganizational group in health and social care integration highlighted group behavior that could point toward darker side of interorganizational relations.

> It's one of those groups where I don't think a decision was ever made, naively when I went into it I thought, right okay, this is a group where you need to go in and say what you think about health, but it was a group where you went into that had made this decision and that what was done and that's the type of group it was. The decision-making took place outside of those groups and it either took place in the silos or collectively on the health and social care integration stuff that fed into it—so there was no decision made really that was the sad thing about it.
>
> (Health and Wellbeing Board Member)

As the above quote illustrates, some of the group processes, such as decision-making, can take place outside of group boundaries, which can have an effect on other group processes, in particular, group membership. This view of group working is inconsistent with the dominant theoretical and empirical view in the literature, which depicts group working as necessary to address 'wicked issues' and where much faith is placed in a multi-agency group response even though the 'assumption that they lead to better outcomes is at best unproven' (Glasby and Dickinson 2008). The emphasis here is on the faith in forms of group working. In addition, this dominant view in the literature considers theoretical explanations and empirical solutions based on voluntary and compliant forms of group working, which are inadequate to explain the processes and interorganizational relations of groups formed on a mandated basis.

Group membership in health and social care integration work is already an integral part of organizational existence. Empirical studies refer to a broad spectrum of interorganizational arrangements, such as strategic alliances (Berlderbos et al. 2011; Albers et al. 2013; Yang et al. 2014), cross-sector partnerships (Bryson and Crosby 2006; Koschmann and Pfarrer 2012; Vangen et al. 2014), networks (Operti and Carnabuchi 2011; Jenssen 2013; Ozmel and Gulatti 2013) and joint ventures (Sun and Lee 2013; Zhao et al. 2013), which provide group membership and working across organizations. Groups also provide members with identities which will define who they are within that group, their attitudes, beliefs and behaviors (Wood 2014). Interorganizational groups within health and social care are groups that have been shown to provide members with positive elements such as innovation in service delivery methods, changing goal perception of partners, creating shared meaning across a diverse membership and the potential for social learning (Shannon 2001; Isett and Provan 2005; Hodges et al. 2003; Rodriguez et al. 2007; Ivery 2008; Brummel et al. 2010; Lewis et al. 2008; Provan and Lemiere 2012). However, they have also been shown to promote inclusiveness, selected membership, self-appointed leadership and imposable governance mechanisms, which can leave members feeling disempowered and isolated, creating suspicion, conflict and distrust and being pressured into behavior they do not fully support, more recently labeled as the darker side of organizational group behavior (Provan 2008). Currently there is little research which attempts to explore the group processes that underpin the darker side of interorganizational group membership and despite the growing recognition that mandated groups are now an established part of health and social care integration work, little is known about these specific processes and how they influence social cognition in individual members and group behavior. Aside from the gap in the knowledge, understanding the darker side to group working is essential if our research is to provide support to health and social car practitioners understand the influence mandating membership can have on group outcomes. The rest of this chapter aims to provide an insight into how certain group processes such as social identity theory, cohesion and pluralistic ignorance can function in darker ways when group membership is mandated as opposed to voluntary. The theoretical constructs that are discussed in this chapter are by no means exhaustive and there is no attempt to suggest that this gives a comprehensive view, instead the aim is to provide an outline of some of the processes that underpin mandated group working and the role that they can play in that darker side.

Wicked Issues and the Darker Side of Organizational Issues

Metaphors such as the 'dark side' of organizational behavior are used to define the more negative processes or outcomes of organization behavior such as misconduct, scandals (Stein 2007), aggressive and violent behavior (Liefooghe and Davey 2010), unethical behavior (Sullivan, Haunschild and Page 2007) and domination and oppression (Westheafer 2000). In other words, the dark side of organizational behavior spans the evil aspects of organizing or the negative consequences to people and outcomes as a result of collective action. There is no distinction in the literature as to the dark side of organizational behavior and the dark of interorganizational behavior, and although there is considerable overlap between these terms, this is not enough to argue that differences do not matter, however subtle or nuanced they are.

Generally, the dark side of wicked issues within the health and social care interorganizational literature is usually external and contextual, referring to the long-term, social, economic, environmental and intractable problems that exist within local communities (Murphy 2013). The organizational equivalent of external wicked issues, conceptualizes the dark side as abusive behavior such as harassment, aggression, mistreatment, victimization, mobbing and bullying (direct or indirect) which has been approached from the pathological side of the employee (Mills 2011). However, the evidence in this study suggests that wicked issues and a dark side exist internally, within the collective leadership and management of external wicked issues and not just from the lived experiences of employees. One of the key reasons for this is that organizations as entities, provide multiple opportunities for interorganizational relations that can bring both intended and unintended consequences (Mills 2011). Where this collective action is mandated, there is a potential that the actions and behaviors of the individual organizations will be constrained, either in the freedom that they have to influence the decisions of the group or the level of transparency they must display toward group members. The result of this is manifestations of dark behavior at the intragroup level to resist the constraint to individual organizational action that a policy mandate can impose. The following sections show how the dark side of interorganizational behavior can be manifest at the intra level through the social processes of group membership, social identity theory, cohesion and pluralistic ignorance.

Group Membership

Although individuals within organizations are not defined by their group membership alone, the importance that members can attach to being part of a group and the way in which constructs part of their organizational identity from it is well documented (Tajfel and Turner 1979; Tajfel and Turner 1986). Groups in health and social care form because they offer organizations something they want or need, such as the increased potential to achieve strategic outcomes, share resources, reduce transaction costs or participate in and influence decisions usually outside of their own organizational boundaries (Levine, Prosser, Evans, and Reicher, 2005; Dyer and Hatch 2007; Capaldo 2014; Wood 2014). The research on voluntary interorganizational relations show that groups offer membership to individuals that are responsible for problems or issues, affected by them and have the resources to block them or implement solutions (Chrislip and Larson 1994). Generally, voluntary groups will offer membership to those that they regard as important to group success (Huxham and Vangen 2000). In mandated interorganizational group relations, membership is not offered but decided by a distant hierarchy, usually mandated via government legislation or organizational policy. Similarly, group membership is generally decided on the basis of individuals that are responsible for problems or issues, affected by them and have the resources to block them or implement solutions.

Group Membership and Social Identity Theory—The Darker Side

In voluntary forms of interorganizational groups, members offer and select membership based on a connection to a shared problem or an interest in an outcome that be gained as a result of the effort they are willing to commit to the group. In contrast, an organization who believes in their own ability to solve an issue, will disengage in group behavior if they believe that outcomes in the form of shared resources comes at a cost to their efforts. In health and social care, organizations that feel uncertain about their individual ability to solve wicked issues for which they may be responsible, become motivated to identify with groups who can reduce this uncertainty. Social identity approaches such as social identity theory (Tajfel and Turner 1986) maintain that when individuals identify with a group, they experience further shaping of their self-view, as a result of identifying with characteristic of the new social group different to that of the self (Tajfel and Turner 1979; Hennigan and Spanovic 2012). Social identity theory also alludes to the perception that individuals have of self, and being part of a group can increase the individual's self-esteem, which helps to embed relations between group members. Organizations and individuals who join a group based on shared similarities perceive some kind of oneness with the group. They perceive themselves as psychologically intertwined with the fate of the group, personally experiencing the failures and successes of the group with other group members (Ashforth and Mael 1989) Hence, the research suggests that the social identity impact of group membership can influence members to a point where they set aside individual and organizational needs in favor of group norms (Hennigan and Spanovic 2012).

Much of what is studied and assumed about the membership of groups in health and social care integration has been explained by social identity theory which defines groups *"as cognitively as collections of individuals who share a common evaluative self-definition—a shared social identity"* (Tajfel and Turner 1979; Goldman, Giles and Hogg 2014). Simply put, individuals and organizations interact when they recognize a common problem or issue and identify with other organizations on this basis. This need to identify with others on the basis of a shared identity in the organizational sense is viewed as imperative to the success and management of an interorganizational relation or intergroup, being the common element that supports group cohesion, trust, loyalty and commitment to the group. When members no longer share that sense of purpose with the group, they retreat from the group finding no need to identify with them any further. If social identity theory as a group process points toward interorganizational groups being a collection of individuals based on common self-identity, the data on mandated interorganizational groups in some ways contradict's this theory.

We are amateurs and they are professionals. That's how I see it but then I am biased.

(Health and Wellbeing Board Member)

There is an assumption with mandated interorganizational groups that an acknowledgment by members that the overall objective of the group aligns to individual organizational goals, group members take on the shared identity of the group and interrelations continue on this basis. This study showed that a having a common goal or shared belief, as in the case of reducing health inequalities, is not enough to ensure that members will interact together in a way that the group literature would suggest. Often, as in the case of this study, mandated group memberships are made up of a range of identities that have common goals but from different orientations. When this is the case, the common purpose is not enough to create a shared sense of identity and in these instances, social identities compete with each other, as opposed to finding common ground over time. Competing social identities occur when members agree on the purpose for which they are together but the orientations from which they view the purpose oppose each other, which can become a source of conflict within the interorganizational relation. Health and Wellbeing Boards are made up of a mandated membership of organizational, democratic and third-sector representation. Orientations are based on the beliefs, attitudes, feeling and values systems that individuals lean toward, the compass which influences how they perceive things, the position from which they act and the action that they take. The integration of health and social care can be advocated from a social justice orientation, where the integration of services comes from an interest that advances the inherent human rights of equity, equality and fairness in social, economic, educational and personal dimensions (Goldfarb and Grinberg 2002). In contrast, it can be advocated from an organizational orientation where the interest in integration comes from the belief that the integration of services should be via order and control and the prescriptive processes of fixed rules and authority. This could suggest that if the orientation of mandated members is so diverse, even when there is a common purpose, the group does not develop a sense of shared identity and instead, identities compete with each other with constrains group action.

This process of competing social identities occurs when individual members judge themselves as to their perception of self and other and sense a level of disparity between what they perceive the social identity of the group to be, compared with their own identity.

> They are professional people who have spent years getting to this level in their profession they feel quite capable of making all these major decisions. They've been used to dealing with all these millions of pounds and now all of a sudden they around a board where you have people like myself.
>
> (Health and Wellbeing Board Member)

When group members sense that their identity does not align to what they perceive the social identity of the group to be, this becomes a source of conflict, which can constrain group action. This type of conflict can be explained as the intrapersonal or intrapsychic conflict, which is defined as the conflict that occurs when an organizational member is required to carry out a role or task that conflicts with their attitudes, values, ethics and professional behavior (Rahim 2010) or as Deutsch (1969) defined it as "the incompatible actions that occur in one individual arising from the differences in beliefs, interests, desires or values." Bringing together professionals, democratically elected members and consumer champions under the guise of health and well-being boards was seen to be one of the more positive elements of the 2012 health reform with the opportunity to create new partnerships and join up local services with greater accountability. However, the evidence from this study suggests that were there incompatibilities at the level where a social or group identity cannot be formed, this becomes a source of conflict which divides the group, causing group members to plot against each other to serve individual priorities rather than collaborative aims.

Cohesion—The Darker Side

Group cohesion is a group process that underpins a group's social interactions and behaviors and is derived from the attraction that members feel toward others members, the motivation members have to participation in group activities and level of coordination across group effort (Klein 1997). Within group research, an interesting conceptualization of cohesion is perceived cohesion, which is "an individual's sense of belonging to a particular group and his or her feelings of morale associated with membership in the group" (Bollen and Hoyle 1990, 482). Group members who show high levels of social identity with the group, experience a higher level of cohesion with their group members which influences the level to which members commit and become loyal to group norms. In organizational groups, high levels of cohesiveness may facilitate high levels of group action toward group goals. From this perspective, cohesion is an important group process for the accomplishment of group aims, suggesting that levels of conflict within the group membership interfere with this aspect (Wood 2014).

The perception that cohesiveness as a group social process that underpins group social interactions and behaviors, derived from the attraction that members feel toward others members, should be viewed with caution when the membership is mandated. Bollen and Hoyle's (1990, 482) definition of perceived cohesion as "an Individual's sense of belonging to a particular group and his or her feelings of moral associated with membership in the group."

> I think it is sometimes difficult, for me as well, because it's taken me . . . you know I don't quite know what my role is, because you can't speak with the professionals of let's say the CCG or the NHS and there are all sorts of under currents that you are aware of and you have seen that happening.
>
> (Health and Wellbeing Board Member)

Group members who compete as to their social identities can feel a lack of cohesion with others in the group. When group members feel a lack of association with what they might perceive to be the assumed social identity of the group, feelings of inadequacy regarding their ability to function as a member within that group can give way to forms of relentless self-surveillance or policing of the self. This study showed that when mandated memberships result in competing social identities, with one of the identities becoming the more dominant or the higher social identity. When this happens, members of the 'lower' social identity can begin to feel uncomfortable and disempowered, perceiving a lack of fit with the higher identity and becoming even less cohesive with the other members through relentless self-surveillance.

The research on groups and cohesiveness as a social process suggest that high levels of cohesiveness facilitate high levels of group action, important for the accomplishment of group aims and effective levels of conflict. However, this research suggests that in mandated group membership, when social identities compete and levels of cohesiveness are low, levels of group action become constrained. Managing low levels of cohesiveness in mandated group membership can be especially important as in this study, this was seen to result in some members acting elsewhere, in secret or behind the scenes.

> Yes, it did go on behind the scenes. The relationship building and the reality of what it all meant went on absolutely behind the scenes.
>
> (Health and Wellbeing Board Member)

> Just because you're round the table it doesn't mean you're really collaborating, so see you can easily have a facade of collaboration when you're in the room, but not really playing an active part.
>
> (Health and Wellbeing Board Member)

Acting behind the scenes in this study was identified as a group strategy belonging to the darker side of interorganizational relations and can happen as a result of mandating group membership. This study showed that low levels of cohesiveness in mandated groups became a source of conflict that constrained group action resulting in some members interacting in from a place located behind the scenes in an attempt to manage this conflict. From this position, instead of all the group members subscribing to the group process such as openness and transparency, some of the members looked to act outside of the formal group processes and from a position that was not open to scrutiny.

Pluralistic Ignorance—The Darker Side

Pluralistic ignorance is a group process that suggests group members will not always agree with group norms but will abide by them publicly, believing that other group members with whom they experience a shared identity, will be in favor of this (J O'Gorman 1986; Shelton and Richeson 2005). Pluralistic ignorance is a term that was originally used to explain the discrepancy between public behaviors and private beliefs (Allport 1954; Katz and Allport 1931 in Shelton and Richeson 2005). When individual members believe they are alone in their disagreement with group norms, they refrain from publicly opposition within the group (Wood 2014). Group research suggests that when an individual's membership is in its infancy, pluralistic ignorance can be experienced if they are uncomfortable with group norms and experience feelings of cognitive dissonance but over time can come to genuinely those norms they would have privately rejected (Klein and Maxson 2010).

The research on voluntary forms of groups and pluralistic ignorance does have certain parallels with mandated groups, however there are still contradictions from which lessons could be learned. The research on voluntary groups suggests that group members will not always agree with group norms but will abide by them publicly, believing that other group members with whom they experience a shared identity, will be in favor of this (O'Gorman 1986; Shelton and Richeson 2005). Group members of mandated memberships can also show engage in acts of pluralistic ignorance, but their act of agreement does not come from agreeing because of an eagerness to adapt group norms and further embed themselves into the groups social identity, but enacting the process of pluralistic ignorance out of a sense of hopelessness that there is no other choice.

> I hadn't been to more than two meetings when the debacle about closing the B wing happened, and we felt people from the local authority and other organizations who were very accountable bodies, we all felt that this had been foisted on us. That there hadn't been any consultation, the decisions had been made.
>
> (Health and Wellbeing Board Member)

This compliance with the actions of other in the group also contradicts what the literature on groups tell us about the compliance of those others' social norms by disagreeing individuals in a group setting (Asch and Guetzkow 1951). Group norms are the informal rules adopted by groups to govern members behavior and can have a powerful and consistent influence on members behavior when the group, however studies show this happens when the members subscribe to a shared social identity and there is a good level of group cohesiveness. This was demonstrated by the findings in this study where a lack of shared identity and cohesiveness lead to individual members adopting their own norms with the rest of the group members becoming complicit only as they perceived their own lack of capability to reverse decisions or hold individual members to account. This sense of extreme discomfort that some members' sense in relation to the behavior of others is also evidence to suggest that mandated interorganizational relations could become places for dark behavior to occur by certain members creating and acting by their own norms and other members involved in a process of pluralistic ignorance almost under duress.

Summary

This chapter has shared some of the insights of a qualitative study into the darker side of interorganizational relations, specifically mandated interorganizational relations and the dark side that can manifest through the social process that occur within this context. Using the concept of groups within interorganizational relations it offers an insight into the dark side of the social processes group membership theory and social identity theory, cohesion and pluralistic ignorance, which adds a further dimension to which these processes are more generally studied in the literature. However, although this chapter offers conceptual insights, it also offers insights for practice. As more and more health and social care practioners are now being mandated into various forms of interorganizational relations, it is important that they are aware of the role that mandate can play in the manifestations of a darker side of the behavior that can occur and use this knowledge to inform the process by which they manage interorganizational relations.

References

Albers, Sascha, Franz Wohlgezogen, and Edward J. Zajac. 2016. "Strategic Alliance Structures: An Organization Design Perspective." *Journal of Management* 42 (3): 582–614.

Allport, Gordon Willard, Kenneth Clark, and Thomas Pettigrew. 1954. *The Nature of Prejudice*. New York: Addison-Wesley.

Belderbos, René, Victor Gilsing, and Boris Lokshin. 2012. "Persistence of, and Interrelation Between, Horizontal and Vertical Technology Alliances." *Journal of Management* 38 (6): 1812–1834.

Bollen, Kenneth A., and Rick H. Hoyle. 1990. "Perceived Cohesion: A Conceptual and Empirical Examination." *Social Forces* 69 (2): 479–504.

Brummel, Rachel F., Kristen C. Nelson, Stephanie Grayzeck Souter, Pamela J. Jakes, and Daniel R. Williams. 2010. "Social Learning in a Policy-Mandated Collaboration: Community Wildfire Protection Planning in the Eastern United States." *Journal of Environmental Planning and Management* 53 (6): 681–699.

Bryson, John M., Barbara C. Crosby, and Melissa Middleton Stone. 2006. "The Design and Implementation of Cross-Sector Collaborations: Propositions from the Literature." *Public Administration Review* 66: 44–55.

Capaldo, Antonio. 2014. "Network Governance: A Cross-Level Study of Social Mechanisms, Knowledge Benefits, and Strategic Outcomes in Joint-Design Alliances." *Industrial Marketing Management* 43 (4): 685–703.

Carnabuci, Gianluca, and Elisa Operti. 2013. "Where Do Firms' Recombinant Capabilities Come From? Intraorganizational Networks, Knowledge, and Firms' Ability to Innovate Through Technological Recombination." *Strategic Management Journal* 34 (13): 1591–1613.

Chrislip, David D., and Carl E. Larson. 1994. *Collaborative Leadership: How Citizens and Civic Leaders Can Make a Difference*. San Fransisco, CA: Jossey-Bass.

Clarke, John, and Caroline Glendinning. 2002. "Partnership and the Remaking of Welfare Governance." *Partnerships, New Labour and the Governance of Welfare*, 33–50.

Cook, Ailsa, Mulherin T., and Seditas K. 2015. *Partnership Working Across UK Public Services*. Edinburgh: What Works Scotland.

Deutsch, Morton. 1969. "Conflicts: Productive and Destructive." *Journal of Social Issues* 25 (1): 7–42.

Dickinson, Helen, and Jon Glasby. 2010. "'Why Partnership Working Doesn't Work' Pitfalls, Problems and Possibilities in English Health and Social Care." *Public Management Review* 12 (6): 811–828.

Dyer, Jeffrey H., and Nile W. Hatch. 2006. "Relation – Specific Capabilities and Barriers to Knowledge Transfers: Creating Advantage Through Network Relationships." *Strategic Management Journal* 27 (8): 701–719.

Genskow, Kenneth D. 2009. "Catalyzing Collaboration: Wisconsin's Agency-Initiated Basin Partnerships." *Environmental Management* 43 (3): 411–424. Accessed April 20, 2018. http://link.springer.com/10.1007/s00267-008-9236-x

Glasby, Jon, and Helen Dickinson. 2008. "Greater Than the Sum of Our Parts? Emerging Lessons for UK Health and Social Care." *International Journal of Integrated Care* 8 (3).

Glendinning, Caroline, Bernard Dowling, and Martin Powell. 2005. "Partnerships Between Health and Social Care Under' New Labour': Smoke Without Fire? A Review of Policy and Evidence." *Evidence & Policy: A Journal of Research, Debate and Practice* (3): 365–382.

Goldman, Liran, Howard Giles, and Michael A. Hogg. 2014. "Going to Extremes: Social Identity and Communication Processes Associated with Gang Membership." *Group Processes & Intergroup Relations* 17 (6): 813–832.

Goldfarb, K. P., and Jaime Grinberg. 2001. "Leadership for Social Justice: Authentic Participation in the Case of a Community Center in Caracas, Venezuela." *Journal of School Leadership* 12: 157–173.

Gray, Barbara. 1989. *Collaborating: Finding Common Ground for Multi-Party Problems.* San Francisco, CA: Jossey-Bass.

Guro Øyen Huby, Ailsa Cook, and Ralf Kirchhoff. 2018. "Can We Mandate Partnership Working? Top Down Meets Bottom Up in Structural Reforms in Scotland and Norway." *Journal of Integrated Care* 26 (2), 109–119.

Hennigan, Karen, and Marija Spanovic. 2012. "Gang Dynamics Through the Lens of Social Identity Theory." In *Youth Gangs in International Perspective*, 127–149. New York: Springer

Hodges, Sharon, Mario Hernandez, and Teresa Nesman. 2003. "A Developmental Framework for Collaboration in Child-Serving Agencies." *Journal of Child and Family Studies* 12 (3): 291–305.

Humphries, Richard. 2013. "Health and Wellbeing Boards: Policy and Prospects." *Journal of Integrated Care* 21 (1): 6–12.

Hunter, David J., Neil Perkins, Clare Bambra, Linda Marks, Trevor Hopkins, and Tim Blackman. 2011. *Partnership Working and the Implications for Governance: Issues Affecting Public Health Partnerships.* Southampton: NIHR Service Delivery and Organisation Programme/HMSO).

Hunter, David J., and Neil Perkins. 2014. *Partnership Working in Public Health.* Policy Press.

Huxham, Chris., and Siv. Vangen. 2000. "Ambiguity, Complexity and Dynamics in the Membership of Collaboration." *Human Relations* 53 (6): 771.

Isett, Kimberley R., and Provan, Keith G. 2005. The Evolution of Dyadic Interorganizational Relationships in a Network of Publicly Funded Nonprofit Agencies. *Journal of Public Administration Research and Theory* 15 (1): 149–165.

Ivery, Jan. 2008. "Policy Mandated Collaboration." *Journal of Sociology and Social Welfare* 35 (4): 53–70.

Jenssen, Jan Inge, and Erlend Nybakk. 2013. "Inter-Organizational Networks and Innovation in Small, Knowledge-Intensive Firms: A Literature Review." *International Journal of Innovation Management* 17 (2): 27–66.

Katz, Daniel, Floyd Henry Allport, and Margaret Babcock Jenness. 1931. *Students' Attitudes: A Report of the Syracuse University Reaction Study*. Syracuse, New York: Craftsman.

Klein, Malcolm W. 1997. *The American Street Gang: Its Nature, Prevalence, and Control*. Oxford University Press.

Klein, Malcolm W., and Cheryl L. Maxson. 2010. *Street Gang Patterns and Policies*. Oxford University Press.

Koschmann, Matthew A., Timothy R. Kuhn, and Michael D. Pfarrer. 2012. "A Communicative Framework of Value in Cross-Sector Partnerships." *Academy of Management Review* 37 (3): 332–354.

Levine, Mark, Amy Prosser, David Evans, and Stephen Reicher. 2005. "Identity and Emergency Intervention: How Social Group Membership and Inclusiveness of Group Boundaries Shape Helping Behavior." *Personality and Social Psychology Bulletin* 31 (4): 443–453.

Liefooghe, Andreas, and Kate Mackenzie Davey. 2010. "The Language and Organization of Bullying at Work." *Administrative Theory & Praxis* 32 (1): 71–95.

McNamara, Madeline W. 2016. Unraveling the Characteristics of Mandated Collaboration. In *Advancing Collaboration Theory: Models, Typologies, and Evidence*, edited by J. C. Morris and K. Miller-Stevens, 65–85. New York: Routledge.

Mills, Colleen. 2011. "Grappling with the Dark Side of Organisations [Paper in special issue]: Exploring the Dark Side of Organisations: A Communication Perspective." *Australian Journal of Communication* 38 (1): 1.

Murphy, Peter. 2013. "Public Health and Health and Wellbeing Boards: Antecedents, Theory and Development." *Perspectives in Public Health* 133 (5): 248–253.

Ozmel, Umit, Jeffrey J. Reuer, and Ranjay Gulati. 2013. "Signals Across Multiple Networks: How Venture Capital and Alliance Networks Affect Interorganizational Collaboration." *Academy of Management Journal* 56 (3): 852–866.

O'Gorman, Hubert J. 1986. "The Discovery of Pluralistic Ignorance: An Ironic Lesson." *Journal of the History of the Behavioral Sciences* 22 (4): 333–347.

Perkins, Neil, Katherine Smith, David J. Hunter, Clare Bambra, and Kerry Joyce. 2010. "'What Counts Is What Works'? New Labour and Partnerships in Public Health." *Policy & Politics* 38 (1): 101–117.

Provan, Keith G., and Patrick Kenis. 2008. "Modes of network governance: Structure, management, and effectiveness." *Journal of Public Administration Research and Theory* 18 (2): 229–252.

Provan, Keith G., and Robin H. Lemaire. 2012. "Core Concepts and Key Ideas for Understanding Public Sector Organizational Networks: Using Research to Inform Scholarship and Practice." *Public Administration Review* 72 (5): 638–648.

Ranade Wendy, and Bob Hudson. 2003. Conceptual Issues in Inter-Agency Collaboration. *Local Government Studies* 29 (3): 32–50.

Rahim, M. Afzalur. 2010. *Managing Conflict in Organizations*. Routledge.

Rodríguez, Charo, Ann Langley, François Béland, and Jean-Louis Denis. 2007. "Governance, Power, and Mandated Collaboration in an Interorganizational Network." *Administration & Society* 39 (2): 150–193.

Shannon, M. M., and Shortell, S. M. 2000. The Governance and Management of Effective Community Health Partnerships: A Typology for Research, Policy, and Practice. *The Milbank Quarterly*, 78: 241–289.

Shelton, J. Nicole, and Jennifer A. Richeson. 2005. "Intergroup Contact and Pluralistic Ignorance." *Journal of Personality and Social Psychology* 88 (1): 91.

Smith, K. E., C. Bambra, K. E. Joyce, N. Perkins, D. J. Hunter, and E. A. Blenkinsopp. 2009. "Partners in Health? A Systematic Review of the Impact of Organizational Partnerships on Public Health Outcomes in England Between 1997 and 2008." *Journal of Public Health* 31 (2): 210–221.

Stein, Mark. 2007. "Oedipus Rex at Enron: Leadership, Oedipal Struggles, and Organizational Collapse." *Human Relations* 60 (9): 1387–1410.

Sullivan, Bilian Ni, Pamela Haunschild, and Karen Page. 2007. "Organizations Non gratae? The Impact of Unethical Corporate Acts on Interorganizational Networks." *Organization Science* 18 (1): 55–70.

Sun, Sunny Li, and Ruby P. Lee. 2013. "Enhancing Innovation Through International Joint Venture Portfolios: From the Emerging Firm Perspective." *Journal of International Marketing* 21 (3): 1–21.

Tajfel, Henri, and John C. Turner. 1979. "An Integrative Theory of Intergroup Conflict." *The Social Psychology of Intergroup Relations* 33 (47): 74.

Tajfel, Henri, and John Turner. 1986. "The Social Identity Theory of Intergroup Behaviour". In *Psychology of Intergroup Relations*, edited by S. Worchel and W. G. Austin, 7–24. Chicago: Nelson Hall.

Taylor, Brian D., and Lisa Schweitzer. 2005. "Assessing the Experience of Mandated Collaborative Inter-Jurisdictional Transport Planning in the United States." *Transport Policy* 12 (6): 500–511.

Tomlinson, Paul, Stephen Hewitt, and Neil Blackshaw. 2013. "Joining Up Health and Planning: How Joint Strategic Needs Assessment (JSNA) Can Inform Health and Wellbeing Strategies and Spatial Planning." *Perspectives in Public Health* 133 (5): 254–262.

Turner, Daniel, Sarah Salway, Ghazala Mir, George TH Ellison, John Skinner, Lynne Carter, and Bushara Bostan. 2013. "Prospects for Progress on Health Inequalities in England in the Post-Primary Care Trust Era: Professional Views on Challenges, Risks and Opportunities." *BMC Public Health* 13 (1): 274.

Vangen, Siv, and Nik Winchester. 2014. "Managing Cultural Diversity In Collaborations: A Focus on Management Tensions." *Public Management Review* 16 (5): 686–707.

Vaughan, Katelyn Suzanne (2012). "Mandated Collaboration as a Strategy of Environmental Governance? A Case Study of the Niagara Peninsula Source Protection Area in Ontario." Master's thesis, University of Waterloo.

Westheafer, Charles. 2000. "Integrating Perspectives Within a Dominant Framework: Taming the Dark Side." *Organization Development Journal* 18 (3): 63.

Wood, Jane L. 2014. "Understanding Gang Membership: The Significance of Group Processes." *Group Processes & Intergroup Relations* 17 (6): 710–729.

Yaffee, Steven L., and Julia M. Wondolleck. 2000. "Making Collaboration Work: Lessons from a Comprehensive Assessment of Over 200 Wideranging Cases of Collaboration in Environmental Management." *Conservation in Practice* 1 (1): 17–24.

Yang, Haibin, Yanfeng Zheng, and Xia Zhao. 2014. "Exploration or Exploitation? Small Firms' Alliance Strategies with Large Firms." *Strategic Management Journal* 35 (1): 146–157.

Zhao, Xianbo, Bon-Gang Hwang, and Gwendolyn Shiyun Yu. 2013. "Identifying the Critical Risks in Underground Rail International Construction Joint Ventures: Case Study of Singapore." *International Journal of Project Management* 31 (4): 554–566.

11 Deficit Discourses and Aboriginal and Torres Strait Islander Disadvantage

A Wicked Problem in Australian Indigenous Policy?

Elizabeth Pyle, Deanna Grant-Smith and Robyn Mayes

Introduction

Aboriginal people and Torres Strait Islander people have experienced significant marginalization as a result of the British invasion of Australia and the manner of continued colonization. Despite numerous government programs and policies designed to remediate what is referred to as Indigenous disadvantage, Australia's First peoples continue to experience disproportionately negative life outcomes relative to non-Indigenous Australians in areas such as education, health, justice and employment. Following an historical overview of Indigenous social outcomes post colonization, this chapter examines the deficit discourse constituting 'Indigenous disadvantage' and informing Australian Indigenous Affairs policy development and implementation. It does so by examining key policy initiatives and reports between the 1890s and 2017.

This deficit discourse is critiqued in the specific and crucially important context of the recent construction of Australian Indigenous disadvantage as a "wicked problem" (Hunter 2007, 35–51; Johns 2008, 65–84; Head 2008, 101–118), one that is framed as intractable, contradictory and difficult to solve (Rittel and Webber 1973, 155–169). We argue this dominant policy framing works against achieving stated policy aims and problematically conflates Indigenous identity and disadvantage situating both as wicked. As a response, we argue the potential merits of adopting a strength-based policy discourse which not only acknowledges policy legacies but is also cognisant that policy constructions of Indigenous disadvantage as wicked are derived from 'whiteness' as an epistemological *a priori* (Moreton-Robinson 2004, 75–88).

An Historical Overview of 'Indigenous Disadvantage'

Aboriginal peoples and Torres Strait Islander peoples currently comprise approximately 3% of the total Australian population. Approximately

65% live outside of capital cities compared to 32% of the non-Indigenous population. Torres Strait Islander people comprise approximately 5% of Australia's Indigenous population, with approximately 4% identifying as Aboriginal and Torres Strait Islander (Australian Bureau of Statistics 2018). English is often a second or third language for Aboriginal and Torres Strait Islander peoples (Department of the Prime Minister and Cabinet 2014, 2), with 10% speaking an Australian Indigenous language in the home (Australian Bureau of Statistics 2018).

Aboriginal people have lived on the Australian continent for around 60,000 years (Dockery 2010, 315–332). Aboriginal Australians are ethnically and culturally distinct from Torres Strait Islander Australians (Anti-Discrimination Commission Queensland 2017). It is estimated that Torres Strait Islander peoples have lived in the Torres Strait for approximately 3000 years (Lawrence and Lawrence 2004, 15–29). European colonization of 'Australia' began in earnest with the invasion of the British First Fleet in 1788. The embedded ontology of a European colonial world view of 'discovery' secured 'whiteness' as the point of reference for what was assumed or known about Indigenous peoples, who were thereby constituted as 'other' (Moreton-Robinson 2004, 75–88). Furthermore, Social Darwinism at the time validated the classification of Indigenous Australians at the base of a human species hierarchy (Rigney 1997, 109–121), allowing colonizers to exert power and control over a group of people defined as biologically inferior (Walker 2003, 27–40).

This othering has had ongoing policy ramifications. Aboriginal academic Professor Michael Dodson notes that as a result of ongoing colonial discourses: "We are constantly defined as 'other,' but we are never permitted to be genuinely independent, genuinely different. In fact, far from being recognized in our difference, in our own terms, we are always defined in terms of the colonising or defining culture" (Dodson 2003, 36). Significantly, as he further points out, it was under that colonial gaze that "Aboriginality changed from being a daily practice to being 'a problem to be solved" (Dodson 2003, 27).

Deficit discourses in Australian Indigenous Affairs policy have been in evidence since the colonization of Australia and "are a key component of racism and prejudice" (Fforde et al. 2013, 164). This is evidenced in the *Aboriginals Protection and Restriction of Sale of Opium Act 1897 (Qld)* (Museum of Australian Democracy 2018) and ensuing amendments, which created the Chief Protector of Aboriginals Office. This Office exercised extensive control over Aboriginal people and Torres Strait Islander people including being able to forcibly remove Indigenous Australians to reserves and prohibit the practice of rites or customs that, in the opinion of the Minister, could be harmful to their welfare (Museum of Australian Democracy 2018). Between the 1890s and 1970s, under various Protection Acts, the Queensland Government directly managed the wages, savings and property of Aboriginal and Torres Strait Islander Queenslanders (State Library of

Queensland 2016) as a form of social, emotional and physical control. The use of tobacco and other rations as 'payment' for Indigenous Australian labor until the 1960s, combined with the withholding of wages by the government, is believed to have contributed to high levels of tobacco use compared with non-Indigenous Australians and poorer financial circumstances generations later (Schofield et al. 2015, 46–57).

Similarly, assimilationist policies between 1910 and the 1970s, allowed governments to remove Indigenous children from their families and send them to institutions and missions or to be fostered by non-Indigenous families (Human Rights and Equal Opportunity Commission 1997). These children were not permitted to continue cultural practices or speak traditional languages and became known as *The Stolen Generations* (Human Rights and Equal Opportunity Commission 1997). A primary motivation advanced for these policies was child protection grounded in a belief that Aboriginal and Torres Strait Islander children were 'naturally' disadvantaged by being Indigenous and that "non-indigenous models of child rearing were superior" (Brown 2009, 1565–1566). Protection and assimilation policies were based on the idea of 'racial superiority' and a belief that Indigenous peoples should be allowed to 'die out' naturally (Brown 2009, 1565–1566).

A key marker of this systemic disadvantage is the over-representation of Indigenous Australians within the penal system. Approximately 27% of prisoners in Australia have Aboriginal and/or Torres Strait Islander cultural backgrounds, despite comprising only 2% of the Australian population aged 18 years and older (Australian Bureau of Statistics 2017). High rates of incarceration have been accompanied by a large number of deaths of Indigenous Australians whilst in custody. Responding to increased public debate regarding the deaths of Aboriginal people in custody, Prime Minister Bob Hawke formed the Royal Commission into Aboriginal Deaths in Custody in 1987. This Royal Commission examined the causes of deaths in custody of Aboriginal people within state and territory prisons occurring between January 1, 1980 and May 31, 1989 (Australasian Legal Information Institute 1998).

Indigenous politician Patrick Dodson, reflecting 25 years on from the Royal Commission into Aboriginal Deaths in Custody, highlighted the disproportionate growth of Indigenous Australians, particularly Indigenous women, within the justice system and noted, "by and large, the problem the Royal Commission was set up to examine and advise governments on has become worse" (Dodson 2016, 24). Dodson, a Royal Commissioner during the enquiry, emphasized the current and persistent 'tough on crime' political discourse that continues to 'criminalise' Aboriginal people and Torres Strait Islander people.

Wicked Deficit Discourses of Indigenous Disadvantage

Policy discourses frame Aboriginal and Torres Strait Islander identities in circumstances of "deficiency and disempowerment" (Fforde et al. 2013,

162). This includes discussing Aboriginal peoples and Torres Strait Islander peoples based on otherness and stereotypes (Coram 2009, 275–287). As a result, policy development and implementation 'for' Indigenous Australians assumes colonial worldviews and knowledges as fundamental to describing and 'solving' the 'Indigenous problem' (Milner 2007, 389). Indeed, discourses around Indigenous Australians, particularly policy discourses, generally do not acknowledge the cultural background and world view of policymakers. In effect, there is a 'racial construct' for Indigenous Australians but not for European Australians (Moreton-Robinson 2004, 82) to which policy responds.

Despite a long history of government investment in human, financial and emotional resources around Indigenous Australian Affairs, disparities in life outcomes between Indigenous and non-Indigenous Australians continue. Explanations for this 'Indigenous disadvantage,' as advanced by Indigenous and non-Indigenous commentators, politicians, academics, evaluators and business leaders, have tended to foreground a number of key areas including deficit discourses (Bamblett 2011, 5–20). Policy challenges around multifaceted issues such as poverty and homelessness are widely constructed as 'wicked problems' (Sherman and Peterson 2009, 87). That is, these 'problems' are understood to be extremely complex, apparently immovable, insoluble and difficult for stakeholders to define and agree upon a course of action; there is no completion point—they are cyclical. Indigenous Australian disadvantage has been described as a wicked problem (Hunter 2007, 35–51; Johns 2008, 65–84). Indeed, the 2012 Australian Public Service Commission's *Tackling wicked problems: A public policy perspective* specifically refers to Indigenous disadvantage as wicked (Australian Public Service Commission 2012). Characterizing Indigenous disadvantage as a 'wicked problem' recognizes the social, cultural and economic lived complexities involved in disparate life outcomes (Prins et al. 2010, 1–42). However, it also has the potential to disempower Indigenous Australians by framing their lived experiences—and Aboriginal people and Torres Strait Islander people themselves—as a permanently unsolvable problem. Approximately 230 years after colonization, there is still a focus on punitive, patronizing and repressive policies based on the hegemonic *a priori* of whiteness (Moreton-Robinson 2004, 75–88).

Deficit Discourse in Practice: The Northern Territory National Emergency Response

An exemplar of deficit discourse in practice can be found in the Northern Territory National Emergency Response Act (Cth), which became widely known as the 'Intervention.' The 2007 "national emergency response to protect Aboriginal children in the Northern Territory" from sexual abuse and family violence (Australian Human Rights Commission 2007) involved the mobilization of the Australian Defence Force to deliver the child protection priorities of the government in remote Indigenous communities in the Northern Territory. The announcement of the Intervention was made within six days of the highly publicized *Ampe Akelyernemane Meke Mekarle: Little Children are Sacred Report* (Board of Inquiry into the Protection of Aboriginal Children from Sexual Abuse 2007). While the *Little Children are Sacred* report found that child sexual abuse was widespread and often went unreported in Northern Territory communities, the report also emphasized the importance of creating genuine partnerships with communities to ensure positive outcomes (Australian Human Rights Commission 2007).

The emphasis on 'emergency response' in the Act's title positions the government action as both immediately necessary and on a 'national' scale, just as it confirms that the situation requires, if not demands, external intervention. Indeed, this emergency discourse is emphasized in Prime Minister John Howard's use of the term 'disaster' to refer to the extent of the child sexual abuse recorded in the report. Further, he described the situation as 'Australia's Hurricane Katrina' (Faulkner 2015, 118). Such a characterization removes agency from Indigenous Australians, cements concepts of Indigenous deficiency in the minds of the broader public, and creates public spectacle from the suffering of individuals. The implementation of the Northern Territory National Emergency Response was supported by the suspension of *Part II of the Racial Discrimination Act 1975*. This suspension denied protections afforded to other citizens to challenge legislation considered to be in breach of the act (Australian Human Rights Commission 2007).

Discussions continue around the legacies of the Stolen Generations, the removal of children until the 1970s and the current upward trend in the number of young Indigenous people in out-of-home care, particularly as a result of the Intervention. Out-of-home care involves placing children and young people aged 0–17 years of age with carers on a short- or long-term basis (Australian Institute of Family Studies 2017), and the number of Aboriginal children in out-of-home care in the Northern Territory has tripled since June 30, 2007. As of June 2016, 89% of the children in out-of-home care in the Northern Territory were Aboriginal children (Royal Commission and Board of Inquiry into the Protection and Detention of Children in the Northern Territory 2017).

The Northern Territory National Emergency Response illustrates contemporary discourse evolving from a long line of policies which have aimed to 'improve lives.' Indeed, the Northern Territory National Emergency Response is reminiscent of the removal and control policies of the 20th century, particularly those associated with child protection as a justification for significant intervention in Indigenous peoples' lives without consent. Recent examples of this include the introduction of several Australian Government community pilot programmes to trial cashless debit cards as a means to quarantine a percentage of peoples' welfare payments (Department of Social Services 2018) and to restrict expenditure to certain stores. The intention has been to reduce the cash available in a community and thus reduce harms perceived to be caused by alcohol abuse, gambling and drug misuse (Department of Social Services 2018). This form of 'compulsory income management' was introduced during the Northern Territory National Emergency Response, and due to the suspension of *Part II of Racial Discrimination Act 1975* Indigenous Australians in the Northern Territory had no legal means of redress for discrimination due to income management (Bielefeld 2014, 288). There have been consequent amendments in 2010 and 2012 to the income management policies. This included, after criticism of human rights violations within the 2007 laws, reinstating *Part II of the Racial Discrimination Act 1975* within these measures. These income management laws impact significantly on Aboriginal and Torres Strait Islander agency and well-being (Bielefeld 2014, 289). In particular, the focus of the policies and strategies has been on those "defined as 'disengaged youth,' 'long term,' or 'vulnerable' welfare recipients, and on instances where there is a child protection issue" (Bielefeld 2014, 288–289).

Although the Northern Territory National Emergency Response has been characterized as 'wicked' (Hunter 2007, 35–51), Johns (2008, 65–67) argues that it is not the Northern Territory National Emergency Response policy per se that is wicked, but rather, it is the underpinning policy vision that is 'wicked.' That is, Australian Indigenous Affairs policy continues to be shaped by either a romanticized or demonizing characterization of Aboriginal peoples and Torres Strait Islander peoples. As a result, there are significant implications associated with the positioning of 'Indigenous disadvantage' as 'wicked'; this deficit affects not just policy framings and action but limits the range of possible policy outcomes and approaches (Van Hulst and Yanow 2016, 102).

The Future of Australian Indigenous Affairs Policy

Following the Northern Territory National Emergency Response, governments at all levels continue, with varying levels of success, to initiate strategies to address disparities between the lived experiences of Indigenous and non-Indigenous Australians. The most prominent of these is the 2008 *Closing the Gap in Indigenous Disadvantage* (Gardiner 2013.) strategy introduced by the Council of Australian Governments, Australia's peak intergovernmental body involving the Prime Minister, State and Territory Premiers and Chief Ministers and the President of the Australian Local Government Association.

The *Closing the Gap* strategy comprised six target areas focussed on reducing the high levels of disadvantage experienced by Aboriginal and Torres Strait Islander peoples in life expectancy, child mortality, education, literacy and numeracy, year 12 school attainment and employment (COAG Reform Council 2014). The Prime Minister's annual *Closing the Gap Reports* have shown uneven outcomes against many of the targets, with the most recent *Closing the Gap Prime Minister's Report* in early 2018 indicating that after ten years only three of the targets are on track to be realized. Reducing the disparities between Indigenous and non-Indigenous Australians in employment, life expectancy and school attendance are not on track (Department of the Prime Minister and Cabinet 2018).

Although these differences in life outcomes cannot be denied, language that implies an assumption of deficit is contradictory to the nature of problem solving and, "may work against achieving the very aims for which it was developed" (Fforde et al. 2013, 166). In the 2017 *Closing the Gap Progress and Priorities Report*, the Closing the Gap Steering Committee, referred to Prime Minister Malcolm Turnbull's ongoing 'doing with' rhetoric, pointing out a 'continuation of imposed, unengaged and often rushed service delivery' (Australian Human Rights Commission 2017, 1). It was during the *2016 Prime Minister's Closing the Gap Report* that Prime Minister Turnbull stated, "it is time for governments to 'do things with Aboriginal people, not do things to them'" (House of Representatives 2016a, 1173). Within six months of this declaration of collaboration, Turnbull had announced a *Royal Commission into Child Protection and Youth Detention Systems in the Northern Territory*. The establishment of this Royal Commission within less than 24 hours of the national airing of a news documentary about the abusive conditions experienced by children in detention in the Northern Territory, and the ensuing public outrage, was publicly welcomed by Indigenous and non-Indigenous commentators. However, the appointment of a Royal Commissioner and the establishment of the Royal Commission Terms of Reference several days later with extremely limited consultation with Aboriginal and Torres Strait Islander community members was loudly and widely condemned. After much publicity, the Royal Commissioner offered his resignation four days after being appointed, citing, amongst other reasons, that he realized he would not necessarily have the full confidence of Indigenous communities while fulfilling this role (Coggan 2016).

In his response to Prime Minister Turnbull's *2016 Closing the Gap Report* to the Australian Parliament, Opposition Leader, Bill Shorten spoke to the imperatives of political bi-partisanship around strategies and service delivery supporting Aboriginal and Torres Strait Islander people and of the need "to redouble our efforts in an equal, engaged and empowered partnership with the First Australians." (House of Representatives 2016b, 1175). The Closing the Gap Steering Committee, though supportive of statements of bi-partisanship around "closing the gap," asserted that "words are not enough"; words "must be backed by action based on meaningful engagement with Aboriginal and Torres Strait Islander people" (Australian Human Rights Commission 2017, 2). Such an approach will require exchanging deficit discourses with more positive discourses (Bamblett 2011, 5–20).

In recognition of this, there is a growing acknowledgment by government of the need for strength-based and inclusive approaches to policy development and implementation (Bamblett 2011, 5–20; Goodwin and Cox 2008,

18–20; Brough, Bond and Hunt 2004, 215–220), particularly approaches couched in language that affirms the strengths of Aboriginal and Torres Strait Islander individuals and communities. This includes the authentic application of co-design and consultation approaches which acknowledge policy development standpoints and the consideration of lived experiences; including the ramifications of past policies (Brown 2009, 1568). Providing a culturally safe policy environment (Downey and Stout 2006, 327–332) requires the use of strength-based discourse that embraces meaningful conversations, democratic listening (Dobson 2012, 843–859) and policy co-design and implementation. It also requires acknowledging responsibility for past decisions and for the deficit legacies of those decisions.

There are promising examples of such practices beginning to be adopted in Australian Indigenous Affairs policymaking. For example, Tony Fitzgerald QC, lead author of the *Cape York Justice Study*, acknowledged in his introduction to the report that as a white Australian his world view and opinions were shaped by "the beliefs and values of mainstream Australian society" (Department of the Premier and Cabinet 2001, 7). Justice Tony Fitzgerald was approached by the Queensland Government to identify the relationship between alcohol, substance misuse and breaches of the law in Cape York Indigenous communities and to identify ameliorating strategies. The introduction to the *Cape York Justice Study* stated: "Well-intentioned initiatives continue to produce unexpected adverse consequences for Indigenous Australians. The tragic consequences of past mistakes provoke concern that future well-intentioned activities might miscarry and cause further damage" (Department of the Premier and Cabinet 2001, 7).

Conclusion

This chapter has argued that deficit discourses and the concept of 'wicked problems' are a major component of Australian Indigenous policy development and implementation. This dominant policy language situates 'Indigenous disadvantage' as broadly defining the identity of Australia's First Peoples. These findings have emphasized the need for public and policy acknowledgment of the devastating effects of past policies and intergenerational trauma (Beresford and Beresford 2006, 65–78), and for policy and programs to be co-designed with Aboriginal peoples and Torres Strait Islander peoples. In doing so, this chapter has contributed to understandings of the role of prevailing discourses in Australian Indigenous Affairs policy development and implementation by identifying racialized language and assumptions of whiteness and wickedness as key policy framing devices. Such an understanding is fundamental to the pursuit of meaningful dialogue and partnerships between policymakers and Indigenous Australians to ensure that "Indigenous people are viewed as part of the solution—not just as problems to be solved" (Dodson 2016, 28).

156   *Elizabeth Pyle et al.*

Acknowledgments

The authors acknowledge the First Peoples of Australia—the Traditional Owners of the land, seas and waterways—and Elders and Spiritual Leaders, past, present and future. The authors also declare that this chapter, which discusses the lived experiences of Aboriginal people and Torres Strait Islander people, is written from the standpoint of three non-Indigenous Australian women who do not intend for their worldviews to speak for Indigenous Australians, and who wish to acknowledge and respect the sovereignty of the First Australians and Indigenous knowledges and ways of knowing (Martin 2003, 203–214; Merton, Cram and Chilisa 2013, 16).

References

Anti Discrimination Commission Queensland, Queensland Government. (2017). "Torres Strait Islander People Today." Accessed May 22, 2018. www.adcq. qld.gov.au/resources/a-and-tsi/torres-strait-islander-people-in-qld/torres-strait-islander-people-today.
Australasian Legal Information Institute. 1998. "Royal Commission into Aboriginal Deaths in Custody: National Report Volume 1–1.10 An Overview of the Recommendations." Accessed May 22, 2018. www.austlii.edu.au/au/other/IndigLRes/rciadic/national/vol1/24.html
Australian Bureau of Statistics. 2017. "Aboriginal and Torres Strait Islander Prisoner Characteristics." Accessed May 22, 2018. http://www.abs.gov.au/ausstats/abs@.nsf/Lookup/by%20Subject/4517.0~2017~Main%20Features~Aboriginal%20and%20Torres%20Strait%20Islander%20prisoner%20characteristics~5
Australian Bureau of Statistics. 2018. "Aboriginal and Torres Strait Islander Population." Accessed May 22, 2018. www.abs.gov.au/ausstats/abs@.nsf/Lookup/2071.0main+features102016
Australian Human Rights Commission, Australian Government. 2007. "Social Justice Report 2007—Chapter 3: The Northern Territory 'Emergency Response' intervention—A Human Rights Analysis." Accessed May 22, 2018. www.humanrights.gov.au/publications/social-justice-report-2007-chapter-3-northern-territory-emergency-response-intervention.
Australian Human Rights Commission, Australian Government 2017. "Close the Gap Progress and Priorities Report 2017." Accessed May 22, 2018. www.humanrights.gov.au/our-work/aboriginal-and-torres-strait-islander-social-justice/publications/close-gap-progress-0.
Australian Institute of Family Studies, Australian Government. 2017. "Children in Care." Accessed May 22, 2018. https://aifs.gov.au/cfca/publications/children-care.
Australian Public Service Commission, Australian Government. 2012. "Tackling Wicked Problems: A Public Policy Perspective." Accessed May 22, 2018. www.apsc.gov.au/publications-and-media/archive/publications-archive/tackling-wicked-problems.
Bamblett, Lawrence. 2011. "Straight-Line Stories: Representations and Indigenous Australian Identities in Sports Discourses." *Australian Aboriginal Studies* 2: 5–20.
Board of Inquiry into the Protection of Aboriginal Children from Sexual Abuse, Northern Territory Government. 2007. "Ampe Akelyernemane Meke Mekarle:

Little Children are Sacred Report." Accessed May 22, 2018. www.inquirysaac. nt.gov.au/pdf/bipacsa_final_report.pdf.

Beresford, Quentin, and Marilyn Beresford. 2006. "Race and Reconciliation: The Australian Experience in International Context." *Contemporary Politics* 12 (1): 65–78.

Bielefeld, Shelley. 2014. "Income Management and Indigenous Peoples: Nudged into a *Stronger Future?*" *Griffith Law Review* 23 (2): 285–317.

Brough, Marl, Chelsea Bond, and Julian Hunt. 2004. "Strong in the City: Towards a Strength-Based Approach in Indigenous Health Promotion." *Health Promotion Journal of Australia* 15: 215–220.

Brown, Ngiare. 2009. "History, Law, and Policy as a Foundation for Health Care Delivery for Australian Indigenous Children." *The Pediatric Clinics of North America* 56 (6): 1562–1576.

COAG Reform Council, Australian Government. 2014. "Indigenous Reform 2012–2013: Five Years of Performance." Accessed May 22, 2018. http://library.bsl.org. au/jspui/bitstream/1/4164/1/Indigenous%20Reform%202012-13%20Five%20 years%20of%20performance_COAG%2030%20April%202014.pdf

Coggan, Michael. 2016. "Brian Martin QC: Meet the Man Who Quit the NT Youth Detention Royal Commission." Australian. www.abc.net.au/news/2016-07-28/ nt-youth-detention-royal-commission-who-is-brian-martin/7670576

Coram, Stella. 2009. "Encountering Disregard in Australian Academe: The Subjective Perspective of a Disaffiliated Racial 'other'." *British Journal of Sociology of Education* 30 (3): 275–287.

Department of the Premier and Cabinet, Queensland Government. 2001. "Advanced Copy Cape York Justice Study Report." Accessed May 22, 2018. http://pandora. nla.gov.au/pan/24611/20020516-0000/www.premiers.qld.gov.au/about/community/capeyorkreport.htm.

Department of the Prime Minister and Cabinet, Australian Government. 2014. "Communicating with Aboriginal and Torres Strait Islander Audiences." Accessed May 22, 2018. https://www.pmc.gov.au/resource-centre/indigenous-affairs/ communicating-aboriginal-and-torres-strait-islander-audiences

Department of the Prime Minister and Cabinet, Australian Government. 2018. "Closing the Gap Prime Minister's Report 2018." Accessed May 22, 2018. https:// closingthegap.pmc.gov.au/sites/default/files/ctg-report-2018.pdf?a=1

Department of Social Services, Australian Government. 2018. "Cashless Debit Card." Accessed May 22, 2018. www.dss.gov.au/families-and-children/programmes-services/welfare-conditionality/cashless-debit-card-overview.

Dobson, Andrew. 2012. "Listening: The New Democratic Deficit." *Political Studies* 60 (4): 843–859.

Dockery, Alfred. 2010. "Culture and Wellbeing: The Case of Indigenous Australians." *Social Indicators Research* 99: 315–332.

Dodson, Michael. 2003. "The End in the Beginning: Re(de)finding Aboriginality." In *Blacklines: Contemporary Critical Writing by Indigenous Australians*, edited by Michelle Grossman, 25–42. Carlton: Melbourne University Press.

Dodson, Patrick. 2016. "Patrick Dodson: 25 Years on from Royal Commission into Aboriginal Deaths in Custody Recommendations." *Indigenous Law Bulletin* 8 (2): 24–29.

Downey, Bernice, and Madeleine Stout. 2006. "Nursing, Indigenous Peoples and Cultural Safety: So What? Now What?" *Contemporary Nurse* 22 (2): 327–332.

Faulkner, Joanne. 2015. "'Our Own Hurricane Katrina': Aboriginal Disadvantage and Australian National Identity." *National Identities* 17 (2): 117–135.

Fforde, Cressida, Lawrence Bamblett, Ray Lovett, Scott Gorringe, and Bill Fogarty. 2013. "Discourse, Deficit and Identity: Aboriginality, the Race Paradigm and the Language of Representation in Contemporary Australia." *Media International Australia, Incorporating Culture & Policy* 149: 162–173.

Gardiner, John. Australian Parliament. 2013. "Closing the Gap." Accessed May 22, 2018. www.aph.gov.au/About_Parliament/Parliamentary_Departments/Parliamentary_Library/pubs/BriefingBook44p/ClosingGap.

Goodwin, Tim, and Adele Cox. 2008. "Demographics of Indigenous Australia." *Reform* 92: 18–20.

Head, Brian. 2008. "Wicked Problems in Public Policy." *Public Policy* 3 (2): 101–118.

House of Representatives, Australian Government. 2016a. "Ministerial Statements Closing the Gap Speech Wednesday 10 February 2016." Accessed May 22, 2018. Accessed May 22, 2018. http://parlinfo.aph.gov.au/parlInfo/genpdf/chamber/hansardr/7ef9bd10-ec92-4de4-9372-a92d6a12d7ef/0040/hansard_frag.pdf;fileType=application%2Fpdf

House of Representatives, Australian Government. 2016b. "Ministerial Statements Closing the Gap Speech Wednesday 10 February 2016." Accessed May 22, 2018. http://parlinfo.aph.gov.au/parlInfo/genpdf/chamber/hansardr/7ef9bd10-ec92-4de4-9372-a92d6a12d7ef/0041/hansard_frag.pdf;fileType=application%2Fpdf.

Human Rights and Equal Opportunity Commission, Australian Government. 1997. "Bringing Them Home: Report of the National Inquiry into the Separation of Aboriginal and Torres Strait Islander Children from their Families." Accessed May 22, 2018. www.humanrights.gov.au/publications/bringing-them-home-report-1997.

Hunter, Boyd. 2007. "Conspicuous Compassion and Wicked Problems: The Howard Government's National Emergency in Indigenous Affairs." *Agenda* 14 (3): 35–51.

Johns, Gary. 2008. "The Northern Territory Intervention in Aboriginal Affairs: Wicked Problem or Wicked Policy?" *Agenda: A Journal of Policy Analysis and Reform* 15 (2): 65–84.

Lawrence, David, and Helen Lawrence. 2004. "Torres Strait: The Region and Its People." In *Woven Histories Dancing Lives Torres Strait Islander Identity, Culture and History*, edited by Richard Davis, 15–29. Canberra, Australia: Aboriginal Studies Press.

Martin, Karen. 2003. "Ways of Knowing, Being and Doing: A Theoretical Framework and Methods for Indigenous and Indigenist Re-Search." *Journal of Australian Studies* 76: 203–214.

Merton, Donna, Fiona Cram, and Bagele Chilisa, eds. 2013. *Indigenous Pathways into Social Research. Voices of a New Generation.* Walnut Creek, CA: Left Coast Press Inc.

Milner IV, H. Richard. 2007. "Race, Culture, and Researcher Positionality: Working Through Dangers Seen, Unseen, and Unforeseen." *Educational Researcher* 36 (7): 388–400.

Moreton-Robinson, Aileen. 2004. *Whiteness, Epistemology and Indigenous Representation.* Canberra, Australia: Aboriginal Studies Press.

Museum of Australian Democracy. 2018. "Aboriginals Protection and Restriction of Sale of Opium Act 1897 (Qld)." Accessed May 22, 2018. www.foundingdocs.gov.au/item-sdid-54.html

Prins, Gwyn, Isabel Galiana, Christopher Green, Reiner Grundmann, Mike Hulme, Atte Korhola, Frank Laird, Ted Nordhaus, Roger Pielke Jnr, Steve Rayner, Daniel Sarewitz, Michael Shellenberger, Nico Stehr, and Hiroyuki Tezuka. 2010. "The Hartwell Paper: A New Direction for Climate Policy After the Crash of 2009." Paper from a meeting convened at Hartwell House, United Kingdom late 2009: 1-42. https://eprints.lse.ac.uk/27939/1/HartwellPaper_English_version.pdf

Rigney, Lester-Irabinna. 1997. "Internationalisation of an Indigenous Anti-Colonial Cultural Critique of Research Methodologies: A Guide to Indigenist Research Methodology and Its Principles." *WICAZO SA Review: Journal of Native American Studies* 14 (2): 109–121.

Rittel, Horst, and Melvin Webber. 1973. "Dilemmas in a General Theory of Planning." *Policy Sciences* 4: 155–169.

Royal Commission and Board of Inquiry into the Protection and Detention of Children in the Northern Territory, Australian Government. 2017. "Report of Royal Commission and Board of Enquiry into the Protection and Detention of Children in the Northern Territory." Accessed May 22, 2018. https://childdetentionnt.royalcommission.gov.au/Documents/Royal-Commission-NT-Final-Report-Volume-3A.pdf.

Schofield, T., T. Sebastian, M. Donelly, and C. Anderson. 2015. "Tobacco Use Among Aboriginal and Torres Strait Islander High School Students: Understanding 'the social' and the Effects of Indigeneity." *Australian Aboriginal Studies* 2: 46–57.

Sherman, John, and Gayle Peterson. 2009. "Finding the Win in Wicked Problems: Lessons from Evaluating Public Policy Advocacy." *The Foundation Review* 1 (3): 86–99.

State Library of Queensland, Queensland Government. 2016. "Queensland Legislation." Accessed May 22, 2018. www.slq.qld.gov.au/resources/atsi/community-history/qld-legislation.

Van Hulst, Merlijn, and Dvora Yanow. 2016. "From Policy 'Frames' to 'Framing': Theorizing a More Dynamic, Political Approach." *The American Review of Public Administration* 46 (1): 92–112.

Walker, Polly. 2003. "Colonising Research: Academia's Structural Violence Towards Indigenous Peoples." *Social Alternatives* 22 (3): 37–40.

12 Unpacking Dependency; Managing 'Becoming'

Supporting the Experiences of Patients Living with Chronic Disease

Will Thomas

This chapter uses findings from a study of the experiences of people living with a diagnosis of Inflammatory Bowel Disease (Ulcerative Colitis or Crohn's Disease) to illustrate a discussion about the management of patients learning to live with a chronic condition. It draws on a broader discussion of dependency in order to offer suggestions for how the process of 'becoming' someone that lives with such a condition should be supported.

Many of the challenges that are faced as we seek to improve the way in which care services are managed share some or all of the characteristics of "wicked problems" (Rittel and Webber 1973; Grint 2010). In this case, it will be claimed that supporting patients as they learn to live with their chronic condition displays wicked features through its highly individualized and constantly shifting nature. These features make it difficult to imagine straightforward, neat solutions to improving the way in which support is provided.

The use of dependency in an analytical way is offered as a tool to support the construction of "clumsy solutions" (Grint 2010, 176)—ways to work with and address problems and their symptoms without trying to provide a solution. As we improve our understanding of the complexities that are hidden within the concept of 'dependency,' we become able to identify ways in which the provision of care might be improved. Indeed, this move also exposes risks that failing to understand these concerns properly may have on the quality of health and social care management. It is suggested, although not explored in detail, that these improvements carry normative value.

The chapter starts with an unpacking of key features of dependency, using Kittay's (1999) terminology of 'inevitable' and 'derivative' (sometimes 'secondary') dependency as a starting point. This framework is used as a foundation and extended so that it can be used to look at the impact of organizational policies and decisions as they relate to the experiences of those they effect. Crucially, dependency is presented as a normal, natural, feature of existence rather than as a way to identify 'otherness.' Rather than seeing dependency as something which must always be avoided, greater nuance and resolution is brought to analysis through considering features of relations which reflect connectedness, power imbalances and, most importantly, the idea of 'necessity.' Following a discussion of an exploratory research study the chapter offers some considerations of the relationship between the wicked features of managing dependency and the efforts of those with a responsibility to organize and manage care services.

Normalizing Dependency

The notion of dependency is often used as a shorthand justification of a normative judgment whereby a situation, policy or action is wrong when it places the subject in a position of being dependent. Brown, Ecclestone and Emmel (2017) make a similar point about the use of the concept of 'vulnerability,' noting that it is often used to justify public policy initiatives (see also Clough 2017). While some of these decisions may prove justified, we should be careful not to confuse a 'rule of thumb' with a carefully considered analysis. To rely on the idea of being dependent to do the work of forming a moral judgment about a situation partly ignores the reality of what it means to be dependent and of the complexities that are hidden behind this term. However, to make independence, the preferred outcome of our actions denies a fundamental truth about our condition—dependency is a component of our natural and necessary state of being. We are relational animals and as such will often find ourselves dependent on others.

Dependency is a normal feature of shared human experiences, particularly the shared experience of weaknesses or challenges. It is not a characteristic of the weak and powerless but rather of the socially connected. Our understanding of this "shared vulnerability" (Fineman 2010, 270) prompts a response to the needs of those around us. Levinas uses the idea of 'the face' to describes this duty: "The Other becomes my neighbour precisely through the way the face summons me, calls for me, begs for me, and in so doing recalls my responsibility" (in Hand 1989, 83). For Schopenhauer, compassion is the primary motivator of moral behavior, as he describes it "the direct participation . . . in the sufferings of another, leading to sympathetic assistance in the effort to prevent or remove them" (1999, Part III, Chapter 5). While we should also acknowledge that our cultural desire to value independence, freedom and autonomy is important and may create a tension for those that are more dependent (Piredda et al. 2016, 125), the need and desire to respond to others are fundamental.

At various points in our lives, each one of us is more or less dependent on those around us. As babies we are dependent on those that care for us—parents, clearly, but also other family members, health care professionals and so on. During periods of illness or if we become frail in older age, we may once again find ourselves in an inescapable position of being dependent. This "ontological shared vulnerability . . . encourages and in many ways necessitates the forming of relationships of care and support" (Clough 2017, 477). Robinson agrees, noting that the concept of the individual is "incoherent unless understood as . . . existing through a series of complex and ever-changing networks of relations with others" (2006, 13) she describes "'webs' relationships . . . thick with responsibilities" (2006, 8; also, Sherwin and Winsby 2011, 184). As we grow into adults we become, and do not begrudge being, the ones on which others depend. The inescapability of this position is highlighted by Kittay (1999) in referring to this type of dependency as 'inevitable,' reminding us that this is not something we can choose to ignore or avoid.

The positions of dependency and independency do not exist as simple binary positions where we have to be in one category or the other (Cloutier et al. 2015). As we go through life we find ourselves in periods of more or less dependency, perhaps being dependent on different people or groups. Frequently, our situation will be complex or partial—we will be somewhat dependent, perhaps in some aspects of our lives. So just as being dependent does not represent an abnormal or problematic characteristic, equally, we should not view it as being static or a permanent feature.

There is no, or at least very limited, fixedness in our position of being dependent. It reflects a set of circumstances which are likely to shift through time. We should be cautious in using a description of someone as being 'dependent' as a label or a shortcut for efforts to understand the individual nature of their circumstances. Kittay reminds us that there is potential for dependency to be a social stigma (2011, 51); suggesting that the use of dependency as a label is more than simply 'unhelpful' but may help to reinforce socially constructed vulnerabilities (Dodds 2013, 191). Neither is it true that being 'dependent' offers a complete picture of an individual's circumstances; individuals are much more than their 'dependency' at any one moment. While it is a useful tool for "examining the intersections between those who require assistance and those who provide it" (Fine and Glendinning 2005, 615), we must be cautious about using it as a label beyond this narrow scope, not least this is because those who have some elements of dependency may also be the ones on whom others rely (Wiles 2011, 578; Fine and Glendinning 2005, 609–610).

Although we should take care in leaping from empirical observation to normative conclusion the evidence suggests that we are secure in conceding that humans are fundamentally connected and that dependency should not be criticized in all cases. During periods where we find ourselves dependent on others, we ought not be regarded as being 'abnormal,' 'repressed' or 'wronged.' Rather, we are likely to be exhibiting a fundamental characteristic of our human condition—the relational nature of our ontology. It follows from this conclusion that aiming to eliminate dependency is more than simply an inappropriate goal, it is one that seeks to encourage us to deny a key feature of our existence. Instead, we should look toward a more nuanced understanding of dependency to help navigate decision-making.

While dependency is a natural feature of the human condition it is not unproblematic. Principle amongst our concerns is the relationship between dependency and autonomy or independence. In the case of health care, the principle of autonomy "assumes that patients are able to . . . deliberate objectively, arrive at independent judgements and communicate their decisions effectively" (Sherwin and Winsby 2011, 184). Clearly, this ideal is not universally achievable: access to information is just one way in which fully autonomous decision-making might be prevented but there are many others. Equally, the process of enacting a decision must be differentiated from the process of making a decision. Kittay reminds us of a distinction between independence as decision-making and as decision-enacting (Kittay 2011, 50), and this is useful to us. Here, our goal is to facilitate and support independence as decision-making (Fine and Glendinning 2005, 610), recognizing that this form of autonomy is more widely achievable and makes a significant difference to people's lives.

Reflecting Decisions and Power Imbalances

While being in a position of dependency is not always problematic, particularly when it is unavoidable through illness, there are times when decisions, policies or actions create a dependency which causes or reflects a power imbalance (for example, Dodds 2013; Oliver 1989). Kittay's (1999) framework distinguishes between dependency of the type explored above, which she terms 'inevitable dependency,' and that which arises from structures, policies and decisions, which she terms 'derivative dependency.'

Inevitable dependency arises in situations where the relationship occurs naturally, such as in the example of a baby being dependent on adults around it. Implicit in this form of dependency is the existence of a dyadic relationship (or series of relationships) between one that is dependent, and one on whom they are dependent (George 1991, 178). In the case of a baby, they are dependent on their parents or perhaps on anyone around who is in a position to support and care for them. In the case of inevitable dependency, the question 'on whom is this person dependent' is answered straightforwardly—they are dependent on anyone that is able to provide them support. In examples of derivative dependency, the answer to the same question is not as clear.

Derivative dependencies are socially constructed—they are instances where one becomes reliant on another for assistance, help or support, not because of some unavoidable physical circumstances, but because of an environment which creates this position. For example, requiring a student to ask permission to visit the toilet during class time creates a dependency on the class tutor that is driven by a policy decision. While it would be possible to allow a student to leave the class without drawing attention to themselves in this way the decision has been taken not to permit it, perhaps for reasons of security or safeguarding. Those decisions create a form of dependency that it is categorically different to our alternative position in that it is the result of choices.

Whether caused by economic, social or political controls, derivative dependencies are made possible by power imbalances (Kittay 2011). Those in power have the ability to create control mechanisms that force those without power into positions of derivative dependency and thus limit their capacity to act freely—in other words their autonomy. While there may be good reasons for curtailing the independence of individuals by placing them in a position of derivative dependency—for example it would be unsafe to allow patients to help themselves to pharmaceutical supplies, the systems we have in place to control supplies *are* examples of derivative dependency. However, that will not always be the case and situations of dependency may arise to protect power and influence, to exert control or even without any very clear justification at all. It is these cases to which we should pay the closest attention.

The same people that are able to create situations of derivative dependency are also, of course, those who are best placed to ease that situation or to support those that find themselves placed in that position. In the example that features in this chapter they are the managers in a care system: a hospital, other health care providers or funders. While they can act to ease the level of dependence caused by policies, procedures and practices it does not follow that they always have a duty to do so. We will return to this issue later in the chapter.

The second way in which this form of dependency differs to inevitable dependency, addressed earlier, is in the answer to the question of 'on whom is this person dependent?' In the case of inevitable dependency, the answer suggested was 'anyone who can help' but here that is not sufficient. In this case, the same decision-making process that creates the dependency also has to answer this question—in setting up a structure to regulate access to certain pharmaceuticals, we must also explain who is responsible for providing help to gain that access (doctor, nurse etc.). In this example, where the fundamental issue is one of professional expertise, these are the only people who are able to provide assistance.

So far we have identified two categories of dependency differentiated through the degree to which they are natural or constructed. At the same time, we have acknowledged that there are some examples of derivative dependency that are necessary (perhaps for safety's sake) and some which exist for some other reason. While it does not follow that the decisions that create these situations are morally problematic, these positions are not necessary in quite the same manner (for example, financial sign-offs). This is also a feature that we will return to later in the chapter.

Moral Harm and Responsibility

An understanding of the possible forms of dependency allows us to begin a process of hypothesizing normative positions in relation to these forms. It is assumed (but not germane to our argument here) that where we find ourselves in a position to help someone in a position of inevitable dependency we are obliged to do so. Our discussion here focuses on derivative dependencies where the nature of any responsibility is more complex.

It is not always true to say that causing someone to be in a position of derived dependency is wrong. While it is true that this will often limit their freedom, autonomy or liberty in some way it is possible to offer justification for this type of action. We might approach this in utilitarian fashion, arguing that to do so promotes the greater good; we might approach from the position of the social contract, thinking that a curtailment of our freedoms is a rational response to the collective threats we face (e.g. Locke, Hobbes); or we might approach from a position of relational ontology, determining that our natural state is one of " 'webs' of relationships which are thick with responsibilities" (Robinson 2006, 8). Here we need only agree that it is possible that some instances of derived dependency might be morally permissible.

However, we choose to present the argument: it is plausible to say that there are some (you may argue there to be few, or a great number) of instances when taking actions that lead to others being in a position of derivative dependency is not 'wrong.' At the same time, we should recognize the impact of our actions and take responsibility for the dependencies caused by our decisions. Failure to do so risks failing to consider whether dependency is justified or whether there are ways to refine, replace or reduce the dependency caused.

Just as in the case of inevitable dependency, where we can reduce the level of derivative dependency, or better support those that are in a dependent position and such a reduction would not create additional risks (for example, in relation to patient safety), we have a duty to do so. Other things being equal, we should not cause or sustain periods of (derivative) dependency beyond the minimum that can be justified.

Outside the realm of health care, we may find dependency being exaggerated or extended through dysfunctional parental relationships. Dodds (2013, 192) describes how parents of a child who seek to limit the contact their child has with other children, adults and social settings in order to protect them. In doing so, they increase the dependency of the child; an example of what Dodds terms 'pathogenic vulnerability.' Care must then be taken to ensure that our actions, however well-meaning, do not make worse a situation that they were trying to improve.

We are now in a position to extend Kittay's (1999) framework of inevitable and derivative dependency in order to highlight some additional features critical to our current project. Both broad categories are useful—and help to draw distinctions which are critical in forming an organizational response. Analytically, the idea of derivative dependency is particularly important, as it highlights the impact of choices and the power relations that make it possible to place others in a position of dependency. From a more critical standpoint, we are able to see derivative dependency as a curtailment of independence which in some circumstances can be justified by its necessity (e.g. in situations where safety is at risk). The category of derivative dependency therefore needs to be further divided into necessary and unnecessary dependencies. Those where we can agree the necessity of the circumstances are likely to be morally justifiable; but those in which the dependence is not 'necessary' are ones to which we should pay closest attention.

Background to the Study

The exploratory study used to illustrate this chapter's arguments focuses on people living with Inflammatory Bowel Disease. Although numerous previous studies have sought to understand the patient experience in quantitative terms (Dudley-Brown and Baker 2012; Iglesias et al. 2010; O'Sullivan et al. 2000) or have evaluated new surgical techniques (Gray, Leung and Scales 2009; Kennedy et al. 2008) or drug regimes (Sewitch et al. 2002), few, if any, have attempted to understand the patient experience from a qualitative perspective.

The study was conducted following a favorable opinion (approval) from the London (Bloomsbury) National Research Ethics Service Committee following a proportionate review. With help from a local hospital, potential participants were selected in order to give a broad range of experiences with the condition and contacted to explain the nature of the study. Interviews were conducted with 15 individuals with a diagnosis of Inflammatory Bowel Disease. The participants exhibited: a range of periods since their first diagnosis; variety in age (from early 20s to late 60s); balance of gender (nine female and six male); and the nature of their diagnosis (ten Crohn's Disease and five Ulcerative Colitis).

Semi-structured interviews were conducted with each of the participants, during which there was discussion of the period up to and including diagnosis; of how they coped following diagnosis; of treatment; and of how their lives have changed since they received their diagnosis. All interviews were audio-recorded and then transcribed prior to analysis.

A lack of prior work on the experiences of patients living with Inflammatory Bowel Disease (IBD) suggested that an approach in which themes were drawn out of and grounded in the interview data was the most appropriate way to analyze these data. The analytical approach drew on the work of Friese (2014), who suggests a "Noticing, Collecting and Thinking" framework to support working from descriptive analysis that reflects themes in the interviews toward an analytical level of analysis in which themes are reanalzsed in more detail and with an eye on the creation of conceptual themes. The analysis of the interview data followed this model, resulting in analytical themes which were derived inductively from the collected data.

The resulting analysis identified common features in the experiences of individuals as well as highlighting areas where participants' accounts were very different. Hence it was possible to describe the experience of diagnosis and how this occurred; the role played by medication in defining their condition; the relationship with hospital staff; changing day-to-day behaviors; and the impact of a lack of public understanding as elements of the experience that were important.

As the iterative nature of the analysis moved to identify analytical themes from the data two broad thematic issues were identified: the importance of 'learning to live' with IBD; and a recognition of a complex feeling of 'otherness' experienced by patients following their diagnosis. The next section focuses on the first of these two thematic areas and is used to highlight how our more nuanced understanding of the nature and impacts of dependency can help to suggest ways to address wicked elements in managing support for patients with complex, chronic conditions. The theme relating to otherness is not considered here for reasons of space but focused on the sense of difference that those living with IBD feel, partly as a result of a lack of general understanding about the condition amongst the public, and partly due to a lack of outward manifestation (for most) of the disease—that often one can look 'well' while suffering badly. For many participants, these issues were isolating and a cause of emotional stress.

Unpicking the Learning Involved

Learning to live with IBD encompasses both abstract learning about the condition (many participants reported never having heard of the condition prior to diagnosis) and learning about how the condition affects them as individuals. Important aspects of this process include learning about the impact of diet; finding an appropriate medication regime; and talking to family, friends and colleagues about the condition. However, most significantly, the study highlighted a key component described as 'becoming someone who has IBD.'

While individual experiences around diagnosis varied, most participants experience a complex transition or series of transitions into someone who has a named chronic condition that will define, or partly define, them for the rest of their life. Amongst the participants there was a very wide range of reported emotions around this time. For some, the diagnosis offered relief that they had an explanation, and a name, for how they felt, or that they did not have Cancer. For others, they were faced with a condition that they had never heard of and knew nothing about. As a result, some participants described feelings of shock, anxiety and denial following their diagnosis.

There were numerous examples of participants changing behaviors following their diagnosis. One of the most commonly discussed changes was a reduction in the frequency with which they would go out and socialize. Others described a reluctance to go shopping or on holiday. In some interviews, there were examples of participants reporting changes that they had made which helped them 'cope' with their condition rather than 'manage' it. For example, one interviewee talked about always keeping a set of clothes in the back of their car in case they needed them to change into while away from home.

Different elements of learning were shown to be components of 'becoming' someone who lives with IBD, namely: learning about their condition; learning to manage their condition; and learning to cope with their condition. As participants describe addressing these components they gradually develop expertise which becomes an important coping strategy in their management of their condition. In participants with a longer period since their diagnosis, the interviews revealed much more about the collaborative practices between medical professionals and the participants themselves. This was characterized by participants being encouraged to take control over some medication decisions (such as when to take short courses of steroids) and having considerable control over discussions regarding future treatment options.

There are practical and moral imperatives to support the process of 'becoming' in patients. Practical imperatives arise simply because greater self-responsibility amongst patients suffering from chronic disease is a requirement of both effective (meeting the needs of the patients well) and efficient (allocating resources well) care (see e.g. Baars et al. 2010; Barlow, Edwards and Turner 2009; Rogers et al. 2005). Moral imperatives arise because the lack of knowledge in these three components places the individual in a state of 'dependency' because, as Kittay (1999) notes, they lack capacities "essential to surviving and maintaining oneself." Kittay goes on to note that the vulnerability of the patient places the professional in a situation of obligation—where they are obliged to respond to the individual's needs. Managing care for these groups of patients therefore requires considering how best to support the acquisition of knowledge in each of the three component areas above.

Learning About IBD

The immediate needs of patients who are diagnosed with IBD are likely to involve access to information and support with the first component area of learning—learning about the condition. The data from interviews suggests that very few participants had heard of Crohn's Disease or Ulcerative Colitis prior to their diagnosis, let alone knew about what living with it would be like or how it might be managed. Each individual has a preference for how they access information, or the pace at which they wish to engage with learning about this new feature of their life. Some of those interviewed described wanting to learn as much as they could as quickly as they could; others report being in denial for some time after diagnosis occurred.

Clearly, there is scope for health care providers to do this more or less effectively, particularly when it comes to considering how best to provide information to people who are likely to be feeling ill, anxious and perhaps shocked at their diagnosis. From a management of care point of view, then, the challenge is in understanding how best to provide this information to patients, and considering the type of support which should be provided in order to help patients process this information as readily as possible.

We might tentatively suggest some principles to guide this process that include 'drip feeding' information so as not to overwhelm the patient; making use of multiple forms of information provision (online, leaflets, conversations); and having counselors or advisors available to support patients, particularly in the period immediately following diagnosis. However, this is a manageable, linear issue—one where we can easily define success and which we can measure progress to confirm patient satisfaction. While it may therefore be difficult, it does not meet criteria for a 'wicked problem' (Rittel and Webber 1973; Grint 2010; Raisio 2009).

Learning to Manage and Cope With IBD

The process of 'becoming' is characterized by two further types of learning: how to manage the condition and how to cope with it. The distinction, drawn for our analytical purposes, between these two types of learning is primarily one of physical versus emotional characteristics. Learning to manage the condition (its physical manifestation) might primarily require learning about methods of control (medication, diet etc.) and the recognition of causes and signs of exacerbations. Learning to cope with the condition (its emotional effects) concerns adjustment to being someone who will live with this chronic condition for the rest of one's life.

The individual nature of IBD makes it difficult to define, in the abstract, what these processes will be like for a newly diagnosed patient. For every patient the personal experience of how the condition will affect them is different. There is a level of complexity, primarily due to a lack of linearity, which does not exist in the same way for learning about the condition. In this latter example, patients with no previous knowledge of IBD can be given access to learning materials and supported as they find out more about what their diagnosis means. In the case of the other two categories of learning the same cannot be said. Rather, these aspects of learning display two characteristics of 'wicked problems': complexity that makes them difficult to fully define, and a multifaceted nature that prevents linear solutions. It is the individual nature of the experience; and dependencies between the person with IBD and supporting/caring individuals or teams that shift over time and which fundamentally define the nature of caring relationships. Increasingly, these patterns are hard to describe and predict, making the task for professionals and managers more difficult.

Taking the case of learning to manage the condition through medication as an example, we see evidence of both these wicked characteristics at play. At first, the patient is entirely dependent on the health care professional for input into potential medication strategies. Protocols will be tried and tested in the hope that one will be found which offers a good level of day-to-day control. If required, steroids may be used to try to bring exacerbations under control. This example highlights the individual nature of the condition because the drug mix that works for one patient may not work for another and because of the dependency of the patient on the consultant. Generalizations about what works are impossible to make given this characteristic.

As those living with IBD become more used to their condition, learn more about it and become used to managing it, the situation changes. Patients may prompt consultants about new drugs, or about different protocols. For example, some participants report having more control over their own medication, particularly in choosing when to self-administer steroids, and becoming more involved in decisions about changes to medication regimes. This prompts us to think about how dependencies might change as patients become more adept at learning to manage and cope with their condition as well as in response to the way that care is organized, managed and delivered. For those that seek to improve the management of care the task is made 'wicked' by the highly individual and constantly shifting nature.

Dependency and Wickedness

Grint (2010) cautions against seeking neat or perfect solutions to wicked problems. Instead, he suggests a need to focus on building relationships and on understanding the situation, seeking 'clumsy solutions' built through 'bricolage' and reflection. Tools which offer ways to generate insight into the nature of the problem, or suggest potential solutions, are valuable in contributing to the information available to decision-makers as they seek multifaceted solutions to these complex problems. In this final section of the chapter, the value of the dependency framework will be presented as a way to increase the insight with which we start to tackle this wicked problem.

The framework presented here facilitates discussion of aspects of the support and management of support that influences the success and speed with which someone can learn to make adjustments that will enable them to live with this chronic condition more comfortably. In this sense, the value of the dependency framework is in exposing hidden assumptions (Wulfekühler and Rhodes 2017, 1) or unexamined crises (Critchley 2001) to proper scrutiny and questioning. In this case, the result of this exposure is to prompt a consideration of the extent to which the decisions that lead to the creation of derivative dependencies are 'necessary.' The model, then, highlights or uncovers opportunities to reconsider the way in which a situation is managed.

Where our model of dependency helps to identify instances of inevitable dependency then the responsibility is clear. Here, it is suggested, care staff and their managers should seek to support and mitigate those effects and to provide the necessary care. We can judge and perhaps even measure the effectiveness of a system insofar as it is able to deliver this care effectively and in a timely fashion. This element of providing care is not 'wicked,' even though individuals will have different preferences and needs. We know how to characterize a successful outcome (patients know about their condition, or know how to access information) and can imagine how such a system could be enacted.

Instances of derivative dependency are not dealt with in such a straight-forward manner. To start, not all these cases will require that action is taken to mitigate or avoid them. Simply being in a state of dependency is not sufficient to require action to be taken—in itself it is not enough to gener-ate a normative claim. Where the idea of derivative dependency is useful is in highlighting and exposing organizational or social structures that cre-ate (derivative) dependencies (Kittay 2011, 50; Fine and Glendinning 2005, 607) and the power imbalances that may create and sustain unhelpful ele-ments of derivative dependency (Robinson 2006). Through this work in considering how dependencies have been established, we are able to begin to identify responsibilities and ways in which approaches could be changed to reduce the level of dependency.

In addition to identifying the presence of a dependency caused by choice or policy, the framework developed from Kittay's original work prompts us to consider the necessity of the dependency relation that results from the decisions of those with power. This characteristic is relevant because we can understand derivative dependency as a curtailment of independence, or autonomy. While there are circumstances in which such a restriction can be justified there is a prima facie assumption against doing so. Our first move, therefore, must be to question the necessity of individual aspects of depen-dency which generates potential starting points for improving the quality of the care and support that is being offered. It opens up a discussion about the degree of independence that is possible and desirable for those in the posi-tion of a newly diagnosed patient, permitting a balance of the requirement for autonomy and patient involvement in decision-making with acknowl-edgment that there are likely to be limits to its scope and extent.

Placing another autonomous being in a position of dependency—that is, limiting their decision-making and/or decision-enacting independence—is justifiable only in circumstances in which this dependency is 'necessary.' A full treatment of the boundaries of this necessity is beyond the scope of this chapter, but it is sufficient to assume that legal, professional and safety grounds are likely to be acceptable grounds for the creation of a derivative dependency. It would, therefore, in our terms be 'necessary.'

If we accept that there will be some derivative (constructed) dependencies that are not 'wrong'—for example, requiring that qualified professionals sign-off on requests for new, potentially dangerous, pharmaceutical treatments—then we might also agree that some of the same types of dependency are less obviously necessary. Such decisions, systems or structures that place individuals in a position of derivative dependency but which fail to meet our standard for 'necessity' are at the very least, morally questionable. This distinction offers another analytical tool for considering the way in which the support for those learning to live with a chronic condition is managed.

It is on unnecessary derivative dependencies that the primary focus of those that seek to improve the way in which care and support are managed for patients following a diagnosis of a chronic disease or condition should be placed. Structures that create derivative dependencies limit autonomy, reinforce power structures and are self-defeating at least within a context of encouraging those living with chronic or long-term conditions to be more effective at managing their own condition. While it might be messy, at least we are in a position to identify the first steps which could be taken in improving the quality of care.

Managers should take note of how structures and decisions cause and sustain dependency—they have a duty to reduce these if it is possible to do so. Even though there are instances where derivative dependency can be justified this does not imply that individuals have no right to self-determination (autonomy). Careful thought should be given to the nature of any curtailment of autonomy: the right to autonomy of decision-making is distinct from autonomy of execution. Cases where the former can be restricted will be far fewer than those in which the latter can.

A working system for supporting those learning to live with a chronic condition must therefore be able to manage two overlapping impulses. We must acknowledge and act upon an understanding that individuals will have different, perhaps very different, needs. Systems that determine whether someone meets criteria for aid and then offer a one-size fits all package fail to do this sufficiently. At the same time, we must be alert to the notion of shifting needs—the position of being dependent is not a permanent state that once entered into cannot be left. Equally, needs may increase or shift in other ways. Well-designed systems must ensure frequent reassessment of needs and recognize independence (in this context) as "control, choice and self-governance in ones life" (Morris 1993 in Power 2008, 834).

Conclusion

This chapter offers thoughts on how attention to the nature of dependency can be used to help identify ways in which wicked problems might be addressed. Kittay's (1999) framework of inevitable and derivative dependency provides a starting point through its useful identification of two forms of dependent relationship: one in which the dependency is natural and the other in which the dependency is caused by choices made by those in power. In this chapter, this framework has been extended and applied to the idea of wicked problems, primarily through the introduction of the ideas of necessary and unnecessary derivative dependency.

As an analytic tool, this revised framework prompts questions about structures and policies that serve to place individuals in positions of derivative dependency. It is sufficiently nuanced to allow acknowledgment of the need to create dependency for reasons of (for example) safety or protection. However, it also reminds health care managers that creating unnecessary dependencies serves to limit the extent to which the person who is coming to terms with a diagnosis of a chronic disease is able to learn to manage and cope with their condition.

The tool, and its resulting analysis of dependency, does not offer easy solutions to complex, wicked problems but it offers some insight into how a clumsy or messy solution might help respond to important aspects of the issue. In this example, clumsy solutions will include straightforward improvements to service delivery and particularly to the format and methods used to provide information. They will also include personalized approaches that take account of the way in which the condition affects each person in a different way with different exacerbating factors or symptoms. Additionally, and less obviously, the framework reminds those in power to seek out and respond to the individual needs of each patient, responding to them uniquely rather than as generic 'patients with condition X.' In taking account of these maxims the resulting approach may start to address the symptoms of the wicked problem even if it is unable to resolve it neatly and completely.

References

Baars, J. E., T. Markus, E. J. Kuipers, and C. J. van der Woude. 2010. "Patients' Preferences Regarding Shared Decision-Making in the Treatment of Inflammatory Bowel Disease: Results from a Patient-Empowerment Study." *Digestion* 81 (2): 113–119.

Barlow, J., R. Edwards, and A. Turner. 2009. "The Experience of Attending a Lay-Led, Chronic Disease Self-Management Programme from the Perspective of Participants with Multiple Sclerosis." *Psychology and Health* 24 (10): 1167–1180.

Brown, Kate, Kathryn Ecclestone, and Nick Emmel. 2017. "The Many Faces of Vulnerability." *Social Policy and Society* 16 (3): 497–510.

Clough, Beverley. 2017. "Disability and Vulnerability: Challenging the Capacity/Incapacity Binary." *Social Policy and Society* 16 (3): 469–481.

Cloutier, Denise S., Anne Martin-Matthews, Kerry Byrne, and Faye Wolse. 2015. "The Space between: Using 'Relational Ethics' and 'Relational Space' to Explore Relationship-Building Between Care Providers and Care Recipients in the Home Space." *Social & Cultural Geography* 16 (7): 764–782.

Critchley, Simon. 2001. *Continental Philosophy: A Very Short Introduction*. Oxford: Oxford University Press.

Dodds, Susan, ed. 2013. *Dependence, Care, and Vulnerability*, edited by Catriona Mackenzie, Wendy Rogers, and Susan Dodds. Oxford: Oxford University Press.

Dudley-Brown, Sharon, and Kathy Baker. 2012. "Ulcerative Colitis from Patients' Viewpoint." *Gastroenterology Nursing* 35 (1): 54–63.

Fine, Michael, and Caroline Glendinning. 2005. "Dependence, Independence or Inter-Dependence? Revisiting the Concepts of 'Care' and 'Dependency'." *Ageing and Society* 25 (4): 601–621.

Fineman, Martha Albertson. 2010. "The Vulnerable Subject and the Responsive State." *Emory Law Journal* 60 (2): 251.

Friese, Susanne. 2014. *Qualitative Data Analysis with ATLAS. Ti*. London: Sage Publications.

George, Steve. 1991. "Measures of Dependency: Their Use in Assessing the Need for Residential Care for the Elderly." *Journal of Public Health* 13 (3): 178–181.

Gray, J. R., E. Leung, and J. Scales. 2009. "Treatment of Ulcerative Colitis from the Patient's Perspective: A Survey of Preferences and Satisfaction with Therapy." *Alimentary Pharmacology and Therapeutics* 29 (10): 1114–1120.

Grint, Keith. 2010. "Wicked Problems and Clumsy Solutions: The Role of Leadership." In *The New Public Leadership Challenge*, edited by Stephen Brookes and Keith Grint, 169–186. London: Springer.

Hand, Sean. 1989. *The Levinas Reader*. Oxford: Wiley-Blackwell.

Iglesias, M., I. Vazquez, M. Barreiro-de Acosta, A. Figuerias, L. Nieto, M. Pineiro, R. Gomez, A. Lorenzo, and J. E. Dominguez Munoz. 2010. "Health Related Quality of Life in Patients with Crohn's Disease in Remission." *Revista Espanola De Enfermedades Digestivas* 102 (11): 624–630.

Kennedy, Erin, Teresa To, A. Hillary Steinhart, Alan Detsky, Hilary Llewellyn-Thomas, and Robin McLeod. 2008. "Do Patients Consider Postoperative Maintenance Therapy for Crohn's Disease Worthwhile?" *Inflammatory Bowel Diseases* 14 (2): 224–235.

Kittay, Eva Feder. 1999. *Love's Labor: Essays on Women, Equality and Dependency*. New York, London: Routledge.

Kittay, Eva Feder. 2011. "The Ethics of Care, Dependence, and Disability." *Ratio Juris* 24 (1): 49–58.

Morris, Jenny. 1993. *Independent Lives? Community Care and Disabled People*. Basingstoke: Palgrave Macmillan.

Oliver, Mike. 1989. "Disability and Dependency: A Creation of Industrial Societies." In *Disability and Dependency*, edited by Len Barton, 6–22. London: Falmer.

O'Sullivan, Maria, Nasir Mahmud, Dermot P. Kelleher, Ella Lovett, and C. A. O'Morain. 2000. "Patient Knowledge and Educational Needs in Irritable Bowel Syndrome." *European Journal of Gastroenterology and Hepatology* 12 (1): 39–43.

Piredda, Michela, Chiara Bartiromo, Maria Teresa Capuzzo, Maria Matarese, and Maria Grazia De Marinis. 2016. "Nursing Care Dependence in the Experiences of Advanced Cancer Inpatients." *European Journal of Oncology Nursing* 20 (February): 125–132.

Power, Andrew. 2008. "Caring for Independent Lives: Geographies of Caring for Young Adults with Intellectual Disabilities." *Social Science and Medicine* 67 (5): 834–843.

Raisio, Harri. 2009. "Health Care Reform Planners and Wicked Problems: Is the Wickedness of the Problems Taken Seriously Or Is It Even Noticed at All?" *Journal of Health Organization and Management* 23 (5): 477–493.

Rittel, Horst W. J., and Melvin Webber. 1973. "Dilemmas in a General Theory of Planning." *Policy Sciences* 4 (2): 155–169.

Robinson, Fiona. 2006. "Care, Gender and Global Social Justice: Rethinking 'ethical Globalization'." *Journal of Global Ethics* 2 (1): 5–25.

Rogers, Anne, Anne Kennedy, Elizabeth Nelson, and Andrew Robinson. 2005. "Uncovering the Limits of Patient-Centeredness: Implementing a Self-Management Trial for Chronic Illness." *Qualitative Health Research* 15 (2): 224–239.

Schopenhauer, Artur. 1999. *On the Basis of Morality*. Indianapolis: Hackett Publishing.
Sewitch, Maida, Michal Abrahamowicz, Alain Bitton, Donald Daly, Gary E. Wild, Albert Cohen, Saul Katz, Peter L. Szego, and Patricia L. Dobkin. 2002. "Psycho-social Correlates of Patient-Physician Discordance in Inflammatory Bowel Disease." *American Journal of Gastroenterology* 97 (9): 2174–2183.
Sherwin, Susan, and Meghan Winsby. 2011. "A Relational Perspective on Autonomy for Older Adults Residing in Nursing Homes." *Health Expectations* 14 (2): 182–190.
Wiles, Janine. 2011. "Reflections on Being a Recipient of Care: Vexing the Concept of Vulnerability." *Social & Cultural Geography* 12 (6): 573–588.
Wulfekühler, Heidrun, and Margaret L. Rhodes. 2017. "Meticulous Thoughtfulness: Cultivating Practical Wisdom in Social Work." *Ethics and Social Welfare* 20 (5): 1–18.

Section 4

Beyond Conventional Methodologies for Understanding Wicked Challenges

Given the intractable nature of wicked problems in health and social care, and the limited success of traditional (often positivistic) approaches to researching how best to organize our responses to the questions they pose, it seems reasonable to consider alternative methods and epistemologies. The fourth part of the book does just that.

We begin with a focus on what are traditionally seen as difficult to research groups with Edmund Coleman-Fountain and Bryony Beresford's account of mental health and Asperger's syndrome. The chapter highlights the manner in which health and social care services struggle to cope with intersecting problems. Worse still, our research often neglects those who are perceived as difficult to research. Coleman-Fountain and Beresford challenge us to think again about who should take part in and indeed shape the very questions and nature of our research. The theme of co-construction is picked up in the next chapter by Marta Strumińska-Kutra, who makes the case for employing action research when tackling complex problems. Here a concern with power (implicit in the prior chapter) is brought to the fore as the strengths and limitations of critical, pragmatic and constructivist research approaches are considered. The idea of multiplicity and competing perspectives is then extended by Anneli Hujala, Sanna Laulainen, Andy Brookes, Maarit Lammassaari and Tamara Mulherin as they seek to explain what multi-paradigmatic research might imply for the consideration of wicked problems—in this case the challenge of encouraging collaborative action. They conclude by reminding us that in research and organizing we often see what we look for. This leads neatly into the final chapter by Jari Martikainen, who introduces visual methods as a powerful way of exploring the hidden side of organizing and being. Together, these chapters invite us to think again about the ways in which we might see, conceptualize and tackle wicked problems in health and social care.

13 Improving Young People's Mental Health?

Understanding Ambivalence to Seeking Support among Young Adults with Asperger Syndrome

Edmund Coleman-Fountain and Bryony Beresford

Introduction

Mental health is a 'wicked problem,' as it cannot be easily defined or resolved through simple linear solutions. Instead, how it is viewed reflects different 'values or prevailing interests' to which solutions are 'inextricably linked' (Hannigan and Coffey 2011, 221–222). Consequently, the 'wicked problem' may be reframed to reflect a distinct set of social arrangements or problematics. Presenting one such reframing, this chapter presents data from a study with 19 young adults with Asperger syndrome (AS).[1] Asperger syndrome shares features in common with other autism diagnoses, such as differences or difficulties linked to the interpretation and processing of 'information specific to communication, social interpretation and interaction' (Beardon 2017, 19), as well as in the experience of sensory stimuli. The Asperger syndrome diagnosis is covered by the term autism, although individuals have typically been diagnosed with AS because they do not have a co-morbidity with a learning disability (Beardon 2017).

The chapter explores the theme of self-reliance among young people with mental health problems and presents a view that draws on the experiences of these young adults with AS. The chapter discusses how self-reliance can be a product of how autism is understood and be a response to an ambivalence about available support. The chapter reflects on the importance of specialist early intervention for this group.

Creating Meaningful Engagement with Mental Health

Young people experience higher rates of mental health problems compared to the rest of the population, but more commonly report preferring to cope alone (Gulliver, Griffiths and Christensen 2010). One reason for this is the perceived stigma associated with the 'mental health/illness' label, which can make young people reluctant to identify distress as more than a minor concern (Wright, Jorm and Mackinnon 2011). Young people's view of mental distress as a threat to their sense of normalcy has been found to underpin a 'cycle of avoidance' (Biddle et al. 2007). In other studies, themes of 'pulling oneself together' (Issakainen 2014, 180) and putting on a 'façade of normality' (Draucker 2005) indicate a tendency to normalize and self-manage distress or to conceal distress that appears 'abnormal' (Prior 2012).

Silence around mental distress can reinforce non-help seeking. Meaningful engagement with services can be inhibited because a young person worries about stigma (Rickwood, Deane and Wilson 2007). A lack of knowledge about mental health and available services can also result in distress being mislabeled and support missed. Researchers and practitioners have suggested ways to promote meaningful engagement with mental health services, including by reframing mental distress as a 'normal but serious' part of life (Issakainen 2014, 180) and creating non-stigmatizing settings in which young people are 'empowered' to talk about distress (Prior 2012). This has involved teaching young people how to recognize mental distress (Kelly, Jorm and Wright 2007) and to challenge their own preconceptions by providing education on the stigma associated with mental illness (Yamaguchi, Mino and Uddin 2011). Interventions that teach family members how to recognize and respond to mental ill health (Harrison, McKay and Bannon 2004) also aims to normalize talk about mental health within families.

Innovation in mental health services is also recommended as a means of promoting meaningful and timely engagement with mental health. Calls for a 'youth-friendly ethos' (Hughes et al. 2017) in mental health services, and for 'stigma-free cultures of care' (McGorry, Bates and Birchwood 2013, s30), promote an approach to mental health care that seeks to be accessible and integrated into young people's lives. Current recommendations include young people shaping services and an enhanced role in supporting mental well-being for other institutions in which young people already participate (Department of Health 2015).

Asperger Syndrome and Mental Distress

As with young people generally (Patton et al. 2016), mental distress in autism represents a 'key' focus of a broader mental health agenda (Autistica 2016). This emerges from the understanding that autistic people experience mental distress as a 'common' feature of their lives (Jones, Zahl and Huws 2001). Exploring how young people with AS respond to distress is another way of approaching the 'wicked problem' of mental health, already reframed as a problem of self-reliance. One impetus for our research is evidence that lack of timely and appropriate support can produce 'reactive' self-management in autistic young people (Trembath et al. 2012). Instead of self-reliance securing a sense of 'normalcy,' it may reflect an inadequate response to the 'normality' of distress in Asperger syndrome.

This contrast reflects how mental distress is linked to Asperger syndrome. For example, vulnerabilities to distress can derive from sensory difficulties

(Smith and Sharp 2013), a tendency to ruminate, and fears around change (Carrington and Graham 2001). Social communication difficulties can also present challenges (Müller, Schuler and Yates 2008) and affect help seeking; as can being treated as 'different' (Huws and Jones 2013). Further studies have linked bullying, isolation and stigma to low self-esteem and depression (Penney 2013). Finally, research on alexithymia shows that some autistic young people may less accurately name and describe emotions (Bird and Cook 2013). As alexithymia can affect how mental distress is communicated, it has been posited as an explanation for heightened levels of mental health difficulties in this group (Erbas et al. 2013).

This chapter explores how young adults with AS manage distress in the absence of external support. It develops two core themes. First, unlike accounts of 'neurotypical' youths (meaning young people who do not display autistic traits) that link self-reliance to a resistance to 'being defined in terms of mental health problems' (Issakainen 2014, 180), this chapter explores how mental distress is conceived as part of or in relation to Asperger syndrome. Second, it addresses what this understanding means for how distress is managed. The chapter thus contributes to discussions around self-management and the role and timing of interventions for young adults with Asperger syndrome.

Methods

The data analyzed in this chapter are from a study of how young adults with AS make sense of mental health difficulties. It formed part of a program of work on autism and mental health (entitled Improving Outcomes for People with Autism Spectrum Disorders by Reducing Mental Health Problems, PI: Professor Emily Simonoff), and included interviews with 19 young adults with AS about managing mental distress. An NHS Research Ethics Committee (Ref: 14/EM/1282) provided ethical approval for the study. Two advisory panels, which included autistic adults and parents of autistic children, supported the study.

Sampling and Recruitment

Recruitment for the study was through an existing research cohort (n = 171) of autistic young adults (aged 23 or 24) living in the South East of England (Baird et al. 2006). The cohort included families who had agreed to contact for future research. The aim was to recruit 20 young adults with an AS diagnosis (in addition to interviewing parents of autistic young adults on their experiences, a study we report separately). A purposive sampling frame was used to support recruitment. The cohort study administrators provided the research team with an anonymized dataset of young adults who had a diagnosis of Asperger syndrome and no additional learning disability. To support identification of young adults who could talk about experiences relating to mental health, scores on mental health outcome measures, collected at one or more waves of cohort data collection were also used (see Table 13.1 for time point and measures). Young adults were not approached if scores on outcome measures suggested they had recently experienced a period of severe mental ill health.

The cohort study administrators approached families by telephone to explain the study and seek consent to share their contact details with the research team. Following that, families indicating an interest received a mailed information sheet highlighting the study's focus and aims. Families who did not decline at this stage (using a supplied 'decline further contact' return slip) were called by a member of the research team a week later to talk about the study and to identify which family member wanted to take part. The cohort study administrators approached 36 families. Six declined to take part (before or after receiving the information pack) due to lack of time or interest. Nineteen young adults from the remaining 30 families participated. Interviews were held within two weeks of arranging the interview. Informed consent was sought before each interview; this

Table 13.1 Parent and Young Adult Completed Mental Health Indicators

	Young adult completed	Parent completed		
	Age 23 yrs (n = 17)	Child aged 23 yrs (n = 19)	Child aged 16 yrs (n = 18)	Child aged 12 yrs (n = 17)
Beck Anxiety Inventory *(Clinical categorization of score*)*				
Minimal	4	10		
Mild	6	4		
Moderate	4	4		
Severe	3	1		
Beck Depression Inventory *(Clinical categorization of score)*				
Minimal	12	15		
Mild	1	2		
Moderate	1	1		
Severe	3	1		
Obsessive Compulsive Inventory				
OCD indicated'	7	3		
Strengths and Difficulties Questionnaire *(Clinical categorization of score)*				
Normal score	8	7	3	8
Raised score	3	7	7	3
High score	6	5	8	6

* Clinical categorizations of symptom severity or 'caseness' were assigned using cut-off points reported in scale manuals and/or associated literature (Beck et al. 1988; Beck, Steer and Carbin 1988; Foa et al. 1998; Goodman 1997)

stated that the participant had the option of ending the interview at any stage.

The Sample

The sample comprised 17 young men and two young women aged 23–24. We sought to recruit positively for young women; however, they were under-represented in the cohort—reflecting a now recognized under-diagnosis of autism in girls in childhood (Baird, Douglas and Murphy 2011). Most had received an AS diagnosis before the age of eight. Eighteen described themselves as 'White British' and one as of mixed ethnicity. Seventeen were living with their parents, and two were in their own rented accommodation. Most had attended mainstream school. Several had completed further and higher education. Nine participants were unemployed or job seeking, with the remainder in some form of paid employment.

Table 13.1 describes the sample in terms of scores on the mental health outcome measures. It demonstrates well-established differences in proxy- and self-reported mental health symptoms (Eiser and Varni 2013). These scores did not form part of the interview. Instead, they point to a range of potential experiences relating to mental distress identified in the sample.

Interview Procedure and Data Analysis

Interviews were held at the participant's place of residence or at facilities at a university campus they were familiar with visiting through the cohort study. Interviews started with a card sorting exercise (developed with the project's two advisory panels) which involved choosing words that they felt described their experiences of distress in the context of their Asperger syndrome diagnosis. Probes were used to explore how they interpreted and managed those experiences. Participants were then asked to describe a time related to one experience of distress. The interview ended with questions related to services and support. Participants were then given time to reflect on and talk through anything that appeared troubling. They were also provided with details of advice and support organizations. Interviews lasted about one and a half hours.

Data were analyzed thematically (Miles, Huberman and Saldana 2013). A thematic framework was developed through a process of data immersion and discussions within the research team. After identifying key themes and sub-themes, each was assigned a unique code. An early version of the thematic framework was shared and discussed with the programme's advisory panels. Transcripts were marked up using the codes (Rapley 2016) and data segments extracted into Word documents in the form of verbatim text. Once complete, one researcher led on a process of making detailed analytical notes that fed into the writing process through which data were further analyzed (Wolcott 2009). To ensure that the data had been fully analyzed and comprehensively reported, the writings were continually refined over several redrafts.

Findings

The data indicated that the young adults had a distinct relationship to distress which was forged in the absence of effective external support. That relationship was one in which mental distress, meaning discomforting experiences associated with stress, anxiety, worry, fear and depression, was interpreted as a 'core' feature of Asperger syndrome, or as the outcome of core characteristics of Asperger syndrome. The young adults talked about how they had learned to manage their experiences.

The Frequency of Distress

One theme that developed in the analysis was the way the young adults linked distress to their understanding of Asperger syndrome. Underpinning the young adult's accounts was the view that Asperger syndrome had a role in producing their experience of distress. For example, some young adults talked about distress as being 'part' of the diagnosis:

> I've always had it, and she [his sister], her's kind of was triggered because . . . things was getting her down. . . . I've always assumed that, cos it was part of my autism
>
> (YA05SM)

The frequency of distress, and the extent to which the young adult's experiences were perceived to be enduring or predictable, appeared to inform the view that distress was rooted in Asperger syndrome. For example, some described distress as something they had 'always' experienced, had experienced lots over a long period of time or had experienced regularly in specific circumstances.

Explaining 'My' Tendencies

These temporalities and frequencies were associated with AS as a 'permanent' condition which they saw as producing tendencies to experience distress or as making them vulnerable due to other characteristics that heightened the likelihood of them facing difficulty. In relation to this, the young adults described learning to explain their experiences as part of Asperger syndrome.

Often, this process involved acquiring a vocabulary related to Asperger syndrome. For example, one young women talked about how her mother and a special education needs coordinator had helped her make sense of her tendency to worry:

INTERVIEWEE: I thought why am I worrying about them. 'Cos I knew I was, but I didn't know why . . . obviously mum . . . she must have had a conversation with the special educational needs coordinator, and that's probably when they decided maybe it was best to tell me. [. . .]

INTERVIEWER: Did you see Asperger's as contributing to that? . . .

INTERVIEWEE: Yeah, but thinking about it now it was a contribution . . . but I just didn't realise . . . obviously that was part of it, that was why I was worrying; if I hadn't had that then I wouldn't have been worrying about those little. . .

(YA01SF)

The process of attribution included making connections between what they understood to be the core characteristics or effects of Asperger syndrome and the content and frequency of their experiences:

> Say obsessional thoughts leads to over thinking things . . . and then it gets me anxious about it and then it becomes even more obsessional and, you know, it just sort of goes round in a bit of a cycle, like, like gets increasingly worse.
>
> (DY08SM)

Making a connection to Asperger syndrome was part of how the participants explained their experiences as part of their everyday lives. It was often by articulating an understanding of what characterized Asperger syndrome that the young adults made sense of their individual tendencies.

Learning to Cope

The young adults also talked about their experiences of managing mental distress (such as stress, worry, anxiety, fear and depression). Responses to distress could be placed in two categories: 'reactive' strategies related to getting by and 'pre-emptive' strategies involving developing skills and techniques (Trembath et al. 2012). These were employed to cope with times of difficulty or to minimize any distress they might experience.

For example, several young adults described learning to distract themselves from 'common' experiences of distress, or of coming to find spaces of comfort to which they could retreat or 'withdraw' (Trembath et al. 2012):

> . . . just ignore it, but that's quite hard . . . keep my mind preoccupied . . . to try and get the anxious out.
>
> (YA05SM)

> . . . you just go into . . . I call it my retreat.
>
> (YA08SM)

The methods they described were usually self-devised and carried out alone. They were implemented in the home. Parents were aware of how they coped and would often support them by giving them space or by talking them through periods of worry:

INTERVIEWER: Who do you typically talk to?
INTERVIEWEE: Well my mum, for starters . . . I find it helps, yeah, getting it out, speaking it out.

(DY06SM)

In other cases, young adults talked about managing emotional experiences which they felt were a consequence of them having Asperger syndrome, such as awkwardness in social interaction or due to communication difficulties. Some felt they had to learn to work around those things, again by developing strategies that they could implement themselves:

I guess you could call them self-help books . . . like Ninety-Six Ways To Talk To People, something like that . . . I picked up a few tips from that, and; or How To Talk To Anyone . . . I found a use of books to . . . little nuggets.

(DY04SM)

Ambivalence to Support

The tendency to self-manage was also shaped by the young adult's views on support. First, many doubted whether professional support would take their Asperger syndrome into account. Asperger syndrome was, for many, a different 'way of being' (what Endow (2017) describes as an 'autistic operating system') linked to underlying tendencies and difficulties. There were concerns that support might not consider the foundations of distress to be 'in' Asperger syndrome:

[I]f you wanted to see like say a psychiatrist for anxiety and you've got Asperger's Syndrome, then ideally, you'd need to see somebody who specialises in that [. . .] going back to how you, the person with autism is generally wired . . . Obviously a specialist would have had more observation on that.

(YA11SM)

[W]ould the treatment just affect the anxiety . . . would that treatment also then get rid of communication problems or would they still be there because they're a core feature of autism?

(DY04SM)

Many participants were reluctant to seek help because they felt that their self-devised strategies were enough to get them through a difficult period. In other cases, it was because a view was held that professional support would not work any better than those strategies.

Quite often this ambivalence was based on past experiences of mental health support. For example, several young adults talked about counseling received in, or via, school during difficult teenage years. Some felt that this had been unsatisfactory and ineffectual:

> I tried seeing the school counsellor once but they were just, oh how does that make you feel . . . it didn't feel like they, that they were sort of taking a lot of it in.
>
> (YA10SM)

In other cases, the ambivalence appeared to be grounded in the fact the support described had been intermittent and not sustained, either because it was not provided on a long-term basis or because changes in staff made developing a therapeutic relationship very challenging for the young person.

> [Y]ou make progress . . . but then that psychologist tries to leave, passes on everything to someone else and then it all gets lost and forgotten about.
>
> (DY01SM)

> [M]y mum deemed it . . . unnecessary . . . cos there wasn't much she [the psychologist] could really do to help me.
>
> (YA03SM)

The interruption of care and lack of continuity generated anxiety and lack of trust at the effectiveness of support and doubt about whether they could be helped as adults.

Concerning current help-seeking, uncertainty was expressed about what could be provided, who would provide it and whether it would work. When asked about sources of support or treatment doctors were mentioned, including GPs and psychiatrists, but the young adults reported being unsure that those professionals had the skills to help them. Similarly, some young adults sensed an ambivalence among their parents about whether they needed professional help; again this view was based on previous conversations with parents:

> I asked mum and dad, I was saying, "Oh do you think I need to see a psychiatrist?" and they said, "No" . . . I've always assumed that I didn't then, but I've always thought that maybe if I did get a psychiatrist it would have helped.
>
> (YA05SM)

Thus, there was a sense that some young adults had developed a strong sense of ambivalence about professional mental health support and that this was keeping them from seeking help, *even* at points when they felt they would benefit from it. There was a danger, therefore, that they might be imagining a world in which they could not be supported. Sometimes the idea of support was abandoned because it had not in the past not yielded results:

> I just saw it as a step back . . . I've always thought it was, oh I've got better, sort of thing, but then getting one again, I've always looked at it as a step back.
>
> (YA05SM)

Discussion

There is an acknowledged need for evidence of how young adults with AS experience support, including support that is targeted at improving their understanding of Asperger syndrome and support aimed at helping them with mental health. This is so given the understanding that autistic adults experience high rates of mental health difficulties (NICE 2012). In this chapter, we have documented understandings around mental distress in the context of a diagnosis of Asperger syndrome. Our aim has been to redefine the 'wicked problem' of mental health to consider solutions that could benefit young people with Asperger syndrome.

Before we provide our conclusions however, we first want to stress that our conclusions are derived from the direct accounts of young adults with AS. We hope it is clear in the findings that we have reported that these accounts are essential. They cannot be replaced by 'proxy informants,' nor can wider evidence on young people and mental health be straightforwardly applied to this particular population. This points to the importance of the direct involvement in research of groups for whom the 'wicked problems' of health care may be 'unique' in some way. Tackling the 'wicked problem' of mental health, we argue, requires understanding the way characteristics such as autism matter for the way mental health issues are experienced and understood. This places importance on exploring how various intersecting characteristics influence health. But it also requires researchers to identify and engage groups who might be commonly overlooked or who are 'harder to reach' owing to socially constructed barriers to participation in research. It is our experience that dedication to such engagement along with the resulting research are a prerequisite to reshaping health and social care provision. In our research, the input from user advisory panels, made up of people who have first-hand experience of the issue being researched (in this case, autistic people or parents of autistic children) help us better understand the main areas of research need, including things that might be overlooked without their involvement.

One way in which we have sought to redefine the wicked problem of mental health is by addressing a well-documented problem in mental health studies: namely, young adult's preference for self-reliance as a barrier to mental health care (Gulliver, Griffiths and Christensen 2010). Our analysis suggests that for the young adults we interviewed, distress did not appear to be uncommon or outside their everyday experience, and they did not conceal their experiences to avoid being stigmatized (Prior 2012) or defined by them (Issakainen 2014). Instead, they described distress as part of 'autistic selfhood,' as something that formed part of how they were 'wired' and who they were. The process of making sense of their tendencies to experience distress was bound up in understanding what it meant to be a person with Asperger syndrome. The young adults sought to respond in ways that made best use of their knowledge about Asperger syndrome.

The young adults' 'normalisation' of distress was not about 'pulling oneself together' (Issakainen 2014, 180). Rather, it was about acknowledging and explaining distress in a way that linked it to their lived experience as people with Asperger syndrome. There was little sense that the young adults were aiming to put on a 'façade of normality' (Draucker 2005). That was not how they saw themselves. However, the young adults were ambivalent about seeking help, and this underpinned their emphasis on self-devised coping strategies. The problem that we may identify is not that the young adults did this to avoid talking about distress. Instead, it was because they did not often feel that they could be helped. Such a view was based on previous experiences of mental health care which were impacting their help seeking as adults. There was an anxiety about whether current support would be effective and whether it would be provided in a way that was right for them. For this reason, the young adults often preferred their own ways of coping. Limited past success with support or treatment also meant that parents could be skeptical about whether their children could be helped.

These issues would seem to provide a different reason for non-help-seeking. For many groups who are vulnerable to experiencing mental distress, including but not limited to young people with Asperger syndrome, we need to acknowledge the importance of early experiences of accessing mental health support (which for this group may be earlier than their neurotypical peers). There is evidence that young people who fail to be supported after a referral can be reluctant to access services again, often because they begin to feel that they cannot be helped (Spence, Owens-Solari and Goodyer 2016). This may be true for young people with Asperger syndrome. Early failure can inform a view that external support may not work for distress on the autism spectrum. The young adult's self-reliance makes sense when we consider that their past encounters with mental health services were not always helpful. The young adults were not unwilling to get help; rather, they doubted the help was there or that they would 'fit' in what was there (Griffith et al.

2012). They may have good reason to be ambivalent. This population are relatively invisible to statutory, or other, services. Some areas of the country do offer access to autism specialist multidisciplinary teams, typically based in community mental health provision (Beresford et al. 2016), but this is not the norm and systemic change is required to ensure that the mental health support needs of young adults with AS do not continue to remain under-supported or unmet (NICE 2012).

What this might point to then is the importance of early specialist inter-vention for young people with Asperger syndrome, including interventions that provide young people with resources around managing distress, and information about where to go when they find their strategies fail them. Indeed, the young adult's experiences were on a continuum, and it was not uncommon for them to feel that they were no longer able to cope. The danger is to what degree their ambivalence about support is reinforced at an early age and their preference for self-reliance overtakes their desire for assistance. The aim should be to ensure that young people with AS feel confident that they can be helped. To this, we may add that our findings also demonstrate the importance of interventions which mean parents of young adults with AS are equipped both to engage in conversations about emotional experiences and well-being and to recognize when it might be advisable to seek support. While some input may be provided regarding this around the time of diagnosis, for parents, the challenges of supporting their child's well-being are enduring. Furthermore, the transition to adult services significantly reduces the routes by which a parent can access such support (Beresford et al. 2013).

Finally, we would note that the sample recruited to this study had very little experience of accessing and using services beyond that they received at school, thus we were not able to explore issues of service use and this remains a further gap in the existing evidence base. More generally, we would also argue that what we describe in this chapter is not only relevant to young adults with Asperger syndrome, but may cut across how any group of young people might interact with health services, and what early experi-ences involving limited outcomes might mean for their later participation. For young people who are more likely to be in touch with mental health services from a young age, it is important that those services are not only 'youth-friendly' but designed in a way that acknowledges the factors that led to their engagement with that service. A 'youth-centered' approach must acknowledge diversity within the youth category.

Note

1 While no longer a recognized label in terms of the American Psychiatric Associa-tion and *DSM 5*, Asperger syndrome (AS) continues to be relevant and preferred as a label by those who have received this diagnosis (Kenny et al. 2016), as is the case for the individuals recruited to this study.

References

Autistica. 2016. "Autism: Top 10 Research Priorities." Accessed July 9, 2016. www. autistica.org.uk/research/top10/.

Baird, G., H. R. Douglas, and M. S. Murphy. 2011. "Recognising and Diagnosing Autism in Children and Young People: Summary of NICE Guidance." *BMJ* 343: d6360. doi: 10.1136/bmj.d6360.

Baird, G., E. Simonoff, A. Pickles, S. Chandler, T. Loucas, D. Meldrum, and T. Charman. 2006. "Prevalence of Disorders of the Autism Spectrum in a Population Cohort of Children in South Thames: The Special Needs and Autism Project (SNAP)." *The Lancet* 368 (9531): 210–215. doi: 10.1016/S0140-6736(06)69041-7.

Beardon, Luke. 2017. *Autism and Asperger Syndrome in Adults*. London: Sheldon Press.

Beck, Aaron T., N. Epstein, G. Brown, and Robert A. Steer. 1988. "An Inventory for Measuring Clinical Anxiety: Psychometric Properties." *Journal of Consulting and Clinical Psychology* 56 (6): 893–897. doi: 10.1037/0022–0006X.56.6.893.

Beck, Aaron T., Robert A. Steer, and Margery G. Carbin. 1988. "Psychometric Properties of the Beck Depression Inventory: Twenty-Five Years of Evaluation." *Clinical Psychology Review* 8 (1): 77–100. doi: 10.1016/0272-7358(88)90050-5.

Beresford, Bryony, Nicola Moran, Tricia Sloper, Linda Cusworth, Wendy Mitchell, Gemma Spiers, Kath Weston, and Jeni Beecham. 2013. *Transition to Adult Services and Adulthood for Young People with Autistic Spectrum Conditions*. York: Social Policy Research Unit.

Beresford, Bryony, Lucy Stuttard, Suzannah Mukherjee, and Tracy Berney. 2016. "Models of Providing Specialist Diagnosis and Support Services for Adults with Asperger Syndrome: The Current Situation." XI Autism-Europe International Congress, Edinburgh.

Biddle, Lucy, Jenny Donovan, Debbie Sharp, and David Gunnell. 2007. "Explaining Non-Help-Seeking Amongst Young Adults with Mental Distress: A Dynamic Interpretive Model of Illness Behaviour." *Sociology of Health & Illness* 29 (7): 983–1002. doi: 10.1111/j.1467-9566.2007.01030.x.

Bird, G., and R. Cook. 2013. "Mixed Emotions: The Contribution of Alexithymia to the Emotional Symptoms of Autism." *Translational Psychiatry* 3: e285. doi: 10.1038/tp.2013.61.

Carrington, S., and L. Graham. 2001. "Perceptions of School by Two Teenage Boys with Asperger Syndrome and Their Mothers: A Qualitative Study." *Autism* 5 (1): 37–48. doi: 10.1177/1362361301005001004.

Department of Health. 2015. *Future in Mind: Promoting, Protecting and Improving Our Children and Young People's Mental Health and Wellbeing*. London: Department of Health.

Draucker, Claire Burke. 2005. "Interaction Patterns of Adolescents with Depression and the Important Adults in Their Lives." *Qualitative Health Research* 15 (7): 942–963. doi: 10.1177/1049732305277859.

Eiser, C., and J. W. Varni. 2013. "Health-Related Quality of Life and Symptom Reporting: Similarities and Differences Between Children and Their Parents." *European Journal of Pediatrics* 172 (10): 1299–1304. doi: 10.1007/s00431-013-2049-9.

Endow, Judy. 2017. "Mental Health Therapy and the Autistic Client: The Autistic Operating System." *Aspects of Autism Translated*, August 22, 2017. www.judyendow.

com/autism-and-mental-health/mental-health-therapy-and-the-autistic-client-the-autistic-operating-system/.

Erbas, Yasemin, Eva Ceulemans, Johanna Boonen, Ilse Noens, and Peter Kuppens. 2013. "Emotion Differentiation in Autism Spectrum Disorder." *Research in Autism Spectrum Disorders* 7 (10): 1221–1227. doi: 10.1016/j.rasd.2013.07.007.

Foa, E. B., M. J. Kozak, P. M. Salkovskis, M. E. Coles, and N. Amir. 1998. "The Validation of a New Obsessive-Compulsive Disorder Scale: The Obsessive-Compulsive Inventory." *Psychological Assessment* 10 (3): 206–214. doi: 10.1037/1040-3590.10.3.206.

Goodman, R. 1997. "The Strengths and Difficulties Questionnaire: A Research Note." *Journal of Child Psychology and Psychiatry and Allied Disciplines* 38 (5): 581–586. doi: 10.1111/j.1469-7610.1997.tb01545.x.

Griffith, G. M., V. Totsika, S. Nash, and R. P. Hastings. 2012. "'I Just Don't Fit Anywhere': Support Experiences and Future Support Needs of Individuals with Asperger Syndrome in Middle Adulthood." *Autism* 16 (5): 532–546. doi: 10.1177/1362361311405223.

Gulliver, Amelia, Kathleen M. Griffiths, and Helen Christensen. 2010. "Perceived Barriers and Facilitators to Mental Health Help-Seeking in Young People: A Systematic Review." *BMC Psychiatry* 10 (1). doi: 10.1186/1471-244x-10-113.

Hannigan, Ben, and Michael Coffey. 2011. "Where the Wicked Problems Are: The Case of Mental Health." *Health Policy* 101 (3): 220–227. doi: 10.1016/j.healthpol.2010.11.002.

Harrison, M. E., M. M. McKay, and W. M. Bannon, Jr. 2004. "Inner-City Child Mental Health Service Use: The Real Question Is Why Youth and Families Do Not Use Services." *Community Mental Health Journal* 40 (2): 119–131.

Hughes, F., L. Hebel, P. Badcock, and A. G. Parker. 2017. "Ten Guiding Principles for Youth Mental Health Services." *Early Intervention in Psychiatry* 12 (3): 513–519. doi: 10.1111/eip.12429.

Huws, Jaci C., and Robert S. P. Jones. 2013. "'I'm Really Glad This Is Developmental': Autism and Social Comparisons—An Interpretative Phenomenological Analysis." *Autism* 19 (1): 84–90. doi: 10.1177/1362361313512426.

Issakainen, Mervi. 2014. "Young People Negotiating the Stigma Around Their Depression." *Young* 22 (2): 171–184. doi: 10.1177/1103308814521624.

Jones, Robert S. P., Andrew Zahl, and Jaci C. Huws. 2001. "First-Hand Accounts of Emotional Experiences in Autism: A Qualitative Analysis." *Disability & Society* 16 (3): 393–401. doi: 10.1080/09687590120045950.

Kelly, C. M., A. F. Jorm, and A. Wright. 2007. "Improving Mental Health Literacy as a Strategy to Facilitate Early Intervention for Mental Disorders." *The Medical Journal of Australia* 187 (7 Suppl): S26–S30.

Kenny, Lorcan, Caroline Hattersley, Bonnie Molins, Carole Buckley, Carol Povey, and Elizabeth Pellicano. 2016. "Which Terms Should Be Used to Describe Autism? Perspectives from the UK Autism Community." *Autism* 20 (4): 442–462. doi: 10.1177/1362361315588200.

McGorry, P., T. Bates, and M. Birchwood. 2013. "Designing Youth Mental Health Services for the 21st Century: Examples from Australia, Ireland and the UK." *The British Journal of Psychiatry Supplement* 54: 30–35. doi: 10.1192/bjp.bp.112.119214.

Miles, Matthew B., A. Michael Huberman, and Johnny Saldana. 2013. *Qualitative Data Analysis*. London: Sage Publications.

Müller, Eve, Adriana Schuler, and Gregory B. Yates. 2008. "Social Challenges and Supports from the Perspective of Individuals with Asperger Syndrome and Other Autism Spectrum Disabilities." *Autism* 12 (2): 173–190. doi: 10.1177/1362361307086664.

NICE. 2012. *Autism Spectrum Disorder in Adults: Diagnosis and Management.* London: NICE.

Patton, George C., Susan M. Sawyer, John S. Santelli, David A. Ross, Rima Afifi, Nicholas B. Allen, Monika Arora, Peter Azzopardi, Wendy Baldwin, Christopher Bonell, Ritsuko Kakuma, Elissa Kennedy, Jaqueline Mahon, Terry McGovern, Ali H. Mokdad, Vikram Patel, Suzanne Petroni, Nicola Reavley, Kikelomo Taiwo, Jane Waldfogel, Dakshitha Wickremarathne, Carmen Barroso, Zulfiqar Bhutta, Adesegun O. Fatusi, Amitabh Mattoo, Judith Diers, Jing Fang, Jane Ferguson, Frederick Ssewamala, and Russell M. Viner. 2016. "Our Future: A Lancet Commission on Adolescent Health and Wellbeing." *The Lancet* 387 (10036): 2423–2478. doi: 10.1016/s0140-6736(16)00579-1.

Penney, Sharon. 2013. "Qualitative Investigation of School-Related Issues Affecting Individuals Diagnosed with Autism Spectrum Disorder and Co-Occurring Anxiety and/or Depression." *Autism Insights* 5: 75–91. doi: 10.4137/aui.s10746.

Prior, Seamus. 2012. "Overcoming Stigma: How Young People Position Themselves as Counselling Service Users." *Sociology of Health & Illness* 34 (5): 697–713. doi: 10.1111/j.1467-9566.2011.01430.x.

Rapley, Tim. 2016. "Some Pragmatics of Data Analysis." In *Qualitative Research*, edited by David Silverman, 331–346. London: Sage Publications.

Rickwood, D. J., F. P. Deane, and C. J. Wilson. 2007. "When and How Do Young People Seek Professional Help for Mental Health Problems?" *The Medical Journal of Australia* 187 (7 Suppl): S35–S39.

Smith, Richard S., and Jonathan Sharp. 2013. "Fascination and Isolation: A Grounded Theory Exploration of Unusual Sensory Experiences in Adults with Asperger Syndrome." *Journal of Autism and Developmental Disorders* 43 (4): 891–910. doi: 10.1007/s10803-012-1633-6.

Spence, Ruth, Matthew Owens-Solari, and Ian Goodyer. 2016. "Help-Seeking in Emerging Adults with and Without a History of Mental Health Referral: A Qualitative Study." *BMC Research Notes* 9 (1). doi: 10.1186/s13104-016-2227-8.

Trembath, D., C. Germano, G. Johanson, and C. Dissanayake. 2012. "The Experience of Anxiety in Young Adults with Autism Spectrum Disorders." *Focus on Autism and Other Developmental Disabilities* 27 (4): 213–224. doi: 10.1177/1088357612454916.

Wolcott, Harry F. 2009. *Writing Up Qualitative Research*, 3rd ed. Thousand Oaks, CA: Sage Publications.

Wright, Annemarie, Anthony F. Jorm, and Andrew J. Mackinnon. 2011. "Labeling of Mental Disorders and Stigma in Young People." *Social Science & Medicine* 73 (4): 498–506. doi: 10.1016/j.socscimed.2011.06.015.

Yamaguchi, Sosei, Yoshio Mino, and Shahir Uddin. 2011. "Strategies and Future Attempts to Reduce Stigmatization and Increase Awareness of Mental Health Problems Among Young People: A Narrative Review of Educational Interventions." *Psychiatry and Clinical Neurosciences* 65 (5): 405–415. doi: 10.1111/j.1440-1819.2011.02239.x.

14 Action Research in the Health and Social Care Settings
A Tool for Solving Wicked Problems?[1]

Marta Strumińska-Kutra

Introduction

Health and social care governance confront 'wicked problems.' Such problems feature substantial interdependencies among multiple systems and actors, have redistributive implications for entrenched interests (Rayner 2003) and create high levels of uncertainty and instability into the socio-political systems.

In the chapter I argue that these challenges call for innovative ways of organizing research, serving not only as a description and explanation of given circumstances, but also as a tool for solving wicked problems. A methodological framework of action research delivers such a tool. It is based on a pragmatist philosophy and methodology, where the same people are both producing and applying knowledge, and indeed the production and application processes are also combined. Knowledge is co-created through the cooperative actions aimed at solving of a given problem (Torrance 2011). Hence research activity can be seen as a scientific tool for enhancing reflexive governance and management, creating a space where researchers, policymakers, health and care workers, patients and their families form 'mutual learning systems' (Robinson 1992).

It seems that this potential has been recognized by practitioners and researchers in health and social services area, where action research is a relatively popular approach (Huzzard and Johansson 2014). On the contrary to the dominant rational and positivist evidence-based approach, the collaborative approaches in health and social services research recognize that scientific knowledge is being implemented in specific cultural, institutional, organizational and social contexts; e.g. many health-related issues like drug addiction, prenatal care, sexual education and palliative care are complex and beset by ideological divisions. On the level of policymaking and implementation, lack of consensus over values and complexity places limits on the use of scientific evidence. The evidence is often inconclusive or cherry picked dependently on political orientations (Ansell and Geyer 2016). On the individual level of patients and their families, or health services professionals, practices prompted by evidence approaches are modified by a totality of everyday situations, by a context, in which things, people, actions and options already matter in specific ways (Sandberg and Tsoukas 2011). Action research offers a way of integrating different types of knowledge, experiences and values in order to advance the quality of health and social services. It provides a positive alternative conception of the relationship between scientific knowledge and decision-making. Action research–based approaches allow to do both: acknowledge the value scientific knowledge, while appreciating its limits (Ansell and Geyer 2016).

Yet action research is filled with important tensions resulting from power differences between actors participating in the process. The chapter uses existing research from the area of health and care services in order to illustrate three types of research-related relationships involving power: 1) between the participatory inquiry and its cultural, institutional and social environment, 2) within 'the community' being studied, which itself is not homogenous in terms of interests, values and ability of their realization and 3) between the researcher and 'the community.' Tensions emerge within each of them and are illustrated by following questions: 1) how to conduct dialogical research based on the idea of equality, within the non-dialogical and hierarchical cultural and institutional environment; 2) how to invite and involve those in power into activities which expose domination and seek ways to reduce it and 3) how to be a genuine partner to a 'community' and simultaneously to adopt a critical stance that presupposes the definition of their problem.

I start with exploring the meta-theoretical inconsistancies of action research (AR), attempting to use the three mutually exclusive approaches of pragmatism, critical theory and constructivism. Later, these inconsistencies are illustrated by tensions and dillemas encountered by researchers in the area of health and social services. Finally, I argue that use of the meta-theoretical triangle (pragmatism, constructivism and critical theory), though not elegant, is beneficial for theorizing and making sense of research experience and as a check and balance tool guiding an ethical and quality inquiry on the one hand and democratic and effective problem solving on the other.

A Meta-Theoretical Inconsistencies

Three philosophical and theoretical traditions important for the AR community (Reason and Branbury 2001) seem to be especially important and fruitful for the exploration of tensions within AR. These are the traditions of critical theory, pragmatism and constructivism.[2]

Critically oriented versions of AR prioritize emancipation as an ultimate goal of research (Johansson and Lindhult 2008, 102). Participatory inquiry challenges the conventional processes of knowledge production, it creates a space in which dominant discourses are questioned and reframed, and it thereby shifts the horizons of the possible. The focus on the relationship between knowledge and power is traceable to the Marxist theory of ideology and to the writers exploring how social location shapes individuals' perceptions of the social world (Abbott 2001). This is the critical theory tradition, which combines epistemological subjectivism, i.e. assumptions about the social construction of knowledge, with ontological realism, i.e. assumption about the existence of a reality independent of human subjectivity (e.g. structures of domination, Duberley and Johnson 2009).

The constructivist tradition is the second important reference point for emancipatory AR (Reason and Bradbury 2013, 18; Grant, Nelson and Mitchell 2013; Hielsen 2006). It posits that realities are local, specific and socially constructed (Lincoln, Lynham and Guba 2011). Exploring and bringing out authentic local knowledge is an important part of the empowerment enterprise, because of the assumption that self-knowledge can be liberating. However—in contrast to critical theory—the constructivist tradition assumes ontological and epistemological subjectivism.

The emphasis on exploring local knowledge and experience makes a connection to the pragmatist tradition. In fact, critically oriented AR approaches the problems of power armed with a methodology originating from Pragmatism. It assumes the necessity of a group process involving diverse stakeholders with different experiences and knowledge of the problems at hand (Levin and Greenwood 2011, 29). Pragmatism assumes that the production of knowledge and its application are intertwined. Hence the crucial epistemological role of action (Johansson and Lindhult 2008). Pragmatically orientated AR aims above all at improving the workability of human praxis, hence participation is here 'not just a moral value' but is essential for a successful inquiry into complexity of the problems addressed (Greenwood 2007, 131). The assumption of the pragmatist approach is that complexity requires the knowledge and expertise of a broad and diverse array of stakeholders and that it is common action on the problem, which enables us to gain valid knowledge and seek an effective solution.

The attempts to use these three perspectives simultaneously create irresolvable tensions. Using a definition of Participatory Action Research, a representative of critically oriented AR, I illustrate how the pragmatist, critical and constructivist perspective are mutually undermining each other within one methodological framework.

> PAR is a research methodology that attempts to address power imbalances and oppressive social structures. It values the 'researched' community as a vital part of the research project and its members as experts of their own experiences. PAR is especially concerned with oppressed communities and [it] attempts to create action as a catalyst for social change [. . .] PAR identifies as goals: emancipation, participatory democracy, and the illumination of social problems and is a cyclical process of research, learning, and action.
>
> (Grant, Nelson and Mitchell 2013, 589)

So, PAR treats the 'researched' community as experts on their own experiences (constructivist perspective) and simultaneously presupposes that relations of domination are an important part of that experience (critical perspective). Thus the critical theory perspective endangers the goals set by the constructivist perspective and vice versa (see Figure 14.1). PAR's orientation toward action (Pragmatism) requires agreement on working within power structures and making use of the same power structures that it tries to challenge. This creates a serious risk of reinforcing the status quo, or at least requires some form of compromise with it (endangering goals set by the critical theory perspective). PAR's orientation toward exploring local knowledge through communication (constructivism), and toward problem solving (pragmatism) makes it prone to overlook the political nature of the cultural, institutional and social environment within which inquiry takes place and by which all inquiry is infiltrated (strongly highlighted by critical theory approach). The constructivist and pragmatist orientation also make the researcher prone to assume that 'the community' is a monolith, just because as a whole it is producing common meanings, and have some common problems to be solved. These tendencies go against the critical perspective, whose basic assumption is that relations of domination are universal, and cannot be organized out of society.

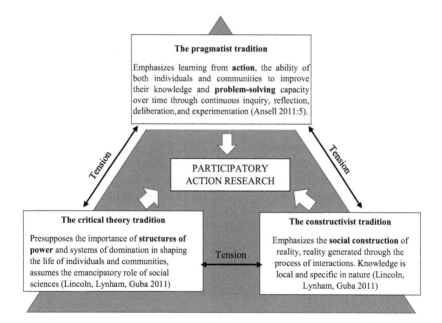

Figure 14.1 Meta-Theoretical Approaches Present in PAR.

Source: Strumińska-Kutra (2016)

On the other hand, separating the three in the name of purism and consistency raises other problems: those of self-reference and power. Logically speaking, a consistent use of critical theory results in imposing the domination framework upon those under research and hence leads researchers to the execution of power (Eikeland 2006). Consistently used constructivism leads a researcher to the crisis of representation questioning the researchers' ability to 'truthfully' describe the perspective adopted by those being studied (Woolgar and Pawluch 1985; Abbott 2001). A consistent pragmatist resolves the crises of representation thanks to the approach of co-creating knowledge (Johnsen 2010). But by emphasizing the cooperation and problem solving action she risks opportunism, at least until she asks how power asymmetries influence the definition and solution of the problem (Duberley and Johnson 2009; Jessop 2011). Hence, a consistent researcher is exposed to the ethical risks of either paternalism (critical theory), relativism, and therefore paralysis (constructivism) or opportunism (Pragmatism).

In the following discussion I will show how tensions between every pair of perspectives, or within every single perspective, can be resolved (or at least softened) by the use of the third one. I propose to analyze these tensions through the lens of power effects connected to social research and present 1) between the participatory inquiry and its cultural, institutional and social environment, 2) within 'the community' being studied, which itself is not homogenous in terms of interests, values and ability of their realization and 3) between the researcher and 'the community.' This kind of anchorage allows us to transform the paradigms' discussion into a creative interplay and useful tool signaling an approaching ethical risk as well as indicating possible ways out.

Praising Equality in Hierarchical and Non-Dialogical Institutional Environment: The Power of Inertia

Participatory methods, emancipatory goals and subversive results of collective inquiry confront dominant non-dialogical discourses and hierarchical modes of governance within private and public spaces. These institutional arrangements mirror and support the relations of power in a particular time and place, privileging purposive and non-purposive actions, which petrify them. Hence the goal and results of critical research are endangered by the problem of inertia. I will first exemplify this problem and then show how it can be answered by the use of a pragmatist approach.

Field-Specific Discourses

Participatory researchers trying to introduce change and facilitate reflection and learning confront discourses dominant in the field of their operation. Conducting research in the non-governmental entities and hospitals, Pedersen and Olesen describe their frustration caused by the inability to open up a dialogue about conflicting interests within organizations being studied. As the main obstacle, they identified specific characteristics of the Danish public discourse, which treats discussion of conflicts of interests as "out-dated, implying disagreement, old-fashionedness, implying socialism and an unwillingness to communicate" (Pedersen and Olesen 2008, 274). Another interesting example of institutional inertia is delivered by Huzzard and Johansson (2014). They present and discuss an action research project that had the initial aim of supporting the development of a number of R&D networks in various domains of health care and raising awareness on the issue of knowledge creation and thereby potentially initiate a process of change. The networks were set up on the local government level in north-east Sweden in order to establish "new arenas for participation and dialogue among health care professionals that straddled existing organizational and occupational boundaries such that the practitioners concerned could develop new forms of knowledge to inform and support their work practices" (Huzzard and Johansson 2014, 87). Despite of the careful design of the process according to the idea of bottom-up transfer of knowledge and participatory logic of knowledge co-production "participants generally eschewed the opportunity to explore new knowledge [including their experiential knowledge] through horizontal relationships in practice and fell back on exploiting the knowledge derived from evidence-based medicine" (Huzzard and Johannsson 2014, 87). Dominant discourse constraint the learning process because it dismisses contextual, local knowledge and privileges 'universal,' rule-based knowledge.

Answers to the Intertia. Toward Radicalization or Pragmatism?

The incongruity between dialogical and emancipatory research and the context of hierarchical, non-dialogical culture of an institutional environment has been recognized within critically oriented AR literature. The fact that participatory projects have developed from marginalized efforts on the part of activists and social scientists to a popular rhetoric of policy arenas, and a commercially driven consultation industry, resulted in calls for 'reclaiming the radical roots' (Brydon-Miller 2013; Chambers 2011; Gaventa and Cornwall 2013; Lykes and Mallona 2013; Wakeford et al. 2013).

But researchers who choose the strategy of scaling back to bottom-up approaches of advocacy will also eventually face dilemmas connected with non-dialogical policymaking patterns. Carr persuasively depicted ethical dilemmas connected to this transition. He started his research as advocacy for public skateboarding facilities on the ground level, involving representatives of local communities. To implement change designed within a critical collective inquiry on the bottom level, he made a pragmatic choice and entered the urban policy arena, where "political conflict is often negotiated through the production of polarized identities, working in that arena often subjects one's research community to essentialized and disempowering representations" (Carr 2012, 62). These circumstances impede context-sensitive dialogue, and the negotiation of solutions in the context of competing interests. He reports experiencing cynicism and frustration caused by attempts to achieve change through the political system, and a simultaneous conviction that there are few other options. One of the options would be a reduction of the pragmatist element and withdrawal to the production of, for example, critical ethnography. In the presented case it would mean giving up hope of having any real influence.

Researchers who find themselves in this kind of dilemma are in fact caught between two perspectives: the pragmatist and the critical one. The first one assumes human willingness to experiment in order to improve practice (Ansell 2011). The second highlights the importance of structures of power and systems of domination in shaping the life of organizations and individuals. They both say something important and both followed in isolation lead the researcher to compromise dangerously near to failure, the first to the risk of opportunism, the second to the risk of impotence.

In order to deal with the problem of inertia, caused by institutional arrangements privileging purposive and non-purposive actions petrifying the status quo, one needs to put the approaches of critical theory and pragmatism into the interplay. John Forester explicitly proposes to merge the two approaches into a critical pragmatism. He points out that the pragmatist perspective is exposed to the danger of naïveté, whereas critical perspective to the danger of cynicism. A critical pragmatism must not just recognize, but also avoid both of these dangers. The action-oriented, pragmatist perspective allows to shift the realm of possible, and explore what seems to work in practice. The supplementation with the critical perspective delivers check and balance mechanism, preventing from creation of dangerous illusions, which, by ignoring power issues, are reinforcing status quo (Gaventa and Cornwall 2013).

Power Asymmetries within 'the Community of an Inquiry'

Even seemingly homogenous communities and organizations are characterized by power asymmetries and diversified in terms of values and interests. Thus the problem solving action recommended by a pragmatist approach is likely become problem solving of elites and bolster dominant position within a given research context (Johansson and Lindhult 2008). The tension between pragmatist and critical assumptions resulted in the evolution of two orientations within AR. The critical orientation includes Participatory Action Research and is associated with the work of Freire (Freire 1970) in its emphasis on the emancipation of underprivileged groups. The pragmatic orientation emphasizes generating local knowledge with practitioners with a view to improving workable praxis, but broadly leaving social relations untouched.

Escaping Opportunism—Toward Critical Theory

Some researchers suggest that the two approaches should be used in different contexts. The pragmatist one is more suitable in contexts where 'concerted and immediate action is needed' (Johansson and Lindhult 2008, 95), and the critical one "where potentially transformative action is needed but has to be preceded by critical thinking and reflection which should reveal dominant ideologies and coercive structures" (Huzzard and Johansson 2014, 85). They further argue that critically oriented AR "recognizes tensions and conflicts between interested parties, and the fact that some interests are dominant. To acknowledge such tensions and conflicts through reflective and self-reflective efforts is crucial, as well as giving a voice to unrecognized groups and interests" (Johansson and Lindhult 2008, 105). In an attempt to escape the risk of opportunism critically oriented AR emphasizes reflection over action. Strengthening of the critical 'leg' raises the feasibility problem: how do invite those in power to deconstruct and minimize their possibilities to influence the decision-making processes? When we convince them, how do we prevent their domination within the dialogue?

Escaping Impossibility—Toward Pragmatism

In areas of management and policymaking, the encouragement for those in power to enter into dialogue would be the perspective of 'getting things done' (Schon and Rein 1994, 157). Thanks to the frame-reflective dialogue on concrete problems those occupying dominant positions can design more effective solutions. This is because the dialogue and self-inquiry enables them to escape from the trap of their own cognitive biases that prevent them from re-defining their own situation. This is all perfect until those privileged within structures of domination discover that their interests and power are endangered. In order to secure the cooperation of strategic stakeholders the researchers will need to cut deals, which is outside of their announced role as knowledge and justice seekers. This particularly concerns critical organization researchers, who do not have much to offer in exchange for a permission to enter an organization. So already at the outset critically oriented AR needs to make a step back in the direction of pragmatism adopting a 'tempered radicalism' perspective implying working for a change 'from within opposing structures' (Meyerson and Scully 1995).

What even more—it often happens that researchers more or less consciously take an advantage from the existence of power assymetries. In their self-inquiring paper on AR projects situated among others in health sector (psychiatric ward) in Denmark, Pedersen and Olesen report this kind of dilemmas. The ward's management initiated the project by seeking and procuring funding for a project concerning the communication of diagnoses and treatment possibilities to schizophrenic patients and their relatives. As it turned out, management and employees did not come to agreement over time and resources investment during the project period. While paying to the researchers the management simply expected that the local participants would 'find time' for their participation by personally 'restructuring' their working hours (282: 262). As a result, the more action researchers insisted on joint knowledge production, the more they pressed workers whose work lives were stressful to begin with. It only escalated the tensions within the working group where the differences of social positons (doctor, the psychologist, nurse, heads of department, employees at 'ground level') could not be discussed openly and were treated as an endangering subject of discussion by both researchers and local participants. In such situations it seems to be justified to ask whose problems are solved by the action research? Asking this question, some observers of critical AR practice question the appropriateness of Habermasian dialogue for critical approaches within AR indicating that in practice, it may not live up to its emancipatory aims (Huzzard and Johansson 2014). In fact, critically oriented AR based on a Habermasian ideal speech situation (e.g. Critical Participatory AR, CPAR Kemmis 2013) is not well equipped to deal with power asymmetries within 'a community of inquiry,' especially because they give little attention to the positionality of those who participate and what this might mean in terms of the versions they present (Gaventa and Cornwall 2013).

Open communicative spaces can be sites of oppression (Wakeford et al. 2013) or create new power inequalities, because participants do not necessarily look for knowledge and learning but can use the participation for self-interest-oriented strategic purposes. Hence tools are needed to deal with the ethical consequences of the fact that similarly as in 'conventional' research, the research projects are used to develop arguments in the political struggle. The frameworks like this one of CPAR, should address these kind of challenges explicitly. To arrive at nonviolent communications critical AR needs a lot of facilitation, and mediation between conflicting interests.

As was illustrated, the influence of domination mechanisms became visible when researchers were trying to change them through action. Interestingly Kemmis's latest display of the CPAR largely omits the action component, so important to anchoring the enterprise in reality and preventing 'flight from it' (Greenwood 2007; Gaventa and Cornwall 2013). Shunning away from 'transformative action' seems to be typical for critical action researchers in general (Johansson and Lindhult 2008) which makes them face the risk of leaving power asymmetries untouched and the participants helpless and frustrated.

Pragmatist Answer to the Impotence

Inability to fulfill the empowering potential of AR may cause frustration and cynicism. In order to avoid that, Forester proposes the following way out: "let's spend less time rediscovering that power of course matters, and let's spend more time exploring how we can do better—less time presuming impossibility and more time exploring actual possibility." (Forester 2013, 7). I partially agree, but add that the exploration of power is important for researchers' ability to design an adequate methodology and for awareness of the fractal power structures in which it is intertwined. That is why, when balancing critical and pragmatist approaches, we need to both explore power relations rhetorically and practically. This is also why we need to research (with) both the excluded and the powerful, trying to balance the power inequalities and recognizing the presence of multiple interest groups. The most fruitful exploration of power and of 'realms of possible' should be situated in a specific problem and should take place in the 'natural space of encounter' (Schon and Rein 1994; Arieli and Friedman 2013).

In conclusion, oppression is complex, nuanced and unstable. There are internal divisions among the oppressed. Researchers who ignore such divisions are liable to be manipulated and corrupted by the more powerful groups/individuals (including amongst the oppressed). Therefore, pragmatist assumptions of deliberation and experimenting with cooperatively designed solutions need to be watched by critical considerations of power issues. And the reverse: critical consideration needs to be supported by transformative action, which facilitates reflection over power inequalities and delivers knowledge on what is feasible.

Researcher as a Subject Enacting Power

The main dilemma addressed here is encapsulated in the question: How to be a genuine partner to a 'community' and simultaneously adopt a critical stance that presupposes the definition of their problem? Within critical action research literature this question was mainly analyzed in terms of balancing between closeness, which suggests maintaining an ethics of care vis-à-vis the actors in the field (Spicer, Alvesson and Kaerreman 2009), and distance, which suggests an ambition to make more critical assessments that can easily compromise the ethical contract (Johansson and Lindhult 2008); (Huzzard and Johansson 2014). It is suggested that this tension can be managed by breaking the research process into the partly overlapping phases of collaboration, where existing knowledge and practice are explored, and of critical interrogation, where knowledge and practice of all involved are critically reflected upon (Huzzard and Johansson 2014). I suggest that this framing, though helpful, is unspecific for critically oriented research. Both pragmatically and critically oriented AR, imply questioning local knowledge and practice. The important difference is that in the case of critically oriented AR the questioning takes place on the ground of the framework delivered by a critical perspective, i.e. through the use of a domination framework. Hence critical action researchers are facing the challenge "common to social reformers and revolutionaries at all times: By what means can we achieve change and promote our goals, without self-destruction, destroying the realization of our goals through the application of our means, through our own practice?" (Eikeland 2006, 44).

Escaping Paternalism—Toward Constructivism

So, the participatory researcher entering the field of study employs the third dimension of power, in Lukes's sense (Lukes 1974). That is, she becomes a subject exercising power by presupposing the framework for the definition of the problem. Many researchers, sensing the tension within the critical perspective, are trying to frame their research in constructivist terms (Grant, Nelson and Mitchell 2013). It enables them to claim that what they are doing is 'illuminating human experience' and undermining relations of power through facilitating individuals in exploring relations of power in their lived experience (Grant, Nelson and Mitchell 2013). This, however, does not solve the problem, since facilitation is inevitably an enactment of power (Olesen and Nordentoft 2013; Kristiansen 2013), more or less conscious, and selective encouragement of certain lines of interpretations, which in turn influence the perception of interests (Schon and Rein 1994). The critical perspective is questioned by the constructivist one. Unfortunately, consistently adopted constructivism informs researchers that they will never be able to produce knowledge reflecting something more than their perception of 'reality' (Woolgar and Pawluch 1985; Abbot 2001). This in turn exposes a critical researcher to the risk of relativism and hence paralysis.

Escaping Paralysis—Toward Pragmatism

One possible way to escape this tension is to make the researcher's agency, values, and agenda (such as the need for publications) visible and open to negotiation. All reports from the project are than perceived as objectifications achieved in the process of interaction between a professional researcher and 'community' representatives (Johnsen 2010). In this sense, the pragmatist approach to AR, concentrated on the co-production of knowledge through problem solving and experimenting, comes to the rescue as a 'third way.' In fact, both pragmatically and critically oriented AR imply that the role of research is not only to listen to the practitioners' voices, but also to be critical and provide contrasting images, reveal new perspectives and problematize established conventions (Huzzard and Johansson 2014; Greenwood 2007).

Escaping the tension between the constructivist and critical perspective, we are moving in the grounds occupied more strongly by pragmatism and constructivism, than by critical theory. We are not safe here either. By restraining ourselves from attempts to introduce power and domination into discussion, we are risking that they will be not discussed at all, because participants themselves may avoid difficult, threatening and painful issues. And by doing this they may "unintentionally contribute to the ability of the dominant group to maintain power and perpetuate inequality while preaching coexistence" (Gawerc 2006).

And here we are at the center of ethical issues. The researcher who is directing individuals into the emancipation becomes responsible for its consequences. To be consistent, one should either take the responsibility and accompany given individuals/community on their long way to emancipation, or start research only when explicitly asked by the community (and after making them aware of the possible risks). Usually, the length of the research projects financed by scientific institutions is very limited. Usually the researcher approaches the community, not the other way around. Usually the community does not really know what it agrees upon when it lets the researcher 'in.' This is partially due to the dominating imaginaries of social research, complying with 'traditional' approaches, and partially due to the inability to predict unintended, adverse consequences. Long lasting commitment can be in conflict with the researchers' agenda which is connected with the pursuit of degrees, publications and funding for new research projects.

Grant et al. emphasizes the imperative of taking the responsibility for possible risks inherent in the commitment to change the world (2013). This is very true but it needs to be highlighted that the risk is to be borne mainly by the community, not by the researcher. That is why the researcher's power must be accompanied by responsibility.

But then again, diving too deep into consideration enhanced by critical and constructivist approaches can be paralyzing. Those who decide to perform critical research involving 'real people,' should not push those problems aside, but should act with careful consideration of them. Here, in turn, what comes to the rescue in the stalemate is the pragmatist perspective. Research should be concentrated on problem solving and action, looking for 'what works' not just on participation and communication of new voices and categories. Critical and constructivist perspectives are important for ethical considerations and research design, but it seems that the pragmatist perspective is the leading one for the actual working of critical AR. But even then, 'what works' depends very strongly on interests and so should be taken as the beginning of a reflection and not the end.

John Carr's conclusions on the ethical consequences of research as advocacy can serve as a good example here. His alignment with the disempowered group strengthened its voice within the urban policy arena. Reflecting on the consequences of his involvement he draws a largely overlooked conclusion: in the world of finite resources a victory for 'us' always has the potential of coming at 'their' expense. Thus, by strengthening one party in the democratic process, we diminish the possibility of other parties realizing their values and interests. The 'covenantal ethic' usually adopted by action researchers, but in fact also by critical researchers in general, indicates that the researcher's work is based in caring relationships between the researcher and researched, with a shared commitment to social justice and cogeneration of knowledge (Brydon-Miller 2013; Hielsen 2006). Carr raises the problem: what are our ethical commitments to the communities/interest groups/individuals outside of our collective inquiry? He proposes the extension of 'covenantial ethics' to those with whom we compete in the political arena. "While we cannot abandon political advocacy work, a commitment to "fairer power relations" and "human interdependency" means taking different and opposing perspectives seriously [. . .] a truly covenantal ethic requires not only trying to understand other voices in the political arena, but to count those voices among the constituency that we seek to serve" (Carr 2012, 75).

While conducting critical AR, researchers are the organizers of the process, who actively manage power differences in order to seek missing voices. One cannot fully comply with the constructivist ideal while doing this. A researcher's knowledge and perception is there, inside of the co-produced knowledge, and she needs to face the risks and responsibilities connected to it. Since the researcher does not observe the objectification process, but actively participates in it, her constant reflection-in-action and on-action builds a safety network, protecting her from failures and helping to balance irresolvable dilemmas. Not recognizing, and therefore not dealing with, one's own agency, values and interests in the process has important and negative consequences for both ethics and the quality of research.

Conclusion

Critical scholars have discussed paradigmatical tensions and power issues for decades. I argue that a simultaneous exploration of the ways in which power infiltrates the critical (action) research, and of meta-theoretical tensions, creates a heuristic structure which gathers these problems together, and enables the systematic exploration and management of uncertainty and ambiguity of a research process.

To deal with the problem of power infiltrating critical action research in the three aspects: the relationship between research and the institutional and cultural context, the relationships within the community of inquiry, and between the researcher and the community, one should cultivate a flexible repertoire of responses balancing pragmatist, critical and constructivist traditions. In this way, strategies can be combined and rebalanced to reduce the likelihood of failure, which could have consequences either for ethics or for the inability to introduce change and most probably for both. As illustrated in the analysis, when confronted with the problem of power each of the perspectives is prone to produce specific failures and at the same time delivers important insights into emancipatory enterprises. The pragmatist perspective is exposed to the danger of naiveté or the risk of cynicism while assuming problem solving action without taking into account power asymmetries. The critical perspective is exposed to the danger of cynicism and the risk of impotence while assuming the universal character of domination and hence refusing cooperation with those in power. Moreover, it is also

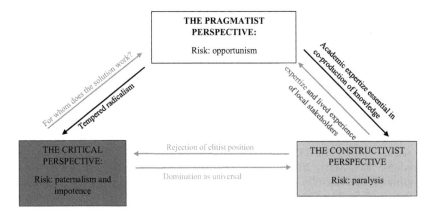

Figure 14.2 Navigating Between Perspectives

Source: Strumińska-Kutra (2016)

exposed to the risk of paternalism while presupposing the definition of the problem and refusing to accept the conservative sensitivity. The constructivist perspective is exposed to the danger of relativism which connects to the risk of paralysis. The weakness of each perspective is exposed and can be managed with the use of the other. Figure 14.2 summarizes the exemplary flows between perspectives which together create the safety network for the scholar trying to navigate between these risks.

Hence the process of research can be described as a constant attempt to avoid failures resulting from the increasing dominance of any of the three perspectives.

The radicalism of critically oriented action research originating from the critical perspective, should be tempered by conclusions drawn from the pragmatist perspective (action orientation—working within the system), and from the constructivist perspective (appreciating and respecting diverse realities and commitments). However attractive it may be for the researcher, the temptation of simplistic radicalism should be resisted. Putting it simply, critically oriented versions of AR should be critical in its aspirations, pragmatic in its practice, and constructivist in its understanding of its self, context and tasks.

Notes

1. This chapter is based on a paper "Engaged Scholarship. Steering between the risks of paternalism, opportunism, and paralysis in Organization" (2016). doi: 10.1177/1350508416631163
2. I distinguish constructivism as a separate tradition, but it is important to note that both critical theory and pragmatism use constructivist subjectivist ontology and interpretive epistemology.

References

Abbott, Andrew. 2001. *Chaos of Disciplines*. Chicago, IL: University of Chicago Press.

Ansell, Christopher, and Robert Geyer. 2016. "Pragmatic Complexity' a New Foundation for Moving Beyond 'Evidence-Based Policy Making'?" *Policy Studies* 38 (2): 149–167.

Ansell, Christopher K. 2011. *Pragmatist Democracy. Evolutionary Learning as Public Philosophy*. Oxford: Oxford University Press

Arieli, Daniella, and Victor J. Friedman. 2013. "Negotiating Reality: Conflict Transformation in Natural Spaces of Encounter." *The Journal of Applied Behavioral Science* 49 (3): 308–332.

Brydon-Miller, Mary. 2013. "Ethics and Action Research: Deepening Our Commitment to Principles of Social Justice and Redefining Systems of Democratic Practice." In *The Sage Handbook of Action Research: Participative Inquiry in Practice*. London: Sage Publications.

Carr, John. 2012. "Activist Research and City Politics: Ethical Lessons from Youth-Based Public Scholarship." *Action Research* 10 (1): 61–78.

Chambers, Robert. 2011. "PRA, PLA and Pluralism: Practice and Theory." In *The Sage Handbook of Action Research: Participative Inquiry in Practice*. London: Sage Publications.

Duberley, Joanne, and Phil Johnson 2009. "Critical Management Methodology." In *The Oxford Handbook of Critical management Studies*, edited by Mats Alvesson, Todd Bridgman and Hugh Willmott. Oxford: Oxford University Press.

Eikeland, Olav. 2006. "Condescending Ethics and Action Research." *Action Research* 4 (1): 37–47.

Forester, John. 2013. "On the Theory and Practice of Critical Pragmatism: Deliberative Practice and Creative Negotiations." *Planning Theory* 12 (1): 5–22.

Freire, P. 1970. *The Pedagogy of the Oppressed*. New York: Herder and Herder.

Gaventa, John, and Andrea Cornwall. 2013. "Power and Knowledge." In *The Sage Handbook of Action Research: Participative Inquiry in Practice*, edited by Peter Reason and Hilary Bradbury-Huang, 172–189. London: Sage Publications.

Gawerc, M. I. 2006. "Peace-Building: Theoretical and Concrete Perspectives." *Peace & Change* 31: 435–478.

Grant, Jill, Geoff Nelson, and Terry Mitchell. 2013. "Negotiating the Challenges of Participatory Action Rsearch: Relationships, Power, Participation, Change and Credibility." In *The Sage Handbook of Action Research: Participative Inquiry in Practice*, edited by Peter Reason and Hilary Bradbury-Huang. London: Sage Publications.

Greenwood Davydd. 2007. "Pragmatic Action Research." *International Journal of Action Research* 3 (1/2): 131–148.

Hielsen, Anne. 2006. "And They Shall Be Known by Their Deeds." *Action Research* 4 (1): 23–36.

Huzzard, T., and Y. Johansson. 2014. "Critical Action Research." In *Critical Management Research: Reflections from the Field*. London: Sage Publications.

Jessop, Bob. 2011. "Metagovernance." In *The Sage Handbook of Governance*, 106–123. London: Sage Publications.

Johansson, A., and E. Lindhult. 2008. "Emancipation or Workability? Critical Versus Pragmatic Scientific Orientation in Action Research." *Action Research* 6 (1): 95–115.

Johnsen, Hans, Ch G. 2010. "Scientific Knowledge Through Involvement—How to Do Respectful Othering." *International Journal of Action Research* 6 (1): 43–74.

Kemmis, Stephen. 2013. "Critical Theory and Participatory Action Research." In *The Sage Handbook of Action Research: Participative Inquiry and Practice*, edited by Maeve O'Grady, 121–138. London: Sage Publications.

Kristiansen, Marianne. 2013. "Dynamics Between Organisational Change Processes and Facilitating Dissensus in Context Inquiring Dialogues." *International Journal of Action Research* 9 (1): 95–123.

Levin, Martin, and Davydd Greenwood. 2011. "Revitalizing Universities by Reinventing the Social Sciences: Bildung and Action Research." In *The Sage Handbook of Qualitative Research 4th Edition*. London: Sage Publications.

Lincoln Yvonna S., Susan A. Lynham, and Egon G. Guba. 2011. "Paradigmatic Controversies, Contradictions, and Emerging Confluences, 97–128." In *The Sage Handbook of Qualitative Research*, edited by Norman K. Denzin, and Yvonna S. Lincoln. London: Sage Publications.

Lukes, Steven. 1974. *Power. A Radical View*. London: Palgrave Macmillan.

Lykes, M. Brinton, and Amelia Mallona. 2013. "Towards Transformational Liberation: Participatory and Action Research and Praxis." In *The Sage Handbook of Action Research: Participative Inquiry in Practice*, 2nd ed. London: Sage Publications.

Meyerson, Debra E., and Maureen A. Scully. 1995. "Crossroads Tempered Radicalism and the Politics of Ambivalence and Change." *Organization Science* 6 (5): 585–600.

Olesen, Brigitte, and Helle Nordentoft. 2013. "Walking the Talk? A Micro-Sociological Approach to the Co-Production of Knowledge and Power in Action Research." *International Journal of Action Research* 9 (1): 67–94.

Pedersen, Christina, and Brigitte Olesen. 2008. "What Knowledge—Which Relationships? Sharing Dilemmas of an Action Researcher." *International Journal of Action Research* 4 (3): 254–290.

Robinson, John B. 1992. "Risks, Predictions and Other Political Illusions: Rethinking the Use of Science in Social Decision-Making." *Policy Sciences* 25: 237–254.

Rayner, Steve. 2003. "Democracy in the Age of Assessment." *Science and Public Policy* 30 (3): 163–170.

Reason Peter, and Hilary Bradbury-Huang, eds. 2001. *The Sage Handbook of Action Research: Participative Inquiry in Practice*. Second Edition. London: Sage Publications.

Sandberg, Jörgen, and H. Tsoukas. 2011. "Grasping the Logic of Practice: Theorizing Through Practical Rationality." *Academy of Management Review* 36 (2): 338–360.

Schon, Donald A., and Martin Rein. 1994. *Frame Reflexion: Toward the Resolution of Intractable Policy Controversies*. New York: Basic Books.

Spicer, André, Mats Alvesson, and Dan. Kaerreman. 2009. "Critical Performativity: The Unfinished Business of Critical Management Studies." *Human Relations* 62 (4): 537–560.

Torrance, Harry. 2011. "Qualitative Research, Science, and Government: Evidence, Criteria, Policy, and Politcis." In *The Sage Handbook of Qualitative Research* 4th Edition, edited by Norman Denzin and Yvonna Lincoln. London: Sage Publications.

Wakeford, Tom, Jasaber Singh, Bano Murtuja, Peter Bryant, and Michel Pimbert. 2013. "The Jury Is Out: How Far Can Participatory Projects Go Towards

Reclaiming Democracy?" In *The Sage Handbook of Action Research: Participative Inquiry in Practice,* edited by Peter Reason and Hilary Bradbury-Huang, 333–349. London: Sage Publications.

Woolgar, S., and D. Pawluch. 1985. "How Shall We Move Beyond Constructivism?" *Social Problems* 33 (3): 159–162.

15 Four Different Ways to View Wicked Problems

Anneli Hujala, Sanna Laulainen, Andy Brookes, Maarit Lammassaari and Tamara Mulherin

Introduction

While the research on management and organizing—including the field of health and social care—is frequently still seen to be based mainly on rational and positivistic reasoning, we want to challenge ourselves to identify other modes of rationality and reality. Through the meta-theoretical reflections presented in this chapter we aim to strengthen the awareness of the 'hidden limitations' underlying our research approaches. Assumptions about what exists (ontology), what can be known and how it can be known (epistemology) are significant for the starting point of any study. Likewise studying wicked problems (Rittel and Webber 1973; Coyne 2005; see also Raisio et al. in this volume), our fundamental conception of their nature really matters: what is the essence of the reality in which wicked problems exist? What is the nature of the knowledge we seek about wicked problems, and how can we access it?

Although ontological and epistemological issues are significant in research, it often seems that individual studies do not sufficiently address them (Hassard and Cox 2013). At least, the assumptions may not be explicitly stated and the connections between meta-theoretical commitments and methodological choices may not be apparent. However, research is always based on implicit assumptions about reality and knowledge, regardless of whether the researcher is aware of them and reflects on them. Researchers need to be aware of these basic assumptions embedded in their studies and to understand that it is on these ontological and epistemological grounds, in particular, that research methods such as collecting and analyzing data are based. As Margaret Archer (1995, 28) has stated, "An ontology without a methodology is deaf and dumb; a methodology without ontology is blind" (Archer 1995, 28).

There are numerous ways in which a researcher can view the world. Depending on the context, these ways are referred to by different names, such as methodological approaches, world hypothesis, philosophy of science, paradigms or meta-theories (Kuhn 1994; Morgan 1997; Pepper 1967; see also Hassard and Cox 2013). In this chapter we will address four non-positivist approaches: critical realism, social constructionism, pragmatism and phenomenology. For the purposes of this chapter we offer a broad sketch of each paradigm, followed by an analysis of its key contributions and weaknesses with examples drawn from research on collaboration in health and social care. These four meta-theories—also illustrated here in pictorial terms—are based on differing understandings of reality and knowledge.

The aim of this chapter is to highlight the potential of meta-theoretical reflection when studying wicked problems in health and social care. The 'unsolvable problem' we specifically address here is cross-boundary collaboration, i.e. the difficulties of enacting collaborative working. While collaboration is often offered as a solution to wicked problems, its complex nature renders problematic fitting it to the Rittel and Webber (1973) definition of a wicked problem. Considering different meta-theoretical perspectives on collaboration and other wicked problems may reveal alternative 'truths' about what these wicked problems are and how they might be solved.

Wicked Problems in Four Seasons

A traditional way for philosophers to call into question the nature of reality is by asking: when we look out of the window and see an apple tree somewhere, what do we actually see? Kenneth Gergen (1999) claims that, depending on the world view from which we look at an apple tree, we perceive totally different kinds of trees. In illustrating the four meta-theories selected from many potential options, as a common-sense orientation we use and extend the metaphor of the apple tree as it appears in four 'seasons' (Hujala et al. 2016):[1] critical realism as 'winter,' social constructionism as 'summer,' pragmatism as 'spring' and phenomenology as 'autumn' (see Figures 15.1–15.4).[2]

To make our considerations more concrete, we address the cross-boundary collaboration of actors in health and social care as an example of a wicked problem to be viewed from these four perspectives. Cross-boundary collaboration, here referring both to interorganizational and multi-professional collaboration, is widely accepted as an important approach for addressing significant social issues, such as the pressures currently imposed on the health and social care system due to population aging (Oliver, Foot and Humphries 2014). The commitment to adopt a more collaborative mode of organizing can be seen in endeavors of many countries to fully join up health and social care, but achieving this aim in practice has proved more difficult than expected. Cross-boundary collaboration is often presented as a solution to wicked problems (Danken, Dribbish and Lange 2016). However, cross-boundary collaboration itself can often be considered as a wicked problem.

Winter: Wicked Problems Are Caused by Underlying Mechanisms

Figure 15.1 describes the critical realist assumptions of the world. The denuded apple tree remains visible on the ground level, although covered and surrounded by snow. It appears to be on its own, yet numerous hidden or unnoticed mechanisms affect the life of the tree. For example, the well-being of the tree is dependent on its invisible roots below ground level. The pressure of the snow coming from above may break a branch, underlying underground structures may collapse or active agency, for example in the shape of a mole, may cause damage.

Critical realism[3] (see e.g. Archer 1995; Fleetwood and Ackroyd 2004) is based on the belief that reality is—at least to some extent—objective, external and independent of human beings. In critical realism the phenomenon to be researched is seen as a 'surface' phenomenon, just like the apple tree in the picture above. What is relevant are 'deeper' underlying mechanisms which produce, generate and affect the phenomenon of interest. According to critical realism the task of research is to study and investigate these underlying mechanisms. A crucial assumption is causality: there are hidden causal relationships between organizational phenomena, and the task of research is to reveal them.

Critical realism would view (any) wicked problem as an issue existing more or less as a separate phenomenon, surrounded by an external reality. This reality, however, exerts an influence. Causal relationships between the phenomenon and its external reality are not so self-evident, predictable or straightforward as causalities in the natural sciences, yet there is still a system of cause and effect, in critical realism called 'underlying mechanisms.'

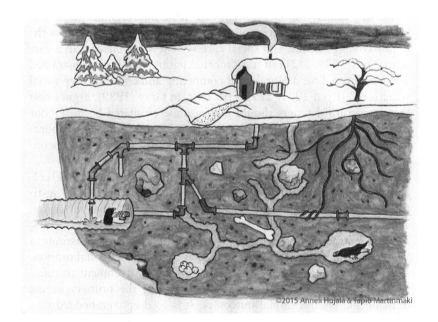

©2015 Anneli Hujala & Tapio Martinmäki

Figure 15.1 Critical Realism

These underlying mechanisms are 'real,' given that for critical realists anything is 'real' if it exists (either materially, ideationally, socially or as an artifact) and if it has a causal effect, that is, if it affects behavior and makes a difference (Alvesson and Sköldberg 2009, 41).

How might a critical realist perspective then look at cross-boundary collaboration in health and social care as an example of a wicked problem? What are the underlying mechanisms in the case of collaboration? It is typical for critical realism to see the world in terms of levels: the macro-level of society, the meso level of organizations, and the micro-level of individual actors. The causes of wicked collaboration problems may be hidden in any of these levels: in societal structures, organizational cultures, management systems or in the behavioral styles of individual actors. The goal of the research is to reveal these deeper connections below the surface and—through abduction, the interplay between empirical and theoretical considerations—create theories to explain these connections.

Box 1 presents an example of how institutionalized ways of thinking and acting can be viewed as underlying mechanisms inhibiting cross-boundary collaboration.

Box 1.   Collaboration Is Inhibited by Deeply Institutionalized Forces

Drawing on a critical realist point of view, the aim of this example is to identify underlying factors that can make interorganizational collaboration difficult to accomplish. Collaborative working across the highly complex health and social care system is not enacted in a vacuum (Gray 1989, 112) but it is "located within, and both constrained and empowered by, a plurality of competing and contradictory social structures" (Reed 2001, 215). Eric Trist, in Gray (1989), argues that these structural barriers should not be underestimated because "our inherited value structure" means that a transition to more collaborative modes will be "profoundly resisted at both conscious and unconscious levels."

It is argued here that interorganizational and multi-professional collaboration in health and social care are inhibited by two deeply institutionalized forces that are essentially anti-collaborative in nature. These forces can be conceptualized as two 'meta-logics' (Scott 2008, 232), a bureaucratic logic and a market logic, which constitute a 'meta-control' system (Storey 1985, 197) that impedes collaboration. The bureaucratic logic can be characterized by 'attachment to rules' (Goffman 1956, 473) and privileges control as the primary means of achieving organizational outcomes. It is so deeply embedded that it is taken for granted as the natural way to organize. The tangible artifacts of this bureaucratic logic are generic management techniques, rules, standardization and hierarchy (Klikauer 2015, 1107). The basic assumption underlying the market logic is that competition and economic reward are the primary motivators of human behavior. It is widely argued that these powerful forces of marketization have "pervaded the public service domain" (Parker 2002, 185) and that within this neo-liberal frame judgments are increasingly being made based on narrow considerations of economic efficiency.

The bureaucratic and market logics provide the guiding organizing principles (Scott 2000, 171) for management practice across the domain of health and social care and they have become deeply embedded in the power structures through roles, identities and privileges. Collaborative actors, as individuals or organizations, are conditioned by these structural forces (Alvesson and Willmott 1996, 57) and they have internalized these logics to the extent that they represent the natural order in the organizing of health care. The depth of institutionalization is also demonstrated by the degree to which the bureaucratic and market logics have displaced the "previous dominant institutional logic of medical professionalism" (Heldal 2015, 190). In contrast to the prevailing institutionalized logics, collaboration is based on a different set of assumptions, with priority placed on the values of trust (rather than control) and cooperation (rather than competition). Attempts to establish a collaborative logic therefore have to confront this pre-existing hierarchy of powerful logics. Institutionalization also serves to reduce critical awareness and constrains the extent to which collaborative actors are capable, or motivated, to perceive alternatives to the current order.

Collaboration is also difficult to establish and sustain because it is a precarious mode of organizing, built on social capital and personal relationships which inevitably take time to establish. An overreliance on control and competition, as is prevalent in health and social care, can also produce an environment of fear and insecurity (Pope and Burnes 2013, 282) which further inhibits collaboration by preventing actors from taking the risks required to build new, trusting relationships.

Although these structural forces are powerful, it does not mean that collaborative actors are totally disempowered or unable to exercise agency. However, it does require actors to approach collaboration in a more reflective, less naïve manner, developing a greater awareness and understanding of the slice of embedded societal structures that they bring into the collaborative space. Productive and meaningful collaboration requires the actors to engage in a process of dialogue where preconceptions and assumptions, such as the bureaucratic and

> market logics, have to be surfaced and confronted in order for the collaboration to mature and develop into a set of relationships and mode of organizing genuinely based on the values of trust and cooperation.
>
> *Andy Brookes*

What, then, are the implications of the critical realist approach to research on wicked problems? By applying a simple version of critical realism we could try to identify the mechanisms underlying problems of collaboration through fairly conventional surveys drawing on causalities between organizational phenomena. However, the real promise of critical realism may reside in novel study designs which could reveal the underlying mechanisms causing problem wickedness. Alvesson and Sköldberg (2009, 43) highlight counterfactual thinking, social experiments and the study of pathological or extreme cases as examples of such innovative research methods drawing on critical realism.

We suggest that many contemporary approaches to wicked problems are grounded in the basic assumptions of critical realism, reasoning that complex problems are generated from 'outside,' 'above' or 'beneath.' For example, in their review article on wicked problems, Danken, Dribbish and Lange (2016, 24) appear to apply critical realist assumptions (albeit not explicitly stated) when they conclude: "In sum, the causes and effects of wicked problems are typically poorly understood, not only because of their complex and distinct nature, but because knowledge and scientific authority tends to be limited and contested."

Critical realism can be criticized for paying too much attention to the assumption of causal relationships between organizational issues. 'Revealing' causality may be difficult, particularly as regards the complexity of wicked problems. In the search for a different basis for understanding problem wickedness, the 'summer approach' based on postmodern social constructionism, introduced in the next part, will offer an alternative to the critical realist winter.

Summer: Wicked Problems Are Constructed in Social Interaction

The sun is shining and family members are enjoying a beautiful summer's day (Figure 15.2). When they look at the very same apple tree, they see and think—and talk about—very different things. The grandmother remembers the apple blossoms on the trees in Karelia, the province which was lost to Russia during World War II. The scientist in the family recalls the Latin names of the flora. The girls speak about the jam the apples produce and the youngster tells a story about exciting apple stealing expeditions.

According to (postmodern) social constructionism[4] (Gergen 1999; Berger and Luckmann 1967), social reality is not external, objective nor independent

Figure 15.2 Social Constructionism

of human beings. Social phenomena can be understood as socially constructed: they are created, maintained and changed in continuous interaction between people through talk and language. Language and words are not only tools for describing the world "as it is"; they also *constitute* the world (Gergen 1999). The result of the social constructionist view of reality is that no single truth of an apple tree can exist. Figure 15.2 illustrates several discourses,[5] such as cultural, academic and functional discourses. All these construct a different understanding of the apple tree.

Social constructionism and critical realism are often represented as opposites (Reed 2005; Fleetwood and Ackroyd 2004). However, there has been contention as to whether the 'discursive or linguistic turn' (Alvesson and Kärreman 2000; Gergen and Thatchenkery 2004), based on postmodernism and manifest in social constructionism, should be replaced by a realist turn or a 're-turn to realism' (Reed 2005; cf. Contu and Willmott 2005).

From a social constructionist point of view, there is no single truth about the wicked problem addressed here, the difficulties in cross-boundary collaboration. The reasons for problems in collaboration are not lurking somewhere beneath the surface, nor caused by underlying mechanisms, nor due to static power dynamics embedded in organizational structures as understood in critical realism. Collaboration problems may be connected, for example, to power positions or differences between cultures, but these positions or differences, like power or cultures, do not exist in isolation; they are constituted, maintained and changed in interaction between people. This construction takes place through talk and language: for example, we draw on macro-level discourses such as fragmented professional knowledge or cultural differences and reproduce these in our micro-level ongoing every-day talk and interaction (Shotter 1993).

In addition, as Gergen (1999, 138) states, "We are made of each other." People at birth are not domineering doctors, difficult nurses or trouble-some social workers. People are different, but their positions in collab-oration are produced by all collaborating participants maintaining—or changing—the ways we interact and talk to each other (or about each other). For example, power is not something a person 'has': we combine to confer power on somebody, we accept it and allow that person to exert influence over us.

Box 2 describes two ways of talking about collaboration between private and public health care. In Maarit Lammassaari's study, managers in private health care organizations drew on these two different discourses when they tried to make sense of the collaboration between the sectors.

Box 2. Discursive Construction of Collaboration Between Private and Public Health Care

The collaboration between public sector and private sector, in Fin-land it (collaboration) has always been . . . a bit . . . bad always. It has been unbelievably bad . . . more because of the attitudes in the public sector.

(Manager in the private health care sector)

The aim of this quote is to illustrate the tension-ridden nature of Finn-ish health care and how it is discursively constructed in the talk of pri-vate health care managers. The quote is an example of how managers in private health care organizations draw on *the blaming the 'other' discourse* to construct collaboration as problematic between the pub-lic and private sectors.

As a business researcher studying health care organizations, I con-sider myself an 'outsider' in the world of health and social care. In order to understand this world it has been useful for me to consider it as a discourse: When actors talk about health and social care, what does that talk tell us about the actors involved, in this example in rela-tion to collaboration.

For decades the dynamics between public and private health care have been at the core of the development of national health care in

Finland (Mattila 2011). Currently an extensive national health and social care reform is being planned to change the roles of public and private actors: freedom of choice opens markets for private actors in a totally new way. In my research, I am interested in what happens when the discursive context of the private world meets the discursive context of the public world. Therefore I study management sensemaking (see e.g. Maitlis and Christianson 2014) in private health care organizations. I am fascinated to understand how and why those managers talk about the same issues in many different ways.

Managers' talk maintains and challenges the construction of collaboration through the dominant social roles in health care, i.e. public and private health care. In my research I have interviewed managers in private health care organizations in Finland. These interviews were analyzed using discourse analysis. I identified two competing discourses, which differ in the ways by which managers make sense of collaboration.

Through the first discourse introduced above, *the blaming the 'other' discourse* management collaboration is constructed as problematique between the public and private health care. This discourse draws on the juxtaposition of the dominant social roles: private is 'we' and public is 'the other.' Through the blaming talk managers maintain and reproduce public and private health care as opposite social roles in Finnish health care and collaboration as a problematic matter between them.

The competing discourse identified in my study is *the collaboration requirement discourse*. This discourse challenges the juxtaposition discourse and calls for collaboration among multiple actors, including not only health care but also social care actors and patient-customers as end-users. "*I think such multiple-provider models (will increase), that not all wisdom concerning social and health related issues is located only in one place (organization). That many times it is this way that we need experts from many areas so that we can help a patient-customer with multiple complex problems. . . .* "

Through this discourse, managers outline cross-boundary collaboration as a critical success factor, not as a problem between competitive forces. The identification of the polyphonic nature of managers' talk is important when developing relations between public and private care and all actors in the care context.

Maarit Lammassaari

Put simply, wicked problems, such as collaboration inertia, exist purely and simply because people constantly produce them. The bad news is that social constructionist thinking confers much responsibility on people in the sense that also problems are created in interaction between them. The especially bad news is that nobody else, either above or outside can be blamed for causing the problems. The good news is that things can be changed in the same way as they are created, by changing the course of interaction and by changing the ways we speak.

From the perspective of research, social constructionism differs fundamentally from critical realism. Instead of attempts to expose the causality underlying wicked collaboration problems, the focus of research should be on identifying and analyzing the discourses constructing wicked problems and the ways how different stakeholders talk about them. Research material can consist of any kind of text such as interviews, blog texts, journal articles or policy papers; these are analyzed by methods like discourse analysis, narrative analysis, category analysis and conversational analysis. A critical orientation (e.g. critical discourse analysis) in particular focuses on whose voice is heeded and whose is not, and on rendering visible the power of language. Accordingly, the management of wicked problems should focus on managing different kinds of discussions and ways of talking. This may sound idealistic, but it is worth acknowledging that talk and language have more power than one might suppose.[6]

It is worth mentioning that criticism of social constructionism addresses how this approach may reduce complex phenomena to 'mere talk.' This may be a good reason to lead us to explore not only talk but also the practice-level doings of people in everyday life.

Spring: Wicked Problems Reside in Everyday Practices

In Figure 15.3 spring has come. The soil smells sweet in the sunshine; nature is just about to begin to bloom. A couple, with itchy fingers, is full of enthusiasm for gardening. They get to grips with the apple tree through concrete practical work, as in its own way does the mole.

In pragmatism (James 2008/1907), see also praxeology, e.g. Nicolini (2017) it is practice that is at the core of understanding reality. It is not underlying mechanisms, not talk and language, but everyday doings that matter, the 'organized constellations of material activities performed by multiple people' (Schatzki 2012). As in Figure 15.3, we get to understand the phenomena only by a hands-on method. Knowledge is born in practice.

Here we do not delve deep into the philosophical underpinnings of pragmatism and praxeology as such, but limit our consideration to the so-called practice turn, which we see as a current manifestation of pragmatism. Practice-based perspectives have recently become increasingly prominent in organization and management research (see e.g. Jonas, Littig and Wroblewski 2017; Miettinen, Samra-Fredericks and Yanow 2009; Shove,

©2015 Anneli Hujala & Tapio Martinmäki

Figure 15.3 Pragmatism

Pantzar and Watson 2012; Simpson 2009; see also Sandberg and Tsoukas 2011). Practice-based studies have become quite popular, particularly in strategy research (Jarzabkowski, Balogun and David Seidl 2007).

Miettinen summarizes the essence of practice-based approach as follows: "the doings of everyday life are seen as constituting a foundation for social order and institutions" (Miettinen, Samra-Fredericks and Yanow 2009, 1312). Even though the everyday practices of people occur at micro-level, they may have a significant effect at meso level (organizations) and macro-level (whole societies). To put it simply, the world around us is based on and made up of small-scale practices,[7] 'all the way down' (Law 2009).

The practice-based approach affords a new perspective on wicked problems in collaboration. It does not matter what formal structures are in place for collaboration, or what talk there is about the value of collaboration if everyday practices inhibit it. Collaboration either evolves (or does not) at the day-to-day, mundane level, in the 'sayings and doings' of actors. Collaboration practices refer to the bundle of 'actual everyday doings' comprising organization members enmeshed in material arrangements, such as meetings, decision-making, planning, service delivery, ways of being present in interaction, physical positioning in management episodes (see e.g. Jarzabkowski and Whittington 2008). From a practice-based perspective, these repeated patterns of routines and practices, embedded in the physical environment, are core elements through which power, hierarchy and control, for instance, are embodied, inscribed, enacted and maintained in organizations, exhibiting structural properties.

The main message—and the big promise—of practice-based orientation is that we ourselves, through our everyday actions, are in a key position to tackle problems of collaboration. We should pay attention what goes on in everyday routines. If we want to change something, we have to start by changing the counterproductive small-scale ways of acting through bodies and things. The possibility for major changes resides in very small changes. From the research point of view, access to the world of practices though diverse data collecting methods is crucial, as described in Box 3.

Box 3.   Tracing Collaboration Practices in Health and Social Care Integration

My research focused on managers working across the organizational boundaries of 'Kintra' Council (social care) and NHS 'Kintra' (health care) involved in Health and Social Care integration (HSCI) in Scotland. I explored how collaborative practices are made sense of and what configuration of practices are shaping HSCI. Understandings of public sector collaborative practices are partial (Thomson and Perry 2006) and too often mirror traditional organizational conceptualizations as fixed, stable entities. This 'entification' of partnership coordinating routines, conceals the processual features of organizing, the messiness and disorder that occurs intra and interorganizationally (Flyverbom 2010).

It is acknowledged that how health and social care has evolved in the United Kingdom since 1948, is not responsive to the needs of the increasing numbers of people with complex, long-term conditions. The Scottish Government introduced legislation, a 'mandated' interorganizing between NHS territorial boards and Local Governments, to address the problem of care for these people (Scottish Parliament 2013).

Central to the research and common to practice studies, is the significance of ethnography as a way of knowing (van Hulst, Koster and Vermeulen 2015). During fieldwork, I shadowed six managers, attended 127 meetings in numerous facilities across eight sites in 'Kintra,' followed specific document development and undertook 20 semi-structured interviews. This provided multiple lines of sight into how managers worked in a partnership (Glasby and Dickinson 2014) and the paradoxes created between different modes of organizing.

Although there is no unified theory of practice (Nicolini 2017) and practices are empirically slippery, in attempting to pin down practices,

I utilized observation, shadowing, interviewing and following an object. Sedlacko (2017) suggests methods, including diaries, manuals, interview to the double (Nicolini 2009), artifact analysis, as well as following ideas or processes. The emphasis on researching practices is attendance to the 'everydayness' of people's situated, interactive doings with materials and how these elements assemble to create, stabilize or dissolve a practice (Sedlacko 2017).

The interorganizational activities of shadowed managers resembled 'typical' administrative, or managerial processes. Inter-organizing elements emerged in the doings of: regular meetings involving two or more organizations; communications via phone and email, creating embodied, material (through documents and technologies); and affective (through listening, or conflict resolution) junctures between organizations. Managers stressed that familiarizing themselves with other forms of organizing, in combination with influencing, not directive conduct, shaped collaborative practice.

However, what appeared to be collaborative was a 'double-doing,' that is, practices undertaken simultaneously. For example, recruitment to joint appointments was regarded as collaborative when both organizations approved and funded positions, yet recruitment was undertaken through two forms of recruitment practice at the same time. This pattern was repeated in relation to other practices, such as, occupational health and safety and financial management. This is not surprising as these generic patterns of organizing shape the distinctive boundaries of organizations. However, for managers, it translated into knowing about and undertaking two parallel procedures – a doubling of work.

Multiple meanings of HSCI were expressed by actors but regarded as comprehensible for programmes, for example, within mental health services. However, HSCI was not perceived as feasible across services and did not encompass corporate practices. Although I was told legislation was the only way to make HSCI happen, various NHS actors expressed apprehensions about the process and legislation. There appeared to be resistance to limit the breadth and depth of HSCI, especially from executives in the NHS.

The mix of practices and multiple meanings associated with HSCI appeared to produce bewilderment amongst the shadowed managers. Within 12 months of HSCI 'going live,' four of the six managers had resigned (three from the NHS, one from the Council). Although it can be argued manager's accomplishments are endowed with a practical sense of opportunities and constraints that enable them to act in skilled ways and maneuver within their own intra-organizational spaces (Bjerregaard 2011), this same experiential knowledge maybe delimited in a partnership context and a 'sense' of collaborative inertia saturates everyday action (Huxham and Vangen 2005).

Analysis showed that despite the ambitions of the legislation, at the early stages of implementation, HSCI was challenging. This situation might be interpreted as more than collaborative inertia, rather revealing the resilience of practice configurations that reinforce the 'stasis' of boundaries between organizations.

Tamara Mulherin

Although a practice-based approach offers interesting insights into wicked problems through searching understanding from the routine actions of people, it may be restricted to explain why people actually do what they do. The following approach leads us to look at reality and knowledge through the lenses of the individual consciousness and subjective, even bodily experiences of human beings.

Autumn: Individual Experiences of Wicked Problems

It is a breezy, chilly autumn day (Figure 15.4). A young woman is walking in a biting wind. The tree, the actual phenomenon of the tree, does not exist in objective reality, nor is it constructed in social interaction or embedded in people's everyday doings. It hides somewhere in the young woman's consciousness. However, when recalling her memory of the once lived experience of the apple tree, she feels the power of the wind all through her body.

Phenomenology leads on to subjectivity: the consciousness and experiences of individuals (Husserl et al. 1995/1950; Schütz et al. 2007/1932; see also Heinämaa 2010). Understanding arises from and through human beings' personal experiences. Phenomenology, in particular the phenomenology of the body (Merleau-Ponty 1993, 2000/1962), also addresses the importance of the physical environment. Experiencing the world does not mean only thinking or speaking of it—above all it is 'feeling' the world. An individual is in contact with the world and with other people through her/his body and embodied experiences, using all five senses. "The world is not what I think, but what I live through" (Merleau-Ponty 2000/1962, xvi–xvii). One's own body is 'the zero point' from and through which the individual experiences the world.

From a methodological point of view phenomenology means that the aim of the research is to achieve and understand the "lived experiences" of the research participants. This is done by trying to step back from the "simplifying everyday attitude" (Husserl et al. 1995/1950; Schütz et al. 2007/1932). The simplifying everyday attitude refers to the way we usually see the world as

©2015 Anneli Hujala & Tapio Martinmäki

Figure 15.4 Phenomenology (of the Body)

taken-for-granted. Everyday life is so close and so familiar as to make it impossible to question the details of the stream of everyday life passing over us.

To study wicked collaboration problems phenomenology thus takes individual experiences as its starting point. Each of us experiences collaboration in her/his own way. Previous experiences may have a major effect. A salient point is that we are not conscious of the reasons for acting as we do. We need to reflect on our feelings about collaboration in novel ways: not only by thinking but, for example, by letting our whole body reveal how we feel. In the world of health care, material artifacts very often relate to hierarchical positions; just think of disempowered patients lying on the hospital bed, surrounded by white-coated all-powerful doctors. Similar unnoticed and unconscious embodied experiences may affect our behavior in demanding collaboration situations.

Research methods based on the phenomenology of the body should help us get rid of our 'simplifying everyday attitude,' which prevents us from seeing the phenomenon for what it is, that is, the real essence of the phenomenon from a Husserlian point of view. Various arts-based methods may be helpful in liberating us from the constraints of our rational minds. The following example (see Box 4) illustrates an experimental study where, instead of an ordinary interview 'an embodied interview' was used to study embodied emotions in workplace interaction.

Box 4. The Dance of a Devil's Advocate

I admit, this is me at my work: becoming frustrated, provoked, annoying colleagues, thirsting for power, feeling happy, enjoying debate, being full of joy. However, in everyday interaction with my colleagues I hardly notice how I feel and I do not pay much attention to emotions. We are supposed to be intellectual members of an academic community, behaving as sensible and rational actors. Only sometimes I notice that my pulse rises, that something tries to come out of me and I feel imprisoned in my own body. Or the opposite: I sometimes feel so happy, so light and free that I am sure I could easily dance on the clouds. If I can feel my emotions in, with and through my body, shouldn't I listen to what it tells to me?

The aim of this example—based on the phenomenology of the body (Husserl et al. 1995/1950; Merleau-Ponty 1993, 2000/1962; see also Heinämaa 2010)—is to consider the question "What does my body reveal to me about my emotions in work-related interaction?" The reflections presented here are based on an experiment in which creative dance was applied as a method in a small-scale study, in which we wanted to question the dominant role of discursive data in organization and management research by focusing on embodied knowledge, (Hujala, Laulainen and Kokkonen 2014; see also Hujala et al. 2016).

The experiment was carried out in the form of a dance session coordinated by a dance pedagogue. The participants, seven female leaders and researchers from the field of health and social care, gave individual performances using 'dance' (creative movement). The session was videotaped. Here I return to my personal experiences in the experiment through an auto-ethnographic orientation, with a focus on embodied emotions. The methodological approach of the experiment was based on the assumptions of the phenomenology of body. By performing my 'lived experiences' (Husserl et al. 1995/1950; Schütz et al. 2007/1932) of the meeting through creative movement, I stepped aside from my 'everyday simplifying attitude,' in which I take my behavior and my interaction with others for granted.

In the experiment I recalled an interaction in a certain recent workplace meeting. In the actual meeting I had felt frustrated and annoyed and missed a sense of freedom without knowing why I felt so. In such situations I often take a very critical position and say straight out things that I think other people lack the courage to say. Through creative movement in my performance, I recalled the frustration I often have when I am forced to sit still on a chair and listen to those in powerful positions, looking at the silent audience consisting of colleagues who I think do not dare to say aloud what they think. In my 'dance' I expressed my frustration by squirming like a snake on the ground. My critical opinions in the meetings were shown through movements of my hands, imitating sharp beak strokes of a bird.

The feelings aroused through the bodily reflection were almost tangible, so much so that the embodied manifestations of my inner consciousness made me frightened. Is it really me, pecking at my bosses and colleagues with my sharp beak? The reflection through my body made me think seriously about my interaction model. I try to raise issues, but I very often end up doing it too critically. A situation where other people stay silent and do not comment anything seems to make me extremely frustrated and this results in excessively sharp comments. My feelings of frustration and distress turned out to be one main constructor of my role as a (wicked) devil's advocate (Janis 1982, 267–268) in the meetings.

It feels that in the workplace meetings we habitually curb our expression: we act our role as obedient followers, not being the professional experts as usual. We are limited by the conventions of a meeting, we get stiff—and often this all takes place unconsciously.

To sum up, why should we be satisfied with mere words if we can harness our whole physical bodies to elicit, express and create new and different kinds of understanding of collaboration?

Anneli Hujala

Different kinds of arts-based methods (see also Martikainen in this volume)—whether drawing explicitly on phenomenology or not—include high potential to reveal knowledge and meanings beyond rational, practical or discursive-level understanding. Such methods are used as tools in organization development, but not so often in research.[8] Regarding wicked problems, Sörensen and Waldorff (2014) conducted workshops, in which theatre sequences based on stories about concrete life experiences were used in a collaborative policy innovation process addressing wicked problems in mental health care in Denmark. Winters, Cushing and Lach (2016) report on designing visualization software in a wicked problem context and suggest that visualization of data enables different stakeholders to make sense of complex scientific data. Grant-Smith and Osborne (2016) state that the unspeakable nature of some wicked policy problems (due to moral, psychological, religious or cultural dimensions of them) further increases their wickedness: re-imagining wicked problems through emotional and embodied talk is needed to open new ways of planning practices.

Phenomenology in general is often criticized for being a difficult approach: to grasp individual consciousness even as a concept is a challenging task, not to speak about the problems of making any generalizations based on individual experiences. However, much potential resides in the notion that the key to understanding wicked problems may reside in understanding ourselves as individuals, in how we feel and 'live through' the world.

Discussion

In order to produce valuable knowledge to support managers and decision-makers in solving wicked problems, we need novel approaches and methods to understand those problems more holistically (Hassard and Cox 2013). As Danken, Dribbish and Lange (2016, 16) state: "There is a broad scholarly consensus around the concern that policymakers run into serious problems when sticking to traditional scientific-rational approaches to policymaking and implementation when dealing with complex issues." This claim poses a serious challenge to us as researchers: Wicked problems challenge us to display creativity and innovation and invite us to use scientific imagination beyond conventional rational reasoning (Brown, Harris and Russell 2010; Sharts-Hopko 2013).

The aim of this chapter was to highlight the potential of meta-theoretical reflection when studying wicked problems in health and social care. We reflected here four different non-positivistic meta-theoretical approaches: critical realism, social constructionism, pragmatism/practice-based approach and phenomenology (of the body). Cross-boundary collaboration was used as an example of problem wickedness.

The issues introduced here through four meta-theories—causalities and connections between different levels of societal structures (critical realism), talk and interaction of people (social constructionism), everyday practices (practice-based approach) and individual experiences (phenomenology)—are invariably likely to be somehow involved when we encounter difficulties in enacting collaborative working. Similarly, in research we may be in danger of ignoring any of these if we contemplate collaboration from one single perspective. This does not mean that we should always do multi-paradigm research. However, it is important to remember that we only 'see' certain kinds of things depending on what kinds of ontological and epistemological assumptions our study designs are based on—either consciously or unconsciously.

Meta-theories do indeed clarify and give structure for basic assumptions regarding ontology and epistemology. However, they may also impair our understanding, because such 'groupings' make the world look simpler than it is. As Deetz suggests (in Newton et al. 2011), being constrained to a particular paradigm, be it critical realist or social constructionist, may represent "less than useful polarization." For example, in approaching the complex and multifaceted phenomena of cross-boundary collaboration in health and social care, how can we know which meta-theoretical approach is best suited for generating warranted or valid insights? Approaching the pre-existing context or structural aspects of the problem lends itself to adopting a critical realist lens. However, it can also be argued that the act of collaboration itself is essentially an exercise in social construction. It could thus be argued that a holistic explanation of the phenomena requires taking advantage of both of these perspectives.

Thus different meta-theories may be contradictory but they are also over-lapping: they can be combined, to some extent even in a single study. Hassard and Cox (2013) refer to this when they speak about multiple paradigm research, paradigm interplay and meta-triangulation. We indeed agree with Hassard and Cox (2013, 717) that meta-theoretical considerations are useful not only for showing differences between research orientations but also in identifying similarities.

Altogether, we are convinced that meta-theoretical thinking can be utilized in generating new research approaches and novel methodologies for studying wicked problems. This may further add value to the currently increasing interest in open science and citizen science: We need to engage not only managers and decision-makers but also care professionals and end-users such as patients, clients and citizens (Hassard and Cox 2013, 1717) as partners to solve wicked problems in health and social care. In future we may probably be able to pay less attention to defining what wicked problems are and, instead, focus more on how to understand them and how to learn more about them by approaching them from different alternative perspectives on the basis of knowledge produced by diverse actors in novel and sometimes even imaginary ways.

Acknowledgments

The authors would like to express their warmest thanks to Tapio Martin-mäki (Turku, Finland) for visualizing the 'four seasons' (Figures 15.1–15.4).

Notes

1. This 'four seasons approach' was originally published in *Organizational Aesthet-ics* (see Hujala et al. 2016) and is re-used here with the permission of the journal.
2. The metaphor of the four seasons is based on experiences of looking out of the window in the context of Finnish nature, where totally different 'seasonal realities' are available depending on the time of year. This season metaphor also conveniently restricts the meta-theories to only four, although there are many others which could also have been addressed here.
3. There is a wide spectrum of approaches within critical realism, for example, from the philosophical production of Roy Bhaskar (1975, 1979) and the social realism

of Margaret Archer (1995) to the methodological realism of Andrew Sayer (1984) and the critical scientific realism of Ilkka Niiniluoto (1999). The approach to critical realism in this paper is not based on one particular orientation, but on the more generally accepted assumptions of critical realism.

4. Social constructionism includes several approaches with different foci. Our interpretation of social constructionism here is based mainly on the ideas and views of Kenneth Gergen (e.g. 1999) and John Shotter (e.g. 1993).
5. For various meanings of 'discourse,' see, e.g. Potter and Wetherell (1987) and Alvesson (2004).
6. It is worth mentioning that from the social constructionist point of view, we can claim that these meta-theories are only social constructs created by academics—as also the concept 'wicked problem,' just one way of speaking of difficult challenges.
7. Discursive practices are often included in the practice-based approach. Here we want to emphasize 'doing' rather than speaking in order to make a clear distinction between discursive and practice turns.
8. For the purposes of this book chapter, we did not conduct a systematic literature review to search for methodological approaches used in research on wicked problems. Thus we have undoubtedly missed many relevant and interesting contributions. Hopefully we will hear of them in future.

References

Alvesson, Mats. 2004. "Organizational Culture and Discourse." In *The Sage Handbook of Organizational Discourse*, edited by David Grant, Cynthia Hardy, Cliff Oswick, and Linda L. Putnam, 317–335. London: Sage Publications.

Alvesson, Mats, and Dan Kärreman. 2000. "Taking the Linguistic Turn in Organizational Research: Challenges, Responses, Consequences." *Journal of Applied Behavioral Science* 36: 136–158.

Alvesson Mats, and Kaj Sköldberg. 2009. *Reflexive Methodology: New Vistas for Qualitative Research*. London: Sage Publications.

Alvesson, Mats, and Hugh Willmott. 1996. *Making Sense of Management: A Critical Introduction*. London: Sage Publications.

Archer, Margaret S. 1995. *The Realist Social Theory: The Morphogenetic Approach*. Cambridge: Cambridge University Press.

Berger, Peter L., and Thomas Luckmann. 1967. *The Social Construction of Reality: A Treatise in the Sociology of Knowledge*. New York: Anchor Books.

Bhaskar, Roy. 1975. *A Realist Theory of Science*. Leeds: Leeds Books.

Bjerregaard, Toke. 2011. Co-Existing Institutional Logics and Agency Among Top-Level Public Servants: A Praxeological Approach." *Journal of Management & Organization* 17 (2): 194–209.

Brown, Valerie A., John A. Harris, and Jacqueline Y. Russell. 2010. *Tackling Wicked Problems: Through the Transdisciplinary Imagination*. London: Earthscan.

Contu, Alessia, and Hugh Willmott. 2005. "You Spin Me Round: The Realist Turn in Organization and Management Studies." *Journal of Management Studies* 42 (8): 1645–1662.Coyne, Richard. 2005. "Wicked Problems Revisited." Design Studies 26 (1): 5–17.

Danken, Thomas, Katrin Dribbish, and Anne Lange. 2016. "Studying Wicked Problems Forty Years on: Towards a Synthesis of a Fragmented Debate." *Der Moderne Staat* 9. Jg. Heft1/2016: 15–33.

Fleetwood, Steve. 2005. "Ontology in Organization and Management Studies: A Critical Realist Perspective." *Organization* 12 (2): 197–222.

Fleetwood, Steve, and Stephen Ackroyd, eds. 2004. *Critical Realist Applications in Organisation and Management Studies*. London, New York: Routledge.

Flyverbom, Mikkel. 2010. "Hybrid Networks and the Global Politics of the Digital Revolution—A Practice-Oriented, Relational and Agnostic Approach." *Global Networks* 10 (3): 424–442.

Gergen, Kenneth J. 1999. *An Invitation to Social Construction*. London: Sage Publications.

Gergen, Kenneth J., and Tojo J. Thatchenkery. 2004. "Organization Science as Social Construction: Postmodern Potentials." *Journal of Applied Behavioral Science* 40 (2): 228–249.

Glasby, Jon, and Helen Dickinson. 2014. *Partnership Working in Health and Social Care: What Is Integrated Care and How Can We Deliver It?* Bristol: Policy Press.

Goffman, Erving. 1956. "The Nature of Deference and Demeanor." *American Anthropologist* 58 (3): 473–502.

Grant-Smith, Deanna, and Natalie Osborne. 2016. "Dealing with Discomfort: How the Unspeakable Confounds Wicked Planning Problems." *Australian Planner* 53 (1): 46–53.

Gray, Barbara. 1989. *Collaborating: Finding Common Ground for Multiparty Problems*. San Francisco: Jossey-Bass.

Hassard, John, and Julie Wolfram Cox. 2013. "Can Sociological Paradigms Still Inform Organizational Analysis? A Paradigm Model for Post-Paradigm Times." *Organizational Studies* 34 (11): 1701–1728.

Heinämaa, Sara. 2010. "Minä, tietoisuus ja ruumillisuus. [Self, Consciousness and Embodiment]." In *Fenomenologian ydinkysymyksiä [Core Issues in Phenomenology]*, edited by Timo Miettinen, Simo Pulkkinen, and Joona Taipale. Helsinki: Gaudeamus.

Heldal, Frode. 2015. "Managerial Control Versus Professional Autonomy in Organizational Change: Tearing Down the Walls and Fighting Fire with Fire." *Journal of Change Management* 15 (3) (September): 188–209.

Hujala, Anneli, Sanna Laulainen, Riitta-Liisa Kinni, Kaija Kokkonen, Katja Puttonen, and Anniina Aunola. 2016. "Dancing with the Bosses: Creative Movement as a Method." *Organizational Aesthetics* 5 (1): 11–36.

Hujala, Anneli, Sanna Laulainen, and Kaija Kokkonen. 2014. "Manager's Dance: Reflecting Management Interaction Through Creative Movement." *International Journal of Work, Organization and Emotion* 6 (1): 40–57.

Husserl, Edmund, Juha Himanka, Janita Hämäläinen, and Hannu Sivenius. 1995/1950. *Fenomenologian Idea: viisi luentoa [The Idea of Phenomenology: Five Lectures, 1950]* [Die Idee der Phänomenologie]. Helsinki: Loki-kirjat.

Huxham, Chris, and Siv Vangen. 2005. *Managing to Collaborate—The Theory and Practice of Collaborative Advantage*. Abingdon: Routledge.

James, William. 2008/1907. *Pragmatismi—uusi nimi eräille vanhoille ajattelutavoille [Pragmatism: A New Name for Some Old Ways of Thinking, 1907]*. Tampere: Eurooppalaisen filosofian seura.

Janis, Irving Lester. 1982. *Groupthink*. Boston: Houghton Mifflin Company.

Jarzabkowski, Paula, Julia Balogun, and David Seidl. 2007. "Strategizing: The Challenges of a Practice Perspective." *Human Relations* 60 (1): 5–27.

Jarzabkowski, Paula, and Richard Whittington. 2008. "A strategy-as-Practice Approach to Strategy Research and Education." *Journal of Management Inquiry* 17 (4): 282–286.

Jonas, Michael, Beate Littig, and Angela Wroblewski, eds. 2017. *Methodological Reflections on Practice Oriented Theories.* Cham: Springer.

Klikauer, Thomas. 2015. "What Is Managerialism?" *Critical Sociology* 41 (7–8) (November): 1103–1119.

Kuhn, Thomas. 1994. *Tieteellisten vallankumousten rakenne [The Structure of Scientific Revolutions].* Helsinki: Art House.

Law, John. 2009. Collateral Realities. http://www.heterogeneities.net/publications/Law2009CollateralRealities.pdf

Maitlis, Sally, and Marlys Christianson. 2014. "Sensemaking in organizations: Taking Stock and Moving Forward." *The Academy of Management Annals* 8 (1): 57–125.

Martikainen, Jari. 2018. "The Promise of Visual Approaches in Organizational and Management Research." (in this volume).

Mattila, Yrjö. 2011. *Major Turning Points or Measured Progress? A Study of Development Trends in Finnish Health Care.* Helsinki: Social Insurance Institution of Finland.

Merleau-Ponty, Maurice. 2000 [1962]. *Phenomenology of Perception.* London: Routledge.

Merleau-Ponty, Maurice, and Kimmo Pasanen. 1993. *Silmä ja mieli [The Eye and the Mind; L'Ceil et l'Esprit].* Helsinki: Taide.

Miettinen, Reijo, Dalvir Samra-Fredericks, and Dvora Yanow. 2009. "Re-Turn to Practice: An Introductory Essay." *Organization Studies* 30 (12): 1309–1327.

Morgan, Gareth. 1997. *Images of Organization.* Thousand Oaks, CA: Sage Publications.

Newton, Tim, Stan Deetz, and Mike Reed. 2011. "Responses to Social Constructionism and Critical Realism in Organization Studies." *Organization Studies* 32 (1): 7–26.

Nicolini, Davide. 2009. "Zooming in and Zooming Out: A Package of Method and Theory to Study Work Practices." In *Organizational Ethnography—Studying the Complexity of Everyday Life,* edited by Sierk Ybema, Dvora Yanow, Harry Wels, and Frans H Kamsteeg. 120–138. London: Sage Publications.

Nicolini, Davide. 2017. "Practice Theory as a Package of Theory, Method and Vocabulary: Affordances and Limitations." In *Methodological Reflections on Practice Oriented Theories,* edited by Michael Jonas, Beate Littig, and Angela Wroblewski, 19–34. Cham: Springer.

Niiniluoto, Ilkka. 1999. *Critical Scientific Realism.* Oxford: Oxford University Press.

Oliver, David, Catherine Foot, and Richard Humphries. 2014. *Making Our Health and Care Systems Fit for an Ageing Population.* London: King's Fund.

Orlikowski, Wanda J. 2010. "The Sociomateriality of Organizational Life: Considering Technology in Management Research." *Cambridge Journal of Economics* 34 (1): 125–141.

Parker, Martin. 2002. *Against Management: Organization in the Age of Managerialism.* Cambridge: Polity Press.

Pepper, Stephen C. 1967. *Concept and Quality: A World Hypothesis.* LaSalle, IL: Open Court Press.

Pope, Rachael, and Bernard Burnes. 2013. "A Model of Organisational Dysfunction in the NHS." *Journal of Health Organization and Management* 27 (6) (October): 676–697.

Potter, Jonathan, and Margaret Wetherell. 1987. *Discourse and Social Psychology. Beyond Attitudes and Behaviour.* London: Sage Publications.

Raisio, Harri, Alisa Puustinen, and Pirkko Vartiainen. 2018. "The Concept of Wicked Problems: Improving the Understanding of Managing Problem Wickedness in Health and Social Care." (in this volume).

"Realist Perspective." *Organization* 12 (2): 197–222.

Reed, Michael. 2001. "Organization, Trust and Control: A Realist Analysis." *Organization Studies* 22 (2): 201–228.

Reed, Michael. 2005. "Reflections on the 'Realist Turn' in Organization and Management Studies." *Journal of Management Studies* 42 (8): 1621–1644.

Rittel, Horst W. J., and Melvin M. Webber. 1973. "Dilemmas in a General Theory of Planning." *Policy Sciences* 4 (2): 155–169.

Sandberg, Jorgen, and Haridimos Tsoukas. 2011. "Grasping the Logic of Practice: Theorizing Through Practical Rationality." *Academy of Management Review* 36 (2): 338–360.

Sayer, Andrew. 1984. *Method in Social Science: A Realist Approach*, 2nd ed. London: Routledge.

Sayer, Andrew. 2004. "Foreword: Why Critical Realism?" In *Critical Realist Applications in Organisation and Management Studies*, edited by Fleetwood Steve and Stephen Ackroyd, 6–20. London, New York: Routledge.

Schatzki, Theodore R. 2012. "A Primer on Practices." In *Practice-based Education: Perspectives and Strategies*, edited by Joy Higgs, Ronald Barnett, Stephen Billett, Maggie Hutchings, and Franziska Trede, 13–26. Rotterdam: Sense.

Schütz, Alfred, Veikko Pietilä, and Tapio Aittola. 2007/1932. *Sosiaalisen maailman merkityksekäs rakentuminen. Johdatus ymmärtävään sosiologiaan [Meaningful Building Up of the Social World: Introduction to Understanding Sociology: Der sinnhafte Aufbau der sozialen Welt: Eine Einleitung in die verstehende Soziologie 1932].* Tampere: Vastapaino.

Scott, W. Richard. 2008. "Lords of the Dance: Professionals as Institutional Agents." *Organization Studies* 29 (2) (February): 219–238.

Scott, W. Richard, Martin Ruef, Peter J. Mendel, and Carol A. Caronna. 2000. *Institutional Change and Healthcare Organizations: From Professional Dominance to Managed Care.* Chicago: University of Chicago Press.

Scottish Parliament. 2013. *Public Bodies (Joint Working) (Scotland) Bill—SPICe Briefing 13/50.* Edinburgh: Scottish Parliament.

Sedlacko, Michal. 2017. "Conducting Ethnography with a Sensibility for Practice." In *Methodological Reflections on Practice Oriented Theories*, edited by Michael Jonas, Beate Littig, and Angela Wroblewski, 47–60. Cham: Springer.

Sementelli, Arthur. 2001. "Distortions of Progress: Evolutionary Theories and Public Administration." *Administration & Society* 39 (6): 740–760.

Sharts-Hopko, Nancy C. 2013. "Tackling Complex Problems, Building Evidence for Practice, and Educating Doctoral Nursing Students to Manage the Tension." *Nursing Outlook* 61: 102–108.

Shotter, John. 1993. *Conversational Realities: Constructing Life Through Language.* London: Sage Publications.

Shove, Elizabeth, Mika Pantzar, and Matt Watson. 2012. *The Dynamics of Social Practice: Everyday Life and How it Changes.* London: Sage Publications.

Simpson, Barbara. 2009. "Pragmatism, Mead and the Practice Turn." *Organization Studies* 30 (12): 1329–1347.

Sørensen, Eva, and Susanne Boch Waldorff. 2014. "Collaborative Policy Innovation: Problems and Potential." *The Innovation Journal: The Public Sector Innovation Journal* 19 (3): 1.

Storey, John. 1985. "The Means of Management Control." *Sociology* 19 (2) (May): 193–211.

Thomson, Ann Marie, and James Perry. 2006. Collaboration Processes: Inside the Black Box." *Public Administration Review* 66 (S1): 20–32.

van Hulst, Merlijn, Martijn Koster, and Jeroen Vermeulen. 2015. "Ethnographic Research." In *Encyclopedia of Public Administration and Public Policy*, edited by Melvin Dubnick, and Domonic Bearfield, 1335–1339. New York: Taylor & Francis.

Winters Kirsten M., Judith B. Cushing, and Denise Lach. 2016. "Designing Visualization Software for Super-Wicked Problems." *Information Policy* 21: 399–409.

16 The Promise of Visual Approaches in Organizational and Management Research

Jari Martikainen

Turn to the Visual in Organizational and Management Research

In work organizations, meanings are created and transmitted not only through language but also through visual means. However, organizational and management research is still largely based on discursive research materials. That said, the current millennium has witnessed a clear increase in research methods using visual materials for organizational and management research (Bramming et al. 2012; Martikainen and Hujala 2014, 2017; Warren 2009), which many believe is due to the fact that the visual element is closely intertwined with contemporary social practices (Clark and Morris 2017; Mannay 2015; Rose 2014). Such methods are diverse in terms of both visual materials and their treatment in research (Rose 2014). Visual research methods therefore refer to a wide variety of research practices which "use visual materials of some kind as part of the process of generating evidence in order to explore research questions" (Rose 2014, 26).

Rose (2014) summarizes the three key strengths of visual research methods as follows: 1) visual materials may encourage participants to discuss issues they might not bring out in talk-only interviews; 2) visual materials may reveal tacit conceptions taken for granted in everyday life; and 3) visual materials may promote collaboration between the participant and the researcher. In addition, participant-created visual materials are often regarded as more authentic, since they diminish the influence of the researcher and concepts used by him/her (Inözu 2017; Mannay 2015; McNiff 2008). Finally, visual materials may generate sensory and emotional experiences that are often lacking in social science research (Banks 2008; Kohler Riessman 2008). According to Mannay (2010, 2015), visual materials have the potential to make the familiar strange, which involves participants observing social phenomena and reflecting on them from an unusual standpoint. It is the reflective combination of visual depiction and verbal explanation that makes visual research methods powerful (Rose 2014). In many cases, visual research methods are therefore multimodal in reality (Clark and Morris 2017).

Inspired by the 'visual turn' in the social sciences (Clark and Morris 2017) and management and organizational research (Dale 2005; Martikainen and Hujala 2017; Warren 2009), this research uses participant-created drawings to examine organizational experiences. Seven persons working in the field of social and health care in Finland—frontline managers at a hospital and university researchers—participated in the research in spring 2013. They were asked to draw pictures of their work organizations. Afterwards, the drawings were discussed collaboratively. The purpose of this article is not to highlight novel results related to the substance of organizational research as such—but to examine and discuss the potential of visual research materials to shed light on problematic aspects of organizational life that are normally hidden and supressed.

Participant-Created Drawings as Research Material

Visual research materials can be classified into researcher-generated, participant-created, and found materials (Clark and Morris 2017; Pauwels 2013; Rose 2014). According to Clark and Morris (2017) and Rose (2014), participant-created materials—especially photographs—are most commonly used in social science research. Drawings have also been used extensively to understand people's lived experiences (Clark and Morris 2017; Huss, Kaufman and Siboni 2013; Mannay 2010).

It is frequently assumed that participant-created visual materials activate participants to discuss a research topic (Rose 2014; Mitchell et al. 2011)—even to the extent of paying more attention to the discussion of the pictures than to the pictures themselves (Rose 2014). However, three focus areas must be considered in research based on visual materials: the production of pictures (participant), the pictures themselves and the interpretation of pictures (researcher) (Clark and Morris 2017; Mitchell et al. 2011; Kohler Riessman 2008). Although some proponents of art-based research argue that visual materials speak for themselves and can express aspects not easily expressed in words, participant-created visual materials are frequently analyzed based on the participants' verbal explanations of them (Clark and Morris 2017; Mitchell et al. 2011).

The relationship between the two above positions is addressed by Mitchell et al. (2011) and Rose (2014) as the distinction between 'the visible' and 'the visual.' In their view, 'the visible' refers to a researcher-driven analysis of participant-created images, which they consider insufficient when the purpose of the research is to gain insights into 'the visual'—that is—into participants' meanings and intentions expressed through visual means. Participants' verbal accounts of the meanings of their pictures are regarded as crucial to gaining insights related to the 'the visual' (Mitchell et al. 2011; Rose 2014). Rooted in the auteur theory (Rose 2001), this approach claims that pictures are not transparent windows into their participants' inner lives, but are created from a number of motivations and positions (see also Mannay 2015;

Mitchell et al. 2011). For this reason, it has become customary to ask picture makers to give accounts of their visual creations (Mitchell et al. 2011).

The act of drawing pictures not only involves visualizing—or visually representing—one's personal views and experiences, but also constructing them visually (Clark and Morris 2017; Mitchell et al. 2011; see also Fairclough 1995). Within this frame rooted in social constructionism, drawing pictures can be conceptualized as a process of visual narration intertwining subjective experiences with social and cultural practices in the research situation (Inözu 2017; Kress and van Leeuwen 2006). Thus, it is assumed in this research that drawing pictures provides a channel for members of work organizations to explore, construct and critically reflect on their experiences of organizational life.

Visually and Verbally Storied Work Organizations

Seven persons working in the field of social and health care in Finland—frontline managers at a hospital and university researchers—participated in the research. They were asked to draw a picture of their work organizations. All of the participants were female and will be referred to using fictitious Finnish women's names.

Before starting to draw, some participants doubted their skills in visual expression. Following the recommendation of Mitchell et al. (2011), the researcher reassured the participants that drawing skills are secondary in this task. In order not to lead the participants verbally, the researcher simply asked them to draw a picture of their work organizations, without further specifying the task. They were provided with papers, pencils and colors—and could themselves decide whether or not they used colors. After the drawing session, the participants elucidated their drawings verbally. These verbal accounts were recorded and transcribed.

The data was analyzed inductively without articulate preconceptions, applying an approach reminiscent of 'Grounded Theory,' which allowed the findings to emerge during the analysis process (Charmaz 2006). At the first stage of the analysis, the researcher observed and analyzed the drawings based on their visual qualities. This was followed by an analysis of drawings based on the participants' verbal explanations. In the next phase, the researcher met the participants again and asked some clarificatory questions generated by the analysis. Such an analysis does not adhere to a rigid model but fluctuates between content analysis, narrative analysis and discourse analysis in order to give a voice to the participants' visual and verbal narrations, as well as the researcher's interpretations of them (see Kohler Riessman 2008; Rose 2001).

In the Shadow of a Bleak House

Two participants depicted their organizations as communities surrounded by beautiful natural scenery. Salla drew her organization as a village by a

river. The sun is shining in the sky and bright colors create a joyful atmosphere. In the village, houses and flowers are depicted in different colors,
expressing the variety of professionals needed in the organization.

> Well, this is my work community. This is a kind of village, where there
> are houses and flowers in different colours . . . let all the flowers bloom
> [. . .] different types of people are needed in an organization.

Anna also drew a picture where a group of colorfully dressed people stand
in a landscape consisting of a lawn, river, trees, flowers and birds. The sky
is blue, and the sun is shining. With these elements of summery nature,
Anna wanted to express the positive way in which she experienced her work
organization.

> I see a lot of good things here. [. . .] In my experience, the atmosphere
> is quite good in my work organization. [. . .] The reason why I drew the
> sun and . . . and trees and birds is that I think [. . .] that you can express
> your ideas and be creative in this organization. There are also work
> organizations that are very routinized.

However, in the middle of the paper, Anna drew a dark, black cottage that
stands out like a fracture in the polished surface of the organization (Figure 16.1). Black smoke comes from the chimney. Nobody is near the cottage, as if everybody was avoiding it. It is isolated and stands out from
the otherwise bright colors in the picture. Whereas the picture is otherwise
drawn and colored in a light and relaxed manner, the coloring of the cottage reveals that Anna had pressed the crayon more strongly against the
paper when coloring it. The cottage draws one's attention. However, when
discussing the picture, Anna began by describing all of the other elements in
the painting, before hesitantly moving on to the meaning of the black cottage, while trying to play down its significance.

> Well, then this black cottage . . . is . . . is . . . in this organization . . . and
> these kinds of cottages are also in other organizations, but I think there
> is this kind of little cottage in this organization too. And . . . we don't
> dare to open its door together. Open the door . . . and these people are
> quiet and . . . and keep quiet. [. . .] Well, it is nothing too dramatic [. . .]
> not a big issue really.

Anna's visual and verbal accounts were contradictory and seemed to refer
to an ambivalent relationship to her organization. It almost seemed as if
she wanted to present a more positive image of her organization than she
had in reality. The eye-catching position of the black cottage in her drawing
and its strong visual expression compared to her hesitant discussion of the
cottage seemed to reveal a tacit issue within her organization that bothered
her more than she admitted—or perhaps realized. Even though Anna didn't

Figure 16.1 A Dark, Black Cottage Visualizing a Problematic Issue in the Work
Organization

specify the meaning of the black cottage when drawings were discussed with all participants, drawing seemed to provide her with means of recognizing and expressing a problematic issue in her organization. Maybe it would have been easier for her to talk about its meaning with the researcher alone, or write about it.

The Sun King and Vampire-Leader

Liisa and Mari depicted their organizations from the perspective of leadership. Liisa divided her picture into two parts: the upper section depicts the sun shining in the sky and the lower section depicts a field full of flowers. The sun is positioned in the middle of the picture, and the entire picture is covered by fog that blurs the contours of the shapes. Liisa explained that the sun depicts the leaders' vision guiding operations within the organization. However, this vision becomes obscured due to various disturbing circumstances symbolized by the fog.

> First, I drew this shining diamond of leadership, which turned out to be the sun. But here we have . . . the problem is that the leaders have a vision, a kind of goal and idea of why we exist as an organization. A clear idea in our minds, but in reality, there is no [such idea]. There is a lot of fog that obscures the leaders' vision . . . our basic idea . . . so that you don't see it clearly.

Because the ultimate vision becomes obscured—and eventually forgotten—there are dozens of competing and even contradictory visions and guidelines among the employees of the organization depicted by the dozens of flowers in the field. Liisa emphasized this multitude visually, through the varying colors of the flowers.

> When the leadership approach is not articulate, or clear for everybody . . . that is why there are different flowers of leadership here. All are different. In a way, it is very varied, the reality . . . very different from the outside image [of the organization].

Visually, Liisa's painting seemed to depict a hierarchical work organization, where the employees are at the mercy of the light provided by the leader who appears as a kind of Sun King. Tied to the soil, the employee-flowers cannot truly influence the course taken by the organization, but only do their best to flourish despite the disorder depicted by the fog.

Mari, for her part, depicted her organization as a theatre in which employees are seated around a circle stage where the leader is performing in the middle. The leader is clearly distinguishable and wears a black suit, but the employees are depicted as generalized forms—seen from the back—without any personal characteristics. On the basis of this visual choice, Mari wanted to express the unimportance of individual employees in the organization as a whole.

> The leader is in the arena, in the middle, in the focal point. [. . .] The leader has sharp contours. S/he has to be clearly distinguishable. [. . .] The leader [. . .] is different from us, the employees, who are depicted

here sitting and watching—which expresses their role in this leadership drama. We are not even targets, targets of leadership, but passive bystanders [. . .]. And then, faces don't matter, we all look similar, and are depicted from behind . . . the leaders think we do not [matter].

At the same time, however, Mari used colors to criticize another aspect of leadership. The employees watching the leader's performance are drawn using a range of colours—blue, red, yellow, green, orange, brown and purple. The colorful outlines of the employee-spectators flow toward the black leader. Mari explained that, just as black is created by mixing all colors, leadership is based on the contribution of all employees.

> But the reason I have coloured everybody with a different colour is that [. . .] for example, when you mix blue and red you get purple and so on, and when you mix all colours you get black. The power of black derives from all these colours. [. . .] I think that true leadership is the contribution of [employees].

Taken together, these two perspectives in Mari's drawing paint a picture of an organization in which the leader takes advantage of the employees' efforts, without giving them credit or publicly acknowledging their contributions. On the contrary, a narcissistic, vampire-like leader of this kind uses them as tools to gain merit and strengthen his/her power position.

An Arena of Competitive Cliques and Self-Interested Loners

Tiina drew a picture in which there are different scenes depicting people doing different things that seem to have nothing in common. In one scene, a group of people is smiling and dancing in a circle holding flowers in their hands; in another, people are digging a dung heap with an irritated expression on their faces (Figure 16.2); in the third scene, a group of people is running on a track wearing doctor's hats. Between these scenes, there is a person sunbathing with a big smile. Tiina used these detached groups of people to express the lack of togetherness in her organization. Instead of working together in order to achieve a common goal, the organization is divided into cliques with their own interests.

> What I find interesting is that in the same work organization some people [. . .] dance happily together [. . .] and others dig a dung heap. [. . .] Nothing in common [. . .]. The boundaries are so strict [. . .] dictating with whom you play and with whom you don't.

In every corner of the paper, there is a person working on his/her laptop and wearing headphones. They are turning their backs toward the groups of people in the center. With these figures in the corners, Tiina wanted to

Figure 16.2 People Are Digging a Dung Heap with an Irritated Expression on Their Faces

express working alone and networking with partners outside the actual work organization, in order to promote one's own interests.

> We have a lot of separateness [. . .] loneliness, working alone [. . .] and then we have those cliques. [. . .] These people are alone in the corners. Some of them may be quite satisfied with being alone [. . .] but others can feel very lonely and gloomy. And they have headphones and

laptops, they can be networked all over the world. [. . .] But they could as well work in another organization. [. . .] I suffer from loneliness in my work, I would prefer teamwork.

In this drawing, the organization lacks a coherent structure, which is expressed through the picture's fragmented composition. Similarly, the organization lacks a physical location. Only the boundaries of the paper keep these people 'together.' Tiina's drawing clearly articulates the absence of a common goal within the organization, employees' unwillingness to adhere to the community, as well as their fierce mutual competition. In this organization, individuals are left to struggle alone.

Keeping Up Appearances

Leena and Maija reflected on the positive and negative experiences in their work organizations, as well as the appropriateness of expressing negative experiences in public. In Leena's drawing, which depicted a group of employees and customers, the overall atmosphere is welcoming, with bright colors and smiling people. However, there are also signs of negative aspects. A crying person is depicted alone, detached from the other people. In addition, three windows in the building in the background are painted black. Despite the presence of these negative aspects, the focus is on the smiling people in the middle of the picture.

> And then [. . .] all these people are smiling. But people don't always feel like smiling. That is why here is this lonely person. And then these windows, there is light in most windows but then there are these dark windows too. [. . .] It could mean that work [in the organization] is not always that pleasant. There are dark moments.

In Maija's drawing, members of the organization are depicted outdoors. On the left the sun is shining, while there are dark clouds and rain on the right. Maija explained that, through these natural elements, she wanted to express the changing conditions within the organization. Despite these conditions, all of the people are smiling—those in the sunshine and those in the rain—as if they were keeping up appearances and unwilling to show their true feelings.

> In a way, we are one big family—but not such a happy family, though. [. . .] Although I suffer mentally all the time [. . .] everybody smiles.

However, there is a detached frame in Maija's drawing, where a person is working alone and sweating under the workload. This frame seems to create a private sphere—a backstage—where this person shows his/her true feelings (Figure 16.3).

Figure 16.3 A Person Is Working Alone and Sweating under the Workload

You should work around the clock. And then there is an exhausted worker sweating alone by the computer.

In their drawings, both Leena and Maija reflected on the appropriateness of showing—genuine—emotions within the organization. The drawings show that the negative emotions and hardship caused by an excessive workload and other unfavorable working conditions are hidden behind a veneer of smiles and calm behavior. Fatigue and stress seem to be signs of weakness, which are concealed in public.

Contribution of Participant-Created Drawings

Drawing pictures of their organizations was rewarding for the participants. Although some participants doubted their drawing skills at first, they were all able to depict and reflect on their work organizations visually. On one hand, this may be due to the reassuring nature of the assignment, which downgraded the role of skills in visual expression, while on the other the drawing process itself seemed to immerse the participants in reflecting on their organizations in a new and unusual—and thus motivating—manner (see also Mannay 2010, 2015; Mitchell et al. 2011). The drawings demonstrated that the participants could modify the meanings of the objects through their choice of colors, sizes, distances from each other, locations in the depicted space as well as overall composition. The participants also creatively harnessed non-organizational elements—such as weather conditions—in order to create a visual narrative of their organizations. This creative aspect seemed to render their consciousness more porous, providing unconscious experiences with representation in their reflections on their organizations (see also Martikainen and Hujala 2014, 2017).

Although most of the participants reported having had a general idea of what they would depict before starting to draw, most also indicated that they had no 'prepared picture' in their minds, but the idea had evolved during the drawing process. Maija, for instance, explained, "*I just thought I would start drawing what came to my mind*," and Leena explained that she had "*started drawing people [. . .] and had no idea how the drawing would proceed.*" This suggests that the drawing process not only represented the subjects' conceptions of their work organizations, but also constituted constructions of them (see also Clark and Morris 2017; McNiff 2008; Pauwels 2012). As McNiff (2008) argues, the most meaningful insights often emerge unexpectedly during the drawing process—growing alongside the creative process itself. This research shows how drawing pictures functioned as a means of visual thinking (Arnheim 1969), intertwining multimodal as well as conscious and unconscious experiences in the processing of the topic.

The data revealed that the participants visualized their organizations from a number of perspectives, ranging from portrait-like depictions of organization members to metaphoric depictions of competing leadership ideas. This variety of approaches is in accordance with research which argues that participant-created visual materials allow the participants to engage in more self-determination due to the reduced influence of the verbal concepts used by the researchers (Mannay 2015; McNiff 2008; Rose 2014). Participant-created drawings seem to produce valuable 'crowdsourcing' insights which challenge the researcher's preconceptions and direct him/her toward more inductive analysis methods and promoting social change.

In accordance with previous studies (Mitchell et al. 2011; Rose 2014), the data and observations of the research situation revealed that visual materials activated both the participants' reflective stance and interaction around the subject matter. This reflective attitude did not, however, seem to result from the visualization of conceptions and experiences alone; the verbalization of visual creations also seemed to play a role in this. This multimodal processing—fluctuation between the visual and verbal—seemed to increase the reflection on the topic (see also Martikainen and Hujala 2017). Another key factor contributing to the reflective stance seemed to be the fact that the drawings concretized, visualized and materialized conceptions and experiences of organizations, which the participants were themselves unaware of. In this research, experiences of detachment—end even loneliness—as well as keeping up appearances despite unfavorable conditions, seemed to become visually articulated and challenge conscious conceptions. This suggests that drawings can reveal both emotional and tacit dimensions that can remain unnoticed when immersed in everyday routines or when they are difficult to articulate verbally (see also Banks 2008; Clark and Morris 2017; Mannay 2015).

When comparing verbal and visual accounts, some participants expressed negative conceptions and experiences of their organizations more courageously when drawing than through talking. In general, drawing seemed to encourage the participants to reflect on their organizations critically—even though this was not specifically requested. Through their drawings, the participants reflected on organizational problems discussed in recent research literature, such as feelings of isolation (Ayazlar and Güzel 2014; Lam and Lau 2012; Wright 2005), problems with teamwork (Caruso, Rogers and Bazerman 2009; Erdil, Oya and Müceldili 2014), suppression of negative emotions (Mastracci, Guy and Newman 2012; Mesmer-Magnus, DeChurch and Wax 2011; Wolf Baily et al. 2016), fear of articulating problems within the organization (Burris 2012; Donaghey et al. 2011) and narcissistic leadership (Braun 2016, 2017; Stein 2013). This research suggests that participant-created drawings may illuminate aspects of these problematic—and often silenced—matters in organizations, beyond the reach of mere verbal materials.

Conclusion

This small-scale research highlighted promising findings on the aptness of participant-created drawings for studying the multiple facets of organizations and generated some suggestions for future studies involving the use of participant-created visual materials. Firstly, ample time should be reserved for the participants to draw the pictures and explain them. Secondly, it would probably be beneficial for the analyser of the drawings not to hear the participants' verbal explanations before the analysis. Instead, it would be fruitful to arrange a further gathering between the participants and researchers, in order to compare the researcher-driven analysis and participant's intentions. Such interaction between 'the visible' and 'visual' (Mitchell et al. 2011; Rose 2014) could provide a means of revealing the tacit meanings and suppressed dimensions of organizations. Finally, the research suggests that, in terms of the analysis, it would be highly beneficial to video-record the act of drawing in order to gain insights into the process of producing pictures (see also Clark and Morris 2017; Mannay 2015). In the same way as recording discussions can reveal important issues, the opportunity to closely observe the act of drawing may provide valuable information on the drawing process, such as the order in which the visual elements are drawn, the enthusiasm for drawing, hesitation, rubbing out and facial expressions. This would help the researchers to relate the act of drawing to the verbally conveyed meanings.

Although the visual may not be fully verbalized or the verbal visualized (McNiff 2008), this research suggests that fluctuation between the visual and the verbal provides a means of articulating unpleasant, stressful and even devastating experiences which are usually repressed, feared and hidden by members of an organization. It is time for the hardships and challenges experienced by such people to be recognized not only as cosmetic cracks in the face of an organization, which can be solved with temporary facelifts, but as expressions of the misery they experience on a daily basis. Participant-created visual materials may provide an authentic insight into such experiences. This insight is needed in order to promote positive social changes in organizations.

References

Arnheim, Rudolf. 1969. *Visual Thinking*. Berkeley, Los Angeles, London: University of California Press.

Ayazlar, Gökhan, and Berrin Güzel. 2014. "The Effect on Loneliness in the Workplace on Organizational Commitment." *Procedia—Social and Behavioral Sciences* 131: 319–325. doi: 10.1016/j.sbspro.2014.04.124.

Banks, Marcus. 2008. *Using Visual Data in Qualitative Research*. London: Sage Publications.

Bramming, Pia, Birgitte G. Hansen, Anders Bojesen, and Kristian G. Olesen. 2012. "(Im)perfect Pictures: Snaplogs in Performativity Research." *Qualitative Research in Organizations and Management: An International Journal* 7 (1): 54–71. doi: 10.1108/17465641211223465.

Braun, Susanne. 2016. "Narcissistic Leadership." In *Global Encyclopedia of Public Administration, Public Policy, and Governance*, edited by Ali Farazmand, 1–9. Cham, Switzerland: Springer.

Braun, Susanne. 2017. "Leader Narcissism and Outcomes in Organizations: A Review at Multiple Levels of Analysis and Implications for Future Research." *Frontiers in Psychology* 8 (773). doi: 10.3389/fosyg.2017.00773.

Burris, Ethan, R. 2012. "The Risks and Rewards of Speaking Up: Responses to Voice in Organization." *Academy of Management Journal* 55 (4): 851–875. doi: 10.5465/amj.2010.0562.

Caruso, Heather M., Todd Rogers, and Max H. Bazerman. 2009. "Boundaries Need Not Be Barriers. Leading Collaboration Among Groups in Decentralized Organization." In *Crossing the Divide: Intergroup Leadership in a World of Difference*, edited by Todd A. Pittinsky, 113–126. Boston: Harvard University Press.

Charmaz, Kathy. 2006. *Constructing Grounded Theory: A Practical Guide Through Qualitative Analysis*. London, Thousand Oaks, CA, New Delhi: Sage Publicaitons.

Clark, Andrew, and Lisa Morris. 2017. "The Use of Visual Methodologies in Social Work Research over the Last Decade: A Narrative Review and Some Questions for the Future." *Qualitative Social Work: Research and Practice* 16 (1): 29–43. doi: 10.1177/1473325015601205.

Dale, Karen. 2005. "Building a Social Materiality: Spatial and Embodied Politics in Organizational Control." *Organization* 12 (5): 649–678. doi: 10.1177/1350508405055940.

Donaghey, Jimmy, Niall Cullinane, Tony Dundon, and Adrian Wilkinson. 2011. "Reconceptualising Employee Silence: Problems and Prognosis." *Work, Employment and Society* 25 (1): 51–67. doi: 10.1177/0950017010389239.

Erdil, Oya, and Büsra Müceldili. 2014. "The Effects of Envy on Job Engagement and Turnover Intention." *Procedia—Social and Behavioral Sciences* 150: 447–454. doi: 10.1016/j.sbspro.2014.09.050.

Fairclough, Norman. 1995. *Media Discourse*. London: E. Arnold.

Huss, Eprath, Roni Kaufman, and Avril Siboni. 2013. "Children's Drawings and Social Change: Food Insecurity and Hunger Among Israeli Bedouin Children." *British Journal of Social Work* 44 (7): 1857–1878. doi: 10.1093/bjsw/bct034.

Inözu, Jülide. 2017. "Drawings Are Talking: Exploring Language Learners' Beliefs Through Visual Narratives." *Applied Linguistics Review*. doi: 10.1515/applirev-2016-1062.

Kohler Riessman, Catherine. 2008. *Narrative Methods for the Human Sciences*. CA: Sage Publications.

Kress, Gunther, and Theo van Leeuwen. 2006. *Reading Images: The Grammar of Visual Design*. London: Routledge.

Lam, Long W., and Dora C. Lau. 2012. "Feeling Lonely at Work: Investigating the Consequences of Unsatisfactory Workplace Relationships." *The International Journal of Human Resource Management* 23 (20): 4265–4282. doi: 10.1080/09585192.665070.

Mannay, Dawn. 2010. "Making the Familiar Strange: Can Visual Research Methods Render the Familiar Setting More Perceptible?" *Qualitative Research* 10 (1): 1–37. doi: 10.1177/1468794109348684.

Mannay, Dawn. 2015. "Visual Methodologies for Communication Studies: Making the Familiar Strange and Interesting Again." *Estudos em Comunicacaio* 18: 61–78. www.ec.ubi.pt/ec/19/pdf/n19a04.pdf.

Martikainen, Jari, and Anneli Hujala. 2014. Piirretty työorganisaatio: Kokeilu kuvalähtöisen menetelmän soveltamisesta organisaatio—ja johtamistutkimukseen." ["Drawing the Work Organization: An Experiment of Applying Picture-Based Methodology in Organization and Management Research."] *Premissi: Terveys— ja sosiaalialan johtamisen erikoisjulkaisu* 9 (5): 35–44.

Martikainen, Jari, and Anneli Hujala. 2017. "Johtajuuden visuaaliset kategoriat." ["Visual Categories of Leadership."] *Sosiologia* 54 (1): 43–62.

Mastracci, Sharon H., Mary E. Guy, and Meredith A. Newman. 2012. *Emotional Labor and Crisis Response: Working on the Razor's Edge*. London, New York: Routledge.

McNiff, Shaun. 2008. "Art-Based Research." In *Handbook of the Arts in Qualitative Research: Perspectives, Methodologies, Examples, and Issues*, edited by Gary J. Knowles and Ardra L. Cole, 29–40. Thousand Oaks, CA, New Delhi, London, Singapore: Sage Publications.

Mesmer-Magnus, Jessica R., Leslie A. DeChurch, and Amy Wax. 2011. "Moving Emotional Labour Beyond Surface and Deep Acting: A Discordance-Congruence Perspective." *Organizational Psychology Review* 2 (1): 1–48. doi: 10.1177/2041386611417746.

Mitchell, Claudia, Linda Theron, Jean Stuart, Ann Smith, and Zachariah Campbell. 2011. "Drawings as Research Method." In *Picturing Research: Drawing as Visual Methodology*, edited by Linda Theron, Claudia Mitchell, Ann Smith, and Jean Stuart, 19–36. Rotterdam: Sense Publishers.

Pauwels, Luc. 2012. "Contemplating the State of Visual Research: An Assessment of Obstacles and Opportunities." In *Advances in Visual Methodology*, edited by Sarah Pink, 248–264. London: Sage Publications.

Pauwels, Luc. 2013. "An Integrated Conceptual Framework for Visual Social Research." In *The Sage Handbook of Visual Research Methods*, edited by Eric Margolis and Luc Pauwels, 3–23. London: Sage Publications.

Rose, Gillian. 2001. *Visual Methodologies: An Introduction to the Interpretation of Visual Materials*. London: Sage Publications.

Rose, Gillian. 2014. "On the Relation Between 'Visual Research Methods' and Contemporary Visual Culture." *The Sociological Review* 62 (1): 24–46. doi: 10.1111/1467-1954X.12109.

Stein, Mark. 2013. "When Does Narcissistic Leadership Become Problematic? Dick Fuld at Lehman Brothers." *Journal of Management Inquiry* 22 (3): 282–293. doi: 10.1177/1056492613478664.

Warren, Samantha. 2009. "Visual Methods in Organizational Research." In *The Sage Handbook of Organizational Research Methods*, edited by David Buchanan and Alan Bryman, 566–582. London: Sage Publicaitons.

Wolf Baily, Elizabeth, Jooa J. Lee, Sunnita Sah, and Alison Wood Brooks. 2016. "Managing Perceptions of Distress at Work: Reframing Emotion as Passion." *Organizational Behavior and Human Decision Process* 137: 1–12. doi: 10.1016/j.obhdp.2016.07.003.

Wright, Sarah L. 2005. "Organization Climate, Social Support and Loneliness in the Workplace." In *The Effect of Affect in Organizational Setting. Research on Emotion in Organization, Vol. 1.*, edited by Neal M. Ashkanasy, Wilfred J. Zerbe, and Charmine E. J. Härtel, 123–142. Bingley: Emerald Group Publishing Limited.

Index

action research: concept of 194–195; constructivism and 204; critically oriented action research 196; critical pragmatism of 199–200, 206–207; critical theory and 201; emancipatory action research 196; field-specific discourses 198–199; meta-theoretical inconsistencies of 195–198; overcoming impotence 202–203; PAR 196–198; power asymmetries within 'the community of an inquiry' 200–203; pragmatically orientated action research 196; pragmatism and 201–202, 204–206; problem of inertia 198–200; researcher as subject enacting power 203–206
arts-based methods 227, 235–247
Asperger syndrome (AS) study: ambivalence to support 186–188; background to study 179–180; coping strategies 185–186; discussion of study 188–190; explaining 'my' tendencies 184–185; findings of study 184–188; frequency of distress 184; interview procedure and data analysis 183–184; mental distress 180–181, 189; methods of study 181–184; 'pre-emptive' strategies 185–186; 'reactive' strategies 185–186; recruitment for study 181–183; sample for study 183
Australian Indigenous policy: *Closing the Gap Report* 154; future of 153–155; historical overview of Indigenous disadvantage 148–150; *Little Children are Sacred* report 152; Northern Territory National Emergency Response Act 151–153; *Part II of the Racial Discrimination*

Act 1975 152–153; wicked deficit discourses of Indigenous disadvantage 150–151
Australia, use of personal budgets 35–36
autonomy 28

blame culture: concept of 119–121; radiographic practice 122–130; safety 121–122
bureaucratic logic 214–216

Canada 36, 37
care: autonomy and 28, 30; caring relationships 28–31; elderly care 21–31, 62–73; equal care 29–31, 43–44; ethic of 27–30; interdependence and 28, 30; marketization of 24–27; personalization of 34–44
challenge of problem definition 5–6
collaboration: cross-boundary collaboration 13–15, 214–216; impact of institutionalized forces on 214–216; nursing home managers 69–70; practices in health and social care integration 222–224; between private and public health care 218–219
collective denial discourse 97–98
communication technology: benefits of 103; Parkinson's Disease and the POHC System 106–115; use and effect on roles of patients 103–115
complex adaptive systems (CAS) 11
complexity 11–13, 16
complex problems 11–12
complex systems 11
complicated problems 11–12

coping 14–15
Critical Leadership Studies (CLS) 52, 59–60
critically oriented action research 196
Critical Management Studies (CMS) 52–53, 59–60
critical realism 213–216, 217
cross-boundary collaboration 13–15, 214–216

dependency: concept of 160–161; derivative dependency 163–166, 172–173; inevitable dependency 163–166, 172–173; moral harm and 164–166; normalizing 161–163; power imbalances 163–164; responsibility and 164–166; study on experiences of patients living with IBD 166–170; wickedness and 170–172
derivative dependency 163–166, 172–173
destructive leadership: categories of 93; collective denial discourse 97–98; features of 92–94; role of employees in 94–100; self-interest discourse 95–97
diversity 39–40

elderly care: impact of funding pressures on 23–24; impact of social care reform on 21–31; increased pressure on budgets for 22–23; marketization of care 24–27; personal budgets 40; study of nursing home managers confronting wicked problems 62–73
emancipatory action research 196
emotional labor 29
employees: collective denial discourse 97–98; crucial role of employees in ethical leadership 85–87; as followers/initiators in ethical leadership 82–85; role in destructive leadership 94–100; role in ethical leadership studies 78–80; role of employees in ethical leadership 80–81; self-interest discourse 95–97
empowerment 103, 113–114
equal care 29–31, 39–40, 43–44
ethical leadership: characteristic features of 78–79; crucial role of employees in 85–87; employees

as followers/initiators in 82–85; relationship between OCB and 76, 79–80, 86; role of employees in ethical leadership 80–81; role of employees in ethical leadership studies 78–80
ethics 10–11

fantasies 58–59
followers 82–83
found materials 236
free association interviews 53–54
fundamental complexity 13

governance 14
'Grounded Theory' 237
group cohesion 141–142
group membership: concept of 138; social identity theory and 138–141

how-to-do action strategies.14
human rights 36–37

identity regulation 105–106
identity work 104–106
independency 162
inertia 198–200, 220
inevitable dependency 163–166, 172–173
Inflammatory Bowel Disease (IBD): background to study 166–167; learning to live with 167–168
Inflammatory Bowel Disease (IBD) study: experiences of patients living with 166–170; learning about 168–169; learning to manage and cope with 169–170
initiators 83–85
interdependence 28
interests 6
interorganizational relations: group cohesion 141–142; group membership 138–141; interorganizational groups 135–137; mandated forms of 134–135; pluralistic ignorance 142–143; wicked issues and the darker side of organizational issues 137–138

laissez faire leadership 94, 96, 97, 99
leadership: destructive leadership 91–100; ethical leadership 75–87; fantasies about 59; laissez

faire leadership 94, 96, 97, 99; management of wicked problems 13–15; self-fantasies 56–58; supportive-disloyal leadership 94, 95–96, 99; team fantasies 58–59; use of free association interviews 53–54; use of photo elicitation methods 54–56; wicked problems in NHS 51–59

management 13–15
managerialism 26
market logic 24–27, 214–216
mental distress 180–181
mental health problems: personal budgets 40; supporting young adults with Asperger Syndrome 179–190
multi-actor environments 5–6

National Health Service (NHS): blame culture in 119–130; elderly care 24; wicked problem of leadership in 51–59
neo-liberal policies 21, 25, 26, 28, 114, 215
Netherlands: personal budgets 35, 36, 37, 42–43; pilot project on POHCs 106–115
non-resolvability 5–6
nursing home managers: caring eye-to-eye 67–68; caring ideals in the abstract 65–66; collaboration 69–70; contested schedules 70–71; everyday vexations 68–71; high workloads 70–71; instruments of caring 66–67; lofty ideals 65–68, 72; staff not following routines/set responsibilities 68–69; temporary staff 70–71; wicked problems for 64–73; wicked problems from the national to the local level 63–64, 71–73

organizational citizenship behavior (OCB) 76, 79–80, 86

paradigm of conscious complexity 11
paradigm of order 11
Participatory Action Research (PAR) 196–198
perceived cohesion 141
personal budgets: availability and quality of support infrastructure 42–43; benefits of 36–37; concept of

35–36; cost-effectiveness of 41–42; critique of 37–43; human rights and 36–37; impact on health outcomes 40–41; issues of equity and diversity 39–40; outcomes for service users and carers 38–39; perceptions of frontline staff? 42; personalization of 34–44; as wicked solution to welfare rights and equity 43–44
Personal Online Health Communities (POHCs): content of postings 110–111; data analysis 108; data collection 107; number of postings 108–110; online-offline intersection 111–112; Parkinson's Disease and 106–115; as vehicles of empowerment 113–114
phenomenology 224–228
photo elicitation 54–56
pluralistic ignorance 142–143
pragmatically orientated action research 196
pragmatism 201–202, 204–206, 220–224
praxeology 220–224
problem governance 14–15
problem-solving 14–15
psychodynamics 56, 59

radiographic practice 122–130
researcher-generated visual research materials 236

safety 121–122
self-fantasies 56–58
self-interest discourse 95–97
simple problems 11–12
social constructionism 217–220
social identity theory 138–141
super wicked problem 9
supportive-disloyal leadership 94, 95–96
Sweden 62–73

tame game 9–10, 10
tame problems 4, 7
taming 14–15
team fantasies 58–59

United Kingdom: blame culture in the NHS 119–130; Care Act 2014 24; Community Care Act 1990 24; personal budgets 35–36; social

care reform in 21–31; supporting
experiences of patients living with
chronic disease 159–173; supporting
young adults with Asperger
Syndrome 179–190; wicked problem
of leadership in the NHS 51–59
United States 36, 37
unknown knows 8
unknown unknowns 8

values 6
visual research methods: contribution
of participant-created drawings
as research material 245–246;
found materials 236; key strengths
of 235–236; participant-created
drawings as research material
236–237; researcher-generated
visual research materials 236; types
236–237; visually and verbally
storied work organizations 237–245

wicked ethics 10–11
wicked game 9–10, **10**
wickedness 6–8, 170–172
Wickedness Cube 6–7, 7
wicked problems: action research
as tool for solving 194–207; in
Australian Indigenous policy

148–155; blame culture in the NHS
119–130; caused by underlying
mechanisms 212–216; characteristics
attributed to 4–5, 5; complexity
and 11–13, 16; concept of 3–8,
15–16; conceptual expansions 9–11;
constructed in social interaction
216–220; of destructive leadership
91–100; of elderly care 62–73;
of ethical leadership 75–87; in
everyday practices 220–224; in four
seasons 212–229; how-to-do action
strategies. 14; individual experiences
of 224–226; interorganizational
relations 134–146; knowledge
challenges 12–13; of leadership in the
NHS 51–59; personalization of care
34–44; problem governance 14–15;
resourcing social care provision
within modern welfare state 21–31;
role of leadership and management
of 13–15; supporting experiences of
patients living with chronic disease
159–173; supporting young adults
with Asperger Syndrome 179–190;
use of health care communication
technology 103–115; use of visual
research methods 235–247
wicked solutions 43–44